Essential Statistics

J. H. Wilson
Georgia Southern University

PEARSON

Prentice
Hall

Upper Saddle River, New Jersey 07458

Library of Congress Cataloging-in-Publication Data

Wilson, Janie H.
　　Essential statistics/J.H. Wilson.
　　　　p. cm.
　　Includes bibliographical references and index.
　　ISBN 0-13-099422-7
　　1. Statistics. 2. Social sciences—Statistical methods. I. Title.

HA29. W5154 2004
519.5—dc22　　　　　　　　　　　　　2004042070

Editorial Director: Leah Jewell
Senior Acquisitions Editor: Jayme Heffler
Associate Editor: Jennifer M. Conklin
Assistant Managing Editor: Maureen Richardson
Production Liaison: Fran Russello
Project Manager: Marty Sopher/Lithokraft
Prepress and Manufacturing Buyer: Tricia Kenny
Cover Designer: Bruce Kenselaar
Director of Marketing: Beth Mejia

Credits and acknowledgments borrowed from other sources and reproduced, with permission, in this textbook appear on appropriate page within text.

Screen captures used throughout this text were created using SPSS 11.5 for Windows with permission from SPSS Inc., Chicago, IL

Pearson Education LTD., London
Pearson Education Singapore, Pte. Ltd
Pearson Education, Canada, Ltd
Pearson Education–Japan
Pearson Education Australia PTY, Limited
Pearson Education North Asia Ltd
Pearson Educación de Mexico, S.A. de C.V.
Pearson Education Malaysia, Pte. Ltd
Pearson Education, Upper Saddle River, New Jersey

10 9 8 7 6 5 4 3 2 1
ISBN 0-13-099422-7

BRIEF CONTENTS

	Preface	xii
	About the Author	xx
Chapter 1	Welcome to Statistics	1
Chapter 2	Variables and Graphing	11
Chapter 3	Measures of Central Tendency	26
Chapter 4	Measures of Variability	51
Chapter 5	Descriptive z-Scores	70
Chapter 6	Inferential z-Scores and Probability	82
Chapter 7	Hypothesis Testing	98
Chapter 8	Three t-Tests	114
Chapter 9	ANOVA: One-Way, Between-Groups	143
Chapter 10	ANOVA: Two-Way, Between-Groups	171
Chapter 11	Correlational Data	201
Chapter 12	Linear Regression	224
Chapter 13	Chi-Square Analyses	242
Appendix A	ANOVA: One-Way, Repeated-Measures Using SPSS	263
Appendix B	Multiple Regression Using SPSS	274
Table 1	z-Table	281
Table 2	t-Table	285
Table 3	F-Table	286
Table 4	q-Table	289
Table 5	r-Table	291
Table 6	χ^2 Table	293
Answers to Odd-Numbered Items		294

CONTENTS

Preface   xii

About the Author   xx

PART I   INTRODUCTION

Chapter 1   **Welcome to Statistics**   1

Building Competence   1
Rationale for Learning Statistics   1
Math   2
    Proportion and Percent   2
    Rounding   3
Symbols   3
APA Style   4
Conducting Research   4
    Experiments   5
    Correlations   6
    The Usefulness of Correlations   6
How to Pick a Sample   7
Analyzing Data Using SPSS   7
Preview of Chapter 2   8
Conceptual Items   8
Application Items   8

PART II   DESCRIPTIVE STATISTICS

Chapter 2   **Variables and Graphing**   11

Measurement Scales   11
    Nominal Variables   11
    Ordinal Variables   11
    Interval Variables   12
    Ratio Variables   12
    Special Case of Rating Scales   12
Qualitative Versus Quantitative Variables   13
Discrete Versus Continuous Variables   14
Picturing Data: Simple Frequency Tables and Graphs   14
    Nominal and Ordinal Data   15
    Discrete Interval and Ratio Data   18
    Continuous Interval and Ratio Data   19
    Grouped Frequency Distributions   20

	Shapes of Distributions	21
	Normal Distributions	21
	Skewed Distributions	22
	Kurtosis	22
	Bimodal and Trimodal Distributions	23
	Preview of Chapter 3	23
	Conceptual Items	24
	Application Items	24
Chapter 3	**Measures of Central Tendency**	**26**
	Summarizing Data	26
	Mode	26
	Median	28
	Mean	29
	Mean Versus Median	30
	Introduction to SPSS	31
	Measures of Central Tendency on SPSS	33
	Summarizing Experiments Using Means	40
	Graphing Means	41
	Graphing Means on SPSS	42
	Preview of Chapter 4	47
	Conceptual Items	47
	Application Items	48
	Computational Formula in This Chapter	50
Chapter 4	**Measures of Variability**	**51**
	Spread of Scores	51
	Range	51
	Sample Variance	52
	Sample Standard Deviation	55
	Estimated Population Standard Deviation	56
	Estimated Population Variance	57
	Measures of Variability on SPSS	58
	Graphing Sample Standard Deviation	61
	Graphs of Standard Deviation on SPSS	63
	Preview of Chapter 5	66
	Conceptual Items	66
	Application Items	67
	Computational Formulas in This Chapter	69
Chapter 5	**Descriptive *z*-Scores**	**70**
	Standardized Scores	70
	Comparing Values From Different Samples	70
	Standardized Distribution	72

Proportion and Percent 73
    Evaluations Based on z-Scores 75
    Comparing Two Values and Probability 76
    Percentile 77
Logical Limits 78
Preview of Chapter 6 79
Conceptual Items 79
Application Items 79
Computational Formula in This Chapter 81

PART III   **INFERENTIAL STATISTICS: EXPERIMENTS**

Chapter 6   **Inferential z-Scores and Probability**   **82**

Probability 82
Sampling Distribution of Means 84
    Creating a Sampling Distribution of Means for Your Research 86
Standardizing the Sampling Distribution of Means 86
    Critical Value and Critical Region 87
Manipulating a Sample 88
    Not Different From Normal 89
    Higher Than Normal 89
    Lower Than Normal 91
    Decreasing the Critical Region 92
Preview of Chapter 7 93
Conceptual Items 94
Application Items 94
Computational Formulas in This Chapter 96
References 97

Chapter 7   **Hypothesis Testing**   **98**

Formalizing the Inferential z 98
Lay Out Expectations 98
    Null Hypothesis 98
    Alternative Hypothesis 99
    Two-Tailed z-Test 99
    μ Rather Than $\overline{X}$ 100
Choose a Statistic 100
Sketch the Normal Distribution 101
Collect Data 101
    Calculate a Statistic 101
    Significance 102
    APA Style 102
    Reject Or Fail to Reject the Null Hypothesis 102
    Inferential Wording 102
    Effect Size 103

	Plain English	104
	Confidence Intervals	104
	One-tailed Test in the Positive Direction	105
	One-tailed Test in the Negative Direction	107
	Hypothesis Testing, Truth, and Power	108
	Preview of Chapter 8	111
	Conceptual Items	111
	Application Items	111
	Conceptual Formulas in This Chapter	113

Chapter 8   Three *t*-Tests   114

	z-Test Versus *t*-Test	114
	The Single-Sample *t*-Test	114
	Hypothesis Testing Using the Single-sample *t*-Test	116
	The Related-samples *t*-Test	118
	The Sampling Distribution of Mean Differences	119
	Hypothesis Testing Using the Related-samples *t*-Test	120
	Related-samples *t*-Test on SPSS	123
	APA-style Results Section	125
	Independent-samples *t*-Test	126
	The Sampling Distribution of Differences Between Means	126
	Hypothesis Testing Using the Independent-samples *t*-Test	126
	Independent-samples *t*-Test on SPSS	130
	APA-style Results Section	135
	Preview of Chapter 9	136
	Conceptual Items	136
	Application Items	136
	Computational Formulas in This Chapter	140
	References	142

Chapter 9   ANOVA One-Way, Between-Groups   143

	t-Test Versus ANOVA	143
	Logic of ANOVA: Hypothesis Testing	143
	One-way, Between-groups ANOVA: Equal *n*	146
	Organizing ANOVA Results	150
	APA Style	150
	Effect Size	150
	Post-hoc Testing: Tukey's HSD	151
	Plain English	152
	Confidence Intervals	152
	One-way, Between-groups ANOVA: Unequal *n*	154
	Summary Table	156
	Effect Size	156
	Post-hoc Testing: Fisher's Protected *t*-Tests	157
	Plain English	158
	Confidence Intervals	158

One-way, Between-groups ANOVA on SPSS 159
APA-style Results Section 165
Preview of Chapter 10 165
Conceptual Items 166
Application Items 167
Computational Formulas in This Chapter 169
References 169

Chapter 10   ANOVA Two-Way, Between-Groups   171

One-way Versus Two-way ANOVA 171
Logic of the Two-way, Between-groups ANOVA 171
Two-way ANOVA Effects 171
Calculating the Two-way, Between-groups ANOVA 174
SS_{tot} 174
SS_{BG} and SS_{WG} 175
Separating SS_{BG} Into Three Portions 176
F-Tests for Each Effect 177
Hypothesis Testing and ANOVA Results 178
First Main Effect 179
Second Main Effect 180
Interaction Effect 180
Post-hoc Testing 181
Post Hoc for a Significant Main Effect 181
Post Hoc for a Significant Interaction Effect 182
Plain English 184
Applying Results 184
Two-way, Between-groups ANOVA on SPSS 185
APA-style Results Section 192
Graphing the Two-way ANOVA 193
Preview of Chapter 11 196
Conceptual Items 197
Application Items 197
Computational Formulas in This Chapter 200
References 200

PART IV   INFERENTIAL STATISTICS: CORRELATIONAL RESEARCH

Chapter 11   Correlational Data   201

Relationships Between Variables 201
Logic of Pearson's r 201
Perfect Linear Relationships 201
Less-than-perfect Relationships 204
Pearson's r Calculations 205
Inferential Correlations: Hypothesis Testing 207

Correlations on SPSS	209
Scatterplot on SPSS	210
Pearson's r on SPSS	212
APA-style Results Section	214
Inaccurate Correlations	214
Artificially Low Correlations	214
Artificially High Correlations	217
Preview of Chapter 12	219
Conceptual Items	220
Application Items	220
Computational Formula in This Chapter	223
References	223

Chapter 12   **Linear Regression**   **224**

Correlation Before Prediction	224
Linear Regression Theory	224
Prediction	225
Error in Predictions	226
Calculating the Regression Equation	226
Graphing the Regression Line	229
Standard Error of the Estimate	230
Standard Error Calculations	230
Prediction on SPSS	233
Correlation on SPSS	233
Linear Regression on SPSS	234
APA-style Results Section	236
Preview of Chapter 13	236
Conceptual Items	237
Application Items	237
Computational Formulas in This Chapter	241
References	241

Chapter 13   **Chi-Square Analyses**   **242**

Simple Frequency Counts	242
One-Way χ^2: Goodness-of-fit Test	242
Null and Alternative Hypotheses	242
Chosen Statistic	243
Sampling Distribution for χ^2	243
χ^2_{obt} Above Zero	244
APA Style	246
Plain English	246
Inferring Back to the Population	246
Goodness-of-fit for Three Levels	246
Goodness-of-fit with Unequal Expectations	248
One-way χ^2 on SPSS	249

APA-style Results Section   249
Two-way χ^2: Test of Independence   250
    Null and Alternative Hypotheses   250
    Chosen Statistic   250
    Sampling Distribution   250
    Significantly Related   251
    APA Style   252
    Strength of Effect   252
    Plain English   253
    Inference to the Real Population   254
Two-way χ^2 in SPSS   254
APA-style Results Section   259
Conceptual Items   259
Application Items   260
Computational Formulas in This Chapter   261
References   262

Appendix A   ANOVA: One-Way, Repeated-Measures Using SPSS   263

Testing the Same Participants   263
One-way, Repeated-measures ANOVA on SPSS   264
APA-style Results Section   271
Summary of the One-way, Repeated-measures ANOVA   271
Conceptual Items   271
Application Items   272

Appendix B   Multiple Regression Using SPSS   274

More Than One Predictor Variable   274
Multiple Regression in SPSS   275
APA-style Results Section   278
Summary of Multiple Regression   278
Conceptual Items   278
Application Items   278

Table 1 z-**Table**   **281**

Table 2 t-**Table**   **285**

Table 3 F-**Table**   **286**

Table 4 q-**Table**   **289**

Table 5 r-**Table**   **291**

Table 6 χ^2 **Table**   **293**

Answers to Odd-Numbered Items   **294**

Index   **343**

PREFACE

To the Instructor

Why Another Statistics Book?

I have been teaching statistics for about ten years, and one thing remains consistent: The majority of psychology students are not overjoyed to learn statistics. When I ask them why, they often tell me they aren't good at math and statistics is a boring course. While I appreciate their candid replies, I don't think their perceptions are accurate. They *can* be good at math, and statistics doesn't have to be a boring course.

In this textbook, every effort is made to

(1) reduce anxiety about statistics,
(2) make statistics relevant and interesting, and
(3) incorporate SPSS to show students how to analyze data efficiently.

To reduce anxiety, Chapter 1 opens with pointers on how to become competent in the course, with the final point reminding students that we're on their side. We want them to succeed and are delighted to record high grades when they are earned. Chapter 1 also contains a section on math, and students can quickly see that calculations required in statistics are quite simple. To further demonstrate that the math required of them is not difficult, over 30 practice items are offered at the end of this chapter. Within the first few class meetings, students should begin to recognize that they can perform well in statistics if they apply themselves, and we are available to help if they need us.

In addition to a simple introduction to the course in Chapter 1, the entire text is written in a conversational style to further reduce anxiety. Although several reader-friendly supplemental statistics texts have become available over the past few years, this book is the first that offers the same readability and covers all information essential to a statistics course, from z-tests to the two-way ANOVA. In fact, I have also included brief Appendices on the repeated-measures ANOVA and multiple regression for instructors who choose to cover them. Every chapter and appendix is written in a straightforward way that my students have found accessible.

Within each chapter, the material is segmented into many sections and subsections to allow students to digest the material at their own pace without stopping in the middle of a long stretch of text. The final section of each chapter is a preview of the subsequent chapter. The Preview summarizes the current chapter and links the material with the next chapter to help students see connections between topics. Finally, anxiety is reduced by offering students many practice items, which have been divided into Conceptual and Application categories. Conceptual Items are definitional or based on theory presented in the chapter.

- "What measure of variability must be used with ordinal data?"
- "When designing an experiment, why do researchers prefer a dependent variable of interval or ratio values?"
- "Why is it illogical to compare diagonal cell means after discovering a significant interaction?"

Answers to these items can easily be found within the chapter to help students test themselves on their memory of the material. Application Items are more involved, requiring students to analyze an example in detail, often including calculations.

"Examine the data below representing several types of punishment used to discipline children and the effect of these punishers on behavior on a scale from 1-10, with higher numbers indicating better behavior. Children were randomly assigned to receive one of the following types of punishers."

A Lecture	Yelling	Time-Out	Spanking
9	4	7	2
8	6	8	1
5	4	5	3
7	8	9	4
6	7	4	3
3	6	2	5

A second Application Item example allows students to explore the relationship between age and respect.

"Based on your knowledge of linear relationships, analyze the following data set and draw conclusions based on your results. Your job is to clearly communicate exactly what this data set reveals about the relationship between age (in years) and the amount of respect given to people in our society. For the respect variable, assume each person was asked to rate the amount of respect received on a daily basis using a scale from 0-100, with higher numbers indicating more respect."

Age	Respect	Age	Respect
39	90	45	87
75	63	12	35
15	48	50	95
62	85	35	81
19	59	67	78
21	60	20	62
26	78	72	66
37	84	29	76
40	96	80	45
82	40		

For both Conceptual and Application Item sections, more challenging items tend to be found toward the end of each category, and answers to odd-numbered items are located at the back of the book. Answers to all even-numbered items are found in the **instructor's manual,** and the **student workbook** provides larger data sets and a look at studies published by undergraduates.

To address students' concern that statistics is a boring course, I have tried to share my passion for teaching statistics in this textbook. For several years, passion in teaching has been a hot topic among instructors, and encouraging student enthusiasm is a primary goal. Discussions have centered around getting and keeping students' attention in order to teach effectively, and we have begun to embrace the idea of entertaining while teaching. In this text, I have tried to entertain through examples that are relevant to most college students, including examples that have made my students laugh, nod their heads in agreement, or analyze enthusiastically to reach the answer. Because students should recognize that scientific knowledge is established through research, several examples are based on the results of published studies, and references are found at the end of relevant chapters.

In addition to interesting examples, the text includes only analyses that (a) are necessary to build skills or (b) will likely be used by students in the future. Many of us can attest to the frustration (and boredom) associated with learning more than we want to know. I had this experience when I was taught how to build a website; to my dismay, I was also taught the inner workings of my computer. I found myself tuning out the information that, by my teacher's own admission, would not be relevant to me. This text presents statistics chosen as highly relevant based on talking with colleagues, reading their research, and experiencing my own needs when analyzing data from my lab. Further, each discussion of inferential statistics contains information that students are likely to need, including effect size, confidence intervals, and a model APA-style results section.

A third goal of this text is to teach SPSS. Most campuses have access to this computer program, and it is currently the most popular program for data analysis. I require my students to learn how to conduct analyses by hand before turning to computers because hand calculations allow students to play an active role in finding the result of an example. Formulas also tend to reflect the logic behind analyses. I've also noticed that the majority of my students have difficulty relating to the material when they stare at a computer screen. However, SPSS offers a level of efficiency students would never enjoy if they continued to rely on hand calculations. To ease the transition from hand computations to computer analysis, SPSS is thoroughly integrated in the text. After each analysis is conducted by hand, the same example is analyzed using SPSS. That way, students can clearly see that the computer provides the same output they calculated by hand. As an added bonus, students will not need to purchase an additional manual on the use of SPSS; every relevant aspect is covered in the current textbook, from data entry to output.

Topics and Organization

This text covers statistics essential to students in the social sciences. I have chosen a slightly unusual chapter organization, with correlation and regression analyses found under *Inferential Statistics*. Traditionally, these analyses are discussed early in the course as descriptive statistics, and students never hear of *p*-values or significant effects. When I taught correlation and regression as descriptive statistics, it was always awkward for me to try to revisit them at the end of the term to let students know these analyses could actually be inferential statistics. I also wanted to avoid putting correlation and regression in the middle of z-scores because the arrangement breaks up the natural flow of discussion from descriptive to inferential statistics.

The first part of the text, INTRODUCTION, welcomes the student, defines many research terms, and introduces math. Chapter 1 shows students that calculations for this course are not difficult; math is simply a tool we use to make sense of data and hopefully learn something new about behavior.

The second part, DESCRIPTIVE STATISTICS, introduces in Chapter 2 classifications of variables, simple frequency tables and graphs, and shapes of distributions. In Chapters 3 and 4, measures of central tendency and variability are explained in detail using examples, and SPSS output is provided where appropriate. In Chapter 5, descriptive z-scores are introduced, and simple frequency distributions are revisited.

Part III, INFERENTIAL STATISTICS: EXPERIMENTS AND QUASI-EXPERIMENTS covers probability, hypothesis testing, t-tests, and ANOVAs by hand and using SPSS. In Chapter 6, probability and inferential z-scores flow naturally from the Chapter 5 topic of descriptive z-scores. Chapter 7 then relies on inferential z-scores to introduce the logic of hypothesis testing. Chapter 8 takes one more step, beginning with the single-sample t-test and moving through the dependent-samples t-test, then to the independent-samples t-test. The one-way, between-groups ANOVA in Chapter 9 is a logical extension of the independent-samples t-test. A significant ANOVA is followed by post hoc testing. Chapter 10 covers the two-way, between-groups ANOVA and post hoc testing of main effects and the interaction. Within this part of the text, I point out that we have true experiments only when participants are manipulated; without manipulation, we only know if variables are related. This point is illustrated by several Application Items in which a quasi-IV (e.g., gender) is used in a study, and students much decide if causation can be established.

The fourth section, INFERENTIAL STATISTICS: CORRELATIONAL RESEARCH, covers correlation, linear regression, and chi squared. My students generally perform well on these topics, easing their stress toward the end of the term and allowing them to get their second wind for the final exam. Just as with Part III of the book, I point out here that cause and effect can in fact be established in correlational research if one variable has been manipulated.

The fifth section offers APPENDICES to cover additional designs students are likely to use as undergraduates. Instructors may choose to discuss the logic of the one-way, repeated-measures ANOVA as well as multiple linear regression. SPSS layout, data analysis, and output for these designs are also covered.

Supplemental Materials

A **Student Workbook (0-13-111705-X),** written by J.H. Wilson, is available for students in this course who want additional practice with conceptual and application items, including SPSS analysis. The workbook showcases student research with articles featured in undergraduate journals. Students will have the opportunity to read work published by their peers as they evaluate data using their knowledge of statistics. Writing this workbook has allowed the author to support student research, always a top priority, as well as make sure the materials are tightly integrated with the textbook.

An **Instructor's Manual (0-13-111706-8)** with sample test items, written by J.H. Wilson, is offered to the instructor of this course. The items have been tested in the author's classes for many years and have improved with student suggestions. The instructor's manual also contains answers to even-numbered Conceptual and Application Items located at the end of each text chapter. In addition, the manual offers various approaches to topics in statistics and presents ways to encourage active participation.

The **NEW Prentice Hall's TestGen (0-13-189667-9)** is available on one dual-platform CD-ROM. This test generator program provides instructor's "best in class" features in an easy-to-use program. Create tests using the TestGen Wizard and easily select questions with drag-and-drop or point-and-click functionality. Add or modify test questions using the built-in Question Editor and print tests in a variety of formats.

Research Navigator™ features three exclusive databases full of source material, including:

- *EBSCO's ContentSelect Academic Journal Database*, organized by subject. Each subject contains 50 to 100 of the leading academic journals for that discipline. Instructors and students can search the online journals by keyword, topic, or multiple topics. Articles include abstract and citation information and can be cut, pasted, emailed, or saved for later use.
- *The New York Times Search-by-Subject One Year Archive*, organized by subject and searchable by keyword or multiple keywords. Instructors and students can view the full text of the article.
- *Link Library*, organized by subject, offers editorially selected "best of the Web" sites. Link Libraries are continually scanned and kept up to date providing the most relevant and accurate links for research assignments.

To see how this resource works, take a tour at **www.researchnavigator.com**, or ask your local Prentice Hall representative for more details.

To the Student

How to Use This Book

While I wrote this book, I tried to always keep in mind how I would talk with you if we were discussing statistics face to face. As a result, I hope you find the conversational style enjoyable and easy to read. For many of us, statistics can be a bit overwhelming, and I didn't want the wording to get in the way of learning the material.

Each chapter begins with a brief overview of what is found in the chapter. It is really the theory of when and why we run certain statistics. Terms that are particularly important are in **bold** type. Next, formulas are introduced with examples rather than alone because *using* the formulas is more important than just looking at them or trying to memorize them with no application. It is useful for you to calculate statistics by hand for at least two reasons: Hand calculations offer an active role in conducting statistics that reinforces the logic behind each calculation, and later, computer output can be examined for errors. The examples calculated by hand should be of interest to most college students. In fact, many examples are based on suggestions from my own students.

- The effect of calling your parents on how much spending money they send you (Chapters 3 & 4)
- Pain ratings of people who get a tattoo at either the Hepatitis Shack or the House of Maim (Chapter 5)
- Students' attitudes toward the DARE program (Chapter 9)
- The relationship between hours of sleep and grades in college (Chapter 11)
- The potential relationship between sexual orientation and creativity (Chapter 13)

As soon as you calculate the answer to an example, you'll learn to make sense of the result and write it in plain English. After all, a statistic is not useful unless it brings us knowledge to share with the world. In fact, psychologists rely on the American Psychological Association to set guidelines for reporting results, and your instructor might ask you to review the APA-style results section in relevant chapters.

At the end of each analysis, SPSS is offered as a way to calculate answers more quickly. SPSS, a computer program used to analyze numerous types of data, was chosen for this text based on its popularity and availability. For every analysis on SPSS, an example that was recently calculated by hand is entered into the computer. The text begins with how to enter numbers in a spreadsheet and covers which options to choose from pull-down menus as well as how to read the output. It might be useful to highlight relevant information on the output to avoid focusing on information you don't need to report.

Because each example on SPSS will have been calculated by hand first, you will be able to check the output from SPSS for reasonable answers. For example, the text indicates that SPSS offers a way to describe a *sample* that in fact is an estimate of the *population*. This type of error will not be understood unless you first complete calculations to describe a sample by hand. Of course, computers are not thinking creatures, so we have to make sure we double-check the logic of all output based on our own experiences with hand calculations. After you feel comfortable with assessing computer output, SPSS will probably replace hand calculations as an efficient way to analyze data. This will certainly be true in later courses like research methods and when you conduct your own research in the future.

Finally, each chapter ends with a preview of the next chapter, but this section also contains a summary of the current chapter. Reading this section carefully will give you an idea of whether or not the overall picture of the chapter is clear.

To further check your grasp of the material, Conceptual Items will test your memory of information found in the chapter. Next, Application Items present examples to be analyzed by hand and on SPSS.

- In Chapter 7, the possibility of an effect of exercise on self-esteem can be examined.
- In Chapter 9, you can analyze a data set of several types of punishment used to discipline children to see if some are more effective than others.
- In Chapter 10, you will have the opportunity to examine the possible effect of alcohol and provocation on aggressive behavior.

Even if your instructor does not assign practice items, you might want to make a habit of completing them to become competent with the material before a test. Additional examples can be found in the **student workbook,** and the workbook also showcases research articles published by undergraduates.

Acknowledgments

I sincerely appreciate the open-minded, friendly approach of Jayme Heffler, Acquisitions Editor for Psychology, and the whole team at Prentice Hall. I also wholeheartedly thank the many reviewers who offered comments and suggestions on drafts of this text. I recognize that only through peer review can we hope to share our knowledge in a clear and effective way.

Jeffrey B. Adams
Saint Michael's College

Barney Beins
Ithaca College

Jacqueline Bichsel
Pennsylvania State University at Harrisburg

Carrie Bulger
Quinnipiac College

Kim Cronise
Oregon Health & Science University

Robert J. Crutcher
University of Dayton

Nancy Da Silva
San Jose State University

Leslie Gill
Eastern New Mexico University

Mark E. Hamlin
University of Central Oklahoma

Scott Hershberger
California State University, Long Beach

Donald Kendrick
Middle Tennessee State University

Ed Lipinski
Mesa Community College

Barbara A. Lounsbury
Rhode Island College

Anna M. Napoli
University of Redlands

Evangeline Wheeler
Towson University

ABOUT THE AUTHOR

Janie Wilson began her adventure in teaching during graduate school and continued in a full-time teaching position at Columbia College before receiving her Ph.D. in Experimental Psychology from the University of South Carolina in 1994. Since that time, she has been teaching and conducting research at Georgia Southern University. Her teaching includes courses in statistics, research methods, large sections of introductory psychology, and physiological psychology. Teaching and research merged when she was awarded a National Science Foundation grant as principal investigator for a physiological teaching laboratory, and a recent grant from the National Institute of Mental Health continues to fund her research program. She works with both undergraduates and graduate students on research projects involving social buffering of stress responses in rats and human adults and children. Dr. Wilson also conducts research on student evaluations of instructor immediacy and their ability to predict students' attitudes, motivation, and grades. She was honored with the College of Liberal Arts and Social Sciences Award for Excellence in 1997, the Award of Distinction in Teaching in 2003, and the Georgia Southern University Award for Excellence in Contributions to Instruction in 2004.

1

Welcome to Statistics

Building Competence

Each of you brings to the course different expectations about statistics and various levels of competence. This chapter will introduce the basics of statistics to guide your expectations and perhaps alleviate anxiety. Below are some suggestions to help you become more competent:

1. Attend every class. Missing a class means missing valuable information and relying on others to provide their versions of the material.
2. Pay attention in class. This sounds easier than it is because we tend to day-dream without realizing it. As soon as you realize you have lost focus, bring your attention back to the class. Eventually you will train yourself to stay in the present.
3. Practice, practice, practice. Nothing builds competence as well as practice. Do not just practice doing statistics; practice doing statistics quickly. Most class periods are not long enough to allow you to trudge slowly through a test.
4. Try to relax. You might use deep breathing and progressive muscle relaxation to calm yourself. A small amount of stress is useful because it keeps you awake, but too much stress can get in your way, especially on a test.
5. Rely on your instructor. You have an expert to help you through the rough spots, and he or she wants you to succeed. Of course, grades have to be earned, but it is always a pleasure when those grades are high.

Rationale for Learning Statistics

First, statistics offer a way to organize information. You have been using statistics for years—every time you calculated your test average by adding test scores and dividing by the number of tests. This average was more useful than individual test scores and is an example of using statistics to summarize data. When your instructor announces the average for a statistics test, he or she is also using statistics to summarize data, and a second purpose is served: communicating information.

Third, statistics can be used to examine the results of a study. For example, if we wanted to know if exercising increases heart-rate, we could measure participants' heart-rate before and after exercising and compare the numbers. All we have to know is how to analyze the data using a specific statistic. (You'll learn that soon.) Fourth, we want to be competent and honest when we analyze data so we can have confidence in our results. Fifth, even if you never do research, you will want to read the research of other people. If you know something about statistics, you will be able to evaluate whether or not researchers are using the right test for their data.

Math

It is no secret that this course involves math, but if you know how to add, subtract, multiply, and divide, the math in this course should not be overwhelming. Most instructors will allow the use of calculators, and many will permit (even encourage) the use of a computer with statistics software.

Regardless of the tools used for data analysis, always simplify formulas. As a general rule, work inside parentheses and deal with exponents first. Since you already know what parentheses are, we will discuss exponents. Exponents are numbers with a small additional number in the upper right corner. In this course, that additional number will always be a two, so you will need to square the main number. An example is

$$2^2 = 4$$

Next, calculate any multiplication and division found in the formula. When you have a fraction, immediately divide the *numerator* (top) by the *denominator* (bottom).

$$\frac{\text{Numerator}}{\text{Denominator}} \qquad \frac{1}{10} = 0.10$$

Fractions are not intuitive to most people; division will create a number that is easier to use.

Finally, complete addition and subtraction in a formula.

One last bit of advice on calculating a formula: Work from the inside out. For example, if you have a formula with addition in the parentheses, do the addition first. (That makes sense because you know to begin inside parentheses.) As another example, if you have subtraction in the numerator of a fraction, subtract before dividing the numerator by the denominator. Again, work from the inside out, simplifying the formula with each step.

Proportion and Percent

A **proportion** is a fraction that indicates what part of the whole is represented by a specific value. The highest possible number for proportion is 1.00. As an example, if your score on a statistics quiz was 9 out of 10 items correct, your proportion correct would be

$$\frac{9}{10} = 0.90$$

Likewise, you could calculate the proportion incorrect:

$$\frac{1}{10} = 0.10$$

Most people prefer to deal with percent instead of proportion. **Percent** is a portion of 100. To change proportion to percent, multiply by 100. For our example above, 90% were correct on the test, and 10% were wrong.

Rounding

One of the first questions that might arise when you start calculating is the number of decimal places to use. Keep at least six decimal places all the way through a calculation, then round to two decimal places at the end. When we round to two decimal places at the end, we are following the guidelines given to us by the American Psychological Association (APA). Since psychologists (and many other people) use APA style, you should begin to get used to this style.

Throughout this text, we will keep six decimal places until we reach the final answer, then we will round to two decimal places. The only exceptions will be when intermediate calculations yield several zeros at the end of the numbers, in which case the additional zeros will not be written while we are calculating. However, keep in mind that the final answer must have two decimal places, even if that means adding zeros. For example, 52.3 should be written as 52.30, and 44 should be written as 44.00. The second exception will be when numbers are put into tables for viewing. In order to fit tables on the pages in an organized way, I will often stop at two decimal places. Your instructor will decide if you should keep six decimal places in your tables.

When rounding to two decimal places, the third number to the right of the decimal dictates whether the second number to the right of the decimal stays the same or is rounded up. If the third number is 0–4, the second number remains the same; however, if the third number is 5–9, the second number is rounded up, or increased by one. For example, when rounding 13.781 to a final answer with two decimal places, the 1 is removed, and the 8 stays the same, for an answer of 13.78. On the other hand, 13.789 is rounded up to 13.79. The same concept applies when rounding to six decimal places prior to the final answer, with the seventh number dictating whether the prior number stays the same or increases. For example, 2.6579333 is rounded to 2.657933, because the seventh number is between 0–4.

Symbols

Each formula in statistics has a name, and that name is represented by a symbol. Symbols are efficient because they take much less time to write than the full names, which can often be quite long. Symbols were meant to reduce work, so we will keep the symbols in this book simple. For example, $\overline{X}$ refers to the mean or average for a group of numbers. It is much more efficient to write $\overline{X}$ than "the average for a group of numbers."

Several symbols used in statistics are altered when reported in APA style. For example, $\overline{X}$ will be used when we calculate an average, but M will represent the average when the number is reported in an APA-style manuscript. In this text, the traditional symbols will be introduced in the chapters, and APA symbols will be explained at the end of the chapters. It is likely that APA-style symbols will be used during calculations in the future, but until that happens, you should become familiar with both types of symbols.

APA Style

APA style governs much more than symbols used in manuscripts. In fact, the scope of responsibilities carried by the APA is far too extensive to be covered here. Discussions in this text will be restricted to the role of this association in reporting statistical results. The APA provides detailed guidelines on how to prepare a Results section, including graphs and tables of statistical information.

Conducting Research

Research occurs in two primary forms: correlations and experiments. For each type of research, **variables** are studied. A variable is anything that varies. That is, a variable is anything that can take on at least two values. For example, a certain number of words are typed on this page. Another page contains a different number of words. The number of words on a page varies, so the number of words on a page is a variable.

No matter what kind of variable is used, it must be clearly defined. For example, aggression can be defined as hitting or any intent to harm, including using harsh words. A variable that is clearly defined is said to be **operationally defined**. Again, aggression might be operationally defined as hitting, touching in anger, or even using insulting words. For each study, the researcher must operationally define the variables used.

Experiments

In an **experiment**, one variable is manipulated, and the effect on a second variable is observed. Keep in mind that a variable is anything that can have more than one value. The manipulated variable is called the **independent variable** because it is not influenced by the behavior of people in the experiment. We usually call this variable the **IV**. For an example, we might examine the effect of room color on mood. Room color would be the IV because we choose the room colors to be used in this experiment. If red and green were chosen, these would be the **levels** of the IV. So our IV is the general term room color, and the levels are red and green. Levels can also be called **conditions**, **groups**, or **treatment groups**.

The variable measured after people have been exposed to the IV is called the **dependent variable (DV)**. It is called the dependent variable because the outcome (like mood) should depend on what level of the IV people had—if our experiment worked. The DV is not manipulated; it is measured across everyone at the end of the experiment. In our example, participants would be exposed to different room colors (IV), then asked to rate their mood (DV).

As another example, perhaps we were interested in the effect of sleep on how tired people are the next day. Our IV would be how many hours of sleep people get, but we still have to manipulate it by choosing levels. We could use four hours and eight hours as levels of the IV. Since each hour of sleep is always 60 minutes, and sleep is a familiar state of consciousness, the IV has been operationally defined. The DV is how sleepy people are the next day. Sleepiness is more difficult to operationalize. It could be operationally defined as the number of times people fall asleep in their 8:00 A.M. class, or participants could rate how tired they feel on a scale from 1 to 7, with 1 being "not tired at all" and 7 meaning "very tired." No matter which of these (or others) we choose for the DV, it will be operationalized, so people will know exactly how we measured tired. Because the variables are operationalized, other researchers could evaluate our experiment and even repeat the study using the same operational definitions to see if they find the same results.

In this example, we have two levels: four and eight hours of sleep. The next step in this experiment is to assign participants to one of the two levels of the IV. We could take the first 20 people who arrived at the experiment and put them in the eight-hour group, and the later participants would be put in the four-hour group. At the end of our experiment, we might find that four hours made people more tired than eight hours. However, if we assign participants to groups this way, other explanations are possible. Perhaps those who arrived early are "morning people" who are always wide awake at 8:00 a.m. On the other hand, the late arrivals could be "night owls" who do not wake up completely until noon. In the end, we cannot say that sleeping four hours made people more tired the next morning than sleeping eight hours as long as other explanations are possible.

The solution is to put participants in groups using **random assignment**. Random assignment to conditions means that everyone in the sample has an equal chance of being put in the levels of the IV. That way we would know if our IV truly caused changes in the DV—like four hours making people sleepier than eight hours. In experiments, if we want to know if our IV caused something to happen to our DV, we could randomly assign participants to conditions of the IV.

Correlations

A **correlational study** examines the possibility of a relationship between two variables: a co-relationship. For example, the price of jeans seems to be related to how popular they are. Using our new terminology, these two variables are correlated. This correlation does not tell us that the cost of jeans *causes* them to be popular; it only says that the two variables are related. That is the main problem with correlational studies: they do not tell us that one variable caused the other one. For jeans, does the price make them popular? Does their popularity affect price? Another possibility is that a third variable we did not measure might have influenced both the cost of jeans and how popular they are. For example, maybe the label on the jeans affects the price, and maybe the label affects how popular the jeans are. In this example, it could actually be the label (a third variable) that caused both the price and the popularity. The bottom line is that correlations cannot reveal that one variable caused the other: a correlation only tells us that the two variables are related somehow.

The Usefulness of Correlations

Because experiments provide information on cause (IV) and effect (DV), and correlations can only indicate if two variables are related, it might seem odd to conduct a correlational study rather than an experiment. However, correlations may be chosen for several reasons. First, correlations can be conducted on data that already exist; this is called archival research. For example, your school's registrar has a computer full of data on thousands of students. It would be simple to look at co-relationships between variables like age and GPA, or SAT score and GPA, or anything else that might be in the data set. Experiments are not possible because the data already exist; we cannot pretend we manipulated people to be a certain age or have a specific SAT score. As an added bonus, archives often contain a large amount of data—much more than we could collect quickly and in a single study.

Second, correlations can be used when we are collecting data and are only interested in relationships between variables; cause and effect are not the goals of the study. Quite often, researchers contact people and collect data on them across several variables, then look for correlations. One example you might have seen is when researchers stand in a shopping mall and stop people to ask a few questions, or have people complete a questionnaire.

A third reason to conduct correlations rather than an experiment is that sometimes it is unethical to force people into levels of the IV. For example, imagine you want to see if smoking and number of coughs per hour are related. You are ambitious and want to find out cause and effect, so you try to design an experiment. You invite people to participate in your study. Some people are handed one pack of cigarettes, and some are handed ten packs of cigarettes. You order them to smoke. Ignoring that we have not operationalized the variables well enough (like how long they have to smoke), this experiment presents an ethical problem. Since most of us believe that smoking is physically damaging, it would not be acceptable to make people smoke, especially ten packs of cigarettes.

It might be tempting to think you could ask people how much they generally smoke and watch how many times they cough. Although the idea is good, it is not an experiment; it is a correlational study. As long as we are not manipulating what happens to people, we are getting only correlations. In cases like this cigarette example, a correlational study is our only ethical option. We ask people how much they smoke and count their coughs, looking to see if number of cigarettes and number of coughs are related. We did not force participants to do anything harmful; those who smoked did it of their own free will.

How to Pick a Sample

Whether we are conducting a correlational study or an experiment, we are interested in learning something about people (or other types of animals). The group of interest is called a **population**. For example, you might be interested in learning about all students at your school. Then all the students at your school would be the population of interest. Perhaps you do not have time to study all the students; you only have time to study some of them. A subgroup pulled from the population is called a **sample**.

When you are picking members of the population for a sample, you hope they will represent the population in which you are interested (in this example, all students at your school). Not surprisingly, a sample that represents the population of interest is called a **representative sample**. Your best bet for getting a representative sample is to not just pick your friends, but pick people in a way that everyone in the population has an equal chance of being selected for your sample. This is called **random sampling**. It is also sometimes called **random selection** from the population.

Random sampling (selection) can be used when choosing a sample for either a correlational study or an experiment. For correlations, a sample is randomly selected, and information is collected to look for correlations. For example, if we learn from a sample of college students that their SAT scores and college GPA are related, we assume the same relationship would be found in the entire population—if we took the time to ask everyone in the population to report their SAT scores and GPAs. For an experiment, we randomly select a sample to split into levels of the IV. Even though we are manipulating people (the IV) and looking at the outcome variable (the DV), we are still using a sample. If different levels of the IV cause changes in the DV, we assume the same effect would be true if we tested everyone in the population. In either a correlational study or an experiment, we hope for a representative sample so we can learn about the population.

In other words, we infer something about the population from the representative sample we are studying. In statistics, numbers are used to help us infer back to the population, and these calculations are called **inferential statistics**. Most of this book will deal with inferential statistics. At first, though, we will describe a sample and not make any guesses about the population from which they were drawn. While that might not sound as exciting as inferring to an entire population, we sometimes only want to describe a sample. Returning to an earlier example, when your instructor goes over a test, he or she might tell you the average grade for the class. Remember that an average is a statistic. As a student in the class, you are not interested in whether or not the average can be expected for a larger population of students; you merely want to know the test average for your class. No inferential statistics are needed. When you are merely describing a sample, the calculations are called **descriptive statistics**.

To revisit our newest terms, we have inferential statistics, with which we learn about a population from a representative sample, and we have descriptive statistics, which simply describe a sample and make no guesses about the population.

Analyzing Data Using SPSS

One of the most efficient tools used to calculate either descriptive or inferential statistics is computers. Some people are good at using computers and others *can* be good at it. The most popular statistics program today is SPSS. When first learning a statistic, completing calculations by hand clarifies the theoretical bases; therefore, hand calculations for each statistic will be covered first. But SPSS will conduct the detailed math after you have had enough practice to know if the output looks logical.

Preview of Chapter 2

In the next chapter, we will cover descriptive statistics. You will learn that variables can represent different levels of measurement, then several types of graphs and graphing rules will be presented. Remember to practice statistics, talk with your instructor, and keep a positive attitude.

Conceptual Items

1. Why are statistics useful?
2. Define each of the following.

   a. APA
   b. experiment
   c. random assignment
   d. correlations

   e. random selection
   f. descriptive statistics
   g. inferential statistics
   h. SPSS

3. Why are symbols used in statistics?
4. Experiments reveal cause and effect, and correlational research primarily communicates a _____ between two variables.
5. Compare random selection and random assignment.
6. Compare experimental and correlational studies.

Application Items

7. Use rounding rules to round the following to two decimal places.

   a. 45.932
   b. 7.5100
   c. 36.8000

   d. 11.355
   e. 2.996
   f. 0.975555

8. Use calculation rules to find answers to the following. Your final answer should be rounded to two decimal places.

   a. 3^2
   b. 33^2

   c. 333^2

9. Divide each numerator by the denominator. Be sure to keep two decimal places in the final answers.

a. $\dfrac{2}{4}$

b. $\dfrac{4}{4}$

c. $\dfrac{3}{12}$

d. $\dfrac{40}{60}$

e. $\dfrac{17}{55}$

f. $\dfrac{9}{80}$

10. Change each answer in Application Item 9 to a percent. Since you already rounded to two decimal places in 9, the answers will be whole numbers.

11. Use calculation rules to find answers to the following.

a. $\sqrt{36}$

b. 6^2

c. $\dfrac{4^2}{3}$

d. $\sqrt{\dfrac{4^2}{3}}$

e. $\dfrac{\sqrt{(2+9)+(2)(9)}}{2^2+9^2}$

f. $\dfrac{5+\dfrac{7}{1}}{\dfrac{12}{5}}$

g. $\sqrt{\dfrac{4}{9}}+9$

h. $\dfrac{(8)(7^2)+1}{27}$

12. Use calculation rules to find answers to the following.

a. If $X = 3$, complete this problem: $2X + X$

b. If $Y = 5$, complete this problem: $\sqrt{Y-\dfrac{Y}{7}}$

c. If $Z = 10$, complete this problem: $(Z+3)(Z^2+8)$

d. If $G = 21.24$, complete this problem: $0.5G + G^2 - G$

13. List at least two levels for each of the following variables.

a. grades
b. hair length
c. baseball scores
d. patience
e. skin color
f. personal hygiene

14. Operationally define:

a. happiness
b. hunger
c. breakfast cereals

15. Identify the IV, IV levels, and DV.

Follow the format of this example:

The effect of halitosis on how far away people stand. One day you brush your teeth before class and measure how far away people stand when you talk to them. The next day, you eat breakfast and don't brush your teeth.

> IV: Brushing your teeth or not
>
> Levels: no brushing and brushing
>
> DV: How far away people stand

a. The effect of violent video games on violence in real life (playing them vs. not playing them).

b. The effect of smiling (none, once, or twice) on how long it takes to get someone to have a conversation.

c. The effect of exercising (3 times a week or 6 times a week) on self-esteem.

d. The effect of not watching TV or watching TV every day on motivation.

e. The effect of taking or not taking this course on happiness.

16. For each of the following, choose whether the item describes an experimental or correlational design. Keep in mind that an experiment requires manipulation of participants. On the other hand, correlation is based on two variables that are not manipulated.

    a. Examine the length of time it takes for students to complete a test and their grades on the test.

    b. Give some students thirty minutes to take a test, and give others sixty minutes to take the test. Examine their grades.

    c. Make some people gamble during the year. The remainder of the participants should not be allowed to gamble. At the end of the year, see how many bills each participant paid late.

    d. Ask people to report how many times they gambled in the past year and how many bills they paid late last year.

    e. Stop people at a coffee shop and ask them to report their age and rate their self-esteem on a scale from 1 to 500.

    f. Randomly assign participants to live either within one mile of an airport or at least ten miles away from an airport, then ask them to report their ability to concentrate.

    g. Ask males and females to write their GPAs on confidential slips of paper for you to analyze.

17. If $\sum$ is a symbol for "sum," N represents the number of values, and X is a symbol for values (numbers), complete the following calculation for the data set provided.

X

3
5
4
5
6

$$\sqrt{\dfrac{\sum X^2 - \dfrac{\left(\sum X\right)^2}{N}}{N}}$$

2

Variables and Graphing

Measurement Scales

In Chapter 1, a variable was introduced as anything that can have more than one value. In other words, variables vary. Although they vary in several ways, the most important descriptions are **scales (or levels) of measurement**. Scales of measurement define variables in one of four types: nominal, ordinal, interval, or ratio.

Nominal Variables

We will begin with the variable of eye color. Some people have brown eyes, and others have blue or green. Because the color of people's eyes can take on more than 1 value, this is obviously a variable. Brown, blue, and green (and other colors) are simply categories, so we can call eye color a **categorical** variable. Another term used more often is **nominal** variable, and it is synonymous with categorical.

Ordinal Variables

Suppose you and a group of your friends enter a weight-lifting contest. Janice wins 1st place, Timmy wins 2nd place, and Patrick wins 3rd place. Their ranking is a variable because ranking can take on more than one value: 1st, 2nd, and 3rd places. Rank is not a nominal variable because 1st, 2nd, and 3rd place are more than just categories; there is a meaningful order to the levels. First place is better than 2nd, and 2nd is better than 3rd place. With meaning to the order, this is called an **ordinal** scale of measurement. As a second example, if five of your friends were standing in front of you, they could be arranged from shortest to tallest (or the other way around, if you'd prefer). The order would have meaning because the second person would be taller than the first, and so on.

Interval Variables

So far, we have covered nominal variables (categorical) and ordinal variables (ranked), but some variables are at a higher level. That is, some variables have a meaningful order (like ordinal variables), *and* they have equal intervals between levels. These properties define an **interval** scale. An example of an interval scale is temperature. Whether temperature is measured in Fahrenheit or Celsius, the intervals across a thermometer are equal. The interval between 10°F and 20°F is the same as the interval between 20°F and 30°F.

Equal intervals allow calculations on the numbers. If you tried to do math with a nominal scale, like gender, it would not work. Adding or subtracting categories is not logical (brown eyes and blue eyes don't equal green eyes). It is the same for an ordinal scale; you cannot do math on place (1st place plus 3rd place doesn't equal 4th place). But with an interval scale, like temperature, morning temperature can be subtracted from afternoon temperature to describe a rise in temperature across the day.

Ratio Variables

Some variables have equal intervals and one more important property: absolute zero. Absolute zero means the absence of the variable measured. For example, imagine that we wanted to look at the number of movies people see in a year. The variable would be the number of movies seen, and it has equal intervals because the interval between three and four movies is one film, and the interval between four and five is one film. We also have an absolute zero point because it would be possible to see no movies at all. A variable with equal intervals and an absolute zero point represents a **ratio** scale, and this type of scale allows you to do math— just like the interval scale. In addition, on a ratio scale, four is twice as many as two, six is twice as many as three, and so on, because every value is relative to the absolute zero point. Using our movie example, someone who saw 100 films in the past year saw twice as many as someone who saw 50.

A second example of a ratio scale would be money in your pocket. Money has equal intervals in pennies, nickels, dimes, or quarters, etc, and it can definitely have an absolute zero point, with that zero point being the absence of money. In addition, $20 is twice as much as $10, and $100 is 4 times as much as $25.

Special Case of Rating Scales

In general, we think of nominal and ordinal variables as similar in that they do not allow math. Likewise, interval and ratio scales have in common that they do allow math, and because math permits us to use more powerful statistics, researchers try to measure variables that are at least at the interval level. It does not matter if a variable reaches ratio level (with an absolute zero); interval is good enough. You will need to know the four scales and examples, but for most data analysis in this book you will only need to know if an outcome variable (e.g., a dependent variable) at least reaches interval level. If it does not, simpler types of statistics for nominal and ordinal outcome data must be used.

As a psychologist, I have encountered one type of variable that forces a difficult choice between a math-based scale (interval) and a non-math scale (ordinal). We must decide if rating scales are only an ordinal scale of measurement or if they reach the higher-level interval scale. For example, when you evaluate your instructors at the end of each term, you probably use a rating scale with several numbers on it. Perhaps the scale ranges from 1 to 7, with 1 meaning "not enthusiastic" and 7 representing "very enthusiastic." Most psychologists would agree that a rating scale is an interval variable because we assume that the number 2 on the sheet is the same distance from the 1 as it is from the 3, etc. It is a large assumption, and many mathematicians would disagree with us. Since you are in a psychology course, your instructor may ask you to accept that rating scales are interval variables.

Qualitative Versus Quantitative Variables

In addition to defining a variable's scale of measurement, you may need to decide whether it is qualitative or quantitative. Those two words are similar, so be careful not to confuse them with each other. It might help to think of the first word as quality and the second as quantity. A **qualitative** (quality) **variable** is one that can be separated into categories with no math properties. For example, ethnicity is a nominal-level variable (e.g., African American, Native American and Asian), and it can be called qualitative because the levels place people in categories. As you know, ethnicity does not have math properties.

The same holds true for a variable like T-shirt size, which is often divided into small, medium, large, and extra large. These are not exact measurements; they are merely ranked in order from smallest to largest. From our previous discussion, you know that this variable represents an ordinal scale of measurement. You also know that ranked data do not have equal intervals, so math cannot be conducted. Ordinal data is then considered to be qualitative. Since nominal and ordinal data do not have math properties, both of these types of variables are qualitative. Their levels have qualities, but no meaningful numbers can be assigned to them.

On the other hand, **quantitative variables** have levels with meaningful numbers that allow calculations. For example, blood alcohol concentration represents a ratio scale of measurement because it has equal intervals per volume of blood, and a zero is the absence of alcohol in the bloodstream. You already learned that interval and ratio data allow math; therefore, it will come as no surprise that these data are quantitative variables.

Here are the main ideas to take away from this discussion of qualitative and quantitative variables: Qualitative variables are simply divided into categories with no math possible. Two types of qualitative variables are nominal and ordinal scales of measurement. Quantitative variables do allow math because the levels are represented by numbers with an underlying quantity. Two types of quantitative variables are interval and ratio scales of measurement.

Discrete Versus Continuous Variables

This section will cover one final way to discuss variables. In addition to deciding the scale of measurement (nominal, ordinal, interval, or ratio) and choosing between qualitative and quantitative, variables can be defined as either discrete or continuous.

Discrete variables do not allow continuity (fractions) between categories. In fact, some discrete variables have levels that are categories and no math properties at all. You already know that nominal and ordinal data (qualitative) fit this definition. One special example of a discrete scale has only two levels. This is called a **dichotomous variable**, since "di" stands for two. It is useful to have a special name for a discrete scale with only two possible categories because many examples of dichotomous variables exist in research. Some popular examples are gender, present versus absent, on versus off, and inside versus outside.

Discrete also applies to numbers with mathematical properties, as long as the numbers are whole numbers with no possibility of fractions (decimals). This means that a discrete variable can be interval or ratio data. For example, the number of people at parties represents ratio data due to equal intervals (four people are twice as many as two), and zero is the absence of people at a party. But only whole numbers are logical. Obviously 22.50 people cannot be at a party, so fractions make no sense on a discrete scale.

Levels of a **continuous variable** are not restricted to whole numbers; fractions between numbers are reasonable. For example, dollars in your pocket represent a continuous scale because you might have 0.50 dollars. Another example is weight. Most people do not weigh pounds in whole numbers. An exact scale might show that a person weighs 175.20 pounds, 120.47 pounds, or 245.85 pounds.

What should be remembered from this discussion of discrete and continuous variables is that nominal and ordinal data are definitely discrete, and interval and ratio scales can also be discrete if the levels can only be represented by whole numbers. When it comes to a continuous scale, nominal and ordinal variables are never continuous. Only interval and ratio scales have the possibility of being continuous—when fractions between numbers are logical.

Picturing Data: Simple Frequency Tables and Graphs

In the second half of this chapter, you will learn how to organize data in simple frequency tables and graphs, both of which are often called **simple frequency distributions**. **Simple frequency** means the number of times (how frequently) an item (or score or number or whatever you're measuring) comes up in a sample. It is symbolized by f. Tables are similar regardless of the type of data represented, but a graph depends on the variable's scale of measurement (nominal, ordinal, interval, or ratio) and whether the variable graphed is discrete or continuous. (Qualitative or quantitative doesn't affect graphing.) First we will create tables and graphs for nominal and ordinal data, then we will cover discrete interval and ratio data, and finally continuous interval and ratio data will be addressed.

Nominal and Ordinal Data

Remember that nominal and ordinal data are both qualitative variables. They are also both discrete. Because these types of variables are so similar, most of the same rules for making tables and graphs can be followed for both.

First, nominal data will be illustrated. Imagine that you walked into a classroom and noticed that nine people had brown eyes, seven had blue eyes, and three had green eyes. In other words, the simple frequency of brown was nine, the simple frequency of blue was seven, and the simple frequency of green was three. You could organize the information in a table this way:

Eye Color	*f*
Brown	9
Blue	7
Green	3

The colors are categories; therefore, their order in the table does not matter as long as the correct simple frequency is across from each color.

In addition to organizing data in a simple frequency table, a graph could be created. A graph is simply a picture of the data set. First, lines for the *x*-axis and *y*-axis are sketched, with the *y*-axis about 75% as long as the *x*-axis. Then the *x*-axis (the one on the bottom) should be labeled with the three colors in your table. Although we know that any order would be fine, we will use brown, blue, then green in this example. So far, the graph should look like this:

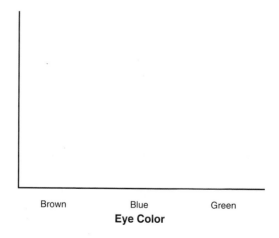

On the *y*-axis (the one on the left side), label what is being measured. In this case, the data are simple frequency counts—how often each color occurs in the data set. Since the most frequent color occurs nine times (brown), the *y*-axis must extend to nine, and I have chosen to count by ones on the *y*-axis. Now the graph should look like this (see next page):

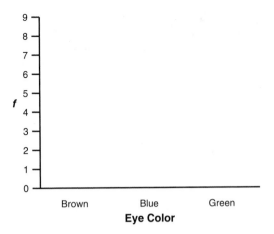

Above each color we will draw a bar to indicate how frequently the color occurs based on the y-axis measurements. We can graph brown first. The color brown occurs nine times in the sample, so the bar above brown should reach to the level of the nine based on our y-axis label numbers. A completely separate bar will be drawn above the color blue, and this one should extend to a simple frequency of seven. Lastly, draw a bar above the color green, but this one only needs to reach a simple frequency of three. The completed graph should look like this one:

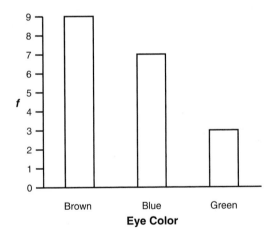

For ordinal data, the rules are the same as nominal, with one exception: The order of levels does matter with ordinal data. Although categories can occur in any order (for nominal data), ranked data are based on a meaningful order. For clarification, we will turn to letter grades as an example of an ordinal variable. They are in a meaningful order: A is better than B, and B is better than C. This scale is not interval because we cannot assume there are equal intervals between each grade. That is, we do not know that an A is exactly 10% better than a B and so on. In fact, we know that an A could be 90% and a B could be 89%.

On the last test you took, if 12 of the students in the class received an A, four received a B, three received a C, and three received a D, the simple frequency of an A was 12; the simple frequency of B was four; the simple frequency of a C was three; and the simple frequency of D was three Here is a simple frequency distribution for these data in table form:

Grades	f
A	12
B	4
C	3
D	3

The grades and simple frequency could also be written in the reverse order, like this:

Grades	f
D	3
C	3
B	4
A	12

When creating a graph of the grades above, label the *x*-axis with grades. Because numbers on the bottom of a graph should get larger from left to right, I prefer to label the D grade near the left side of the *x*-axis as the lowest grade. Then the C and B grades are placed in the middle of the *x*-axis, and the A is on the right side. The labeled *x*-axis is illustrated below:

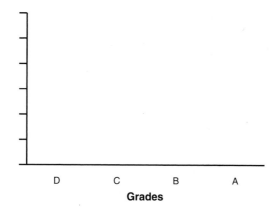

Now that the *x*-axis is labeled with grades, the *y*-axis must be labeled. The most frequently seen score among the grades happened 12 times; therefore, the *y*-axis needs to extend at least to 12 so we will be able to graph all of the A grades. On the bottom of that line, where it touches the *x*-axis, write a zero. I have chosen to count by two for my increments, labeling the *y*-axis from 0 to 12 (notice that numbers increase from bottom to top on this axis), and we are ready to create the inside of this graph. First depict the D grade. It happened three times and can be graphed with a bar from the D area on the *x*-axis up to where the *y*-axis indicates three. A grade of C also occurred three times. Use the same procedure with the B grade, allowing this bar to reach slightly higher to a frequency of four. Finally, the A bar extends all the way up the graph to a frequency of 12.

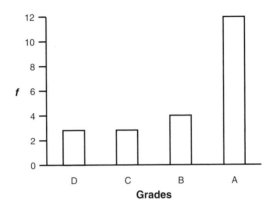

When graphing nominal or ordinal data on the *x*-axis (as we did above), use a bar graph. The bars must not touch each other; each level is separate and independent.

Discrete Interval and Ratio Data

We know that bar graphs are used when we have a nominal or ordinal variable on the *x*-axis, and the bars may not touch since we obviously have discrete data. But our graphing procedure changes slightly with discrete interval or ratio data. Remember that interval or ratio variables allow math to be conducted on the data, but discrete variables do not allow fractions. We can still create a bar graph—since the data are discrete—but allow the bars to touch to indicate that our variable is interval or ratio data.

For example, you could graph the number of classes students in your statistics course miss this semester. (I'm making the assumption that no one would miss a fraction of a class period, because that would mean arriving very late or walking out in the middle of lecture.) Your data might look like this:

Classes missed	f
0	5
1	12
2	6
3	5
4	2

The number of classes missed is a discrete, ratio variable, requiring that you create a bar graph for discrete but make the bars touch for ratio-level data.

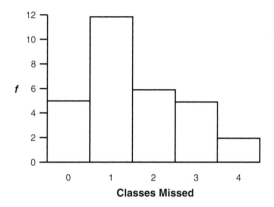

This type of graph is called a **histogram.**

Continuous Interval and Ratio Data

When interval or ratio data are continuous (allow fractions), the continuity between values is represented by a **line graph**. A line graph of simple frequency data is sometimes called a **simple frequency polygon**. For an example, hair length is a continuous ratio variable. The data might look like this:

Hair Length (in)	f
3	4
4	8
5	3
6	1

To graph these data, label the x-axis from 3 to 6, and label the y-axis with f. Since the simple frequencies range from 1 to 8, label the y-axis from 0 to 8. I have chosen to count by intervals of two from 0 to 8. When graphing the simple frequency for each hair length, do not use a bar; instead, put a dot at the place where the top of the bar would have been. Above the 3-inch length on the x-axis, place a dot at a frequency of four. Continue for hair lengths of four through six until four dots are drawn across the graph, then connect each dot, beginning with the first dot on the graph and ending with the one above the 6-inch hair length. (See graph on next page.)

Keep in mind that line graphs are used when a continuous variable on the x-axis is either interval or ratio. Histograms illustrate discrete interval or ratio variables. And bar graphs are used to depict nominal and ordinal discrete variables on the x-axis.

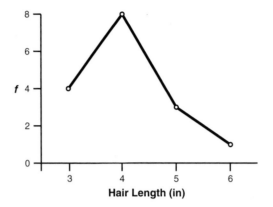

Grouped Frequency Distributions

In the examples thus far, only a few values were used to make it easier to create tables and graphs. But very often you will have too many different values to make a useful table or fit all the values on the *x*-axis of a graph. This problem can be solved by grouping values together in equal intervals. For example, if your instructor wanted to tell you about grades in the class on the first test but did not want to use letter grades, he or she might use number grades clumped together in groups of 10 (or whatever he or she wanted to use, as long as they were equal intervals). The raw data might look like this:

89	92	77	65	91	58	73	82	88	90
62	73	95	84	87	89	78	63	80	79

A table or graph of these data would be crowded and difficult to read. Too many different values are in this data set to treat it the way we have the previous examples. If the instructor grouped them in intervals of 10, the simple frequency table might look like this:

Scores	*f*
50–59	1
60–69	3
70–79	5
80–89	7
90–99	4

Notice that since we must have equal intervals, the lowest and highest numbers might not exist in the data set. For example, scores of 50–57 did not happen, but the interval had to be 10 numbers to be consistent across all intervals in the data set. Group the data any way you choose, but remember to set up a manageable number of groups (from about 3 to 7), and make sure each interval span is the same.

These data are continuous, because, although the professor may round to whole numbers, fractions in grades are certainly possible. To graph continuous ratio data, we should create a line graph. In this example, the middle numbers of each interval are decimals: 54.50, 64.50, 74.50, 84.50, and 94.50.

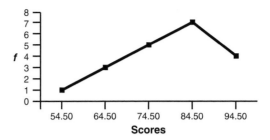

If these data had represented a discrete interval or ratio variable, a histogram would have been used. Labels on the *x*-axis would also have changed. Because discrete data can only be represented by whole numbers, the entire range of each group would have been written; the middle number of each interval was a fraction. However, when the middle number of each interval is a whole number, each bar on a histogram can be labeled with the middle number.

You are never going to create a grouped frequency distribution for nominal data, because it does not make sense to group certain colors together or any other categorical data. It is also unlikely that you will ever create a grouped distribution for ordinal data, but it would be possible. For example, we could group together T-shirt sizes of small and medium and create a separate group of large and extra large, placing the frequencies of each group in a table. To graph, we would use a bar graph to represent ordinal data, and the bars would not touch. We would need to show the range of each group, because a mathematical middle would not be appropriate with ordinal data.

Shapes of Distributions

When you look at graphs, you will notice that they can have different shapes. It does not matter if the figure is a bar graph or a line graph; you will still see a shape. In this section, the names of some shapes will be presented. The shape is determined by the point in the graph with the highest frequency (the hump).

Normal Distributions

The shape you have probably seen most often is when the highest part of the graph is in the middle, and the bars on the right and left (or the continuous line for a line graph) slope off gently toward the *x*-axis. The figure is most often called a **normal curve**, but it has also been called a bell-shaped curve. A normal curve is symmetrical around the middle. This means that the left side of the graph is the mirror image of the right side, with the highest point in the exact center of the distribution. The further the slopes extend to the ends of the graph, the lower the simple frequencies. These ends look a bit like tails, so they are often referred to as the tails of the distribution. On the next page are bar and line normal distributions, respectively:

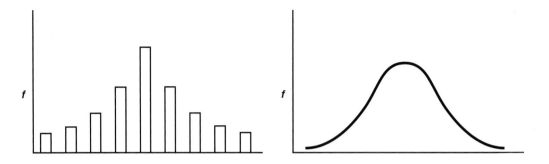

Skewed Distributions

Although the normal curve is the most popular type of graph, and we will use it often in later chapters, you should become familiar with a few other shapes. If the high point on the graph is pushed over to one side, the graph is called **skewed**. If the high point is closer to the right side of the graph, the data are **negatively skewed**; if the high point is to the left, the graph is **positively skewed**. Remember how we said that numbers always increase from left to right on the *x*-axis? That is why we refer to the left side of the *x*-axis as the negative side, and the right side as the positive side. So when the tail on the left side appears to push the high point to the right, we can think of the left tail as skewing the distribution, making a negative skew. When the right-side tail appears to push the high point to the left, the positive tail is skewing the data, creating a positive skew. The following sketches show you a negative skew and a positive skew:

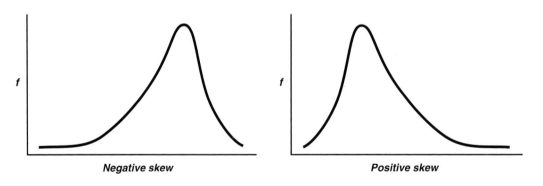

Negative skew   **Positive skew**

Kurtosis

Other shapes you might see are a short, flat graph or a tall, thin graph. A short, flat graph is called **platykurtic**. Since *plat* sounds like *flat*, the term is not too difficult to remember. A tall, thin graph is called **leptokurtic**. Maybe the tall, thin *l* at the beginning of the word will help you remember what this word represents. A medium-type of high point (not too thin, not too fat) is called **mesokurtic**, with *meso* meaning *middle*. Defining a shape by how thin or fat the hump is means defining by **kurtosis**, which explains why the three terms above end in *kurtic*. Platykurtic, leptokurtic, and mesokurtic shapes are normal distributions if they are symmetrical about the middle (as in the sketches below):

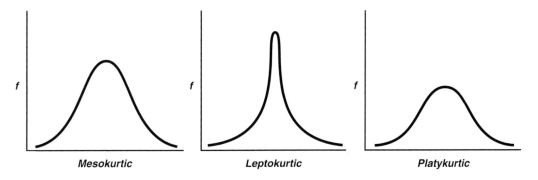

| Mesokurtic | Leptokurtic | Platykurtic |

Bimodal and Trimodal Distributions

Two final distribution shapes might be seen on occasion. You might see graphs with two high points instead of one. If the high points are approximately the same height, the shape is called **bimodal.** Below is an example of a bimodal distribution.

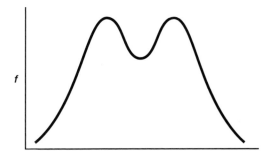

Likewise, if you see a graph with three distinct high points, it is called **trimodal.**

With these terms for shapes of distributions, you can talk intelligently with people about data. For example, if your instructor told the class that the shape of the distribution for an exam was negatively skewed, most students would be concerned because they heard the word negative. Now you would know that negatively skewed means the grades were on the high end, so most people did well.

Preview of Chapter 3

In the next chapter, you will learn how to provide one piece of information to tell people about an entire data set. You will summarize where most of the values in your data are found with measures of central tendency.

Conceptual Items

1. Define the following:
   a. nominal variable   c. interval variable
   b. ordinal variable   d. ratio variable
2. Which two scales of measurement are qualitative?
3. Which two scales of measurement are quantitative?
4. Would it be possible for a nominal or ordinal variable to be continuous? Explain.
5. Would it be possible for an interval or ratio variable to be discrete? Explain.
6. Which of the following does *not* affect graphing?
   a. scale of measurement   c. discrete vs. continuous
   b. qualitative vs. quantitative
7. When are the following types of graphs used to illustrate data?
   a. bar graph   c. line graph
   b. histogram
8. Grouped frequency distributions must have equal _____.
9. Define simple frequency polygon.
10. Sketch a trimodal graph.

Application Items

11. For each variable, choose the appropriate classifications.

Variable	Nominal, Ordinal, Interval, or Ratio	Qualitative vs. Quantitative	Discrete vs. Continuous
Ink colors			
Number of research paper rough drafts			
Time spent writing research paper			
Rank boyfriend/girlfriend from best to worst			
Gallons of water in the bathtub			
Test difficulty on a scale from 1–10			
Number of notebooks in a book bag			
Price the bookstore pays to buy back used textbooks			

12. Several people from your Taekwondo school of martial arts recently competed at a national championship. Create a simple frequency table and graph for the trophies they brought back:

2nd	4th	3rd	2nd	3rd	4th	1st	2nd	3rd	1st
2nd	3rd	3rd	2nd	2nd	2nd	4th	1st	3rd	1st

13. If we asked students how many times a month they attend church, we might find the following sample data. Based on the assumption that it would not be reasonable to attend church a fraction of a visit, prepare a simple frequency table and graph for these data.

0	4	0	3	5	0	1	4	1	2
2	2	8	2	3	0	3	4	8	4
6	4	0	4	1	4	4	5	0	4

14. A sample of people told you the names of their poodles. Illustrate these data in table and graph form.

Fluffy	Fluffy	Princess	Fluffy	Fifi
Princess	Trixie	Fluffy	Fifi	Princess
Fifi	Fluffy	Fifi	Fluffy	Butch

15. A sample of college students in your classes told you how many hours a week they talk on the phone. Sketch a simple frequency table and graph of these data.

7	1	2	7	3	3	0	5	3	4
6	4	6	4	5	3	7	5	5	5
5	6	0	6	4	6	4	6	6	7
7	6	7	2	4	5	6	7	5	3

16. You want to organize data from a sample of students who told you how many hours of TV they watch each week. Create a grouped simple frequency distribution table and graph for the following data. Use intervals of five.

29	19	12	9	0	23	25	5.5	7	29
17	14	28	13	8	20	10	15	22	26

17. After a party with odd-tasting punch, you and your friends rate head pain on a scale from 1 to 100, with higher numbers indicating more pain. Create a grouped simple frequency distribution table and graph using intervals of 10.

90	62	77	78	42	55	69	41	99	100
86	62	56	87	44	61	97	92	91	79

18. Imagine that you asked people in your class to report their shoe size, with the assumption that size changes in equal intervals. The data are below:

7	7	13	6	8	9	8	6	10
9	8	9	7	11	10	8	13	8

   a. What scale of measurement do these data represent?
   b. Is this a continuous or a discrete variable?
   c. Choose the best way to organize these data in table form, and create the table.
   d. Choose the best way to organize these data in a simple frequency graph, and sketch the graph.

CHAPTER 3

Measures of Central Tendency

Summarizing Data

Now that simple frequency bar graphs and line graphs have been examined, we will cover where the majority of values fall when taking into consideration the entire data set. It might be tempting to say the highest point on a simple frequency graph illustrates the majority of values, but this is not always the best way to indicate a representative value. Picture a severely skewed distribution. Summarizing the data set with the highest point would ignore the scores in the tail of the distribution. Thus, each **measure of central tendency** presented in this chapter offers one number to best summarize and represent a data set. The measure of central tendency chosen relies on the shape of the distribution and the variable's scale of measurement.

Mode

As presented in Chapter 2, the highest point on the graph is the value of the variable that occurs the most often. A formal name for the highest point is the **mode.** By definition, the mode is simply the value that occurs most often.

Although the mode does not seem very sophisticated, it offers one piece of information to summarize the entire data set. It is convenient to get one piece of information and learn something about most of the values, and this one value can be used to tell others about the data set. Rather than listing all values in a data set, we can share the mode to communicate where most of the scores fall. Here is an example of how the mode might be used: Imagine you asked your friends what their favorite type of music is. Ten of your friends said pop; 15 said rap; and four of them said country. Since most of them said their favorite music was rap, the modal type of music is rap.

As a reminder of what you learned in Chapter 2, you could graph the data for pop, rap, and country. As you can see in the following figure, the highest bar is above rap. You might also recall that this must be a bar graph because type of music is a nominal variable.

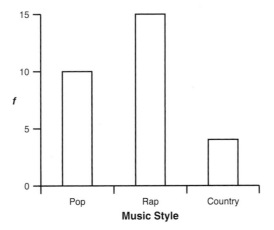

Here is one more example before we leave the straightforward mode: If you asked students in your class how many carbonated beverages they drink each day, two might say they consume two drinks a day; no one drinks one and a half sodas; nine of them might drink one carbonated beverage a day; eight drink half of a soda a day; and four of them drink none. In this example, the modal number of softdrinks is one, since most of your classmates drink one soda a day. The highest point on the simple frequency graph should be above one drink.

The correct type of graph must be chosen based on the characteristics of the variable. A can of soda is a standard size, giving this variable equal intervals. In fact, this is ratio data, because the variable also has an absolute zero point, meaning the absence of the variable being measured (sodas consumed). Finally, four cans are twice as many as two, and so on. You also need to decide whether sodas characterize discrete or continuous data. Since fractions are possible (like half of a can of soda), you have continuous data. Remember that continuous ratio data are illustrated using a line graph.

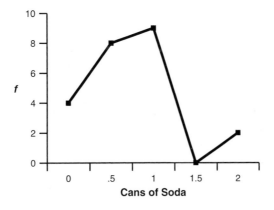

Communication about data becomes more efficient when we can communicate one piece of information—such as the mode—to summarize a group of data. Although the mode is a useful tool, it does not take into consideration all other values on the variable being measured. Look at that last example again. Some people drank two sodas, half of a soda, or none, but we lose that knowledge when only the value at the highest point (with the highest simple frequency) is used. If you report that most members of your class drink one carbonated beverage, you are neglecting to tell them that almost as many only drink half of a soda, and several do not drink sodas at all. To solve this problem, we will need to move on to a second measure of central tendency, remembering that we are still looking for one number to summarize the entire data set.

Median

Still using the soda example, instead of just using the mode to tell where most of the values are (1 drink), the middle value could be reported. The middle score is the one you would find if all of the values were arranged in order from lowest to highest number of drinks consumed (or highest to lowest) and the value halfway through the data was chosen. Fifty percent of the values are at or below the middle, and 50% are higher than the middle value. Instead of calling this value the middle, it is called the **median**, abbreviated *Mdn*.

To locate the median number of sodas consumed, put all the values (of cans) in order and pick out the middle one to find a value of 0.5.

2	2	1	1	1	1	1	1	1	1	1	*0.5*
0.5	0.5	0.5	0.5	0.5	0.5	0.5	0	0	0	0	

If the data set contains an even number of values, you can use the lower of the two numbers in the middle. (Your instructor might prefer for you to average the two middle numbers together when it's possible.) In the beverage example, the middle value is 0.5 of a soda per day, so that is the median. Notice that the mode and the median were different. The mode was 1 can, and the median was 0.5 of a can. Given the entire data set, with several people drinking 0.5 of a can or no soda at all, 0.5 would perhaps offer a better summary of the entire distribution.

You might be wondering when the mode should be used and when the median should be used. The mode works well with nominal data. It would be impossible to use the median for nominal data since categories (like favorite type of music) do not have a meaningful order. For graphing, categories on the *x*-axis can be placed in any order.

To use the median, because the values of a variable must first be put in a meaningful order, only ordinal, interval, or ratio data would be appropriate. For an example of an ordinal scale, you could examine restaurant ratings in your town. In this example, we will use the A, B, C, D ratings rather than the numbering system on which the letters are based. The letters for restaurant ratings are an ordinal scale, since we cannot assume that every A is exactly 10 points higher than every B, etc. Perhaps your town has 17 restaurants with an A rating, 21 with a B rating, 13 with C ratings, and 1 with a rating of D. To use the median, first put the ratings in order: A, B, C, and D (or vice versa). Then find the letter in the middle, which in this case is two letters, since the data set has an even number of values. The 26th and 27th letters are exactly in the middle. This is not a problem given that both of these letters are B values.

A	A	A	A	A	A	A	A	A	A	A	A
A	A	A	A	A	B	B	B	B	B	B	B
B	*B*	*B*	B	B	B	B	B	B	B	B	B
B	B	C	C	C	C	C	C	C	C	C	C
C	C	C	D								

A few paragraphs ago, I wrote that if you had an even number of values, you could either take the lower of the two values or average the two middle values together to get one score. In the restaurant-ratings example, you can see that averaging is not an option. If a B and a C were the two middle restaurant ratings, it would not have made sense to average them because you cannot calculate an average between two letters. (You couldn't guess at something like a C+.) The bottom line is that you can calculate the average between the middle two numbers as long as the variable is interval or ratio (an example of ratio was the soda example), but an ordinal variable requires taking the lower of the two values.

Mean

The final measure of central tendency in this text is the average, a statistic you have been calculating in classes for many years. As mentioned earlier, every time you added all of your test grades and divided by the number of tests, you were calculating your average grade. We also call that the **mean**, with the formula

$$\overline{X} = \frac{\Sigma X}{N}$$

Since you are already familiar with the mean, we will take this opportunity to examine symbols.

First, notice the X. The letter X stands for scores. Nothing has been done to them, so they are called **raw scores.** Sometimes you will use a Y to represent raw scores, but it would be equally reasonable to use a Q, P, or any other English letter. Most people who conduct research use X first and Y second. Next, look at the N symbol. A capital N is the symbol for the number of values in a data set. The Greek symbol (sigma) means "add up," so you will need to sum all X values (like test scores) and divide by N (the number of tests). When the calculation is complete, the answer is the mean of X values, symbolized by an X with a line (or bar) across the top of it. Some people call it X-*bar*, but that sounds more difficult than its real name (the mean). When reporting results in APA style, $\overline{X}$ is written as M.

The mean is a useful measure of central tendency because it represents the exact mathematical center of a distribution. Recall from Chapter 2 that math can be used only when we at least have equal intervals; therefore, our variable must be interval or ratio data to calculate the mean. Think back to the restaurant-ratings example with letters A–D. We agreed that these ordinal data did not allow averaging because two letters cannot be averaged. In others words, we cannot get a mean of ordinal data. Interval or ratio data are required.

Below is an example of the mean to use the new symbols just covered. We could analyze fictional data about the age at which women get married. We hypothetically select a sample of women from a grocery store and ask them how old they were when they married. The ages are:

$$X$$

30
21
27
23
34
28
24
26
18
25

Before we calculate, make sure these data reach *at least* interval level. The variable is age. Age has equal intervals regardless of the units chosen: years, days, months, or decades. In addition, zero is the absence of years, and a 40-year-old person is twice as old as someone at 20. Ratio data allow use of the mean.

$$\overline{X} = \frac{256}{10}$$

$$\overline{X} = 25.60$$

The bottom line for when to use the mean as a measure of central tendency is when the data are at interval or ratio level, but there is one exception.

Mean Versus Median

When we have a skewed distribution of interval or ratio scales, we generally use the median. The reason for that goes back to the whole purpose of any measure of central tendency: We are trying to get a single number that best represents the entire data set. In a skewed distribution, the extreme values in the tail will pull the mathematical average (mean) in their direction, bringing the mean too far from the majority of the values to accurately reflect the distribution. For practice, refer to the ages in the previous example and add an extreme value. Imagine we found one woman at the grocery store who married at the age of 105. Calculate the mean again and find the new average age of marriage for women.

$$\overline{X} = \frac{361}{11}$$

$$\overline{X} = 32.818182$$

The mean is no longer an accurate reflection of the age at which women marry. The extreme value pulled the mean too high to represent the data set.

Instead, we can turn to the median, arrange the ages in order—including the 105—and find the middle age at marriage.

X
18
21
23
24
25
26
27
28
30
34
105

The median is 26. You can see that 26 is a much more accurate reflection of the age at which most women marry than the mean (32.82), which was pulled up by the extreme score.

To review the rules for measures of central tendency one last time, the mode is used with nominal data to simply indicate which value occurs most often in a data set. The median is used with ordinal data to represent the middle value in a data set. If the ordinal data set has an even number of values, choose the lower of the two values as the median. The median is also used with skewed interval or ratio data. If an interval or ratio data set has an even number of values, average the two values together and give the mean of the two middle values. The mean is used with interval or ratio values that are not very skewed.

Introduction to SPSS

If your computer has a red and white SPSS icon on the screen, simply double-click on it with the mouse. If there is no icon, your computer screen will show Start in the lower left corner. Using your mouse, click Start + Programs + SPSS Windows + SPSS for Windows Student Version.

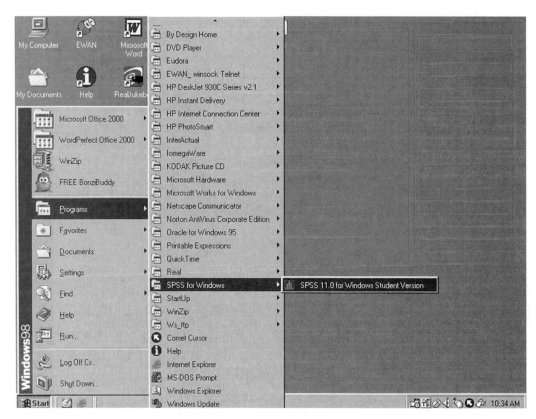

You should see a spreadsheet of blank boxes with the title SPSS Data Editor at the top. If a gray box is covering the middle of your spreadsheet, click Cancel to have a clear view of the spreadsheet.

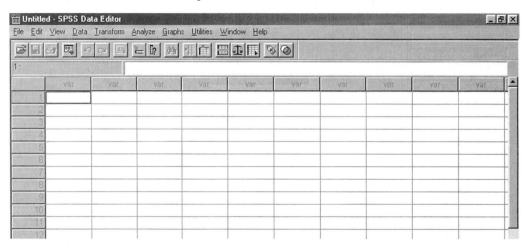

For the rest of this introduction, we'll enter the data from our last example of the ages at which women marry—including the woman who married at the age of 105.

Measures of Central Tendency on SPSS

Label the first column with the variable name. Do this by pointing to View, then selecting Variables.

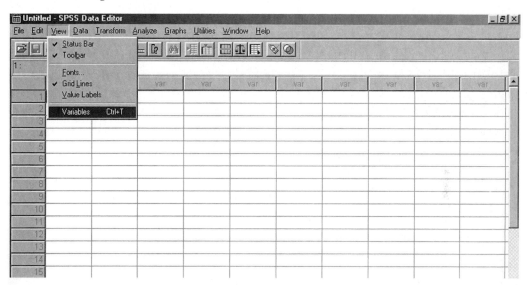

Your entire spreadsheet will change to show each variable (column heading) in row form.

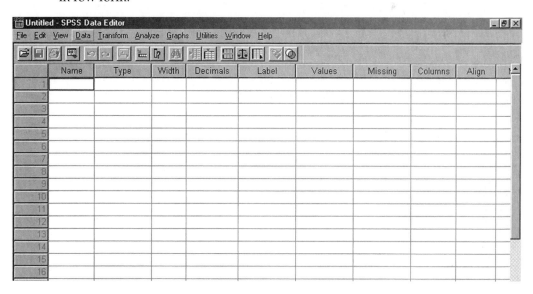

Type **age** in the first box, then press Enter.

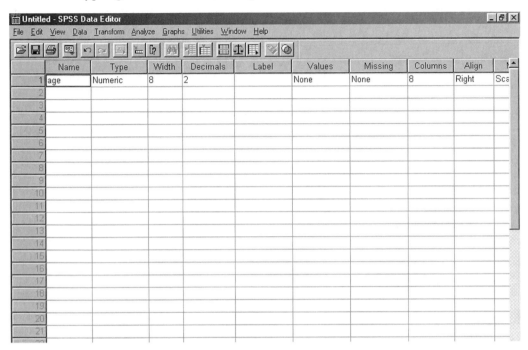

Return to your data by pointing to View, then selecting Data.

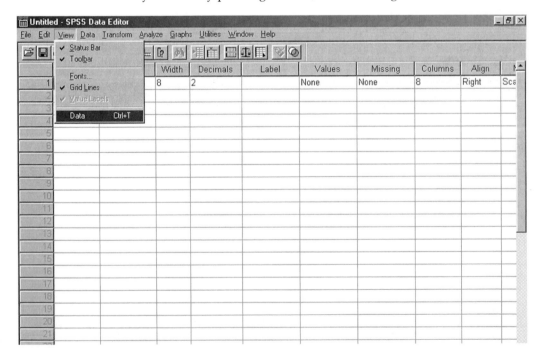

The column heading age should be seen at the top of the first column.

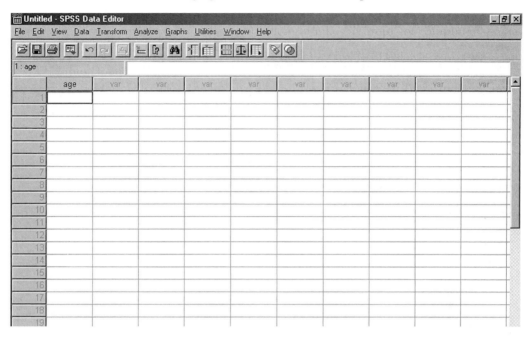

To get measures of central tendency for the data set, enter the ages from our example in any order in the first column of the spreadsheet. The spreadsheet should look like this:

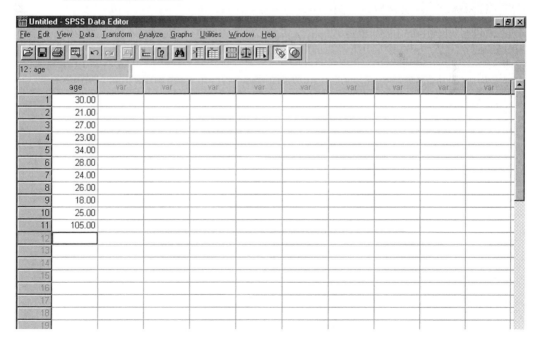

Now point to Analyze, then select Descriptive Statistics + Frequencies.

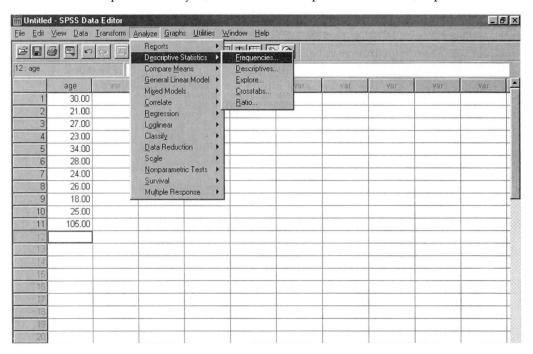

When a box opens in the middle of your screen, select the word age on the left.

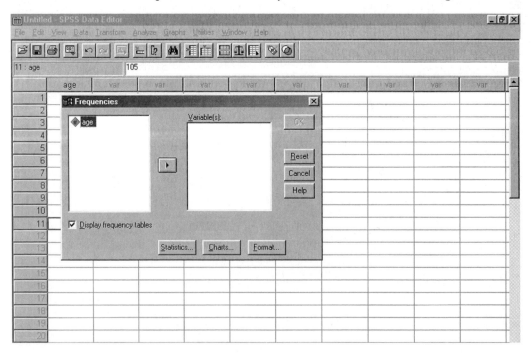

Move age to the box on the right by clicking the arrow key in the middle of the box.

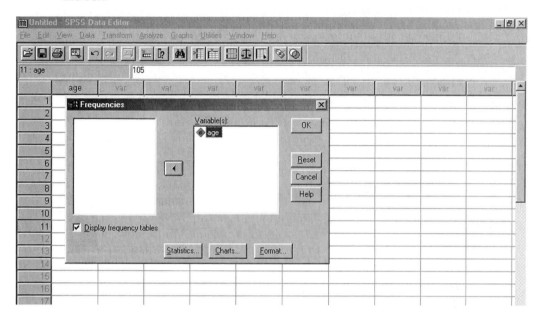

Then click Statistics. A new gray box will open on top of the old one.

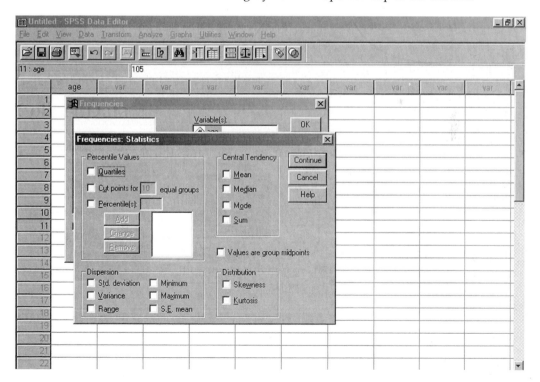

On the right side of the new box, check Mean + Median + Mode.

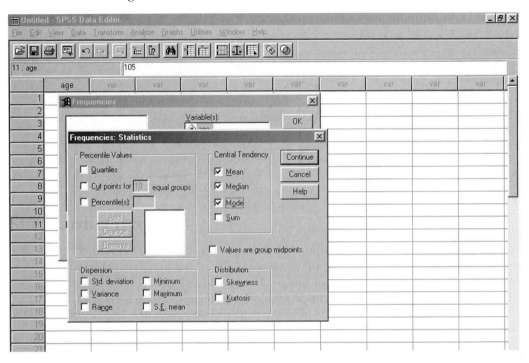

Click Continue + OK.

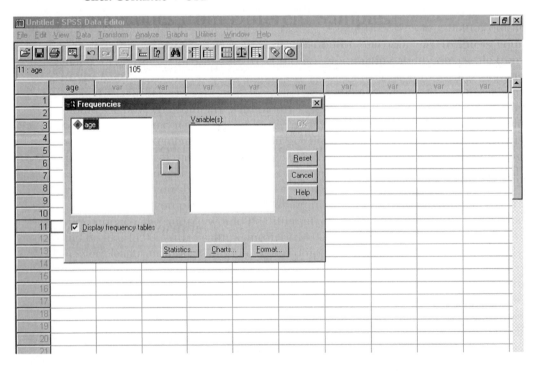

The output will open automatically.

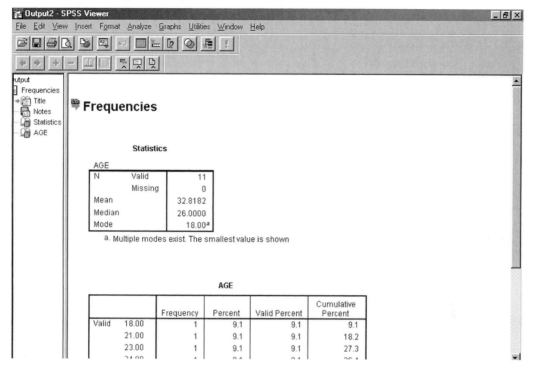

To view the bottom parts of the output, click the vertical bar on the right-hand side of the screen and drag it down while still holding the mouse button down.

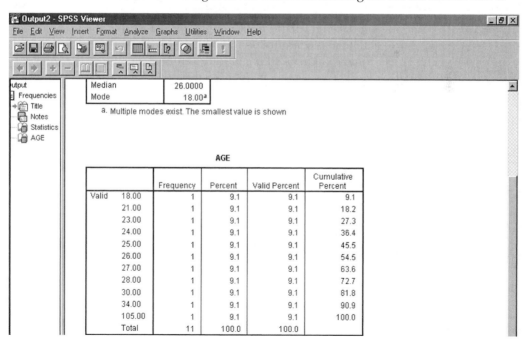

You can print the output by clicking the printer button at the top of the screen. (Clicking the printer button will also allow you to print your data layout.)

Frequencies

Statistics

AGE

N	Valid	11
	Missing	0
Mean		32.8182
Median		26.0000
Mode		18.00[a]

a. Multiple modes exist. The smallest value is shown

AGE

		Frequency	Percent	Valid Percent	Cumulative Percent
Valid	18.00	1	9.1	9.1	9.1
	21.00	1	9.1	9.1	18.2
	23.00	1	9.1	9.1	27.3
	24.00	1	9.1	9.1	36.4
	25.00	1	9.1	9.1	45.5
	26.00	1	9.1	9.1	54.5
	27.00	1	9.1	9.1	63.6
	28.00	1	9.1	9.1	72.7
	30.00	1	9.1	9.1	81.8
	34.00	1	9.1	9.1	90.9
	105.00	1	9.1	9.1	100.0
	Total	11	100.0	100.0	

In this data set, 18 is listed as the mode, but no mode actually exists in the data set; all values occur with the same frequency of one. SPSS simply reports the lowest number in the data set and then notes that there are multiple modes.

From the output, use the most appropriate measure of central tendency to summarize the data set. Because you know that not every measure of central tendency is the correct one to use, choose what you want based on your knowledge from the chapter. For this data set, we know to use the median since we have ratio data with an extreme value (105).

Summarizing Experiments Using Means

You can use the mean to summarize an interval or ratio data set as long as it is not very skewed (has no extreme values), and that is fine if you only plan to collect data on one variable across a group of people. But in psychology we often want to go further than that; we often want to conduct a study of how one variable affects a second variable. We talked about this kind of situation in Chapter 1 under Experiments. The IV was one variable (the one the researcher manipulates), and the DV was the other variable (the one measured across everyone at the end of an experiment). An example would be the effect of calling your parents on how much spending money they give you. Suppose we decided on three levels of the IV: talking 1 hour a week, 2 hours, and 3 hours. We randomly assign participants to conditions and tell them how long they are allowed to talk to their parents. At the end of the week, we see how much spending money their parents give them (the DV).

1 Hour	2 Hours	3 Hours
$28.50	$52.00	$25.50
$20.00	$49.50	$19.00
$26.00	$64.50	$30.50
$23.00	$62.00	$20.50
$17.50	$57.00	$32.00

We could communicate the results of our experiment in several ways. One way would be to list the amount of money given to each participant in each condition. Those would be the raw data, and it is not a very efficient plan. Or we could get the average (mean) amount of spending money given to students who talked to their parents for 1 hour a week, the average amount given to those who talked 2 hours, and the mean amount given to students who talked 3 hours. So, means can be used to communicate a lot of information quickly and easily.

As a review, make sure we are allowed to calculate the mean for these groups. Under each level of the IV, we are calculating the mean amount of spending money given to students by their parents. The level of measurement is at least interval (pennies, nickels, dimes, etc.), and since zero on the scale would mean no money from parents, this scale reaches all the way to ratio. (Remember, interval level is as far as we needed to get to be allowed to calculate a mean.) Is it okay to calculate the mean DV for each level of the IV? Yes, as long as that DV is an interval or ratio variable, and no obvious outliers are present.

Because we want to be able to calculate the mean for the IV levels of our experiments, the vast majority of studies have interval or ratio DVs.

Graphing Means

Communicating the results of an experiment using the mean amount of spending money for each group is an excellent idea, but we have one more option: we could graph the data. We have covered graphing with simple frequency bar and line graphs, so you already know about graphing one variable by putting the levels on the x-axis and simple frequency on the y-axis. When the results of an experiment are graphed, the IV goes on the x-axis, and the DV goes on the y-axis.

Using the example we just discussed, the length of time students talk to their parents will be on the x-axis, with 1 hour a week toward the left, 2 hours in the middle, and 3 hours toward the right side below the x-axis line. Label the y-axis

Mean Dollars (not that you couldn't use pennies if you wanted to). We cannot call it Dollars because that makes it sound like we are trying to graph all the raw data. Using the word Mean in our label indicates that we will be graphing only the group means. The y-axis should begin at 0 and extend to the highest mean of the three groups on the graph. It is fine to count by five or ten or any other number, as long as the intervals are equal all the way up the y-axis. The only exception is the beginning of the y-axis, where it is often useful to skip some numbers after the 0 and before the first interval. In this case, use two forward slash marks to indicate that numbers were skipped.

The mean amount of spending money given to students who talk to their parents 1 hour a week is $23.00; the average given to those who talk 2 hours a week is $57.00; and the average given after 3 hours a week is $25.50. Before we graph these data, think back to simple frequency graphs and remember that the level of measurement of the x-axis variable makes all the difference in whether a bar graph or a line graph is created. The IV is on the x-axis; the variable Hours Talked to Parents has equal intervals, and interval data require a line graph (in fact, hours reaches to ratio data). The graph you create could look like the one below, or you might use slightly different intervals on the y-axis.

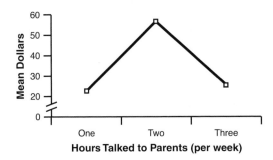

You can see that I used $10 for my intervals after skipping the first 20 and replacing them with the two forward slash marks. If numbers had not been skipped, the line of data would have seemed to float at the top of the graph. When creating a graph, try to utilize the entire area.

Graphing Means on SPSS

When you have a blank SPSS spreadsheet ready, we can graph the last example we were using. For graphing, we must string out the data. That is, we must first lay out a column for the IV (in this case, number of hours spent talking with parents), which we can call "hours." Then, type **dollars** in the second column to label the DV (dollar amount). Because the IV has three levels, SPSS requires numbers to represent these levels. Fortunately, hours talked with parents was already in number form: 1, 2, and 3 hours a week. In the first cell, type **1** for the first person in the first level of the IV. To the right of that number, type the dollar amount the person received, which was **$28.50** (omit the dollar sign in SPSS). The second person under the IV also talked for 1 hour, and he or she received $20.00, and so on.

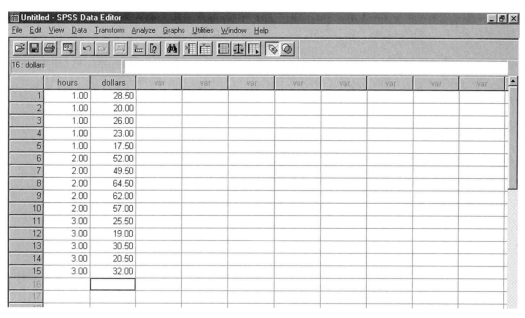

The numbers 1, 2, and 3 in the first column represent the three levels of hours talked, and we could make note of which level is represented by a 1, which is represented by a 2, and what a 3 represents. However, it is more effective to change the numbers to names in SPSS by pointing to View, selecting Variables, then clicking under the heading Values, which currently says None. A small gray box will appear to the right of the cell. Left click with the mouse to open a larger gray option box. In the box beside Value, type the number **1** for the first level of the IV. Then type **one hour** in the box next to Value Label.

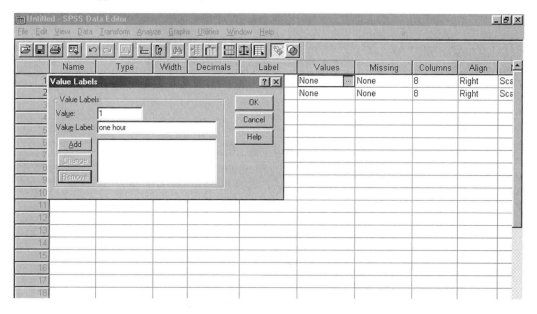

Click Add to allow the number to be labeled in the system.

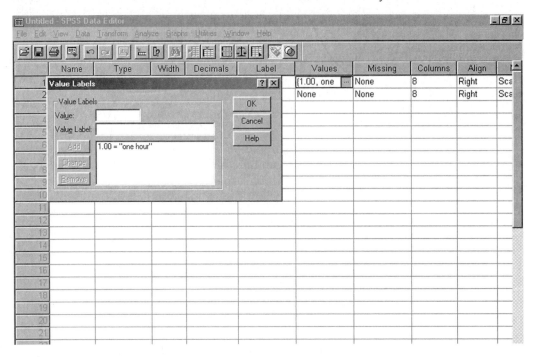

Label the remaining two levels of the IV.

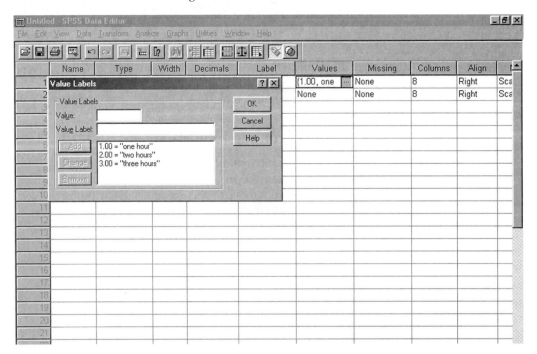

Point to View, then select Data to return to the spreadsheet. The three levels of the IV should now be represented by names instead of numbers. If your screen does not show the labels you just typed in, point to View, then select Value Labels.

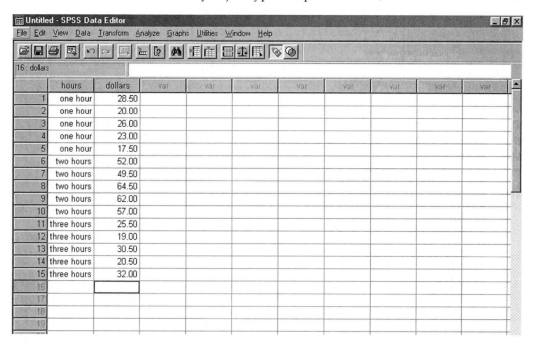

Point to Graphs, then select Interactive + Line.

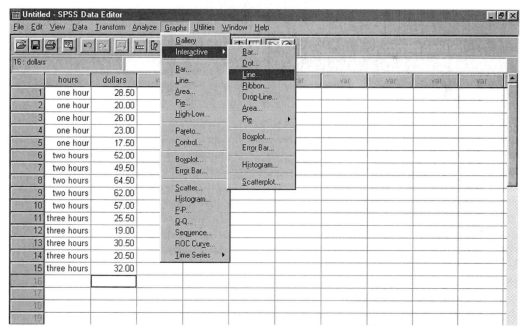

A large gray box will open. Remove the labels already placed in the boxes that represent the *x*-axis (horizontal line) and the *y*-axis (vertical line) by clicking on each label and dragging it to the left column in the gray box.

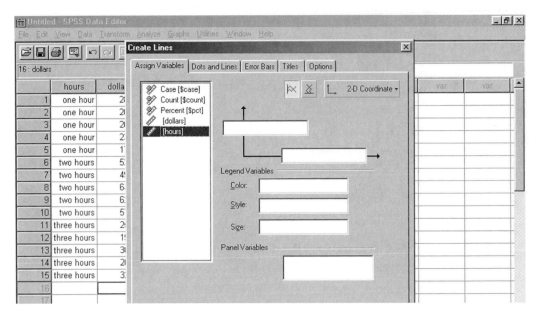

Instead, label the *x*-axis with hours, and label the *y*-axis with dollars by selecting the words in the left column and dragging them to the appropriate axis. Right click hours and choose categorical, rather than the default scale variable. (Although hours is not a categorical or nominal variable, the labels on the *x*-axis are interpreted by SPSS as categories.)

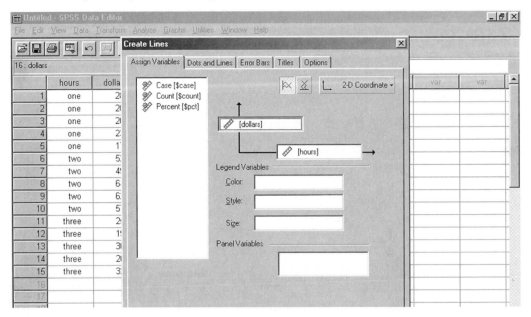

Click OK to reveal a line graph of your data.

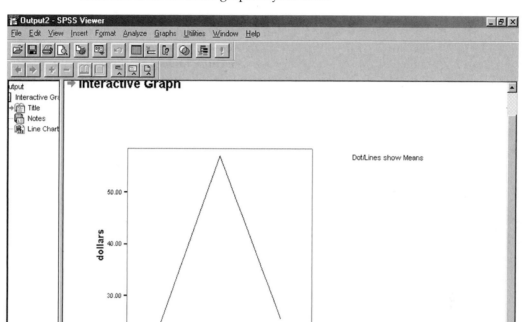

In an APA-style manuscript, a graph is called a **figure.**

Preview of Chapter 4

Now that you are comfortable with measures of central tendency, the next chapter will cover variability. As you know, central tendency is a number that best summarizes an entire data set—one number to represent all values in the data set. Variability will indicate how spread out those values are. Both pieces of information are generally needed to describe data.

Conceptual Items

1. Define measure of central tendency. (What do measures of central tendency tell you?)
2. Define the mode. What type(s) of data is/are best represented by the mode?
3. Define the median. What type(s) of data is/are best represented by the median?
4. Define the mean. What type(s) of data is/are best represented by the mean?
5. When a data set is composed of an even number of interval or ratio values with clear outliers, how is the measure of central tendency calculated?

6. When designing an experiment, why do researchers prefer a dependent variable of interval or ratio values?

7. How does a simple frequency distribution graph of interval or ratio values differ from a graph of experimental data with an interval or ratio dependent variable?

8. What type of graph is used when the independent variable is (a) nominal or ordinal data, and (b) interval or ratio data?

Application Items

9. Using the data below, please answer the questions that follow.

X
50.80
58.42
60.00
43.18
55.37
56.81
58.42

   a. What is the mode?

   b. What is the median?

   c. What is the mean?

10. If the data above are the length of newborn babies in centimeters,

   a. What level of measurement do you have?

      (*Hints:* Does the variable have equal intervals? Does zero mean the absence of infant length? Is a 70cm baby twice as long as a 35cm baby?)

   b. What is the most appropriate measure of central tendency? Why?

   c. Calculate the most appropriate measure of central tendency.

11. Use SPSS to check your answers to Application Item 10. Turn in the data layout and output.

12. For these data, answer the following questions.

X
.57
1.25
2.03
.66
1.25
1.97
20.80
1.25

   a. What is the mode?

   b. What is the median?

   c. What is the mean?

13. Use SPSS to check your answers to Item 12. Turn in the data layout and output.

14. Now suppose the data above represent how many hours a day students generally spend in their apartments (or rooms) alone and awake.
    a. What level of measurement do these data represent?
    b. What is the most appropriate measure of central tendency and why?
    c. What is the value of the most appropriate measure of central tendency?

15. If the president of your school wanted to tell prospective students the approximate class size, he or she could collect a sample of class sizes that might look like the following data of number of students enrolled per class:

35	78	60	42	45	37	25	30	32
24	22	51	34	49	298	30	25	39

    a. What level of measurement do these data represent?
    b. What is the most appropriate measure of central tendency and why?
    c. Provide a single number that best represents class size.

16. If you went to a cosmetologist and wanted to choose the hair color that most people choose, you could collect information on hair colors and find the measure of central tendency.

blonde	red	black	red	red
brown	black	blonde	red	red

    a. What measure of central tendency would you use, and why?
    b. Calculate the value chosen as the best measure of central tendency.

17. Below are means from an experiment on the effect of whether or not people are alone in their apartments on how long they stay there. Suppose we used two levels of the IV: alone in the apartment or with a friend. To make sure we manipulated the IV, we forced participants to either go to their apartment alone or with a friend. Then we sat back (with our hidden camera) to see how long each of our participants stayed in the apartment. Here is what we found:

Alone	With a Friend
2 min	20 min
5 min	17 min
8 min	60 min
3 min	80 min
9 min	32 min

    a. What level of measurement is the IV?
    b. What type of graph is needed?
    c. Sketch a graph of these means.
    d. Create a graph using SPSS. Turn in a printout of the SPSS graph.

18. Imagine that you wanted to know if females indeed have more pairs of shoes than males. Of course, you could not force (manipulate) people to be male or female, so gender is not truly an independent variable. We could call this a quasi-IV, because it might look like an independent variable, but we know that it

is not manipulated. However, the data could still be graphed with no problem. (In statistics, a quasi-IV can be analyzed as a true independent variable; you would just need to be careful about how you discuss your results. True IVs allow a discussion of cause and effect; quasi-IVs limit the discussion to a relationship between the quasi-IV and the DV.)

For our example of gender and number of pairs of shoes owned, we might collect the following data:

Females	Males
20	3
12	8
10	2
26	5
19	7
21	6

a. What level of measurement is the quasi-IV?
b. What type of graph is needed?
c. Sketch a graph of these means.
d. Create a graph using SPSS. Turn in a printout of the SPSS graph.

Computational Formula in This Chapter

Mean (average) $$\overline{X} = \frac{\Sigma X}{N}$$

CHAPTER 4

Measures of Variability

Spread of Scores

When summarizing a data set, it is useful to provide one number to represent the data, and the mode, median, or mean from the previous chapter provides this information. In addition to a measure of central tendency, a second piece of information is often needed: a measure of **variability.** Measures of variability summarize how spread out the values are.

Before we begin variability, examine the following examples to see that summarizing a data set with a measure of central tendency is not enough information. First, calculate the mean for quiz scores of 70, 70, 70, 70, and 70 to get an average quiz score of 70. Now, get the mean of quiz scores 80, 60, 70, 65, and 75. The calculation reveals a mean of 70 again, but these two sets of numbers are very different from each other. Finally, calculate the mean of quiz scores 100, 40, 70, 95, and 45. The mean for this data set is also 70. Raw scores on the three sets of quizzes were different, even though the measure of central tendency (the mean) was the same for all of them. As a result, we cannot summarize a set of numbers using only a measure of central tendency; we also must obtain a number to indicate how distributed the values are.

Range

Recall from Chapter 2 the four levels of measurement: nominal, ordinal, interval, and ratio. Remember that the measure of central tendency for nominal data was the mode, and the mode represented which category occurred most often. The mode allowed you to say that most of your friends chose rap as their favorite music. Now imagine trying to tell someone how spread out the choices were. It would not make sense to say they were spread out from pop to country. You cannot calculate a measure of variability for nominal data, because categories of music type (or any other categories) are not represented by numbers. The bottom line is that nominal data are summarized by the mode, and measures of variability are not possible.

However, ordinal data are ranked in a meaningful order, therefore a measure of variability is possible. Variability can be assessed with the **range** of values, which includes the lowest and highest values. The easiest way to discuss the range of values on an ordinal variable is to state the lowest and highest values. For example, house numbers on a street could range from 192 to 255. Or restaurant ratings could range from A to D. Done this way, the range is two values rather than one; it is defined by the values at both ends of the variable. If variability is reported with the appropriate measure of central tendency for ordinal data from Chapter 3, ordinal data can be summarized: The measure of central tendency is the median, and the measure of variability is the range, the end values on the variable's scale.

In addition to ordinal data, remember that skewed interval and ratio data generally utilize the median as the measure of central tendency. Since the median and range are used in combination, the range is also the measure of variability for skewed interval and ratio data. But the range for interval and ratio data is actually a bit different from the range used for ordinal data. Because interval and ratio data have math properties, it is possible to subtract the lowest value on the variable from the highest value to get the range. For example, if scores on a test ranged from 50% correct to 90% correct, the range would be 90–50, and the final answer would be 40. So, remember that the range of an ordinal set of values includes the low and high numbers, but the range for a skewed interval or ratio set of values involves subtraction and provides only one number for variability.

The range is useful when we want to communicate the spread of scores. Whether we report that the range of an ordinal set of numbers is from A to D, or the range of a skewed interval or ratio set of numbers is 40, it is more efficient than listing all the raw data, especially since data sets can be quite large.

Sample Variance

So far, we have covered the measure of variability for ordinal data and skewed interval or ratio data (the range), and you already know that nominal data does not allow a measure of variability. The only remaining possibilities are interval and ratio data that are not very skewed. Recall that since interval and ratio data have equal intervals, the mean can be used as the measure of central tendency. Because the math properties of interval and ratio data make them highly desirable, we have *four* measures of variability to indicate the spread of scores. All four measures are similar, but the theory behind each one is unique.

We will begin with an example before new formulas are introduced. If we measured how long a sample of eight people held their breath under water, we might find the following: 50, 22, 25, 62, 48, 60, 33, and 56 seconds. Since number of seconds people hold their breath under water is at least interval data (in fact, it is ratio), and the data are not skewed, our measure of central tendency is the mean. In this data set, the mean is 44.50 seconds.

One way to look at the spread of scores is to assess how far each score deviates from the mean. Not surprisingly, each score subtracted from the mean is called a **deviation score** and is symbolized by x. A deviation score is calculated for each raw score in a data set by subtracting the mean from each raw score.

$$x = X - \overline{X}$$

Here is how we might lay out the data so the deviation scores have their own column:

X	$\overline{X}$	x
50	44.5	5.5
22	44.5	−22.5
25	44.5	−19.5
62	44.5	17.5
48	44.5	3.5
60	44.5	15.5
33	44.5	−11.5
56	44.5	11.5

We end up with many deviation scores, but remember that our goal was to summarize the variability in the data set. We have not accomplished our goal by getting a deviation score for each raw score; in fact, we have as many numbers as the original data set.

Think back to Chapter 3. When we wanted the average value on a variable, we calculated the mean, which involved adding all the values and dividing by the number of values. Based on that logic, we could sum all the deviation scores to get one number for average variability in the data set.

X	$\overline{X}$	x
50	44.5	5.5
22	44.5	−22.5
25	44.5	−19.5
62	44.5	17.5
48	44.5	3.5
60	44.5	15.5
33	44.5	−11.5
56	44.5	11.5
		0

Unfortunately, the deviation scores always sum to zero, and zero divided by anything is zero. Even though this approach did not give a useful measure of variability, we can work with the logical beginning.

Squaring a negative number removes the negative sign, always yielding a positive value, and of course, squaring a positive number also provides a positive number. If we square each deviation score, we will have a column of positive numbers: x^2.

X	$\overline{X}$	x	x^2
50	44.5	5.5	30.25
22	44.5	−22.5	506.25
25	44.5	−19.5	380.25
62	44.5	17.5	306.25
48	44.5	3.5	12.25
60	44.5	15.5	240.25
33	44.5	−11.5	132.25
56	44.5	11.5	132.25
		0	1740.00

Now we can follow the averaging logic to add all squared deviation values and divide by the number of values for an average variability. Divide 1740 by 8 to get a final answer of 217.50. This number is called the **sample variance,** the variability for a sample of numbers. The sample variance has the symbol S_x^2 to indicate that the deviation scores were squared. The formula for sample variance is as follows.

$$S_x^2 = \frac{\Sigma(X - \overline{X})^2}{N}$$

For our example, the calculation is:

$$S_x^2 = \frac{1740}{8} = 217.50$$

We squared all the deviation values and divided by the number of values to get the sample variance. Sample variance is introduced with this formula because the logic of an average deviation score is logical if we use the same approach as the mean.

   Now that the logic of the sample variance has been introduced, the definitional formula will no longer be needed. Instead, we will use the computational formula from now on.

$$S_x^2 = \frac{\Sigma X^2 - \frac{(\Sigma X)^2}{N}}{N}$$

This formula will produce the same answer as the definitional formula, but in the long run, the computational formula will be easier to calculate—especially when we have a large data set. Notice that the symbol is still S_x^2 and still stands for the sample variance.

   Before we go any further, see that the commonsense definitional formula and the calculational formula we will use from now on do yield the same answer. The calculational formula does not deal with deviation scores. Instead, the formula requires the raw scores themselves to be squared. (Note that we've already saved a step by not calculating deviation numbers before we began squaring values.)

X	X^2
50	2500
22	484
25	625
62	3844
48	2304
60	3600
33	1089
56	3136
$\Sigma X = 356$	$\Sigma X^2 = 17582$

Then insert the numbers for $\sum X^2$ (the second column), $\sum X$ (the first column), and N (8). Finish the calculation, and be sure to square the $\sum X$ to get 126736 for the $(\sum X)^2$ part of the numerator.

$$S_x^2 = \frac{17582 - \frac{(356)^2}{8}}{8} = 217.50$$

The answer using the computational formula is the same as the number for the definitional formula we first calculated. Now that you know for certain that they give the same answer, remember the logic of the definitional formula, but calculate answers from now on using the calculational formula.

The sample variance reflects the average amount of variability in the data set. In the above example, the variability among the number of seconds that participants in your sample held their breath is 217.50.

Sample Standard Deviation

So far we approached our search for average variability using the same logic as the mean. Then we noticed that adding all the deviation scores equaled zero, so we squared each of them before dividing by N. Unfortunately, squaring increases the variability number massively. We should now shrink the final number (sample variance) back down to make it a more accurate reflection of the average variability. Since the opposite of squaring is taking the square root, change the sample variance the same way. The square root of sample variance is the **sample standard deviation**. The formula is the same as the one for sample variance, but with a square root sign over it. Likewise, change the variance symbol by removing the 2 in the upper right corner, and the new symbol is S_x.

$$S_x = \sqrt{\frac{\sum X^2 - \frac{(\sum X)^2}{N}}{N}}$$

Using our previous example about how long people can hold their breath, take the square root of the sample variance to get the sample standard deviation.

$$\sqrt{217.50} = 14.747881 = S_x$$

The sample standard deviation communicates how spread out, on average, the values are in a data set. We can use the number to further summarize where most of the values fall. The majority of values are found about one standard deviation on either side of the mean, so we can subtract one standard deviation from the mean of 44.50 seconds (44.50–14.75) and add one standard deviation to 44.50 (44.50 + 14.75). These data tell us that the average length of time people in our sample can hold their breath is 44.50 seconds, with most people able to hold their breath between 29.75 and 59.25 seconds.

As you can see, the standard deviation provides concrete information about the spread of scores by allowing us to add and subtract one standard deviation from the mean. The variance would not have provided this useful information, because the number was inflated by squaring.

As another example, if we wanted to summarize the heat index in Georgia across a sample of summer days, we might start with these raw data in Fahrenheit: 95, 110, 120, 97, and 115. Since these data are values on an interval variable and are not very skewed (show no obvious outlier), first summarize with the mean as a measure of central tendency. The mean would be 107.40°F.

$$\overline{X} = \frac{\Sigma X}{N} = \frac{537}{5} = 107.40$$

Of course, we will also need to summarize the spread of scores by completing the calculational formula for the sample standard deviation (S_x).

X	X^2
95	9025
110	12100
120	14400
97	9409
115	13225
537	58159

$$S_x = \sqrt{\frac{58159 - \frac{(537)^2}{5}}{5}} = 9.850888$$

For this sample of summer days in Georgia, most of the temperatures fell around 107.40°F, with the majority of them falling within 9.85 degrees on either side of the mean. In other words, the heat-index temperatures in the sample average 107.40°F, give or take 9.85 degrees, making most summer temperatures in our sample between 97.55°F and 117.25°F. It would not be accurate to report that *all* of the temperatures in the sample fell within one standard deviation of the mean (on either side of it), but the standard deviation indicates that most of them did. So the average amount of variability in the data set is 9.85 degrees.

Estimated Population Standard Deviation

In the prior example (heat index in GA), we were trying to summarize our sample with two pieces of information, but psychologists often want to go beyond describing the sample; we want to make guesses about what the entire population would be like. For the example of summer temperatures in Georgia, a weatherperson would not be very interested in a sample of temperatures, but (s)he would be interested in using those temperatures (the sample) to make general statements about summer temperatures in Georgia. This discussion is based on terms introduced in Chapter 1, where you learned about random samples and representative samples. If we have a representative sample (chosen randomly), we can feel confident when making guesses about the population based on what we learn from the sample. From this heat-index example, you can see that a sample does not have to involve people; it can be a sample of temperature across summer days.

When we are interested in predicting information about the population from a sample (of interval or ratio values), we should predict that the population mean is the same as the sample mean because it is the best guess we have. The **population mean** is symbolized by μ, pronounced "mew." For our temperature example, we would estimate that in general, summer days in Georgia average a heat index of 107.40°F.

We will also want to estimate the population standard deviation from a sample, but the sample standard deviation cannot be used because it underestimates all the variability possible in an entire population. That makes sense because our sample only has a few values, but the population usually has a large number of values, so more variability among values is possible in the population. It does not mean that the sample variability is off by a great deal; it underestimates the variability in the population by a small amount. To solve this problem, the denominator of the formula is changed slightly. Instead of dividing the numerator by N, divide by $N - 1$. Of course, whenever the denominator is reduced, the final number increases.

$$\mathscr{S}_x = \sqrt{\frac{\Sigma X^2 - \frac{(\Sigma X)^2}{N}}{N - 1}}$$

With this slight change to the formula, we now have the **estimated population standard deviation**, symbolized by $\mathscr{S}_x$. Using the Georgia temperatures, change the denominator to estimate the average variability for all summer temperatures in the state. It would not be 9.85 degrees, which was the sample standard deviation. The estimated population standard deviation should be a bit larger to reflect that there are more extreme temperatures in the summer than might have been indicated in our small sample.

$$\mathscr{S}_x = \sqrt{\frac{58159 - \frac{(537)^2}{5}}{4}} = \sqrt{121.30} = 11.013628$$

Use the estimated population standard deviation to guess beyond the sample of five temperatures. Now we can say the average summer heat-index temperature in Georgia is 107.40°F, and most temperatures tend to fall between 96.39 degrees and 118.41 degrees. Notice that we are making a statement about a population of summer temperatures based on a sample.

Estimated Population Variance

One final formula will be covered before learning how to get these answers efficiently using SPSS. Recall that we did not want to rely on the sample variance, because we had squared all the deviation scores before getting the average variability. We realized that it was more useful to take the square root of the sample variance to reduce our final number back down where it began, providing the sample standard deviation. Following that logic, it was only natural for us to estimate the population variability using standard deviation, too. However, later in this book, estimated population variance will be needed, so we will cover it now. As you might have guessed, **estimated population variance** is the same as sample variance, but the numerator is divided by $N - 1$ rather than N. Looking at it another way, we could square the estimated population standard deviation to increase it to variance. Here is the formula for the estimated population variance:

$$\mathcal{S}_x^2 = \frac{\Sigma X^2 - \frac{(\Sigma X)^2}{N}}{N - 1}$$

Compare and contrast the four formulas presented in this chapter.

	Sample	Estimated Population
Standard Deviation	$S_x = \sqrt{\dfrac{\Sigma X^2 - \frac{(\Sigma X)^2}{N}}{N}}$	$\mathcal{S}_x = \sqrt{\dfrac{\Sigma X^2 - \frac{(\Sigma X)^2}{N}}{N - 1}}$
Variance	$S_x^2 = \dfrac{\Sigma X^2 - \frac{(\Sigma X)^2}{N}}{N}$	$\mathcal{S}_x^2 = \dfrac{\Sigma X^2 - \frac{(\Sigma X)^2}{N}}{N - 1}$

Notice that the formulas look highly similar, and their slight differences are based on theory we have covered in detail. As a final reminder, these formulas can only be used when the variable we are summarizing represents interval or ratio data that are not skewed (have no obvious outliers).

Measures of Variability on SPSS

Soon you'll want to save yourself the work of calculating by putting your data on SPSS and letting the program calculate measures of variability. On a new spreadsheet, point to View, then select Variables and type **heat** in the first column. Return to the spreadsheet to enter the numbers from our most recent example: heat index in Georgia.

Point to Analyze, then select Descriptive Statistics+Descriptives.

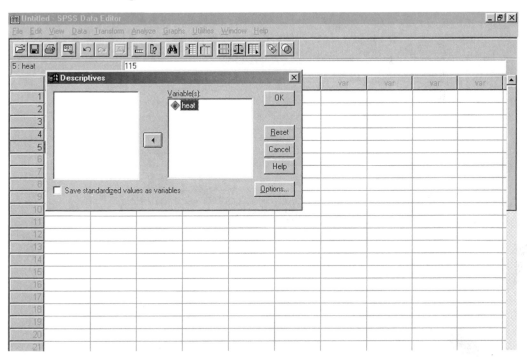

On the left side of the gray box, select the variable(s) of interest and click it over to the right.

Click Options and choose any measures you want, then click Continue+OK. Most of the time, you will want the sample standard deviation, since you're trying to describe your sample using the computer, but be careful; SPSS provides the estimated population standard deviation rather than the sample standard deviation. The good news is that the estimated population standard deviation and the sample standard deviation are very similar, since the denominator is only slightly different for each calculation.

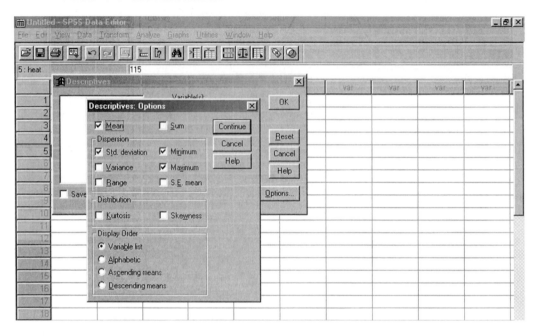

The output printed from SPSS should match the output below.

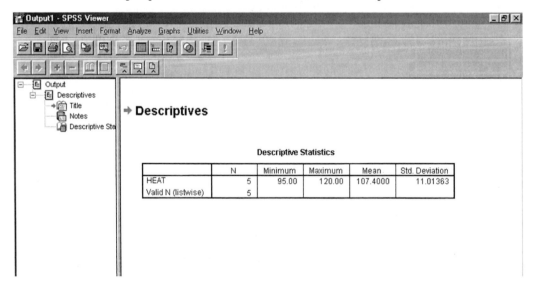

Descriptive Statistics

	N	Minimum	Maximum	Mean	Std. Deviation
HEAT	5	95.00	120.00	107.4000	11.01363
Valid N (listwise)	5				

Graphing Sample Standard Deviation

Chapter 3 introduced graphing group means in an experiment using SPSS. On a graph, the standard deviation of each group (level of the IV) will also be needed. This is accomplished by calculating the standard deviation (preferably for the sample, but if you rely on output from SPSS, you'll be using the estimated population standard deviation). Standard deviations are calculated separately for each level of the IV, then each standard deviation is sketched on the graph using an **error bar** (also called a **T-bar**). Beginning at the mean, which will be the top of the bar in a bar graph or the point (dot) on a line graph, we will draw a line to cover the distance of the standard deviation.

We will return to the example from the end of Chapter 3 and add error bars. Recall that we assessed the effect of number of hours spent talking to parents on how much spending money they send. We used one, two, and three hours a week, and found that parents sent $23.00 for one hour, $57.00 for two hours, and $25.50 for three hours. To calculate the sample standard deviation for each group, you need the raw values (of spending money) again.

One	Two	Three
28.50	52.00	25.50
20.00	49.80	19.00
26.00	64.50	30.50
23.00	62.00	20.50
17.50	57.00	32.00

One column at a time, calculate each sample standard deviation. We will go through the calculations together here.

The first column:

1 (X)	X^2
28.50	812.25
20.00	400.00
26.00	676.00
23.00	529.00
17.50	306.25
115.00	2723.50

$$S_x = \sqrt{\frac{2723.50 - \frac{(115)^2}{5}}{5}} = 3.962323$$

The second column:

2 (X)	X^2
52.00	2704.00
49.80	2480.04
64.50	4160.25
62.00	3844.00
57.00	3249.00
285.30	16437.29

$$S_x = \sqrt{\dfrac{16437.29 - \dfrac{(285.30)^2}{5}}{5}} = 5.622668$$

The third and final column:

3 (X)	X^2
25.50	650.25
19.00	361.00
30.50	930.25
20.50	420.25
32.00	1024.00
127.50	3385.75

$$S_x = \sqrt{\dfrac{3385.75 - \dfrac{(127.50)^2}{5}}{5}} = 5.186521$$

From Chapter 3, the line graph of the means looked like this:

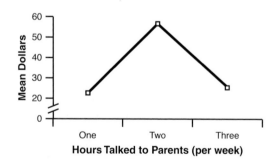

The only change is to add error bars to the graph. Because the mean of the first group was $23.00, with a sample standard deviation of $3.96, draw a line from the top of the point up 3.96 units to the number 26.96 on the *y*-axis. Then make the line look like a *T* by putting another line across the top of it. This first *T*-bar should look like it ends at about $27.00 based on the *y*-axis. If the second point is at $57.00, and the standard deviation is $5.62, the *T*-bar cannot be drawn upward because it would dangle off the top of the graph. Instead, draw the *T*-bar down to the number 62.62 as measured against the *y*-axis. (Extending the *y*-axis to 70 would also solve the problem.) Finally, if a third point is at $25.50 on the *y*-axis, and the standard deviation is $5.19, draw a line up to 30.69 based on the numbers on the *y*-axis. Below is a graph of this example.

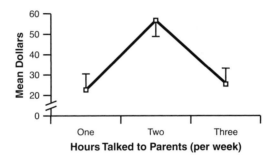

Whether the error bars go up or down does not matter because they both provide the same information: The *T*-bar represents one standard deviation away from the mean (above or below), and that is where most of the values fall. Just as we should always summarize data using a measure of central tendency and a measure of variability, we always need to have both pieces of information on a graph of data.

Graphs of Standard Deviation on SPSS

At the end of Chapter 3, graphing through Interactive in SPSS was introduced, but only means were graphed; no standard deviations (error bars) were added to the graph. Review Chapter 3 to enter data for the example of talking to parents and money received. Then point to Graphs and select Interactive+Line. After entering **hours** as the IV and **dollars** as the DV, be sure to right click and change hours to categorical.

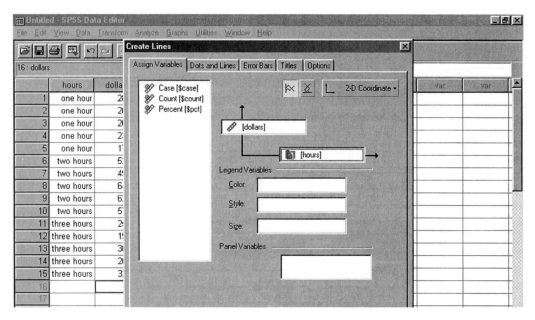

Before you click OK, point to the tab labeled Error Bars across the top of the box. Check Display Error Bars and change Confidence Interval Limits to Standard Deviation, to allow SPSS to graph standard deviation error bars. Notice that the default is 1 standard deviation from the mean, which is exactly what we want. Remember that we can have the error bar drawn upward, downward, or in both directions. Because error bars above and below the mean of each group should be exactly the same size, some researchers prefer to simply graph T-bars in one direction. At the bottom of the box, under Direction, select the second graph (showing error bars drawn in the positive direction).

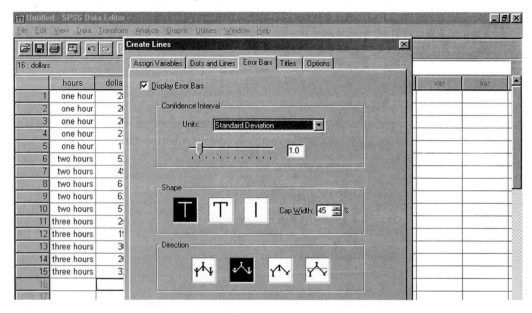

Click OK to see the following output.

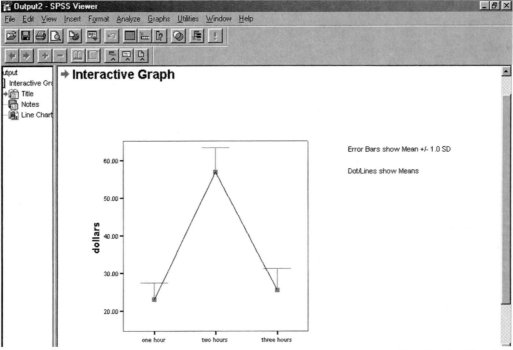

The graph looks fine, but I prefer to make a few changes. To edit, double-click on the graph. Next, right click on each error bar, select Properties, and change the color of the error bar and symbol from red (the default) to black. I also like to label the *x*- and *y*-axes more clearly by double-clicking each one and adding more detailed information. After a change has been made, click anywhere in the graph for the words to move to their proper location.

To print, click outside of the graph once (closing the editing program), then click in the graph, then Print.

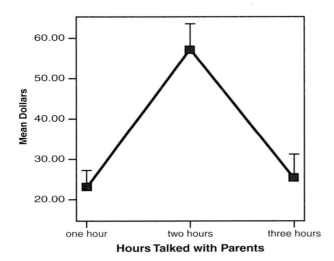

Error Bars show Mean +/− 1.0 SD

Dot/Lines show Means

A graph of group means and group variability (standard deviation in this example) provides a useful figure for an APA-style manuscript.

Preview of Chapter 5

In the past few chapters, you have learned how to illustrate data using graphs. You have also learned how to describe a sample using central tendency and variability and can find those answers using SPSS. In the next chapter, z-scores will be presented, a descriptive statistic that relies on the normal curve we covered in Chapter 2.

Conceptual Items

1. All of these graphs have the same mean. What makes them different? (Hint: Several answers are correct, so use a few of your new terms.)

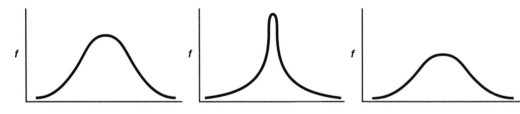

2. Define the following:
   a. range
   b. sample variance
   c. sample standard deviation
   d. estimated population standard deviation
   e. estimated population variance
3. If you just want to describe a sample, which measure of variability would you use?
4. If you want to use a sample to infer something about the population from which the sample was drawn, which measure of variability would you use?
5. Why would it be important to learn about definitional formulas as well as calculational formulas?
6. What measure of variability must be used with ordinal data?
7. What measure of variability is used with skewed interval or ratio data?
8. What measure of variability is used with normally distributed interval or ratio data? Explain your answer.

Application Items

9. In this example, values indicate how long it takes a sample of computers to connect to the Internet in seconds.

X
7.1
5.5
9.4
12.6
6.0
11.2
7.7
6.4
8.3

   a. What is the range?
   b. What is the sample variance?
   c. What is the sample standard deviation?
   d. What is the estimated population variance for all computers?
   e. What is the estimated population standard deviation for all computers?
   f. Which measure of variability would you choose to describe these data and why?

10. If we collected school newspapers from several schools, we might get an idea of how many sports articles are written. The data on the next page might be found:

Sports Articles
5
7
5
9
4
7
7
6
8

   a. What is the range?
   b. What is the sample variance?
   c. What is the sample standard deviation?
   d. What is the estimated population variance for all college newspapers?
   e. What is the estimated population standard deviation for all college papers?
   f. Which measure of variability would you choose to describe these data and why?

11. A group of students presented their research at an undergraduate poster session. They competed in several categories and brought home the following awards:

1st place	1st place	3rd place	4th place	2nd place
1st place	2nd place	1st place	2nd place	3rd place

   a. What type of data are these?
   b. Report the value of the appropriate measure of variability for these data.

12. Below are fictional data of student attitudes toward their instructor after receiving papers graded in black, red, or purple ink. Students' attitudes are on a scale from 1 to 15, with higher numbers indicating a more positive attitude toward the instructor.

Black	Red	Purple
11	5	9
8	6	6
7	9	6
13	4	8
9	7	7
15	6	11
9	8	4
14		13

   a. What level of measurement is the IV?
   b. What type of graph is needed?
   c. Sketch a graph of these means, and be sure to include an indication of variability.
   d. Create a graph using SPSS, and turn in a printout of the SPSS graph.

13. If you owned a company that sold novelty sweaters, you might be interested in knowing what age group spends the most money on your clothing. With this information, you could target a specific group with your advertisements. Suppose you broke down age groups into 21–35, 36–50, and 51–65, and asked customers in these three age groups to report how much they spent in the past month on your company's novelty sweaters. Keep in mind that you did not manipulate people's ages, so this is not a true IV; it is another example of a quasi-IV, and you know it is treated just as an IV would be treated. You simply must be careful not to talk about cause and effect. Our question is whether or not there is a relationship between age and money spent (in dollars) on novelty sweaters.

21–35 years	36–50 years	51–65 years
45	85	70
30	120	96
42	98	111
67	104	56
53	156	81
	95	76

a. What level of measurement is the quasi-IV?
b. What type of graph is needed?
c. Sketch a graph of these means, including error bars.
d. Create a graph using SPSS and turn in a printout of the SPSS graph.

Computational Formulas in This Chapter

Deviation value

$$x = X - \overline{X}$$

Sample variance

$$S_x^2 = \frac{\sum X^2 - \frac{(\sum X)^2}{N}}{N}$$

Sample standard deviation

$$S_x = \sqrt{\frac{\sum X^2 - \frac{(\sum X)^2}{N}}{N}}$$

★Estimated population variance

$$\mathscr{S}_x^2 = \frac{\sum X^2 - \frac{(\sum X)^2}{N}}{N - 1}$$

★Estimated population standard deviation

$$\mathscr{S}_x = \sqrt{\frac{\sum X^2 - \frac{(\sum X)^2}{N}}{N - 1}}$$

5

Descriptive z-Scores

Standardized Scores

In the first part of this text, we described samples of data using central tendency, variability, and graphs. In this chapter, values from different samples will be compared. For example, you normally could not compare your grade on a test in calculus with your younger brother's grade on a test of addition and subtraction. However, a comparison can be made if the scores are first changed to **standardized scores**, which involves transforming values so they fall on the same scale. Next, standardized scores will allow us to find the likelihood of getting a specific value based on the sample's descriptive statistics.

Comparing Values from Different Samples

Suppose you want to act in a local production of *American Pie*. To guess your chance of getting a starring role, we could rate your acting ability on a scale from 1 to 20, with higher numbers meaning better acting. Imagine your acting ability is rated at 15.00. Since you will be competing with other hopeful actors in town, you should see how you compare with them.

First, we would need the average acting rating for the entire sample of people who audition. (Remember that we can get the average, because a rating scale is considered interval data by psychologists.) Perhaps the average rating for acting is 12.00. Your rating of 15.00 is quite good compared with the sample's acting ability of 12.00, and you should have an excellent chance of getting a starring role.

However, if you planned to audition with a group of actors with many years of experience, the sample would be different. The average acting ability might be higher, like 14.00. With a sample mean of 14.00, you might not get a good part. At the very least, auditions would be more competitive with this sample.

The problem is that we need to evaluate your acting score of 15.00 across two different distributions. The good news is that statistics gives us a convenient way to make the comparison: standardize your acting score against each distribution. Standardizing a score is accomplished by changing your raw score of 15.00 into a

z-score (or standardized score) using a formula that incorporates your score, the sample mean, and the sample standard deviation.

$$z = \frac{X - \overline{X}}{S_x}$$

For the first example of amateur actors, standardize the 15.00 using the sample mean of 12.00 and a sample standard deviation of 2.00. Subtract the mean of 12.00 from the raw score of 15.00. Then divide by the sample standard deviation of 2.00. The z-score (standardized score) is a positive 1.50. Because the z-score is a positive value rather than negative, your score is above the group average. The absolute value of the z-score indicates how far from average a score falls.

$$z = \frac{15.00 - 12.00}{2.00} = 1.50$$

Now calculate the standardized score for your raw score of 15.00 in a sample of seasoned actors. Subtract the sample mean of 14.00 from your raw score of 15.00, then divide by the sample standard deviation of 2.00. (To keep these calculations simple, I've chosen 2.00 as the standard deviation for both examples.)

$$z = \frac{15.00 - 14.00}{2.00} = 0.50$$

The z-score for your raw score in this distribution is 0.50. Your score of 15.00 was only slightly above the average acting ability for the talented sample. As a result, your chance of getting a starring role is not as good with such tough competition.

Based on your raw score of 15.00 in the two groups of actors, you might have originally thought that your score was excellent in both samples. But that would not be accurate. Even though in both groups you had a score of 15.00 for your acting ability, the rating ended up being quite different in the two samples. With standardized scores (z-scores), you know that your acting score of 15.00 was much better in the first sample than in the sample of talented actors.

The outcome of this example might seem like common sense, because it is reasonable that you would have a lower chance of getting a starring role when competing with experienced actors. The next example is not as obvious, and you will have to rely on standardized scores to understand the meaning of the values.

Imagine that you and your friend bet on who could make a higher grade on the first test—you in psychological statistics or her in a math statistics course. On the first test in psychological statistics, you earned a 70%. Your friend made a 75% on her math statistics test and believes she won the bet. Since you both have information on class averages and standard deviations, you could standardize the scores by changing them to z-scores. A comparison between two standardized scores would be more appropriate than comparing raw scores, since you and your friend are in different classes taking different tests. In other words, the raw scores come from different distributions. The test average in your friend's class was 85%, with a sample standard deviation of 12%. Her z-score is −0.83.

$$z = \frac{75 - 85}{12} = -0.83$$

Your score was 70%, and your class average on the test was 65%, with a sample standard deviation of 10%. Your z-score is 0.50.

$$z = \frac{70 - 65}{10} = 0.50$$

Most people in your friend's class actually scored higher than her, therefore she is not doing as well as the average student in her class. You, on the other hand, are doing better than the average student in your class. Compared with the others in your class, you are performing better with the material. Based on standardized scores, you earned a higher grade.

A lingering question you might have is why you only scored 70% if you had a firm grasp of the material. As an added insult, your roommate received a higher raw grade. Two explanations could be that the test in your class was particularly challenging, or the test in her class was incredibly easy.

Even when values from different samples are not being compared, raw scores cannot be evaluated clearly; information must be provided concerning how most people perform on the same test and how much variability is in the sample. Only after standardizing a raw score can we understand its true value. Now that you know this, if you earn a low grade, look beyond the raw score. Ask for information about the sample mean and standard deviation from your class. Then if your standardized score is a positive number (above the sample mean), you can feel better about your performance. If the z-score is a high positive value, your performance on the test was excellent.

Standardized Distribution

So far, we have discussed standardizing a single value against a sample. If we changed all of the raw scores in a normally distributed sample to z-scores, we would have more than just a standardized score; we would have an entire **standardized distribution**. Not surprisingly, it is also called a z-distribution. A **z-distribution** is a normal curve (symmetrical around the middle) with two useful properties that make it easy to use: the z-distribution has a mean of 0.00 and a standard deviation of 1.00.

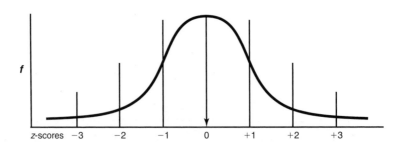

The mean of zero is logical, because a raw score equal to the mean will be zero when the mean is subtracted from the raw score. For example, if a raw score was 10.00 and the sample mean was a 10.00, the z-score would be zero.

$$z = \frac{10.00 - 10.00}{(\text{any number})} = 0.00$$

The standard deviation of a z-distribution is always 1.00. You might be thinking of the examples we just covered in which the sample standard deviations were numbers other than 1.00, but those were from raw scores. After you standardize all of the raw scores, the standard deviation for the new distribution (z-distribution) is 1.00. Most of the standardized scores fall between a z-score of ± 1.00 (one standard deviation on either side of the mean).

From earlier acting examples, your standardized score against untrained actors was 1.50, meaning your acting ability was 1.50 standard deviations above the mean. Because most values in a distribution fall within one standard deviation of the mean, your score of 1.50 was impressive.

Proportion and Percent

On any distribution, or curve, all of the space under the curve is 1.00. In Chapter 1, this was introduced as proportion. If we multiply proportion by 100, we get 100% of the distribution.

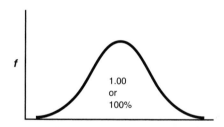

The 1.00 (or 100%) can be divided into segments based on standard deviations. Researchers know what part of a normal distribution is found between one standard deviation, two standard deviations, and so on. The proportions are below.

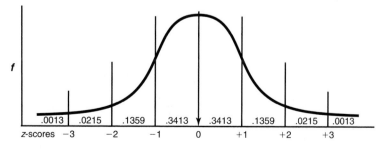

With a standardized distribution, we already know that the standard deviation is 1.00, so each z-score falls exactly on a standard deviation. Thus, a z-score of +1.00 or −1.00 falls at a standard deviation of 1.00; a z-score of +2.00 or −2.00 falls at a standard deviation of 2.00; and a z-score of +3.00 or −3.00 falls at a standard deviation of 3.00.

Given this information, we can use the segments under the curve to answer questions like:

(1) What proportion of the distribution (curve) is found between the mean of a z-distribution and a z-score of 1.00?

Answer: 0.3413 (or 34%, if the question asked for percent)

(2) What proportion of the distribution is found between the mean and a z-score of −1.00?

Answer: 0.3413 (since the distribution is symmetrical)

(3) What proportion of the distribution is found between the mean and a z-score of 2.00?

Answer: 0.4772

(4) What proportion of the distribution is found between the mean and a z-score of −3.00?

Answer: 0.4987

(5) What proportion of the distribution is found above a z-score of 2.00?

Answer: 0.0228

If a raw score can be standardized, questions about proportions above and below that score can be addressed. Looking back at (5) if your z-score on a final exam was 2.00, approximately what segment of the class earned higher scores than you? Only 0.0228, or about 2% received a better grade than you.

In the examples above, whole numbers were used for z-scores. Realistically, when a z-score is calculated, it is rarely a whole number. When the z-score involves decimals, we can turn to a table in the back of the book to look up the z-scores and address questions about proportion and percent.

Recall our earlier example of getting a role in a play when auditioning with inexperienced actors. If you wanted to know what proportion of novice actors had higher acting scores than you, knowing that your raw score was 15.00 does not answer the question. In fact, the sample mean of 12.00 and the sample standard deviation of 2.00 do not help either. However, if you use all three pieces of information to calculate a z-score, you will have a useful tool. We already know that the z-score in this example was 1.50, but what does that mean?

To answer this question, we will need to turn to the z-table in the back of the book. This table shows the proportion of values above (or below) any z-score. Because the entire distribution has a proportion of 1.00, any piece of it will have to be a proportion less than 1.00. When you look for areas under the curve, all values in the table are less than 1.00. In fact, all of the values are less than 0.50, because the table only illustrates half of the distribution. From the pictures at the top of the columns, you can see that the upper half of the distribution is represented, but since the z-distribution is symmetrical around the middle, the same proportions would be found in the lower half of the distribution. This does not mean proportions can be negative. But z-scores can be negative—when they are below the mean of the distribution.

Remember our question: What proportion of the values are above your acting score of 15.00 when the sample mean is 12.00 and the sample standard deviation is 2.00? Since your z-score is 1.50, look up a z-score of 1.50 in the first column of the table. Then look over to the third column, which represents the proportion of values above a z-score of 1.50. The answer is 0.07 (0.0668), which means 0.07 of the acting scores were higher than yours. Or you could say that 0.07 of the people who auditioned were better actors than you in this sample.

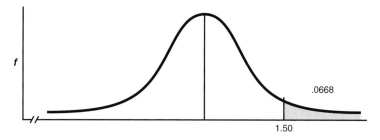

A term you might hear instead of proportion is **area**. For the example we are using, the area between a z-score of 1.50 and the upper end of the distribution is 0.07. Proportion (area) can easily be changed to percent by multiplying by 100. If the entire distribution is a proportion of 1.00, multiplying by 100 means 100% of the distribution. For your z-score of 1.50, since 0.07 proportion of scores/actors fell above you, multiplying by 100 reveals that only 7% of the actors in this sample performed better than you.

$$0.07 \times 100 = 7\%$$

Evaluations Based on z-scores

Another example will help build competence using the z-table. Assume that you have to choose a date from your school based on his/her z-score for kindness. Imagine that all students at your school are the sample, and the sample has a mean and sample standard deviation to calculate z-scores. You can choose among kindness z-scores of -1.65, 0.00, or 1.65. Assuming all other things are equal, you would choose the date with the kindness z-score of 1.65, because that person is above average. But how far above average is the person? What percent of the sample is less kind than your date?

You have a choice of two ways to approach this problem. First, you could look up the z-score of 1.65 and see what proportion of the values are higher by using the third column again. Then subtract the proportion from 1.00, given that you want to know what proportion is lower than 1.65, not higher. Your answer would be $1.00 - 0.05$ (0.0495, to be exact) $= 0.95$. The question asked for percent, so multiply 0.95 by 100 to get an answer of 95% of the people at your school are less kind than your date.

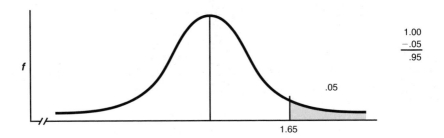

A second way to approach the problem is to look up the z-score of 1.65 and move to the second column to find the proportion of values between the mean of the distribution (the high point) and the z-score of 1.65. You will find that the proportion is 0.45. But people in the lower half of the distribution also have kindness ratings lower than your date. If people in the lower half of the distribution are less kind, the proportion found there is 0.50. That is always the case in half of the distribution, because half is 50%—or 0.50 for proportion.

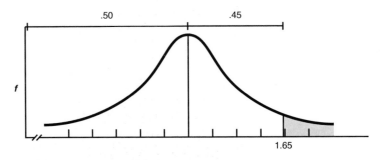

Now add the 0.50 and the 0.45 together to get the proportion of people who are rated as less kind than your date. Then multiply the proportion of 0.95 by 100 to get your answer: 95% of the people at your school are less kind than the person with whom you will spend an evening.

Comparing Two Values and Proportions

In the first half of this chapter, we discussed z-scores as a way to compare values from two different samples. In the second half, values were evaluated based on proportions. Here is an example that does both.

Two of your friends got tattoos on their arms. You want to know which one of them had higher pain tolerance, so you ask them to rate the pain of the needle on a scale from 1 to 40. Callie rated her pain as a 25, and Devon rated his pain as a 30. You realize that you might have a problem comparing their pain ratings because Callie got her tattoo at the Hepatitis Shack, and Devon got his tattoo at the House of Maim. Because it is a small town, you are able to contact the 30 people who received tattoos at the Hepatitis Shack, and you find out that the average pain rating for the sample is 22.00, with a standard deviation of 2.32. That makes Callie's standardized score a 1.29.

Callie's standardized score:

$$z = \frac{25.00 - 22.00}{2.32} = 1.29$$

The 55 people who purchased tattoos at the House of Maim rated their pain average as 26.99, with a sample standard deviation of 2.33.

Devon's standardized score:

$$z = \frac{30.00 - 26.99}{2.33} = 1.29$$

What can we conclude about Callie's pain rating of 25 and Devon's rating of 30? Does Callie have a higher tolerance for pain than Devon? No, because the House of Maim was just more painful overall—for everyone. Callie was simply more fortunate that tattoos at the Hepatitis Shack did not hurt as much. Their standardized scores were identical, leading us to conclude that they both experienced the same amount of pain relative to customers at their tattoo parlors.

With a standardized pain score of 1.29, neither of them tolerates pain well. We can use the z-table to find out exactly where their pain perceptions fell. What proportion of each sample had lower pain ratings than Callie and Devon? Look up the z-score of 1.29, move one column to the right, and see the area (proportion) between the mean and a z-score of 1.29: 0.40 (0.4015). Add the bottom half of the distribution; all of those people also handled pain better than your two friends. The lower half of the distribution is 0.50. Add the 0.40 between the mean and the z-score of 1.29 to get 0.90.

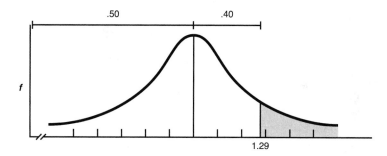

If the question asked for percent, multiply 0.90 by 100 to get the result that 90% of the people from the Hepatitis Shack and the House of Maim rated their pain as less than Callie and Devon.

Percentile

One final way to evaluate a value is by changing it to a percentile. **Percentile** is the percentage of values found at or below a specific z-score. We just figured out that 90% of the people who received tattoos rated their pain lower than your friends did, meaning they fell at the 90th percentile. In other words, a z-score of 1.29 is at the 90th percentile.

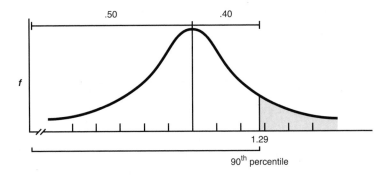

As a final example, if your standardized score on a final exam was 2.00, only 0.02 proportion made better scores than you. To find your percentile, the simplest approach is to subtract 0.02 from 1.00 (for the whole distribution), to get 0.98 proportion with scores lower than you. Then multiply 0.98 proportion below you by 100, to get 98% making scores lower than you. That puts your grade at the 98th percentile.

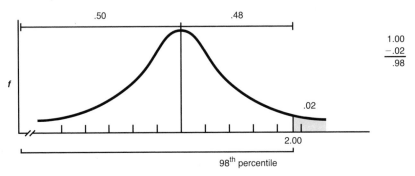

Logical Limits

If a z-score is beyond ± 5, there is probably an error in the calculation. In fact, a z-score will almost never be further into the tails of a distribution than ± 3. Look up a z-score of +3 in the z-table to find that only 0.0013 proportion of the values fall above it. Of course, the same is true for the lower end of the distribution; only 0.0013 proportion of scores fall below a z-score of −3. The proportion of z-scores above a +3 or below a −3 is 0.0013. Put another way, the percent of scores that might actually fall above a +3 or below a −3 is far less than 1%, a very unlikely possibility.

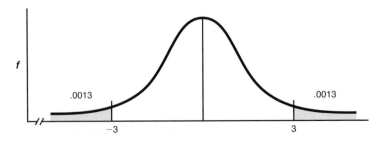

Preview of Chapter 6

In this chapter, we changed raw scores to z-scores, and even changed all raw scores from a sample to z-scores to create a standardized distribution. Since we were only dealing with samples, we were calculating descriptive statistics; the z-scores we used were called descriptive z-scores. In the next chapter, you will learn about z-scores again, but this time they will be inferential z-scores. Instead of comparing a raw score to a sample, we will compare a sample mean to an entire population. Thus, Chapter 6 will open with a discussion of probability and how we learn about a population of interest.

Conceptual Items

1. Why are standardized values often more meaningful than raw values?
2. What is the difference between a z-score and a z-distribution?
3. A z-score is rarely beyond what 2 values? In other words, only 0.13% of the distribution is located beyond each value.
4. Why does the z-table contain only positive values?
5. Can percent be a negative value? Why or why not?
6. Can proportion be a negative value? Why or why not?
7. Can a z-score be a negative value? Why or why not?

Application Items

8. A z-value of -2.00 is how many standard deviations from the mean?
9. Change the following raw scores to z-scores based on a sample mean $(\overline{X})$ of 200 and a sample standard deviation (S_x) of 39. (That is, standardize the following scores.)
   a. 150
   b. 265
   c. 310
   d. 175
   e. 200
10. For a–e above, what proportion of the distribution falls above each standardized score?

    (*Hint:* Each time you search for an area under the normal curve, draw a normal distribution, place the z-score on the x-axis, and shade the area of interest.)

11. Still using a–e from Application Item 9, what proportion falls below each standardized score?
12. For a–e, what percent of the distribution falls below each score?

13. Use the following information to decide which test has a higher standardized score.

Stats Test 1	Stats Test 2
score = 77	score = 77
$\overline{X} = 70$	$\overline{X} = 70$
$S_x = 7$	$S_x = 15$

14. What percent of a distribution falls
    a. above a z-score of 0.92?
    b. below a z-score of −0.92?
    c. between the mean and a z-score of 0.92?
    d. beyond (away from the mean, in the tails) a z-score of 0.92?
    e. beyond the z-scores of −0.92 and 0.92?

15. What is the area on a z-distribution
    a. above 1.84?
    b. below 1.84?
    c. below −1.84?
    d. between −1.84 and 1.84?
    e. beyond −1.84 and 1.84?

16. For each of the following z-values, find the percentile.
    a. 0.92
    b. −0.92
    c. 1.84
    d. −1.84

17. Find the percentile of a score of 50, when the mean is 40 and the standard deviation is 10.

18. Calculate the percentile of a score of 83, when the sample mean is 85 and the sample standard deviation is 6.

19. Find the raw score at the 10th percentile, when the mean is 30 and the standard deviation is 5. (Hint: Change the z-score formula to solve for X.)

20. Calculate the raw score at the 95th percentile, when the mean is 90 and the sample standard deviation is 3.

21. Find the area between the $\overline{X}$ and z when $z = 2.08$.

22. Find the area corresponding to numbers greater than a z of 2.14.

23. Above what z-score are 45.62% of the scores in a distribution found?

24. Below what z-score are 3.29% of the scores in a distribution found?

25. If you had a raw score of 265, and the class average was 200 with a standard deviation of 39, what percent of the class scored higher than you?

26. If your friend had a raw score of 150 on the same test (see Application Item 25), what was her percentile?

27. If you had a raw score of 81, and the class average was 88 with a sample standard deviation of 5, what percent of the class scored lower than you?

28. If your friend had a raw score of 94 on the same test (see Application Item 27), what was his percentile?

Computational formula in this chapter

Descriptive z-value

$$z = \frac{X - \overline{X}}{S_x}$$

CHAPTER **6**

Inferential *z*-Scores and Probability

Probability

When we conduct inferential statistics, the goal is to learn something about a population. Specifically, we would like to know the likelihood or chance of an event occurring in the population. As with proportion, likelihood (and chance) can range from 0-1.00, with 0 indicating that the event will not occur, and 1 indicating that the event will definitely occur. The simplest example is flipping a coin, because only two options can occur: heads or tails. To calculate the likelihood of the coin falling as heads, put the number of times the option occurs on the coin (1 head per coin) over the total number of options on the coin (2 sides per coin).

$$\frac{1 \text{ head}}{2 \text{ sides}} = 0.50$$

Likelihood and chance are often termed **probability**, the likelihood of a given event occurring. Thus, 0.50 is the probability of the coin falling as heads. Similarly, the probability of the coin falling on tails is 0.50.

$$\frac{1 \text{ tail}}{2 \text{ sides}} = 0.50$$

Both probabilities sum to 1.00, because either heads or tails will definitely occur.

Moving beyond an example with only two possibilities, a die has six sides, with six different numbers, one through six. The probability of rolling a six is:

$$\frac{1 \text{ six}}{6 \text{ sides}} = 0.1666667$$

And the probability of not rolling a six is:

$$\frac{5 \text{ numbers other than six}}{6 \text{ sides}} = 0.833333$$

Numbers can be combined to answer additional questions. What is the probability of rolling a five or a six?

$$\frac{1 \text{ five} + 1 \text{ six}}{6 \text{ sides}} = \frac{2}{6} = 0.333333$$

The discussion of probability might help you understand why casino owners will often ask customers to leave if they appear to be counting cards in a game such as blackjack. Someone with a good memory who understands probability can calculate the likelihood of getting a ten-point card (10, jack, queen, king) if one is needed. Based on a full deck with four possible cards per suit,

$$\frac{4 \text{ ten-point cards} \times 4 \text{ suits}}{52 \text{ cards in deck}} = \frac{16}{52} = 0.307692$$

The probability of getting a ten-point card is 0.31. However, if only 20 cards remain in the deck, and 12 ten-point cards remain in that deck, the probability of getting a ten-point card increases.

$$\frac{12 \text{ ten-point cards remaining}}{20 \text{ cards remaining in deck}} = 0.60$$

This situation looks much better for the customer, with a 0.60 probability of getting a ten-point card. Of course, the same calculation of probability would tell the customer when a card is *not* likely to appear, so if a ten-point card would put the customer over the 21 points needed in blackjack, it would be useful to know the 0.60 probability that such a card would be dealt. Either way, the gambler stands a much better chance of winning with knowledge of probability.

For the card example, the possibility of drawing a specific card from a full deck is the same regardless of the card. This also holds true for the coin example; the probability of getting heads or tails in each toss of the coin is equally likely. In real life, however, events do not always occur with the exact same probability. For example, if I generally trip six out of 10 times when I walk up a flight of stairs, the probability of tripping is 0.60. It is not equally likely that I will *not* stumble, which has a probability of 0.40.

Even though the probability of stumbling and not stumbling are not equal, as long as we know the likelihood of an event, guesses can be made about future performance. The probability that I will trip the next time I walk up stairs is 0.60. This also means that if you watched me walk up stairs 10 times, it is likely that I would trip six of those times. However, I might have a good week in which I only stumble five out of 10 times. As you can see, I would not be living up to the normal probability of 0.60, even though a 0.60 would certainly be the most likely number to happen, based on the general knowledge that I normally trip six out of 10 times I walk up stairs. Over a long period of time, if we kept track of number of trips per 10 times walking up stairs, the number 0.60 would indeed be the most likely, or probable. But a proportion of 0.50 could happen every once in a while, and so could a proportion of 0.70. I can even imagine that on those rare, coordinated weeks, I might trip once out of every 10 times, with a proportion of 0.10, but that would be unusual, given that my normal proportion of tripping is 0.60.

The bottom line is that life does not always live up to expectations, but most of the time, it does. Or at least it is pretty close. The true representation of my performance, tripping six out of every 10 times, does indeed occur most often.

The same holds true when learning about any population of events. For example, if we randomly sampled a group of college students from a population of students with an average IQ of 100, a sample mean IQ of 100 is highly likely. After all, the population IQ of 100 is the event that occurs most often in the normal population of college students. It is our best guess. Will the sample mean IQ always be 100? No, just as we would not always find that I trip six out of 10 times up the stairs. But chance assures us that the most likely sample mean will be the population mean.

Sampling Distribution of Means

If many samples were pulled from a population, we would gain a clearer view of the population mean. For example, suppose we wanted to know how much time students spend in chat rooms on the internet. We might select a sample of 10 college students and ask them how many minutes they chat each week. Then we could get an average for that sample—perhaps about 90 minutes. Does that mean all students chat an average of 90 minutes each week? Maybe, or we might have collected a sample that chats a lot (or a little). In a different sample of 10 college students, imagine that the mean was 95 minutes. Another sample, 100 minutes. Another one, 95 minutes. One more, 20 minutes each week. The more samples we pull, the more likely we are to find out how much time most students spend in chat rooms. In other words, we would eventually get a good idea of the population mean.

Look at the averages (sample means) again: 90, 95, 100, 95, and 20. If we ignore the 20 for now, it looks like the population average might be around 95 minutes of chatting each week. Remember from Chapter 4 that the population mean is called mu, symbolized by μ.

The sample mean of 20 looks unusual, but it is a legitimate mean obtained by randomly sampling 10 students and asking them how much they chatted. It is unusual, though, and 20 does not accurately reflect the population mean, so it is called sampling error. **Sampling error** is when chance gives us a value (like a sample mean of 20) that does not accurately reflect the entire population. Sampling error does not mean we made an error; it means chance did. The good news is that most of the time we will pull a sample of students and find their sample mean to be close to the population mean of 95 based on chance. If we randomly select from a population of students with an average chat time of 95 minutes ($\mu = 95$), the sample average is likely to reflect that number. Even if an odd student in the sample chatted 200 minutes and another did not chat at all, averaging brings them back near the population mean of 95 minutes.

With a population mean of 95, how likely would it be for a sample of 10 students to chat an average of 150 minutes? Not very likely. Another way of asking the question would be: What is the probability that we would choose a sample with a mean of 150? A low probability. It is possible that we would pull a sample with a mean of 150, but it is not likely (not probable). If we did obtain a mean of 150 for a sample, we would have extremely bad sampling error.

The point is that all means are possible, but one is most likely: the population mean of 95. Is a sample mean of 92 likely? Yes, because it is close to 95. Likewise, a sample mean of 97 is likely. Sample means of 92 and 97 are not as likely as 95, but they will be found fairly often. Because they are not exactly 95, means of 92 and 97 reflect a small amount of sampling error. If we look at all possible means in a simple frequency distribution (even the rare ones), we can see that the shape is normal. The middle part is the highest—with a sample mean of 95 occurring the most frequently. Slightly to the left and right of the high point we will find our 92 and 97, as well as other means close to the 95, with each mean further away from the high point occurring with a slightly lower frequency (resulting in the sloping curves on both sides of the middle). In the tails of the distribution are the sample means that do not occur often. Remember that when they do occur, it is due to extreme sampling error.

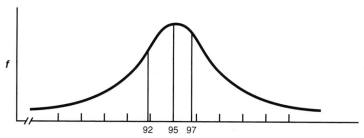

Theoretically, all sample means are possible, but those near the middle of the distribution are most likely. The further the means get in the tails, the less likely they are. Notice on the distribution above that the tails do not actually touch the *x*-axis, which further indicates that all means are possible, even extremely rare ones that we may never see. They would be the result of huge sampling error indeed.

The normal distribution we have just created using a large number of sample means is called the **sampling distribution of means**.

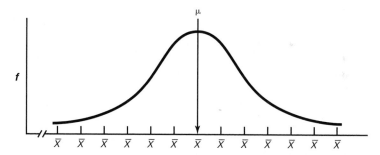

We can create a sampling distribution of means for any interval or ratio variable (because this is a line graph), and the means will always form a normal distribution. Even if the raw scores are from a skewed distribution, pulling entire samples of raw scores and graphing simple frequencies of means will create a normal-shaped distribution. That is because extremely low values and extremely high values will balance each other out when the mean for a sample is calculated. The fact that sampling means always results in a normal distribution characterizes the **Central Limit Theorem.**

One way to test this concept for yourself is to write scores between the values of 0 and 10 on 50 individual scraps of paper and put them in a bowl. You can even make sure you have a skewed distribution by writing more high scores than low ones (or more low than high). Since you know the 50 scores you wrote, you can calculate the true population mean (μ). Pull a sample of 15 pieces of paper, calculate the mean, and write it down. Do this dozens of times using 15 pieces for each sample (any sample size will work as long as the same number of scores is selected every time). Each time you select a sample, write down the sample mean. When you have a page-full, sketch a simple frequency distribution to see if a normal distribution is created. Further, the mean with the highest frequency should be the mean for the entire population of values in the bowl (or close to μ). The more samples you select, the more the graph will resemble a normal distribution.

Creating a Sampling Distribution of Means for Your Research

Other than creating a sampling distribution of means to demonstrate the Central Limit Theorem, will we ever pull dozens or thousands of samples, measure them for a variable of interest (a DV), and graph the means in a simple frequency distribution? No. But if you understand the concept, then you will understand that anything you could measure across thousands of samples would fall into the shape of a normal distribution because of the Central Limit Theorem. We never need to create our own sampling distributions, because they all end up looking the same—normal distributions—and we have statistics to make any normal distribution useful to us.

Standardizing the Sampling Distribution of Means

The sampling distribution of means can be transformed into a standard distribution using z-scores. The new distribution is called a standardized distribution or a z-distribution. In Chapter 5, we standardized a distribution of sample raw scores rather than sample means, but both distributions look the same and answer the same questions. The main difference is that we will be learning about a sample mean compared to a normal population (μ), rather than learning about a single raw score compared to a sample ($\overline{X}$).

In the last chapter, we needed a couple of pieces of information to calculate a z-score. First, we needed the sample mean. In this chapter, the population mean is needed instead. For our example of time spent in chatrooms, μ was 95 minutes per week. In real life, the population mean is rarely available, but it will be provided in this chapter for calculations. Remember from Chapter 5 that we also needed the sample standard deviation to calculate a z-score, so we will need a variability term here, too. Since we are trying to learn about a population rather than a sample, the variability term is the population standard deviation. The symbol for the population standard deviation is σ_x, and it will be provided, since the population standard deviation is rarely known in real life either. For the chat room example, the population standard deviation is 27.48.

The one extra step we have in the inferential z that we did not have with the descriptive z is changing the variability term. The population standard deviation is divided by the square root of N ($N = 10$ in our chatroom example, the number of values in the sample). This simple calculation creates the **standard error of the**

mean, and the symbol is $\sigma_{\overline{X}}$. The standard error of the mean is used because the sampling distribution of means is not based on the variability of single scores, but of means. For our example, take the population standard deviation of 27.48 and divide by the square root of N (10), which is 3.162278. The standard error of the mean is 8.689938, our variability term for the inferential z in this example.

$$\sigma_{\overline{X}} = \frac{\sigma_X}{\sqrt{N}}$$

$$\sigma_{\overline{X}} = \frac{27.48}{3.162278} = 8.689938$$

The last piece needed is a sample mean to compare with the sampling distribution of means as an indication of whether or not the sample is unusual. If it falls in the middle of the distribution, it will not be considered unusual; if it falls in the tails, we will think the sample mean is unusual when it comes to how much time per week students spend in chat rooms.

A sample of 10 students is selected from a computing course and asked how many minutes each day they chat. The average of their responses is 114 minutes. Now we have a sample mean to change to a z-score.

$$Z = \frac{\overline{X} - \mu}{\sigma_{\overline{X}}}$$

$$z = \frac{114 - 95}{8.689938} = 2.186457$$

Rounded to 2 decimal places, the z-score for the sample mean of 114 is 2.19. This number is often called the **z-obtained** value, and it can be symbolized by z_{obt}. Are students from the computing course different from "normal" students? Do they chat more than the general population of students? A z-score of 2.19 is certainly above the mean of the z-distribution, but is it high enough to say that computing students are different from normal? Or is the difference merely sampling error?

Critical Value and Critical Region

Long ago, psychologists embraced the idea that if a sample mean is so far out in the tails that it only happens in the normal population 5% of the time or less, the sample would be considered truly different from normal. We must find out if a specific z-score is so far in the tail that it rarely occurs in the normal population. Recall that we used the z-table to address this issue in Chapter 5. It does not matter that z-scores in the last chapter were descriptive and these are inferential; we still have a normal distribution with a mean of 0 and a standard deviation of 1. All of the proportions (area, chance, probability) are the same.

Returning to the question, is a z-score of 2.19 far enough in the tail to be considered truly different from normal? We need to find out what z-score cuts off the upper 5% of the tail. This z-score is called the **critical value** (symbolized by z_{crit}), and the 5% region is called the **critical region**.

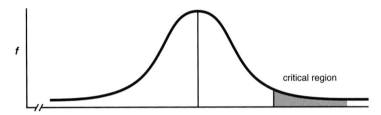

If our value of 2.19 is at or above the cut-off value (z_{crit}), we know we are in the 5% region, and can say our sample of computing students is different from the normal population of students.

In the z-table, the third column represents proportions for the tail region. We need 5%, but the table only has proportions. To change a percent into a proportion, divide by 100. Five percent becomes 0.05, and the relevant number can be found in the third column. If the exact number is not there (and it isn't), choose the closest number without going over 0.05. If we choose a number over 5% (0.05), we are giving ourselves too much leniency to say the computing students are different from normal. In the table we will find 0.0495, which is as close to 0.05 as possible without going over. Look two columns to the left to locate the z-value that cuts off 0.05 (0.0495) of the tail. The answer is 1.65; the z_{crit} is 1.65. Any z-score at or above the cut-off value of 1.65 will be considered unusual.

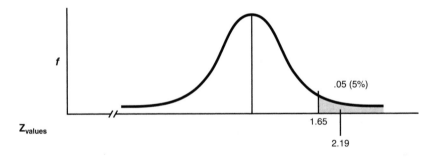

Is our sample of computing students unusual? Yes. With a z-score of 2.19, they are further out in the tail than the minimum value of 1.65, meaning they do spend more time in chat rooms than the general population of college students.

Manipulating a Sample

Most of the time, we are not simply interested in discovering if a sample is different from normal (like selecting a sample of computing students to see if they're different from the normal population). In psychology, we enjoy trying to make change happen. For example, we might be interested in randomly pulling a sample from the population (like college students) and doing something to them to see if they become different from normal.

Not Different from Normal

Suppose we pulled a sample of 36 students and lectured to them about how they could meet the person of their dreams in chat rooms. We could lecture the 36 students, and ask them a few weeks later how many minutes they spent per week in chat rooms to see if they are different from normal college students. If the sample mean for the group was 102, we could put it into our z-score formula to see if the calculated (obtained) value is at or beyond the critical value of 1.65 (the cut-off value we already looked-up for the last example).

We are still using our normal population mean of 95 minutes and a population standard deviation of 27.48. To get the standard error of the mean, divide 27.48 by the square root of N (N = 36 in this example) to get 4.58. Complete the calculation by subtracting 95 from 102, then divide by 4.58. The z-obtained value is 1.53.

$$\sigma_{\overline{X}} = \frac{\sigma_X}{\sqrt{N}} = \frac{27.48}{6} = 4.58$$

$$Z_{obt} = \frac{102 - 95}{4.58} = 153$$

The z-score for our sample (1.53) does not make it past (or to) the cut-off value (1.65); therefore, we have to say that our lecture about meeting someone special in a chat room did not alter the time spent chatting.

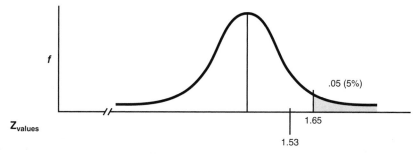

You might be thinking that 1.53 was close to 1.65, and you might also be tempted to conclude that our sample spent slightly more time than average in chat rooms. Yes, it was close, but it was not close enough for us to take credit for making people different—not even slightly. We have to conclude that we had sampling error; when we drew our sample, we must have accidently selected a couple of people who chat a lot, and they pulled the sample mean up a bit. We can only take credit for actually making them different if they get into that rare 5% region of the tail. If the sample mean does not fall in the critical region, we have to say the sample is like the normal population.

Higher Than Normal

A new example might lead us to a different conclusion. Imagine a population of adults from which someone has pulled thousands of samples and measured them on how afraid they are when swimming in the ocean. Since we need a way to measure fear, we can use a rating scale from 1 to 15, with higher numbers meaning more fear. In real life, we would not pull thousands of samples to learn all about the population's fear while swimming in the ocean, so I need to give you the population mean and the population standard deviation. Assume that the μ is 7.53 and σ_x is 2.08. Now that we have the normal population's level of fear while swimming, we are ready to select one sample from that population and do something to them to see if we can make them different from normal.

Randomly sample 100 people from the population of adults and make them watch *Jaws* 5 times. Then ask them to rate their fear while swimming in the Atlantic. Average all 100 ratings of fear to find that the mean fear level for our sample is 8.12. Here is the question of interest: Is this group more afraid of swimming in the ocean than people in the normal population of people who did not sit through 5 runs of *Jaws*? They certainly seem to be more fearful based on their sample mean, but is the sample mean of 8.12 enough above the normal population mean of 7.53 to say that people who watched *Jaws* are truly more fearful than people who were not forced to watch it? To answer this question, we need to turn to *z*-scores.

Subtract the population mean of 7.53 from the sample mean of 8.12 to get a numerator of 0.59. Next, simply divide 0.59 by the standard error of the mean. We have not calculated the standard error of the mean for this example, so take a minute to divide the sample standard deviation of 2.08 by the square root of N, with the N being the 100 people in your sample. The standard error of the mean comes out to be 0.208. Finally, divide the numerator of 0.59 by the denominator of 0.208 to get a final *z*-score of 2.84.

$$\sigma_{\overline{X}} = \frac{\sigma_X}{\sqrt{N}} = \frac{2.08}{10} = 0.208$$

$$z_{obt} = \frac{8.12 - 7.53}{0.208} = 2.836538$$

A *z*-score of 2.84 is in the upper tail of the distribution of the normal population. We must decide if this *z*-score is far enough in the upper tail to say that watching *Jaws* made these people more fearful of swimming in the ocean than people from the normal population. Compare the z_{obt} of 2.84 with the z_{crit} that cuts off 5% of the distribution. We already know that a z_{crit} of 1.65 cuts off 5%, and 2.84 is above 1.65. We can conclude that our sample of 100 people is more fearful of swimming than normal.

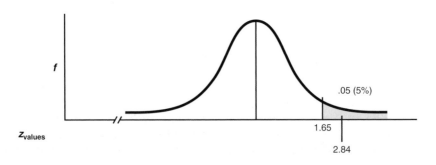

In other words, a z-score of 2.84 (and a raw fear score of 8.12) is rare in the normal population of adults swimmers. That score happens less than 5% of the time normally. It is so rare, in fact, that we can take credit for making this sample of people more fearful than normal by showing them *Jaws* five times.

If you are thinking that we might have made people more fearful or we might be seeing incredibly bad sampling error because we accidentally selected some overly-fearful people in our sample, you would be correct. Both explanations are possible. But psychologists are willing to take credit for any sample mean that happens less than 5% of the time in the normal population. A sample mean extremely far into the tail of the distribution is so rare normally that we feel confident in saying that we truly made the sample different from normal.

Lower Than Normal

A sample mean could also be lower than the population mean. Imagine that your friends between the ages of 17 and 25 talk on their cell phones throughout the day. If a sampling distribution of means from this population was created, we might find that the average amount of time people in this population talk on their cell phones each day is 64 minutes, and the standard deviation among values is 14.70 minutes. Using our symbols, μ is 64, and σ_x is 14.70. Now that we have the population information needed, we could collect data. We could randomly choose a sample of 50 people between the ages of 17 and 25 who have cell phones, and show them a recent report that cell phones might cause cancer (French, Penny, Laurence, & McKenzie, 2001). We want to know if the information will decrease the amount of time people in our sample spend on their cell phones. We could follow people around for the next day and keep track of how many minutes each person in the sample spends on the phone. Then we might average the 50 values together to get a sample mean of 53.63. Did the report about cell phones and cancer reduce the time participants spent talking on their cell phones?

The sample mean of 53.63 minus the population mean of 64 yields a numerator of -10.37. For the denominator, divide the population standard deviation of 14.70 by the square root of 50, giving us 14.70 divided by 7.071068, for a standard error of the mean value of 2.078894. The numerator of -10.37 divided by the standard error of the mean, equals a rounded z-value of -4.99.

$$\sigma_{\overline{X}} = \frac{\sigma_X}{\sqrt{N}} = \frac{14.70}{7.071068} = 2.078894$$

$$z_{\text{obt}} = \frac{53.63 - 64}{2.078894} = -4.988229$$

So far, our cut-off value (z_{crit}) has been 1.65, but it can also be a negative value, because the z-distribution is a normal distribution, and the sides are symmetrical about the middle. If a z_{crit} of 1.65 cuts off 5% of the upper tail, a z_{crit} of -1.65 cuts off 5% of the lower tail. Returning to the cell phone question, since a z_{obt} of -4.99 falls at or below the z_{crit} of -1.65, we know the cell phone report made a difference. (You should also see that we're on shaky ground with a z-score of −4.99, since we agreed that a z-score beyond ±5.00 is nearly impossible. In real life, a z-score beyond ±3.00 is highly unlikely.)

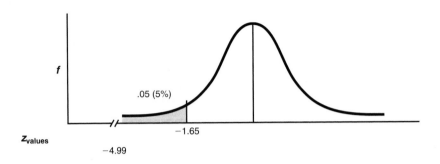

A z-score of −4.99 occurs so rarely in the normal population that we can say with confidence that we must have actually made our sample talk less by showing them the report about cancer.

As these examples have illustrated, we can get a sample mean higher than the population mean, which results in a positive z-value, or we can get a sample mean lower than the population mean, which results in a negative z-value. Either way, we want to know if our sample is different enough from normal to claim that a real difference exists. We will only make that claim if the sample mean happens less than 5% of the time normally.

Decreasing the Critical Region

In some studies, researchers choose a critical region smaller than 5%; the sample mean must be so different from normal that it occurs only 1% of the time (or less) normally. The sample mean must fall even further into the tail of the distribution to take credit for making our sample different from normal.

For example, imagine that the federal government is considering a pre-kindergarten program for at-risk children to get a head start on learning. They decide to test the program on a sample of at-risk pre-kindergarten children before spending billions of dollars on a national program. In fact, taxpayers would be happy to know that the program must improve children's performance in kindergarten enough to put the sample in the upper 1% (rather than the usual 5%) of at-risk kindergarten children who did not have the program.

Picture the sampling distribution of means. Thousands of samples of at-risk kindergarten children are theoretically collected, and the score averages are graphed. The mean grade for this normal population is 89%, with a population standard deviation of 20%. (Don't let percent confuse you; analyze these data using the numbers, and simply keep in mind that they represent percent.)

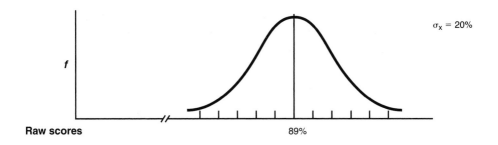

Raw scores   89%

The next step is to picture all of the sample means changed to z-scores to create a standardized distribution.

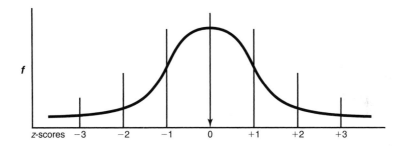

Now we take one sample (we'll use $N = 200$) of at-risk children and put them in the special pre-kindergarten program designed to give them a head start on learning. Then the children are put into a regular kindergarten class, and we ask teachers for the children's scores at the end of the school year. As it turns out, the scores of the children who were in the special pre-kindergarten program were quite high. The sample mean was 92%. We will not know if 92% is truly better than 89% until we calculate a z-score and see where it falls on the distribution.

$$\sigma_{\overline{X}} = \frac{\sigma_X}{\sqrt{N}} = \frac{20}{14.142136} = 1.414214$$

$$z_{obt} = \frac{92 - 89}{1.414214} = 2.121320$$

Remember that the z-value must be so rare that it only happens 1% of the time or less in the normal population of at-risk children. If the sample is that unusual, we can take credit for truly making our sample different from normal with our special pre-kindergarten program.

We now need a z_{crit} value from the table at the back of the book. But instead of looking at a tail region of 0.05 (for the top 5%), look at a tail region of 0.01 (1%).

Since 0.01 is not available, use the next lowest number, which is 0.009. Then look two columns to the left to find the z_{crit} of 2.33.

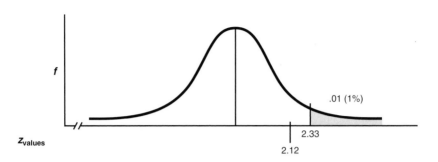

Clearly, our z_{obt} of 2.12 is not at or above the z_{crit} of 2.33, compelling us to say our sample was not different from normal.

Before we started this example, we decided that the program must work so well that at-risk children with a head start in pre-kindergarten would make substantially higher grades in kindergarten than at-risk children who had not attended the special pre-kindergarten program. Although children in the program had a higher average grade, the difference was not enough to say they were truly better than the normal population of at-risk students who did not participate in the program. In fact, we have to say that their average of 92% (which is a z-score of 2.12) was only different from the normal 89% because of sampling error. Based on our analysis, the government should not spend billions of dollars on this program.

You might be thinking we were too hard on ourselves with the 2.33 z_{crit} value, since a 1.65 value would have allowed a z_{obt} of 2.12 to fall in the critical region, and we would have been able to say the program worked. That is true. But we originally decided to use a conservative value of 0.01 because we wanted to be confident that the program substantially improved scores before we spent taxpayers' money.

(Although this example is fictional, you might be interested in reading evaluations of the Headstart Program funded by the Federal Government. Several sample references pertaining to this program are found at the end of the chapter.)

Preview of Chapter 7

In this chapter, you learned to apply the z-distribution to inferential statistics with the sampling distribution of means. Inferential z-scores allow us to decide if a sample is truly different from the normal population or if we simply have a sampling-error difference. In the next chapter, this process will be formalized using hypothesis testing.

Conceptual Items

1. Define the following:
   a. probability
   b. sampling error
   c. critical region
   d. critical value
   e. obtained value

2. Is a sampling distribution of means generally created from a population for each research project? Why or why not?

3. A sampling distribution of means is a simple frequency distribution of means on what variable? That is, are values on the manipulation in a study being graphed, or does the distribution represent values on the dependent variable?

4. How does the Central Limit Theorem define the shape of the sampling distribution of means?

Application Items

5. If a children's board game contains a wheel of color options including red, green, blue, and yellow, what is the probability of the arrow landing on yellow? Show the calculation as well as your answer.

6. Based on Application Item 5, what is the probability of the arrow landing on red or blue? Show the calculation as well as your answer.

7. Find the area between the mean and a z-score of 1.25.

8. What is the probability of getting a z-score between the mean and a z of 1.50?

9. What is the probability of getting a z-score beyond 1.65?

10. What's the probability of getting a z-score beyond 1.96?

11. What's the probability of getting a z-score beyond $\pm$1.96?

12. I want to know if completing statistics homework helps you make a better grade in the class. Of people who don't do homework, the average grade is 73% at the end of the term, with a standard deviation of 12%. A sample of 18 people completed all homework assignments, and the sample average at the end of the term was 80%.
    a. Calculate the standard error of the mean ($\sigma_{\overline{X}}$).
    b. Calculate the z_{obt}.
    c. Sketch a normal distribution with the upper 5% shaded.
    d. Find the z_{crit} in the z-table.
    e. Put the z_{crit} and the z_{obt} on the sketch.
    f. Does completing homework increase grades?

13. Rework the above example using a z_{crit} for only 1% of the upper tail (a more conservative test).

    a. Sketch the distribution.

    b. Put the z_{crit} and the z_{obt} on the sketch.

    c. Does completing homework increase grades?

14. What proportion of sample means would fall between a population mean of 400 and a sample mean of 700 if the standard error of the mean was 200?

15. What proportion of the sample means would fall between a population mean of 600 and a sample mean of 800 if the standard error of the mean was 250?

16. Assume that the mean I.Q. score of a population of 6-year-old children is 100 ($\sigma_{\overline{X}} = 10$). Find out if teaching a sample of kids how to play computer games will improve their I.Q. Here are the I.Q. scores of the sample after they learned how to play computer games:

100	90	95	110	105	115	98	111	107	99

17. You think you have found a drug that will increase memory capacity in patients with memory difficulties. We'll say the average capacity for short-term memory in this population of patients is usually 5 items, with a standard deviation of 0.5. Your job is to find out if the drug is effective, showing all of your work. You administer the drug to your sample and find the following memory capacities:

4	3	4	5	5	4	3	6	4

18. Let's say the average Graduate Record Exam (GRE) verbal score is 400, with a standard deviation of 120. You take a sample of 50 people from the population and make them stay awake all night before the test to see if it reduces their verbal score. The sleepy sample made an average GRE verbal score of 352. Find out if you truly impaired scores, or if their sample mean is simply different from 400 because of sampling error, and show all work.

19. An accountant for a large insurance company knows that the average office visit to a family practice physician is $175.00, with a standard deviation of $65.00. The company suspects that a certain physician is overcharging. From a sample of 100 bills received from this physician's office, the average cost of an office visit is $195.00. Is this physician overcharging? How did you decide?

Computational formulas in this chapter

Standard error of the mean

$$\sigma_{\overline{X}} = \frac{\sigma_X}{\sqrt{N}}$$

z-obtained value

$$z = \frac{\overline{X} - \mu}{\sigma_{\overline{X}}}$$

References

In Text:

French, P. W., Penny, R., Laurance, J. A., & McKenzie, D. R. (2001). Mobile phones, heat shock proteins and cancer. *Differentiation: Research in Biological Diversity, 67*, 93–97.

Related Articles:

Frumkin, H., Jacobson, A., Gansler, T., & Thun, M. J. (2001). Cellular phones and risk of brain tumors. *CA: A Cancer Journal for Clinicians, 51*, 137–141.

Knave, B. (2001). Electromagnetic fields and health outcomes. *Annals of the Academy of Medicine, Singapore, 30*, 489–493.

Nordenberg, T. (2000). Cell phones & brain cancer. No clear connection. *FDA Consumer, 34*, 19–23.

Headstart Program Studies:

Barclay, A. G. (1982). Effect of Headstart programs on the factor structure of mental ability. *Psychological Reports, 51*, 512–514.

Dodd, J. M., & Lipka, R. P. (1966). The Comparative Peabody Picture Vocabulary Test performance of one Headstart Program. *Child Study Center Bulletin, 2*, 116–118.

Vane, J. R., & Hofstra, U. (1971). Importance of considering background factors when evaluating the effects of compensatory education programs for young children. *Journal of School Psychology, 9*, 393–398.

7

Hypothesis Testing

Formalizing the Inferential z

The purpose of this chapter is to formalize the inferential z-test from Chapter 6. A procedure called **hypothesis testing** is used to state expectations about the outcomes of a study and test to see which expectation is supported by the results.

Lay Out Expectations

In the last chapter, we discussed whether or not a sample mean was truly different from the population mean. Recall that it depended on whether or not the z_{obt} was further out in the tail than the z_{crit} value. The examples illustrated that the sample mean can fall in either of the two tails.

Even before collecting data, we should state our expectations for results. Another term for expectation is **hypothesis**. In statistics, the two types of expectations are the null hypothesis and the alternative hypothesis.

The Null Hypothesis

The word "null" means "nothing," so the **null hypothesis** is what we would expect if nothing happened in our study. If manipulation of participants in a study does not make them different from normal, then nothing has happened, and the null hypothesis has been supported. In other words, the sample mean is not far enough in the tail of the sampling distribution of means to take credit for making the sample different from normal.

In Chapter 6, we relied heavily on the sampling distribution (and z-scores); we can look back now and see that we were actually testing the null hypothesis. In every example, we were looking to see if a sample mean fell far enough into the tail to say the sample was unlikely to be normal. If the sample mean falls near the high point of the graph (the middle), we fail to reject the null hypothesis. Failing to reject the null hypothesis means we tried to change members of a sample—tried to make them different from normal—and failed.

Although failure sounds negative, it might simply mean that our manipulation did not work, which is valuable information. For example, if we were testing the effect of a new type of therapy on alleviating depression, we would want to know if the therapy did not work. On the other hand, failure to find an effect could mean that our particular manipulation or sample did not reveal an effect, but an effect might actually exist. For example, the new therapy for depression might not have worked in our study because the therapist was insensitive; another clinician might have been able to help people using the new therapy.

So, failing to reject the null hypothesis does not necessarily mean the manipulation does not work. It might not work, or it might not have worked in this one study. That is why it is rare to see a published study that fails to reject the null hypothesis. The editor cannot know if there was truly no effect, or if the failure to find an effect was due to sloppy research, a poor sample, or some other snag in the study.

The symbol for the null hypothesis is H_0, with the 0 representing zero effect in the study.

The Alternative Hypothesis

In contrast to the null hypothesis, the **alternative hypothesis** is the expectation we hope will be supported in our study. In other words, we hope whatever we do to make people in our sample different actually works. If it does, their sample mean will fall far into a tail of the sampling distribution.

The symbol for the alternative hypothesis is H_1.

Two-tailed z-test

Our expectation (alternative hypothesis) may be that a sample will be different from normal, but perhaps we do not know if the mean will be higher than μ or lower than μ. For an example, we could examine school spirit among college students with an average school spirit (μ) of 35 on a scale from 0 to 100, with higher numbers indicating more school spirit. We could force students to attend football games each Saturday. This manipulation might increase school spirit, but we also realize it might decrease school spirit, because people do not like to be forced to do anything. When thinking of our alternative hypothesis, a two-tailed test is appropriate, because we do not have a good idea about where our sample mean will fall. A two-tailed test is used when we are unsure whether our manipulation of the sample will cause participants to have a higher mean than the population mean, or a lower average.

Hypotheses are stated this way:

H_0: μ = 35.00 school spirit (Football games will not alter school spirit. If attending games doesn't change the school spirit of our sample, the rating will remain at 35.00—just like students from the normal population who don't attend games.)

H_1: μ ≠ 35.00 school spirit (Games will change school spirit. If attending games changes school spirit, we will see either an increase or a decrease from normal.)

μ Rather Than $\overline{X}$

Before we move beyond hypotheses, let me explain why the null and alternative hypotheses use μ rather than the sample mean $(\overline{X})$. In our hypotheses, we are stating that the sample mean might be the same as μ (the null hypothesis), or the sample mean might be different from μ (the alternative hypothesis) after we force students to attend football games. It might seem reasonable to write the hypotheses like this:

$$H_0: \overline{X} = 35.00$$
$$H_1: \overline{X} \neq 35.00$$

The sample mean is not used because we are conducting inferential statistics, not descriptive statistics. We are trying to learn from a sample what the entire population would be like if we treated them the same way. So the null hypothesis is saying more than *the sample mean might be the same as the population mean*; it is indicating that if nothing happens in our sample, nothing will happen in the population, either. In other words, if making students attend football games does not change school spirit among members of our sample, making everyone in the population attend football games would not change school spirit for them either. Likewise, the alternative hypothesis is indicating more than *the sample mean might be different from the normal population mean*. If the students who are forced to attend football games report a change in their school spirit, we assume the same would be true for the entire population. We are never just interested in a sample when conducting inferential statistics; we infer back to the population from which the sample was drawn.

Thus, μ is written with hypotheses to communicate inferential statistics. We understand that the sample should be telling us what would happen to the entire population of college students if we forced them to attend football games. Perhaps we should write our hypotheses as

$$H_0: \mu_{new} = 35.00$$
$$H_1: \mu_{new} \neq 35.00$$

to indicate that we are making assumptions about what the new population mean would be if everyone in the population was treated like participants in the sample.

Choose a Statistic

After hypotheses are stated, we must decide how the data will be analyzed. An inferential statistic will be chosen, and at this point we have covered only 1: inferential z-scores. Keep in mind, though, that the next chapters hold more statistics.

Be as specific as possible when deciding how the data will be analyzed. In this example, we will not simply use a z-test. For the example we are using, our alternative hypothesis is that students who attend football games will report changes in school spirit. That is, we expect the sample mean to fall either in the lower or upper tail of the distribution. A *two-tailed z-test* will be used to analyze these data.

Sketch the Normal Distribution

Because some of the critical region is placed in both tails, we cannot use 0.05 in the lower tail and 0.05 in the upper tail. That would mean we are allowing ourselves 10% of the distribution to take credit for making people different from normal, which is twice as much room to reject the null hypothesis as allowed. Thus, we cannot use ± 1.65 as we did in the previous chapter; −1.65 and +1.65 would segment 5% in each tail.

If we choose a two-tailed test for our alternative hypothesis (as in the present example), the 5% must be split in half, leaving 2.5% (0.025) in each tail. Look up 0.025 in the z-table and move two columns to the left to find a z_{crit} of 1.96. Since this is a two-tailed test, we also need to cut off 0.025 (2.5%) in the lower half of the distribution with a z_{crit} of −1.96. Each tail contains a critical region of 2.5%, with a total of 5%. Thus, the probability used in this test remains 5%. The way to write the probability value in shorthand is $p < 0.05$, where p is the symbol for probability. Notice that we are promising not to take credit for making our sample different unless the sample mean occurs less than or equal to 5% of the time in the normal population. We will not take credit for changing people unless we get a very rare sample mean—one that happens 5% of the time or less normally.

Below is the distribution for a two-tailed z-test.

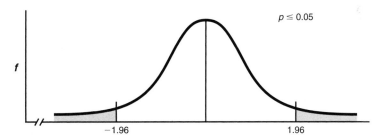

Collect Data

We have stated the null and alternative hypotheses, decided on the best statistic to use, and sketched the appropriate distribution. Data collection is the next step. We might randomly choose 95 college students and force them to attend football games every Saturday for three months. At the end of three months, we could ask the people in our sample to rate their school spirit, perhaps revealing an average school spirit of 42.10.

Calculate a Statistic

The calculations are the same formulas covered in Chapter 6.

$$\sigma_{\overline{X}} = \frac{\sigma_X}{\sqrt{N}} \qquad z_{obt} = \frac{\overline{X} - \mu}{\sigma_{\overline{X}}}$$

For this example, the calculations are

$$\sigma_{\overline{X}} = \frac{29.68}{\sqrt{95}} = 3.045104 \qquad z_{obt} = \frac{42.10 - 35.00}{3.045104} = 2.33$$

Significance

With a z-value of 2.33, we can decide if our sample is different from the normal population of students who were not forced to attend football games. The z_{obt} of 2.33 is beyond 1.96, and is therefore located in the critical region.

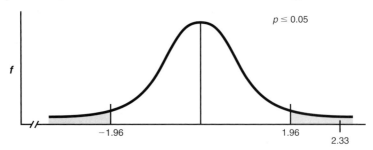

Forcing students to attend football games significantly changed their school spirit ratings.

APA Style

The results of this study are reported in APA style below.

$$z_{obt} = 2.33, p < 0.05$$

Use two decimal places on both the z_{obt} value and the p value, and notice that the z and p are italicized, which is the APA way of showing that they are statistical symbols (or abbreviations). When final results are shown in APA style in this text-book, two decimal places will be used, and symbols will be italicized. APA style for our sample indicates that the probability (p) of getting a z-score that far out in the tail of the distribution is less than 0.05 normally.

Reject or Fail to Reject the Null Hypothesis

Because we are testing the null hypothesis each time we analyze a study, we must decide if we failed to reject the null or rejected the null. If the sample mean falls in the critical region, we reject the null hypothesis. As a result, the critical region is also termed the **rejection region**. In the school spirit example, the null was rejected; our sample fell in the rejection region. The people in our sample were different from the normal population. We reject the idea that nothing happened in our study, because something obviously did.

Inferential Wording

Remember that we are conducting inferential statistics, and the sample was only used to tell us what would (should) happen if we treated the entire population of college students the same way; therefore, we must infer back to the population. Start with "if we went back to the population," then state what would be done to them (the same manipulation as our sample), and what the expected outcome would be (the same outcome as our sample). For this example, we would state: *If we went back to the population and forced students to attend football games, their school spirit would change.* In fact, based on the z_{obt} falling in the upper tail of the sampling distribution, we know that school spirit scores would increase.

What we are saying is that all students in the normal population would have more school spirit if they were forced to attend games, so the entire population of school-spirit scores would shift upward. On the sketch below, the old population is on the left, and the new population (attending games) is on the right.

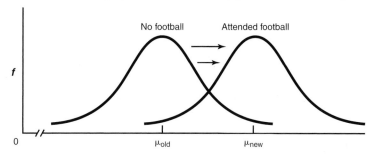

Notice that the people on the far left tail of the old population had low school spirit. When the distribution shifts to the right (attending games), the people with low school spirit from the old population would still be expected to have lower school spirit than the other students in the population. The same would be true for students who have high school spirit when they do not attend games. They should still have more school spirit than others in the new population after they have all attended games. Being forced to attend football games increases everyone's school spirit, but those with low school spirit remain the lowest on the new distribution, and students with high school spirit still have the highest. The entire population simply shifts to the right.

For this example, what would we expect the new population mean to be? We only have one piece of information to use: the mean of our participants who were forced to attend games. Their average school spirit was 42.10. With no other information, we would guess that the new μ if everyone attended games would be a school-spirit average of 42.10.

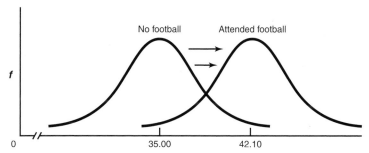

Effect Size

We are confident that attending games would increase school spirit; rejecting the null hypothesis is evidence that our manipulation (study) produced an effect. The effect size can be quantified to indicate how different the two populations (no games and attending games) would be.

To calculate effect size,

$$d = \frac{\mu_{new} - \mu_{old}}{\sigma_{old}}$$

Cohen's d involves subtracting the original population mean from the sample mean (estimated μ_{new}) and dividing by the original population standard deviation. A positive value represents an increase in values based on the study, and a negative value means a decrease based on the study. The absolute value of d indicates the size of the effect. For this example, the effect is

$$d = \frac{42.10 - 35.00}{29.68} = .24$$

Dividing by the standard deviation creates a standardized effect size, allowing effect sizes from different studies to be compared. For our sample above, the effect size is 0.24, a small but significant effect. (A -0.24 would also have been a small effect—with a decrease caused by the study.) An effect size of ± 0.50 is considered moderate, and an effect of ± 0.80 and beyond is strong.

Plain English

Finally, we need to communicate the results of our study in plain English. After all, the point of research is to learn and then share results in a straightforward way. For example, we could say: Being forced to attend football games increased school spirit among college students. In fact, we can estimate that attending football games would increase school spirit ratings to 42.10 on a 1–100 scale.

Confidence Intervals

In addition to estimating a μ of 42.10 if all students were forced to attend football games, we can estimate the range of school spirit values with a 95% likelihood using a **confidence interval**. Confidence intervals provide a strong indication of school spirit for 95% of the population after attending football games.

Based on hypothesis testing, z-scores of -1.96 and $+1.96$ are critical values which cut off 2.5% in the lower tail and 2.5% in the upper tail, respectively. Thus, 95% of the distribution is found between z-scores of ± 1.96. To locate the range of possible values of school spirit if everyone attended football games, first change the z-scores of ± 1.96 to raw scores. The formula requires each score to be changed individually.

$(z)(\sigma_{\overline{X}}) + \overline{X}$, where $\overline{X}$ is the sample mean and also the estimated μ_{new}

For a z-score of -1.96,

$$(-1.96)(3.045104) + 42.10 = 36.131597$$

For a z-score of $+1.96$,

$$(+1.96)(3.045104) + 42.10 = 48.068403$$

Based on these two values, after attending football games, 95% of the population would have school spirit scores between 36.13 and 48.07. Notice that the old μ— the population mean of school spirit for students who did not attend football games—was 35.00, a value below the projected range of those who attend football games. This is a reasonable outcome, given that hypothesis testing indicated a significant increase in school spirit—significantly higher than 35.00.

One-tailed Test in the Positive Direction

Two-tailed tests are used when we are unsure in which tail of the distribution the sample mean will fall, and one-tailed tests are chosen when we have a strong idea about the direction of an effect. For example, assume that college students generally take 4.50 years to complete their education, with a population standard deviation of 1.25 years. We plan to give some students a child to raise to see if they take longer to finish college. We expect that the additional responsibility will increase the length of time it takes to complete college (the alternative hypothesis), but there is always the possibility that they will graduate in 4.50 years with students who do not have to raise a child (the null hypothesis). Because we strongly believe that students will take longer to finish college, the possibility of graduating earlier (a smaller sample mean) is placed with the null hypothesis as an outcome we do not expect.

We can lay out hypotheses this way:

H_0: $\mu \leq 4.50$ years (If raising a child doesn't change the length of time it takes students in our sample to graduate, the sample mean will stay at 4.50—just like students from the normal population. In addition, we consider the possibility of graduating sooner highly unlikely.)

H_1: $\mu > 4.50$ years (We think raising a child will take students longer than 4.50 years to complete college.)

Notice that we set up our expectations (hypotheses) before we conduct the experiment. We cannot examine the data first to decide if we expect students with a child to graduate sooner or later than childless undergraduates.

An inferential statistic is needed to compare a sample mean to the population mean of 4.50 years. Choose a *one-tailed z-test*, because the alternative hypothesis states that we expect our sample to take longer to graduate than students in the normal population (who don't have a child to raise). Recall from Chapter 6 that the z_{crit} for a one-tailed z-test in the positive direction is 1.65. The distribution is as follows.

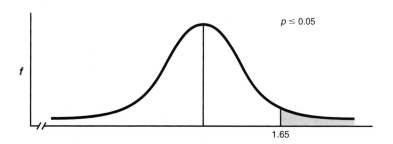

Assume we collected data, and the sample mean after we gave 81 students a child to raise was 4.92 years in college. The z_{obt} is

$$\sigma_{\overline{X}} = \frac{1.25}{\sqrt{81}} = 0.138889 \qquad z_{obt} = \frac{4.92 - 4.50}{0.138889} = 3.023998$$

Place the z_{obt} value on the x-axis of our distribution as indicated below.

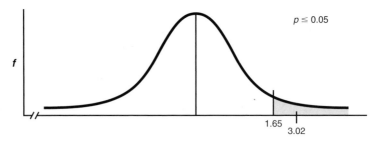

The z_{obt} is beyond (further in the tail than) the z_{crit} value, so it is likely that we made participants in our sample different from normal.

In APA style,

$$z_{obt} = 3.02, p < 0.05$$

The probability of getting a z_{obt} that far out in the tail of the normal population is rare. It happens less than 5% of the time; the probability is less than 0.05. We must have made the sample different by giving them a child to raise.

Choose to reject or fail to reject the null hypothesis. In this case, reject the null hypothesis. Reject the idea that nothing happened, since we obviously made our sample different from normal. Something did happen.

Now infer back to the larger population of all students. If we went back to the population of college students and gave them all a child to raise, they would take longer to finish their degree. In fact, the two populations would likely have an effect size of 0.34, as indicated in the calculation below.

$$d = \frac{4.92 - 4.50}{1.25} = 0.336$$

An effect of 0.34 is a weak to moderate effect, and hypothesis testing illustrated that it is also a significant effect.

In plain English, we could claim: Students take longer than normal to complete a college degree when they have a child to raise. We could estimate how long it would take them to graduate based on the sample mean; students would take about 4.92 years to graduate. The confidence interval indicates

$$(-1.96)(0.138889) + 4.92 = 4.647778$$

for the shortest period of time most undergraduates would take to graduate if they raised a child, and

$$(+1.96)(0.138889) + 4.92 = 5.192222$$

for the longest period of time most students would take to graduate with the added responsibility. That is, if everyone in the population of undergraduates raised a child while trying to earn a degree, 95% of the students would take between 4.65 and 5.19 years to graduate.

One-tailed Test in the Negative Direction

Hypothesis testing can be applied to a new example in which the rejection region is placed in the lower tail. The z-distribution is symmetrical, therefore a z_{crit} of -1.65 delineates the lower 5%.

Imagine we knew that the average speed for drivers who like to break the speed limit is 76.44 miles per hour, with a standard deviation of 30.92 miles an hour. Law enforcement officers think that giving these people tickets will slow them down, and we are going to test that expectation. To do that, we plan to give speeding tickets to a sample of speeders.

Before we collect data, we can begin with our hypotheses, chosen statistic, and z-distribution.

H_0: $\mu \geq 76.44$ miles per hour

H_1: $\mu < 76.44$ miles per hour

Statistical test to be used: one-tailed z-test

Distribution:

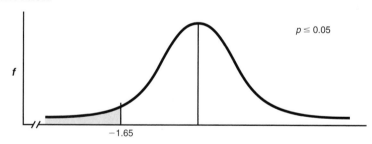

To collect data, we might randomly choose 100 speeders and give them speeding tickets. Then we monitor their speed of driving, perhaps revealing an average speed of 70 miles per hour. Complete the calculations using μ of 76.44 and σ_X of 30.92.

$$\sigma_{\bar{X}} = \frac{30.92}{\sqrt{100}} = 3.092 \qquad z_{obt} = \frac{70.00 - 76.44}{3.092} = -2.08$$

Place the z_{obt} on the distribution.

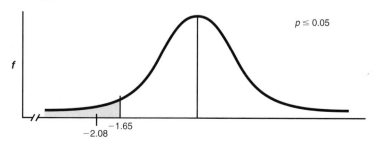

APA style:

$$z_{obt} = -2.08, p < 0.05$$

(1) Did we make people in our sample different from normal?

Yes.

(2) Should we reject or fail to reject the null hypothesis?

Reject H_0.

Inferential Wording: *If we went back to the population of speeders and gave them all tickets, they would slow down.*

Effect Size:

$$d = 70.00 - 76.44/30.92 = -0.208279, \text{a weak but significant effect}$$

Plain English: *Giving speeders tickets slows them down. In fact, their speed decreased to approximately 70.00 miles per hour.*

Confidence Interval: For this example,

$$(-1.96)(3.092) + 70.00 = 63.93968$$

represents the lower end of how fast people drive after getting a speeding ticket, and

$$(+1.96)(3.092) + 70.00 = 76.06032$$

represents the upper end of the range. In other words, if everyone in the population of speeders was given a speeding ticket, 95% of the population would drive between 63.94 and 76.06 miles per hour. Since members of the population used to drive 76.44 miles per hour, did they slow down? Not much, but then we already established this as a weak effect (-0.21).

Hypothesis Testing, Truth, and Power

After hypothesis testing, we have two choices: reject or fail to reject H_0. Similarly, the truth is one of two things: the null hypothesis was false (meaning something unusual happened) or the null was true (meaning nothing unusual happened in a study). Likewise, we could make two kinds of mistakes: rejecting the null hypothesis when it was true (also called **Type I error**) and failing to reject the null hypothesis when it was false (also called **Type II error**). All possibilities are below:

	Your Decision	
	Reject H_0	**Fail to reject H_0**
Truth: H_0 was false	A correct decision	A mistake Type II error
Truth: H_0 was true	A mistake Type I error	A correct decision

We obviously want to make correct decisions, but which one of the above correct decisions is preferable? Since we want to find something unusual and interesting in a study, we want people to be different from normal. In other words, rejecting the null hypothesis is preferable. The upper left box represents **power**, the ability to reject the null hypothesis when it is false.

	Your Decision	
	Reject H_0	**Fail to reject H_0**
Truth: H_0 was false	A correct decision ***POWER***	A mistake
Truth: H_0 was true	A mistake	A correct decision

We will not actually know the hidden truth; we will not know how much power we have. Instead, rely on rejecting the null hypothesis after following the rules in this chapter. For example, use a 0.05 rejection region to make sure the sample is extremely different from the normal population before taking credit for a significant finding. If we are careful about following the rules, we assume we are making the correct decisions.

Based on never really knowing truth, the definition of power can be changed slightly. Power can be stated as the ability to reject the null hypothesis when the rules of hypothesis testing are followed.

Regardless of the definition your instructor asks you to learn, you should know that statistical power is different from the way you have used power in the past. Use the statistical definition to answer the next three questions.

(1) Which kind of test is more powerful between a 0.05 rejection region and a 0.01 rejection region?

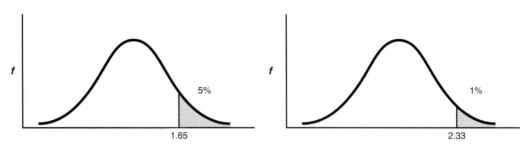

You might have been thinking that the 0.01 is a more powerful test, because if a sample mean falls way out in that very small region, the test must indeed be powerful. But remember the definition of statistical power: The ability to reject the null hypothesis. Which test provides more ability to reject the null hypothesis? The 0.05 test. Using a rejection region of 0.05 is a more powerful test than a rejection region of 0.01.

(2) Which kind of test is more powerful between a one-tailed and a two-tailed test?

If you chose a one-tailed test, you are correct. A one-tailed test has all 5% (0.05) in one tail, but a two-tailed test requires the 5% to be split between the two tails, leaving only 2.5% (0.025) in each tail, offering less chance of getting the sample mean into one of the smaller critical regions. This explains why a one-tailed test is preferable to a two-tailed test, as long as you have reason to believe in which tail $\overline{X}$ will fall.

(3) Would a small number of participants (N) in a study increase or decrease power? (Hint: Examine the formulas.)

$$\sigma_{\overline{X}} = \frac{\sigma_x}{\sqrt{N}} \qquad z_{obt} = \frac{\overline{X} - \mu}{\sigma_{\overline{X}}}$$

In the first formula, as N (the denominator) increases, the standard error term ($\sigma_{\overline{X}}$) decreases. In the second formula, as ($\sigma_{\overline{X}}$) decreases, the absolute value of the t_{obt} increases, forcing it further into a tail of the sampling distribution and increasing the chance of rejecting the null. In summary, a higher N translates into a more powerful test.

Preview of Chapter 8

Remember that in real life, we will rarely know the population mean and standard deviation, so we will rarely do a z-test. The z-test was presented as a simple way to learn about probabilities, obtained and critical values, rejection regions, and hypothesis testing. Throughout the remaining chapters, we will cover various statistics that rely on these concepts. In the next chapter, you will learn three types of *t*-tests. You might be surprised to find how similar they are to the z-test.

Conceptual Items

1. Define the following:
   a. H_0
   b. H_1
   c. rejection region
   d. confidence interval
   e. statistical power
2. What are the z_{crit} values for (a) a one-tailed test and (b) a two-tailed test?
3. Why is μ used rather than $\overline{X}$ when stating hypotheses?
4. What is the difference between μ_{old} and μ_{new}?
5. Why are editors unlikely to publish studies that fail to reject the null hypothesis?
6. Why would you choose a one-tailed test rather than a two-tailed test? Which is generally preferred and why?

Application Items

7. Based on Cohen's *d*, label the following as weak, moderate, or strong effects.
   a. 0.50
   b. −0.29
   c. 0.78
   d. −0.78
   e. 0.65
8. You've decided to test the effect of procrastination on self-esteem. You expect people to have lower self-esteem if you make them procrastinate. Self-esteem is measured on a scale from 0 to 400, with 400 being extremely high self-esteem. Let's say I happen to know that the average self-esteem rating for Americans is 250, and the standard deviation is 50.
   a. What is the population mean?
   b. What is the population standard deviation?

    c. Lay out the null and alternative hypotheses.

    d. Choose the statistic you will use to analyze your data.

    e. Sketch a normal distribution, shade the critical region, and put your critical value on the x-axis.

Now pretend you have forced 100 Americans to procrastinate on an important task and asked each of them to rate their self-esteem. The self-esteem average for your sample turns out to be 240.

    f. What is the sample mean?

    g. Calculate the standard error of the mean and the z_{obt}.

    h. Go back to part e (above), and put your obtained value on the x-axis.

    i. Based on your sample, is there an effect?

    j. Write your result in APA style.

    k. Reject or fail to reject the null hypothesis.

    l. Infer back to the population from your sample.

    m. Calculate effect size.

    n. Write your results in plain English.

    o. Calculate the 95% confidence interval.

Use parts a-o from Application Item to complete the following examples (9–13).

    9. Using the same population of Americans as Application Item 8, the same measure of self-esteem, mean, and standard deviation, you have decided to do a different study; you will force people to exercise. You think exercise will increase self-esteem, but you realize that some people might have a physical limitation that will lower their self-esteem after you make them exercise. After you make 100 people exercise, you calculate their average self-esteem rating to be 260.

  10. One more example using self-esteem and the same mean and standard deviation: You want to see if people who win the lottery have higher self-esteem than normal people. You don't see any way they can have lower self-esteem, so you assume the sample mean will be higher than the population mean of 250. Your sample of 90 lottery winners has a mean self-esteem score of 257.

  11. Moving away from self-esteem, here is an example of the speed of rats' movement. Imagine that a population of rats moves at 15 miles per hour, with a standard deviation of 7. You take a group of 49 rats and encourage them to move faster by telling them how swift they are, with the expectation that they will increase their speed. When you averaged the sample's speed during encouragement, it was 17 miles per hour.

  12. Assume the average number of times a population of college students presses the snooze button on an alarm clock is 7, with a standard deviation of 1.34. Students were asked to listen to nature sounds so we could see if the sounds facilitated or attenuated their ability to wake up in the morning. The data follow:

    5   6   6   8   7   8   5   6

13. Based on the same population as Application Item 12, we might imagine that students given new, soft mattresses would want to sleep longer than normal, causing them to press the snooze button more often.

4	5	7	6	7	9	4	5	8

Computational formulas in this chapter

Standard error of the mean

$$\sigma_{\overline{X}} = \frac{\sigma_x}{\sqrt{N}}$$

z-obtained value

$$z_{obt} = \frac{\overline{X} - \mu}{\sigma_{\overline{X}}}$$

Effect size

$$d = \frac{\mu_{new} - \mu_{old}}{\sigma_{old}}$$

Confidence interval

$$(\pm z)(\sigma_{\overline{X})} + \overline{X}$$

8

Three *t*-tests

z-test Versus *t*-test

In Chapters 6 and 7, we covered the first type of inferential statistics: the *z*-test. Because it was an inferential statistic, we were able to learn about an entire population based on what happened to a sample randomly selected from that population. If the sample was changed, we assumed that the entire population would also change when we treated them all the same way.

Recall that the inferential *z*-test could not be completed unless we had the population mean and standard deviation for our dependent variable. For example, if we wanted to try to change school spirit by sending students to football games, we first had to know the average amount of school spirit in the normal population as well as the population standard deviation. Then we tried to change our sample and compared the sample mean to the normal population mean. But in real life, the normal population mean and standard deviation usually will not be available.

The first *t*-test in this chapter moves us toward a real-life situation by providing only the population mean; the population standard deviation is not given. The **single-sample *t*-test** is used when the population mean is known and the population standard deviation is estimated from the sample.

The Single-sample *t*-test

Using symbols to reword what was stated above, in the *z*-test, we had to know μ and σ_X. In the single-sample *t*-test, μ will be provided, but σ_X must be estimated. Estimating the population standard deviation was covered in Chapter 4 when we talked about measures of variability.

Estimated population standard deviation:

$$s_x = \sqrt{\frac{\sum X^2 - \frac{(\sum X)^2}{N}}{N - 1}}$$

Now that you know the slight difference between the *z*-test and the single-sample *t*-test, we can evaluate an example. If you are employed at a demanding job while taking a full load of courses, you might want to know if students who work jeopardize their grade point average (GPA) by forcing too many responsibilities into each week. Suppose the average GPA for the normal population of college students is 2.31 on a 4.0 GPA scale. Because we are using a *t*-test, that is all the information we will get—and all the information we need—before selecting a sample and making participants work for a semester.

At the end of the term, we could have the 12 students in our sample report their GPAs and get the sample average (hopefully you'll never actually do a study with only 12 people in your sample, because you won't have much power to reject H_0). Here are the 12 GPAs from participants:

2.20   1.54   1.78   1.22   2.00   1.30   2.08   1.01   3.18   3.23   1.76   2.01

The sample mean, obtained by averaging the 12 numbers above, is 1.9425.

Think back to the *z*-test. The first piece of information we needed was a variability term. It was the population standard deviation, and it was provided. With the *t*-test, we must estimate the population standard deviation.

$$s_x = \sqrt{\frac{50.6879 - \frac{(23.31)^2}{12}}{11}}$$

$$s_x = 0.694673$$

In the *z*-test, the variability term was divided by the square root of *N*. Follow the same procedure with this example, but use the estimated population standard deviation in the numerator. In the *z*-test, this piece of information was called the standard error of the mean. In the single-sample *t*-test, we call this formula/symbol by a very similar name: the ***estimated* standard error of the mean**.

$$s_{\overline{X}} = \frac{s_x}{\sqrt{N}}$$

$$s_{\overline{X}} = \frac{0.694673}{\sqrt{12}} = 0.200535$$

Think back once more to the *z*-test. After we calculated the standard error term, we placed it in the denominator of the z_{obt}. Follow the same procedure now, but call it the t_{obt}. The formula for the t_{obt} is

$$t_{obt} = \frac{\overline{X} - \mu}{s_{\overline{X}}}$$

$$t_{obt} = \frac{1.9425 - 2.31}{0.200535} = -1.832616$$

Our final t_{obt} answer is -1.83. The only remaining step is to see if -1.83 is far enough in the tail of the *t*-distribution to be able to say working changed GPA. To do that, we will turn again to hypothesis testing.

Hypothesis Testing Using the Single-sample t-test

First, set up hypotheses. The null hypothesis is that GPAs will not be affected by working; the sample mean will be the same as the population mean of 2.31. In addition, it is highly unlikely that working will increase GPA, so we designate that possibility in the null as well.

$H_0: \mu \geq 2.31$

We also need to set up our alternative hypothesis, which is the one that says how we believe our sample will be changed. In this example, we believe that working while taking classes will reduce GPA, so we have a one-tailed test in the lower tail of the distribution.

$H_1: \mu < 2.31$

Next we choose a statistic to analyze the data. We have a choice this time since we know about both the z-test and the single-sample t-test. Because we are estimating the population standard deviation, we must choose the single-sample t-test. Be as specific as possible about the statistic to be used: one-tailed, single-sample t-test.

Now sketch the distribution of GPAs in the normal population. In theory, we rely on a sampling distribution of means created from numerous samples of college GPAs. But of course the Central Limit Theorem ensures that the sampling distribution would have a normal shape, allowing us to simply rely on a t-distribution. The t-distribution looks like the z-distribution, because they are both symmetrical about the middle with tails that slope downward on each side; however, t_{crit} changes with N. Therefore, we cannot use the z-table for this example, but a different table is available specifically for the t-test.

Cutting off 5% (0.05) in one tail (or splitting it between both tails when a two-tailed test is needed) is not as simple as memorizing a critical value such as the z_{crit} of ±1.65. On the t-distribution, t_{crit} is based on the number of values in the sample minus one ($N - 1$). This is called degrees of freedom and is often symbolized by df. For each study conducted, we must look up a t_{crit} based on the df in our sample. In this example, N is 12, so df is 11. Look up 11 df in the first column of the one-tailed t-test. Move one column to the right for a p-value of .05 to locate a t_{crit} of 1.796. As you know, the distribution is symmetrical, therefore -1.796 defines the lower 5% of the left tail.

A distribution with the t_{crit}, p-value, and df is below:

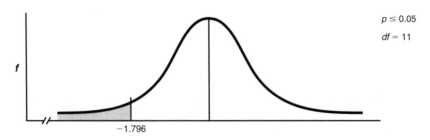

$p \leq 0.05$

$df = 11$

f

-1.796

For this example, we already have the t_{obt} that we would usually calculate at this point. The t_{obt} was -1.83. We can place it on the *x*-axis of the distribution we recently sketched.

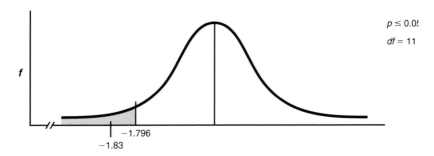

Notice that the t_{obt} fell beyond the t_{crit}.

In APA style we add the *df* information in parentheses after the t_{obt}.

$$t_{obt}(11) = -1.83, p < 0.05.$$

Do we reject or fail to reject the null hypothesis?

Reject the null hypothesis—reject the idea that nothing happened—because the sample mean was far from the population mean.

Was the sample mean significantly different from the population mean?

Yes, the sample mean of 1.9425 was significantly lower than a population mean of 2.31.

In Inferential Wording: If we went back to the population and made all students work a demanding job, their GPAs would suffer.

To calculate effect size, use the same formula from Chapter 7, but change the population standard deviation in the denominator to the estimated population standard deviation.

$$d = \frac{\mu_{new} - \mu_{old}}{\hat{s}_X}$$

where μ_{new} is the hypothesized new population mean, and μ_{old} is the old population mean.

$$d = \frac{1.9425 - 2.31}{0.694673} = -0.529026$$

The effect size is a moderate one, and because it is a negative value, working reduces GPA.

In Plain English: Working a demanding job while taking a full load of college courses reduces GPA below the normal GPA. In fact, it reduces GPA to approximately 1.94.

To find a range of scores that would encompass 95% of the population of students who maintained a full-time job, calculate the confidence interval. The lower limit is calculated using t_{crit} for a two-tailed test, regardless of whether or not hypothesis testing was a one-tailed test. In the table, t_{crit} for a two-tailed t-test with 11 degrees of freedom is ± 2.201.

$$(-t_{crit})(\sigma_{\overline{X}}) + (\overline{X}) = (-2.201)(0.200535) + 1.9425 = 1.501123$$

$$(+t_{crit})(\sigma_{\overline{X}}) + (\overline{X}) = (+2.201)(0.200535) + 1.9425 = 2.383878$$

Based on these calculations, GPA with a full-time job would range from 1.50 to 2.38 for approximately 95% of the population.

The Related-samples *t*-test

The second t-test is one we are more likely to use. Instead of comparing a sample mean to μ, two samples are compared to each other. This test is called the **related-samples *t*-test**. (Please notice that *samples* is plural.) Neither the population mean nor the population standard deviation is given. Like the single-sample t-test, the population standard deviation will be estimated.

Rather than take one sample, manipulate participants, and see if they are different from normal, we will have two samples, do something different to each sample, and compare them to each other. With two conditions in an experiment, we can now return to the term independent variable, which relied on having at least two levels manipulated by the researcher. It would also be reasonable to compare two groups that were not manipulated, such as short people vs. tall people, and their popularity. Because we can clearly see two levels, we might call height a quasi-IV. The ability to use a t-test does not rely on having a true IV, but we would need to be careful not to assume cause and effect. If participants were not forced into conditions, they were not manipulated. A significant effect would merely indicate that height and popularity are related, but the use of a t-test to learn this information is fine.

The samples in the related-samples t-test are called related because participants in one group have something in common with participants in the other group. For example, people in the second group might be brothers of people in the first group. Another example would be if people in the second group were married to people in the first group. The ultimate in related samples is when the same people are tested under both conditions. Obviously, if the same people are tested under two conditions, some type of manipulation took place, meaning we would have a true IV. Regardless of how people are placed in the two groups, a t-test can address whether or not an effect (for an IV) or a relationship (for a quasi-IV) exists.

The Sampling Distribution of Mean Differences

The z-test and the single-sample *t*-test were both based on the sampling distribution of means. You probably remember that the sampling distribution of means was a simple frequency distribution of means theoretically pulled from the population. But the related-samples *t*-test uses two samples; therefore, a sampling distribution of means will no longer apply—we need a distribution based on two samples. The following example will move us toward forming a distribution.

If we randomly pulled a sample from the population, then went back and selected their brothers, we would have two related samples. We might want to know if there is a difference in weight between our two groups. Since the two groups have something in common (they're siblings), we place the weights side-by-side this way:

Sample 1		Brothers of Sample 1	
Fred	185 lbs.	*Fred's brother*	185 lbs.
John	210 lbs.	*John's brother*	210 lbs.
Casey	190 lbs.	*Casey's brother*	190 lbs.
Jack	165 lbs.	*Jack's brother*	165 lbs.
Dan	177 lbs.	*Dan's brother*	177 lbs.

Notice that each person is in the same line as his brother. That is one of the rules. We cannot pair up Jack with Dan's brother.

Now that participants are paired, we can examine the difference between the two samples, by subtracting across rows and placing the difference in a third column. Difference is symbolized by *D*.

Sample 1		Brothers		D
185	−	185	=	0
210	−	210	=	0
190	−	190	=	0
165	−	165	=	0
177	−	177	=	0

First, we did not do anything to these samples, so there is no reason to think that the brothers' weight would differ from each other. (Even though slight weight differences would be perfectly reasonable.) Second, if we do not expect the two samples to be different from each other, the average of the *D* column should be zero.

Of course, the *D* column could be greater than zero by chance. Once in a while we could pull a first sample that just happens to have higher numbers than the second sample, and when we subtract across we would get positive numbers and a positive *D* average. It is also possible that we could pull a first sample with lower numbers than our second sample, making the $\overline{D}$ a negative value. But the most likely value is a $\overline{D}$ of zero when nothing has been done to people in the normal population. Anything else is sampling error, with extremely bad sampling error resulting in $\overline{D}$ values far in the upper tail (when the mean of *D* is positive), or far in the lower tail (when the $\overline{D}$ is negative). All possibilities of $\overline{D}$, from high *f* (simple frequency) values to low f values, create the **sampling distribution of mean differences.** Based on the previous discussion, we would expect the highest point in the distribution (highest f) to be at zero.

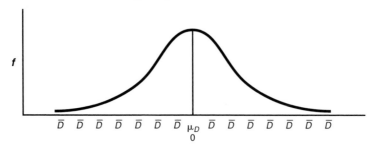

Just as the sampling distribution of means had an error term (the estimated standard error of the mean), the sampling distribution of mean differences has an error term: the **estimated standard error of the mean difference.**

$$s_{\overline{D}} = \frac{s_D}{\sqrt{N}}$$

Notice that the word *difference* was added to both the sampling distribution and the error term to indicate that we are looking at differences between two samples. Similarly, the symbol for the standard error of the mean difference has a subscript $\overline{D}$ rather than an $\overline{X}$, because we are dealing with a mean difference score instead of a mean of X scores.

Hypothesis Testing Using the Related-samples t-test

Returning to our related samples of brothers, we can design an experiment in which the first sample will be given water with dinner every night for a month. The second sample—the brothers—will be forced to drink a milkshake with dinner every night for a month. At the end of the month, we can measure who weighs more. Assume that we think milkshakes could increase weight because they are high in calories, or milkshakes could decrease weight because they are filling and may not allow room for dinner. Thus, a two-tailed test is needed.

Our hypotheses would look like this:

$H_0: \mu_D = 0$

$H_1: \mu_D \neq 0$

When choosing a statistic, be specific: a two-tailed, related-samples t-test. Next, lay out the distribution of mean differences in the normal population, all changed to t-scores. Then place the 5% in two tails (2.5% in each tail). The final component we needed is the df, and the formula is $N - 1$, where N is the number of values in the D column.

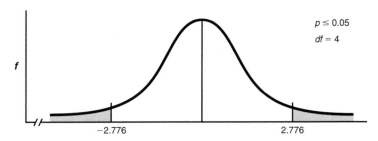

Our data are as follow:

Water	Milkshakes
186	195
200	202
190	196
162	165
175	183

The math is exactly like the single-sample t-test, but use the D column instead of the X column. As a result, the variability term will be δ_D instead of δ_X, and estimated population standard deviation is calculated using the D column.

Water	Milkshakes	D	D^2
186	195	−9	81
200	202	−2	4
190	196	−6	36
162	165	−3	9
175	183	−8	64

$$\Sigma D = -28 \quad \Sigma D^2 = 194$$
$$(\Sigma D)^2 = (-28)^2 = 784$$

$$\delta_D = \sqrt{\frac{\Sigma D^2 - \dfrac{(\Sigma D)^2}{N}}{N-1}}$$

$$\delta_D = \sqrt{\frac{194 - 156.80}{4}} = \sqrt{9.30} = 3.049590$$

As with the z-test and the single-sample t-test, get a standard error term by dividing the estimated population standard deviation by the square root of N. Remember, this is called the estimated standard error the mean difference, because it is based on difference scores (the D column).

$$\delta_{\bar{D}} = \frac{\delta_D}{\sqrt{N}}$$

$$\delta_{\bar{D}} = \frac{3.049590}{2.236068} = 1.363818$$

Finally, calculate the t_{obt} value and compare it with the t_{crit} of ± 2.776. To get the t_{obt}, complete the following formula:

$$t_{obt} = \frac{\overline{D} - \mu_D}{s_{\overline{D}}}$$

The mean of the D column is the first piece entered, then subtract μ_D, which we have not yet discussed. But remember, we are always testing the null hypothesis, and the null hypothesis indicates that μ_D is 0. So subtract 0 from the mean of the D column. Then divide the numerator by the estimated standard error of the mean difference calculated earlier.

$$t_{obt} = \frac{-5.60 - 0}{1.363818} = -4.11$$

On the normal distribution, we can see where the t_{obt} falls.

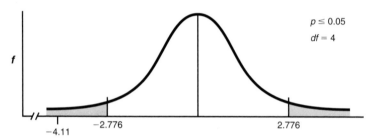

Because the t_{obt} of -4.11 does fall in the region of rejection, we can reject the null hypothesis. The probability of getting a t_{obt} that far in the tail of a distribution of normal people is pretty low—an unusual mean difference. Putting the result in APA style,

$$t(4) = -4.11, p < 0.05$$

Another way of saying it is: The two groups were significantly different from each other.

The size of this effect is calculated using the estimated population standard deviation for the difference column (s_D)

$$d = \frac{\mu_1 - \mu_2}{s_D}$$

where μ_1 is the sample mean difference ($\overline{D}$) and μ_2 is the null mean difference, which of course is 0, based on no difference being expected prior to a manipulation.

$$d = \frac{-5.60 - 0}{3.049590} = -1.836312$$

An effect size of -1.84 is obviously a strong effect, illustrating a large weight change between drinking water and drinking milkshakes with dinner.

We can feel confident that drinking milkshakes every night changes weight. Does it make men gain weight or lose weight? Look back at the two columns of numbers to see which ones weigh more. The milkshake drinkers do. So we can say that drinking milkshakes every night makes men gain weight.

The mean of the difference column in this example was −5.60, but the mean difference in the real population could fluctuate around this number. The confidence interval will indicate approximately how much fluctuation would be expected. To calculate the range of values, $s_{\overline{D}}$ is used. For the range,

$$(-t_{\text{crit}})(s_{\overline{D}}) + \overline{D} = (-2.776)(1.363818) + (-5.60) = -9.385959$$

$$(+t_{\text{crit}})(s_{\overline{D}}) + \overline{D} = (+2.776)(1.363818) + (-5.60) = -1.814041$$

Thus, the average of the difference column is −5.60 (less weight for water than for milkshakes), with a potential range of mean difference values of −1.81 (not a great deal of difference) to −9.39 (a substantial difference).

The related-samples *t*-test is sometimes called a **matched-, paired-,** or **dependent-samples *t*-test.** All four names for this test refer to the fact that the two samples begin with something in common—even before the experiment begins.

Related-samples t-test on SPSS

We can analyze this example efficiently using SPSS. Enter the data just as you see it in the text. The first column will be **water,** and the second column will be **milkshakes.** When you enter information in the columns, make sure your pairs of brothers stay together. Fred and his brother should be across from each other on the first line; John and his brother should be across from each other on the second line; and so on.

Point to Analyze, then select Compare Means + Paired-Samples *t*-test.

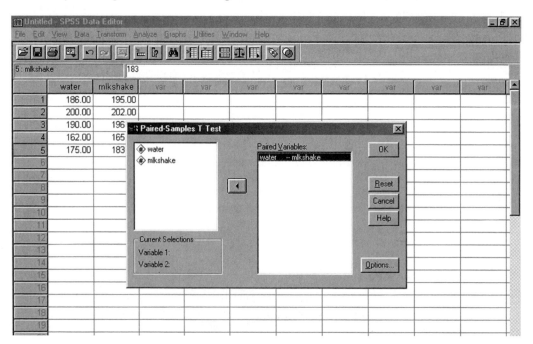

In the gray box, select both variables on the left, then move them to the right by clicking the arrow to the right.

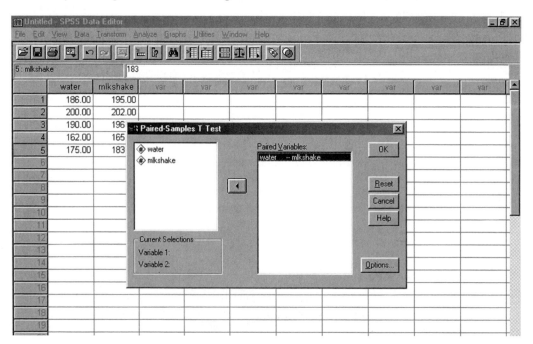

Click OK for data output.

T-Test

Paired Samples Statistics

		Mean	N	Std. Deviation	Std. Error Mean
Pair 1	WATER	182.6000	5	14.58767	6.52380
	MLKSHAKE	188.2000	5	14.68673	6.56810

Paired Samples Correlations

		N	Correlation	Sig.
Pair 1	WATER & MLKSHAKE	5	.978	.004

Paired Samples Test

		Paired Differences					
					95% Confidence Interval of the Difference		
		Mean	Std. Deviation	Std. Error Mean	Lower	Upper	t
Pair 1	WATER-MLKSHAKE	-5.6000	3.04959	1.36382	-9.3866	-1.8134	-4.106

Paired Samples Test

		df	Sig. (2-tailed)
Pair 1	WATER-MLKSHAKE	4	.015

On the output, the important information includes the *t*-value of -4.11, the *df* of 4, and the significance value of 0.015. Significance is the same as *p*-value, and SPSS automatically conducts a two-tailed test. Since 0.015 on this output is less than 5%, the two groups are significantly different from each other, just as you decided when you calculated this example by hand. The confidence interval has also been provided by SPSS.

APA-style Results Section

Using the computer output (or hand calculations), we can prepare an APA-style results section for a manuscript. On the next page is a simple results section for our example.

> **Results**
>
> A two-tailed, related-samples *t*-test was used to analyze these data. The type of beverage consumed affected weight, $t(4) = -4.11, p < 0.05$, with a Cohen's *d* effect size of -1.84. Men who drank milkshakes before dinner for a month weighed more ($M = 188.20, SEM = 6.57$) than their brothers who drank water before dinner ($M = 182.60, SEM = 6.52$).

Notice that the first sentence states the statistical analysis used. The second sentence reports the general effect of the IV on the DV, followed by the obtained value and *p*-value in APA style as well as effect size. The final sentence describes the effect in detail, explaining which group was higher and which was lower based on the means (*M*). Variability in each group is represented by *SEM*, the APA abbreviation for estimated standard error of the mean, an inferential value based on the group standard deviation divided by the square root of *n* (the number in each group). All symbols and abbreviations are italicized.

Independent-samples *t*-test

In the **independent-samples *t*-test**, two samples are used again, but this time participants enter the experiment with nothing in common with each other. They are not brothers, cousins, spouses, or related in any way (and they are not the same people tested under both levels of the IV). One way to get independent groups is to randomly assign people to conditions of an IV such that everyone who comes into the experiment has an equal chance of being placed in each of the levels of the IV. But recall from earlier examples that a quasi-IV, such as height (short or tall), can also be analyzed with a *t*-test.

The Sampling Distribution of Differences Between Means

The **sampling distribution of differences between means** is theoretically created by selecting a sample of people from the population and measuring them on a variable of interest, then pulling a second, unrelated sample and measuring them on the same variable. Even though we have two groups of people, if nothing has been done to these two groups, we would not expect them to be different from each other. The sampling distribution of differences between means is based on a mean of one sample minus a mean of a second sample.

$$\overline{X}_1 - \overline{X}_2$$

(Remember that the sampling distribution of mean differences was based on a mean difference column, rather than two separate sample means subtracted from one another.) The sampling distribution of differences between means is a normal distribution with a mean of 0, because we have no reason to think two normal samples from the same population would differ if they have not been manipulated in any way.

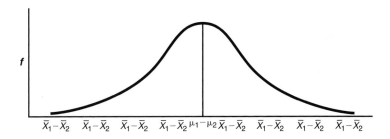

$\bar{X}_1 - \bar{X}_2$ $\bar{X}_1 - \bar{X}_2$ $\bar{X}_1 - \bar{X}_2$ $\bar{X}_1 - \bar{X}_2$ $\mu_1 - \mu_2$ $\bar{X}_1 - \bar{X}_2$ $\bar{X}_1 - \bar{X}_2$ $\bar{X}_1 - \bar{X}_2$ $\bar{X}_1 - \bar{X}_2$

Hypothesis Testing Using the Independent-samples t-test

For an example, we could study the effect of completing college on job salaries. We think people who graduate from college will earn a higher salary than those who drop out of college.

First, set up the null and alternative hypotheses:

H_0: $\mu_1 - \mu_2 \leq 0$ (where 1 is finish college and 2 is drop out of college)

H_1: $\mu_1 - \mu_2 > 0$ (since we expect higher numbers in group 1)

Choose a statistic:

One-tailed, independent-samples *t*-test.

Sketch a normal distribution, and shade the rejection region. Write the *p*-value and *df* in this part, too. Degrees of freedom are calculated this way:

$df = (n_1 - 1) + (n_2 - 1)$ (where *n* is the number of values in each column)

If we decide to test 10 people in our study, *df* is 8, and t_{crit} is 1.860 based on 8° of freedom.

$$df = (5 - 1) + (5 - 1) = 8$$

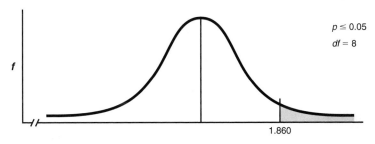

$p \leq 0.05$
$df = 8$

1.860

We might select 10 people from the population and randomly assign them to levels of the IV. A year after either completing college or dropping out of school, we ask participants to report their salaries per year in ten-thousand units. Although each number on the next page represents units of ten thousand (e.g., 5 represents a salary of $50,000), we can work with the numbers as they are listed and return them to large numbers after analysis.

College degree	Drop-outs
5	3
7	2
3	3
5	0
4	1

As in the case of the z-test and both t-tests we have already covered, analysis begins with a variability term. The problem is that we have two columns of numbers instead of one, and we want only one value for variability. First, get a measure of variability for each column of numbers individually. Instead of standard deviation, this time we use the variance. (You already learned that both standard deviation and variance measure variability.) Calculate the estimated population variance for each column of numbers.

$$\mathcal{S}_X^2 = \frac{\sum X^2 - \frac{(\sum X)^2}{N}}{N - 1}$$

Estimated population variance for college graduates:

$$\mathcal{S}_{X_1}^2 = \frac{124 - 115.20}{4} = 2.20$$

Estimated population variance for students who drop out:

$$\mathcal{S}_{X_2}^2 = \frac{23 - 16.20}{4} = 1.70$$

We still need a way to combine these two values into one number for variability, and we do that by calculating a number that pools variability, the **variance pooled:**

$$\mathcal{S}_{pool}^2 = \frac{(n_1 - 1)(\mathcal{S}_{X_1}^2) + (n_2 - 1)(\mathcal{S}_{X_2}^2)}{(n_1 - 1) + (n_2 - 1)}$$

$$\mathcal{S}_{pool}^2 = \frac{(4)(2.20) + (4)(1.70)}{4 + 4} = 195$$

Next, the standard error term is calculated (as with every previous inferential statistic). This time the standard error term is called the **estimated standard error of the difference between means,** to reflect that we are working with two separate means rather than a D column.

$$\mathcal{S}_{\overline{X}_1 - \overline{X}_2} = \sqrt{(\mathcal{S}_{pool}^2)\left(\frac{1}{n_1} + \frac{1}{n_2}\right)}$$

$$\mathcal{S}_{\overline{X}_1 - \overline{X}_2} = \sqrt{(1.95)\left(\frac{1}{5} + \frac{1}{5}\right)} = \sqrt{.78} = .883176$$

Finally, the t_{obt} is calculated using the following formula.

$$t_{obt} = \frac{(\overline{X}_1 - \overline{X}_2) - (\mu_1 - \mu_2)}{\mathcal{S}_{\overline{X}_1 - \overline{X}_2}}$$

Notice that the second half of the numerator again refers to μ, but recall that we are always testing the null hypothesis, which in this example contains the possibility that $\mu_1 - \mu_2 = 0$. Thus, the second half of the numerator is simply zero. Calculate the first sample mean, minus the second sample mean, divided by the estimated standard error of the difference between means.

$$t_{\text{obt}} = \frac{(4.80 - 1.80) - (0)}{0.883176} = 3.40$$

Putting the t_{obt} on the distribution of normal people, we find that it falls in the rejection region, allowing us to reject the null hypothesis.

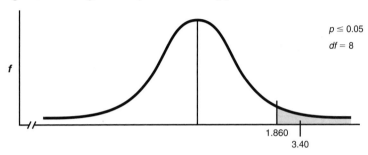

APA style is:

$$t_{\text{obt}}(8) = 3.40, p < 0.05.$$

The two groups were indeed significantly different from each other. The size of this effect can be calculated using the square root of the variance pooled in the denominator $\left(\sqrt{\mathscr{S}_{\text{pool}}^2} \right)$.

$$d = \frac{\mu_1 - \mu_2}{\sqrt{\mathscr{S}_{\text{pool}}^2}}$$

where μ_1 is the hypothesized new μ for the first group, and μ_2 is the hypothesized new μ for the second group. The sample mean from each group is placed in the numerator.

$$d = \frac{4.80 - 1.80}{\sqrt{1.95}} = 2.148345$$

With such a strong effect, it is clear that students who complete college earn vastly different salaries from those who drop out.

Further, we know from the original data and group means that those who finished college earned higher salaries than those who dropped out of college. In fact, based on the difference between the two group means, we would assume that dropping out would decrease salaries by $30,000 (a difference of 3 multiplied by $10,000, to return to the original increments). The plausible range of values can be found in a 95% confidence interval using the estimated standard error of the difference between means $(\mathscr{S}_{\overline{X}_1 - \overline{X}_2})$ and $\pm t_{\text{crit}}$ for a two-tailed test. For the lower and upper ends of the range,

$$(-t_{\text{crit}})(\mathscr{S}_{\overline{X}_1 - \overline{X}_2}) + (\overline{X}_1 - \overline{X}_2) = (-2.306)(0.883176) + (4.80 - 1.80) = 0.963396$$

$$(+t_{\text{crit}})(\mathscr{S}_{\overline{X}_1 - \overline{X}_2}) + (\overline{X}_1 - \overline{X}_2) = (+2.306)(0.883176) + (4.80 - 1.80) = 5.036604$$

Change the resultant values back to their original increments by multiplying each by $10,000, to provide a range from $9,600 to $50,400. Thus, according to this example, students who drop out of college are likely to earn $30,000 less than those who complete college, with an approximate range of potential salary loss from $9,600 to $50,400.

Independent-samples *t*-test on SPSS

When we enter these data into SPSS, we cannot put them in columns next to each other as we did with the related-samples *t*-test. Instead, we return to stringing out the data as we did for graphing at the end of Chapters 3 and 4. First, lay out a column for the IV, with numbers to represent the levels of the IV. Completing college will be changed to a 1 so the computer can read it, and dropping out will be changed to a 2 to reflect the second level of the IV in this study. In the second column, the DV, put the salary (values representing tens of thousands) of each person based on what level of the IV he or she was under. Salaries of participants who completed college are typed beside the first level of the IV; salaries of participants who dropped out of college fall beside the second level of the IV.

With appropriate data names for the IV and DV columns, the data will look like this:

Change level 1 of the IV (college) to graduated, and level 2 to dropped out under Variable View.

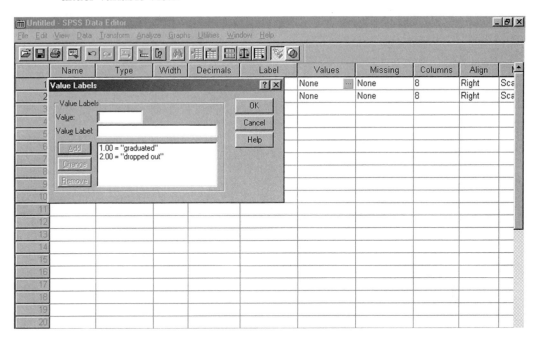

Return to the sheet, then Data View. Point to View and select View Labels to see the IV level names (as in Chapters 3 and 4).

To analyze, point to Analyze, then select Compare Means + Independent-Samples *t*-test.

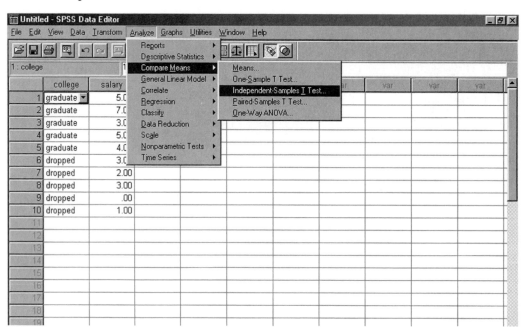

In the gray box, select the IV (college) and move it to Grouping Variable.

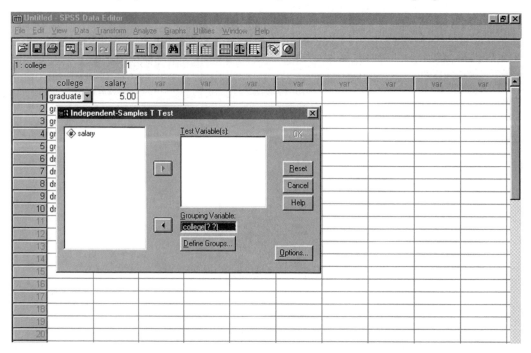

While college is still selected, click Define Groups and enter **1** for Group 1 and **2** for Group 2.

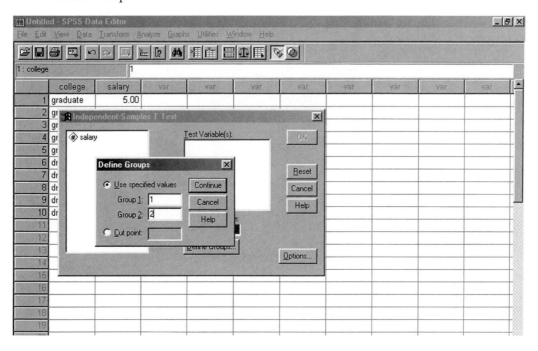

After typing a **1** and a **2** on the appropriate lines, click Continue.

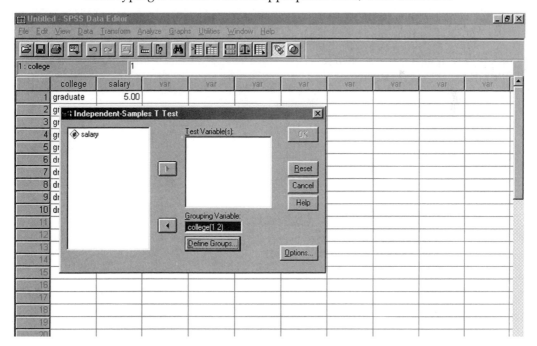

Select the DV (salary), and move it to the right, under Test Variable.

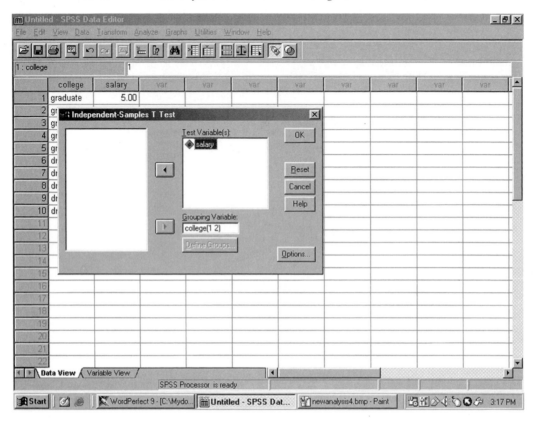

Click OK for the output.

Group Statistics

	COLLEGE	N	Mean	Std. Deviation	Std. Error Mean
SALARY	graduated	5	4.8000	1.48324	.66332
	dropped out	5	1.8000	1.30384	.58310

Independent Samples Test

		Levene's Test for Equality of Variances	
		F	Sig.
SALARY	Equal variances assumed	.000	1.000
	Equal variances not assumed		

Independent Samples Test

| | | \multicolumn{4}{c}{t-test for Equality of Means} |
		t	df	Sig. (2-tailed)	Mean Difference
SALARY	Equal variances assumed	3.397	8	.009	3.0000
	Equal variances not assumed	3.397	7.871	.010	3.0000

Independent Samples Test

| | | \multicolumn{3}{c}{t-test for Equality of Means} |
| | | | \multicolumn{2}{c}{95% Confidence Interval of the Difference} |
		Std. Error Difference	Lower	Upper
SALARY	Equal variances assumed	.88318	.96339	5.03661
	Equal variances not assumed	.88318	.95755	5.04245

On the output, focus on the Equal variances assumed row of data (the first row). The main information we want from the output is the t value of 3.40, the df of 8, and the p-value of 0.009. Since the p-value is less than 0.05, the two groups are significantly different from each other. In fact, 0.009 is a bit too conservative, since we had a one-tailed test in mind rather than a two-tailed test. Although 0.009 is certainly significant, if you ever find a significance value just above 5% (0.05) when you had planned for a one-tailed test, look up df in the t-table for a one-tailed test to locate the t_{crit} and significance level.

The confidence interval has also been calculated by SPSS, and you can see that the results match those we calculated by hand. Many researchers argue that confidence intervals will replace hypothesis testing when analyzing and reporting results, but at this point, hypothesis testing is still used more often than confidence intervals.

APA-style Results Section

An APA-style results section for this example is below:

Results

A one-tailed, independent-samples t-test was used to analyze these data. Whether or not students completed college affected yearly salary, $t(8) = 3.40$, $p < 0.01$, with a Cohen's d effect size of 2.15. People who graduated from college earned more dollars per year ($M = 48,000.00$, $SEM = 6,633.20$) than those who did not earn a college degree ($M = 18,000.00$, $SEM = 5,831.00$).

When reporting the probability value, $p < 0.01$ in the above results section is based on the computer output of a significance value of 0.009. Not only is 0.009 less than the 0.05 needed for a significant effect, it is also less than 0.01 and can be reported as such. For the sake of clarity, dollars were returned to their true value by multiplying each mean and standard deviation from the output by $10,000.

Preview of Chapter 9

At this point, you are familiar with testing hypotheses, conducting two t-tests that will be useful when analyzing data, and reporting outcomes in an APA-style results section. In the next chapter, your knowledge will be expanded to encompass a statistic that can analyze larger designs than one IV (or quasi-IV) with only two levels.

Conceptual Items

1. When the population mean is known and the population standard deviation is estimated from the sample, the statistic used is _____.
2. When two samples of people with something common are compared with each other, the statistic used is _____.
3. When two samples of people with nothing common are compared with each other, the statistic used is _____.
4. For t-tests, effect size for a significant result is calculated using _____.
5. Write the symbol for each of the following:
   a. estimated standard error of the mean
   b. estimated standard error of the mean difference
   c. estimated standard error of the difference between means
6. Why must you use the t-table to look up t_{crit}, rather than simply memorizing a few values as you did with the z-test?
7. In the formula for the independent-samples t_{obt}, why is $\mu_1 - \mu_2$ always 0? (The same answer would explain why μ_D is 0 in the related-samples t_{obt} formula.)

Application Items

8. You may have heard that eating salt makes people retain water, and water weight is quite heavy. If you are skeptical, you might want to know if eating salty foods

truly makes people gain weight (at least temporarily), or if the weight gain is so small that it should not be of concern to people. Assume that the normal weight of 20-year-old females is 150 pounds. Rely on the following sample data of people who consumed salty foods to answer the question of weight gain:

155	160	140	145	180
190	120	85	175	130

a. Lay out the H_0 and H_1 hypotheses.
b. Choose a statistic to analyze this study (be specific).
c. Sketch the distribution of normal people, and include the *p*-value, degrees of freedom, and t_{crit}.
d. Analyze these data, put your answer in APA style, and reject or fail to reject the null hypothesis.
e. Did you find a significant effect?
f. If appropriate, calculate effect size and confidence interval(s).
g. Based on your results, what did you learn from this study?

9. My son loves baseball, and he often asks me to watch games with him. Unfortunately, I don't like to watch baseball—perhaps because I don't understand the game. A study could address the question of whether or not learning the rules of baseball increases enjoyment of the game. It would also be possible that learning the rules decreases enjoyment by making it seem more like "work" to watch sports. Suppose the average enjoyment of baseball (prior to knowing much about it) is 8 on a 15-point scale. The following fictional ratings of enjoyment are from a sample of people who were taught the rules of baseball. Complete parts a-g from Application Item 8.

Learned baseball rules

9
12
8
15
14
7
8
10
13
7
10
12
14

For the remaining items, complete parts a-g from Application Item 8, and verify your work on SPSS.

10. You want to know if clothing that a woman wears has anything to do with how attractive men rate her. Based on a study by Williamson and Hewitt (1986), you suspect that men will rate the woman as more attractive when she is pictured in skimpy clothing than when she is pictured in conservative clothing. You ask each man (each participant) to rate both pictures, and here are the data:

Skimpy clothing	Conservative clothing
10	6
8	5
3	10
5	8
4	7

11. Your roommate smokes two packs of cigarettes a day. She does it in your apartment, so your clothes always smell horrible. You've never smoked, so you don't like the smell all over you. Although you have asked her to smoke outside, she refuses. Because you are locked in to a lease, you decide to try a different approach. You ask her if she'll quit if you can provide evidence that smokers cough and choke more than nonsmokers. She agrees, so you conduct the following experiment, with the DV being the number of times people cough or choke during a 16-hour period after they have either not smoked for 1 month or smoked 2 packs a day for 1 month. (Of course, it would be unethical to make participants smoke cigarettes in an experiment.)

People you did not allow to smoke	People you forced to smoke 2 packs a day for one month
0	20
2	15
16	35
3	12
0	32
6	24
3	45

12. If you wanted to know the effect of friend vs. mother on how often middle-school students recycle, you might ask participants to either listen to a lecture from a friend or from their mother about how recycling benefits the environment. You randomly assign participants to the two conditions, and you don't have an expectation for which will be more effective. After a week, you ask participants to estimate the percent of potential recyclables they recycled in the past week. The following numbers are percent, even though the symbol (%) has been omitted.

Lecture by friend	Lecture by mother
50	95
65	80
75	90
70	95
60	99
40	85
85	75
80	70

13. After examining the question of recycling, you decided it might be interesting to know if middle-school students would be more influenced by their mothers than friends on other issues, such as how much television they watch after school. You choose participants who have a sibling (younger or older) who attends the same middle school. Participants spend after-school hours with a friend who asks them not to watch much TV, and participants' siblings spend after-school hours with their mothers (who ask them not to watch much TV). The data below are number of minutes of TV watched after school.

With friend	With mother
60	75
90	150
30	60
75	120
20	30
75	165

14. If we wanted to know the importance of intimate conversations for men and women, we could ask participants of each gender to rate the importance of emotion-filled conversations on a scale from 1 to 20, with higher numbers indicating higher perceived importance. We might expect women to rate intimate conversations as more important than men rate them.

Men	Women
5	17
3	18
10	12
4	15
2	20
9	19
17	16
4	20
3	14
6	

After completing parts a-g from Application Item 8, address the following question:

For this example, why would it be a mistake to say that gender caused differences in ratings of the importance of intimate conversations?

Computational formulas in this chapter

Because three types of t-tests were covered in this chapter, computational formulas and review information are provided.

single-sample *t*-test	related-samples *t*-test	independent-samples *t*-test
given: μ	given: no population information	given: no population information

single-sample *t*-test

variability term:

$$s_X = \sqrt{\frac{\sum X^2 - \dfrac{(\sum X)^2}{N}}{N-1}}$$

standard error term:

$$s_{\bar{X}} = \frac{s_X}{\sqrt{N}}$$

obtained value:

$$t_{obt} = \frac{\bar{X} - \mu}{s_{\bar{X}}}$$

related-samples *t*-test

variability term:

$$s_D = \sqrt{\frac{\sum D^2 - \dfrac{(\sum D)^2}{N}}{N-1}}$$

standard error term:

$$s_{\bar{D}} = \frac{s_D}{N}$$

obtained value:

$$t_{obt} = \frac{\bar{D} - \mu}{s_{\bar{D}}}$$

independent-samples *t*-test

variability term(s):

$$s_{X_1}^2 = \frac{\sum X^2 - \dfrac{(\sum X)^2}{N}}{N-1} \qquad s_{X_2}^2 = \frac{\sum X^2 - \dfrac{(\sum X)^2}{N}}{N-1}$$

$$s_{pool}^2 = \frac{(n_1 - 1)s_{X_1}^2 + (n_2 - 1)s_{X_2}^2}{(n_1 - 1) + (n_2 - 1)}$$

standard error term:

$$s_{\bar{x}_1 - \bar{x}_2} = \sqrt{s_{pool}^2 \left(\frac{1}{n_1} + \frac{1}{n_2}\right)}$$

obtained value:

$$t_{obt} = \frac{(\bar{X}_1 - \bar{X}_2) - (\mu_1 - \mu_2)}{s_{\bar{x}_1 - \bar{x}_2}}$$

single-sample *t*-test	related-samples *t*-test	independent-samples *t*-test
given: μ	given: no population information	given: no population information
sampling distribution:	sampling distribution:	sampling distribution:

single-sample *t*-test

effect size:

$$d = \frac{\mu_{new} - \mu_{old}}{\varnothing_X}$$

confidence interval:

$$(\pm t_{crit})(\varnothing_{\bar{x}}) + (\bar{X})$$

related-samples *t*-test

effect size:

$$d = \frac{\mu_1 - \mu_2}{\varnothing_D}$$

confidence interval:

$$(\pm t_{crit})(\varnothing_{\overline{D}}) + \overline{D}$$

independent-samples *t*-test

effect size:

$$d = \frac{\mu_1 - \mu_2}{\sqrt{\varnothing_{pool}^2}}$$

confidence interval:

$$(\pm t_{crit})(\varnothing_{\bar{x}_1 - \bar{x}_2}) + (\bar{X}_1 - \bar{X}_2)$$

References

In Text:

Williamson, S., & Hewitt, J. (1986). Attire, sexual allure, and attractiveness. *Perceptual & Motor Skills, 63,* 981–982.

Related Articles:

Baenninger, M. A., Baenniner, R., & Houle, D. (1993). Attractiveness, attentiveness, and perceived male shortage: Their influence on perceptions of other females. *Ethology & Sociobiology, 14,* 293–303.

Barber, N. (1999). Women's dress fashions as a function of reproductive strategy. *Sex Roles, 40,* 459–471.

CHAPTER 9

ANOVA: One-Way, Between-Groups

t-test Versus ANOVA

The related- and independent-samples *t*-tests are useful for a great deal of research, but *t*-tests are restricted to one independent variable with two levels. Limiting a study to one IV and only two levels will not always be the best choice; often three or more levels of an IV must be examined. In this chapter, we turn to a statistic called the ANOVA. Specifically, we will focus on the one-way, between-groups ANOVA, a statistic used to analyze one IV with two or more levels. Although the ANOVA can analyze one IV with two levels, we generally use the simpler approach of the *t*-test and reserve the ANOVA for more than two levels of an IV.

Logic of ANOVA: Hypothesis Testing

Before we discuss the logic behind the ANOVA, you need to become familiar with a few terms and definitions. When discussing ANOVA, an IV or quasi-IV is often called a **factor**. **One-way** simply means one factor, with as many levels of this variable as needed. A **two-way** ANOVA would label a design with two factors, each having at least two levels. A three-way ANOVA has three factors, with at least two levels each. This chapter will not go beyond the one-way ANOVA, but the two-way ANOVA will be covered in Chapter 10.

Between-groups means people in the levels of the factor come to the experiment with nothing in common. In a between-groups design, the best way to put participants in levels of an IV is through random assignment to conditions, so cause and effect can be established. A quasi-IV (such as short, medium, and tall) will also be analyzed as a between-groups ANOVA, with a significant result indicating a relationship, rather than cause and effect.

A second way to run participants is using a **within-groups** design by exposing each person to every level of the IV. The within-groups design is similar to the related-samples *t*-test, because participants in the two groups have something in common before the experiment begins. Although the related-samples *t*-test allows people to have anything in common to be considered related (e.g., cousins, brothers, or spouses), the within-groups ANOVA is more restricted. A design is considered a within-groups ANOVA only if the same people are tested under every level of the IV. Another name for the within-groups test is **repeated-measures** ANOVA, a term to indicate repeatedly measuring the same people. Both the within-groups and repeated-measures label the same type of ANOVA; participants are exposed to all levels of the IV. This chapter will focus on the between-groups ANOVA, but the repeated-measures ANOVA is addressed in Appendix A.

ANOVA stands for **analysis of variance**. It might be more intuitive if the ANOVA stood for analysis of variability, since this statistic examines two types: variability based on the IV manipulation and variability based on differences not associated with the IV. The term variance (and standard deviation) are simply mathematical ways to define variability.

Variability associated with manipulation of the IV is characterized by differences across IV levels. In other words, we want an IV manipulation to cause a difference in participants' behavior. That is why we put people in different groups and expose them to different situations in an experiment. Variability between the levels of the IV is often called **between-groups variability**, and can be abbreviated **BG**.

Variability not associated with levels of the IV is quantified by differences in behavior (the DV) *within* each group. Since participants within each individual level of the IV experience the same situation in your experiment, we would not expect their behaviors to be vastly different from each other. Another name for this type of undesirable variability might be individual differences. Even though everyone in a specific level of the IV is treated the same way by the experimenter, they respond as individuals, allowing DV outcomes (behavior) to vary within a group. Variability among numbers within each group is called **within-groups variability**, and can be abbreviated **WG**.

If undesirable variability, or individual differences, is found within each level of the IV, of course that same amount of individual differences will be found between the groups. We hope the useful variability—the variability caused by what we do to people across different groups—will be so large that it overshadows the differences in numbers associated with individual differences.

These ideas can be written in a formula (one we won't actually calculate) using a symbol for variability. Even though the population variance is symbolized by a Greek letter here, any variability term at this point would be appropriate, because the goal is to illustrate the theory of useful variability and variability associated with individual differences:

$$\frac{\sigma^2_{useful} + \sigma^2_{individual\ differences}}{\sigma^2_{individual\ differences}} = \frac{BG_{variability}}{WG_{variability}}$$

Another way of writing the logic of ANOVA would be to call useful variability treatment variance or effect variance. Undesirable variability or individual differences could be termed error variance. Then the formula would look like this:

$$\frac{\sigma^2_{treatment/effect\ variance} + \sigma^2_{error\ variance}}{\sigma^2_{error\ variance}} = \frac{BG_{variability}}{WG_{variability}}$$

Imagine for a moment that we pulled people from the population, randomly assigned them to groups, but did nothing to them before measuring them on a variable. Would we expect any treatment or effect variability? Because there was no treatment, we certainly would not expect the numbers to be different from each other. Then in the normal population (when nothing is done to them), we would expect treatment/effect variability to be 0, and we would end up with error over error. Any number over itself equals 1:

$$\frac{BG_{\text{variability}}}{WG_{\text{variability}}} = \frac{0 + 27.33}{27.33} = \frac{27.33}{27.33} = 1.00$$

(In this example, I used 27.33 as the error variance, but of course we will need to calculate variance for each example with raw data.)

Using your knowledge of the null hypothesis, what number would you expect to find for the ANOVA if the IV has no effect? Based on our discussion above, you would expect to find error over error, which would equal 1. The ANOVA value, theoretically, will not be less than 1, since treatment/effect variability cannot be less than 0. In other words, if nothing happens in an experiment (the null hypothesis is true), treatment/effect will be 0. If an effect occurs, the effect will be larger than 0. It should be obvious that when you conduct an experiment, you want treatment/effect variability to be large, so you hope for a number far above 1.

Based on this logic, it would be impossible for the distribution to have a normal shape (symmetrical about the middle). Because the numbers can only be 1 or greater, the distribution must be positively skewed, where obtained values only in the upper tail are possible. You no longer have to choose between a one-tailed or two-tailed test; every test of the ANOVA will be one-tailed.

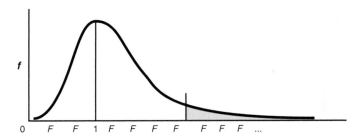

A small proportion of the distribution is below a value of 1, because occasionally a number slips below 1. This can occur when error variability between groups is a bit smaller than error variability within groups—just sampling error differences. Even though a number between 0 and 1 is theoretically impossible, sampling error sometimes allows it to happen. However, it is mathematically impossible for the ANOVA number to slip below 0, so if the ANOVA ever yields a negative number, something definitely went wrong during calculations.

The null hypothesis indicates that if nothing happens, numbers under all levels of the IV will be the same. If the IV has three levels, write that all three groups are equal (that is, all three groups would be expected to be equal in the population if no effect was found).

$$H_0: \mu_1 = \mu_2 = \mu_3$$

The alternative hypothesis indicates that at least two of the groups are different from each other, and no symbols are needed.

H_1: At least two of the groups are significantly different from each other.

It would not be accurate to write

H_1: $\mu_1 \neq \mu_2 \neq \mu_3$

As written, this indicates that all three groups must be significantly different from each other to accept that something happened in the experiment. However, it would not be necessary to find that all of the groups are different. If at least two of the groups are significantly different from each other, the IV caused changes in the DV (or the quasi-IV and DV are related), and we have something interesting to report. That is why we leave it open with

H_1: At least two of the groups are significantly different from each other.

One-way, Between-groups ANOVA: Equal *n*

This section will cover ANOVA calculations, but keep in mind the logic discussed above. As an example of an ANOVA design, imagine that one of your friends wears too much perfume. You would like to let her know that people find the smell unpleasant, but you think she might not believe you; therefore, you conduct a study to try to indicate that too much perfume is offensive. On the first day of the experiment, you wear no perfume and ask students to rate your odor on a scale from 1 to 5, with 1 being very unpleasant and 5 being very pleasant. On the second day, you put on a small amount of perfume and ask a different group of students to rate how you smell. On the third day of the experiment, you wear as much perfume as your friend and ask different students on campus to rate your scent. Note that different people sniff, which means this is a between-groups design. The IV is amount of perfume, and the DV is ratings of odor. Below are your data:

No perfume	A small amount of perfume	A large amount of perfume
3	4	1
4	2	2
3	5	1
5	4	1
4	5	3
3	4	2
3	3	1
4	5	2

Before we examine the between-groups and within-groups variability, the first step is to calculate all of the variability in the data set (total variability). Then we will figure out the between-groups variability (which contains effect variability and some error/individual differences). Finally, we will calculate the within-groups variability (a pure measure of error/individual differences).

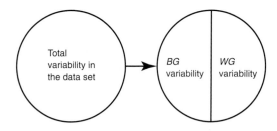

$$Total_{variability} = BG_{variability} + WG_{variability}$$

Total variability is divided into *BG* and *WG* variability. Although the null hypothesis states that *BG* and *WG* variability will be equal, we hope *BG* takes a greater portion of Total variability than *WG*, because *BG* contains any treatment effect.

Variability in ANOVA is called **sum of squares**, abbreviated **SS**. The formula for total variability is:

$$SS_{tot} = \sum X_{tot}^2 - \frac{\left(\sum X_{tot}\right)^2}{N}$$

This should look familiar to you because it is the numerator for variance (from Chapter 4).

Prepare the data with squared columns and sums.

X_1	$X_1{}^2$	X_2	$X_2{}^2$	X_3	$X_3{}^2$
None		*Small*		*Large*	
3	9	4	16	1	1
4	16	2	4	2	4
3	9	5	25	1	1
5	25	4	16	1	1
4	16	5	25	3	9
3	9	4	16	2	4
3	9	3	9	1	1
4	16	5	25	2	4
29	**109**	32	**136**	13	**25**

Add all bolded numbers together (109, 136, 25) to get the total sum of X^2. Then put the number in the first part of the formula. Likewise, add the unbolded numbers (29, 32, 13) to get the sum of *X*; the number goes in the second part of the formula—squared and divided by *N*, which is 24 for the whole data set:

$$SS_{tot} = 270 - \frac{(74)^2}{24} = 270 - \frac{5476}{24} = 270 - 228.1666667 = 41.833333$$

Because all of the variability in the data set is 41.833333, the between-groups variability we will soon calculate cannot possibly be higher than 41.833333.

Now calculate the between-groups variability using this formula:

$$SS_{BG} = \sum \left(\frac{(\text{Column Total})^2}{n} \right) - \left(\frac{(\sum X_{tot})^2}{N} \right)$$

The formula can be rewritten to show each column (in this example, three):

$$SS_{BG} = \left(\frac{(\sum X_1)^2}{n_1} + \frac{(\sum X_2)^2}{n_2} + \frac{(\sum X_3)^2}{n_3} \right) - \left(\frac{(\sum X_{tot})^2}{N} \right)$$

Remember that $\sum$ means to add, and small n is the number in each column. Simplifying the formula reveals SS_{BG}:

$$SS_{BG} = \left(\frac{(29)^2}{8} + \frac{(32)^2}{8} + \frac{(13)^2}{8} \right) - \left(\frac{(74)^2}{24} \right)$$

$$SS_{BG} = \left(\frac{841}{8} + \frac{1024}{8} + \frac{169}{8} \right) - \left(\frac{5476}{24} \right)$$

$$SS_{BG} = 105.125 + 128 + 21.125 - 228.166667 = 26.083333$$

We now have a number for all of the variability in the data set and a number for between-groups variability. Find within-groups variability using subtraction:

$$SS_{tot} - SS_{BG} = SS_{WG}$$

$$41.833333 - 26.083333 = 15.75$$

The total variability was merely used as a stepping stone to calculate the within-groups portion, and we will not use the total variability again. Focus on the two important sources of variability: between-groups and within-groups. The final calculation for each of these portions of variability involves dividing SS by the appropriate degrees of freedom to get a **mean square**, abbreviated **MS**. Dividing by degrees of freedom to complete each variability term is not new; variability terms in all three t-tests (Chapter 8) contained degrees of freedom as the denominator. In the estimated population standard deviation of both the single-sample and related-samples t-tests, df was calculated with $N - 1$ (using the number of values in the D column for related samples). In the independent-samples t-test, the estimated population variance pooled contained a denominator of $(n_1 - 1) + (n_2 - 1)$ for degrees of freedom. The same logic is followed to complete the MS_{BG} and MS_{WG} for ANOVA, with slight changes in the df formulas.

For between-groups variability, divide the SS_{BG} by $k - 1$, where k is the number of levels of the IV. In this example, $k = 3$, so $k - 1 = 2$ ($df_{BG} = 2$):

$$MS_{BG} = \frac{SS_{BG}}{k - 1} = \frac{26.083333}{2} = 13.041667$$

MS_{BG} is the variability between the conditions of the experiment—between the levels of the IV. Recall that this type of variability contains any treatment effect, as well as some individual differences.

For a measure of pure individual differences (error), divide the within-groups variability by its degrees of freedom. The formula for df_{WG} is $N - k$, and you already know that N is the number of values in the entire data set (24) and k is the number of levels of the IV (3). For this example, within-groups $df = 21$:

$$MS_{WG} = \frac{SS_{WG}}{N - k} = \frac{15.75}{21} = 0.75$$

Before we began these calculations, our goal was to get a numerator for between-groups variability and a denominator for within-groups variability to create an ANOVA ratio. We now have the two sources of variability and can complete the final calculation for ANOVA:

$$\frac{MS_{BG}}{MS_{WG}} = \frac{13.041667}{0.75} = 17.388889, \text{rounded to } 17.39$$

This final number is called the **F-ratio**, and it is the obtained value in ANOVA: F_{obt}.

Following the same procedure as the *t*-test, the next step is to find a critical value, put it on the distribution, and see where the obtained (calculated) value falls. To get the F_{crit}, we look up degrees of freedom for between-groups and within-groups numbers. The between-groups df was 2, and the within-groups df was 21. On the *F*-table, between-groups df is across the top of the chart, and within-groups df is down the left side of the chart. The column and row intersect in the table, with most researchers focusing on a 0.05 level of significance. The bolded number in the table is the F_{crit} for 0.05 and can be placed in the upper tail of the distribution:

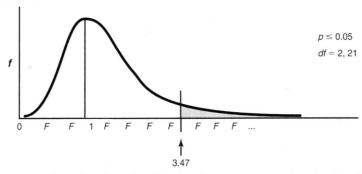

When the F_{obt} is also placed on the distribution, we can see that the F_{obt} falls in the rejection (critical) region:

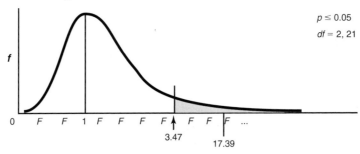

A significant *F*-test means we reject the null hypothesis. At least two of the groups (levels of the IV) were significantly different from each other.

Organizing ANOVA Results

The calculations for ANOVA can be organized using a summary table, a chart produced by SPSS when data are analyzed using the computer.

Source	SS	df	MS	F_{obt}	p
BG	26.083333	2	13.041667	17.39	<0.05
WG	15.75	21	0.75		
Total	41.833333	23			

Notes

1. "Source" refers to sources of variability. We calculated three pieces (sources) of variability: total variability in the data set, between-groups, and within-groups variability.
2. The formula for *df* of total variability is simply $N - 1$, since total variability deals with the entire data set.
3. The SS numbers for BG and WG can be added to get SS_{tot}. The *df* numbers for BG and WG can also be added to get the *df* total.
4. MS numbers are never added together; there is no MS for total.
5. After SS_{tot} and SS_{BG} are calculated, remaining values in the summary table can be obtained quite easily. Take a moment to notice the relationships among numbers in the table. SS divided by the *df* to the right provides MS. MS_{BG} divided by the MS_{WG} below it will yield the F_{obt}.

APA Style

APA style must include both *df* in parentheses, rather than the one number we have seen with *t*-test *df*. For the perfume example, APA style is:

$$F(2, 21) = 17.39, p < 0.05.$$

The null hypothesis is rejected, and the alternative hypothesis remains:

H_1: At least two groups were significantly different from each other.

Effect Size

To find the size of a significant effect, eta squared is calculated to learn how much of SS_{tot} can be attributed to between-group variability:

$$\eta^2 = \frac{SS_{BG}}{SS_{tot}}$$

For this example:

$$\eta^2 = \frac{26.083333}{41.833333} = 0.623506, \text{ rounded to } 0.62$$

Eta squared represents the proportion of variability in the DV accounted for by changing the levels of the IV. Values range from 0 to 1, with a higher number illustrating a larger effect. A small effect would be approximately 0.10; a moderate effect would be around 0.30; and a strong effect would be about 0.50 and greater. For this example, a large amount of variability in the DV is explained by knowing what level of perfume is being examined.

Eta squared multiplied by 100 provides the percent of variability in the DV explained by knowing the IV level. In this example, 62% of the variability in ratings of odor can be explained simply by knowing how much perfume a person is wearing. Again, 62% is a large amount of explained variability and indicates a strong effect.

Post-hoc Testing: Tukey's HSD

Based on our analysis, we know that people rated you as smelling significantly different across levels of perfume. Unfortunately, the ANOVA does not tell us which amounts of perfume were different from each other. With the *t*-test, a significant difference was easy to understand; because we only had two groups, we knew which two groups were different from each other. Since we have three groups in this example, we are not sure which groups are significantly different, and we have three possible combinations of group pairs:

No perfume – A small amount
No perfume – A large amount
A small amount – A large amount

Only after the ANOVA is significant are we allowed to compare the group means to find out which pairs are significantly different from each other. This is accomplished with **post-hoc tests**—tests named for being conducted after (post) the ANOVA. One type of post-hoc test is used for equal *n* across conditions (like this example, where the *n* of each column is 8), and a different type of post-hoc test is used for unequal *n* across conditions. We will begin with the one for equal *n* to complete this example.

Tukey's HSD is the post-hoc test used to analyze a significant ANOVA with more than two groups and equal *n*. HSD stands for honestly significant difference, to indicate that the means being compared are truly different (not just sampling error). After we calculate the HSD value for this example, any groups that are different by at least the HSD value will be considered to have an honestly significant difference.

Because we want to know if groups differ, we have to first calculate the differences between pairs of means using subtraction. Absolute values are fine and will reflect how different two values are. The means and their differences can be represented this way:

Amount of Perfume

None	Small	Large
3.625	4.00	1.625

0.375   2.375

Mean Differences

2.00

Tukey's HSD value is calculated using the following formula:

$$\text{HSD} = q\left(\sqrt{\frac{MS_{WG}}{n}}\right)$$

The q is found in a table at the back of the book; find it using k and $N - k$. Across the top of the table, locate the 3 (for k). Be careful not to look up $k - 1$ across the top of the table, as we did for the F value. Down the left side of the table is $N - k$, which is 21 for this example. The table does not have 21, therefore the next lowest *df* number is chosen to maintain a conservative test. The closest number below 21 in the table is 20. The 3 and 20 intersect in the table at a bolded q value of 3.58, for a significance level of 0.05: The remaining pieces of information for the following formula are already known for this example.

$$\text{HSD} = 3.58\left(\sqrt{\frac{0.75}{8}}\right) = 3.58\left(\sqrt{0.09375}\right) = 1.096147$$

Now that we know how different two groups have to be for an honestly significant difference, we can look back at the group differences to see which pairs were different enough. Placing asterisks in the upper right-hand corner of mean differences identifies them as at or above the HSD value:

Amount of Perfume

	None	Small	Large
Means	3.625	4.00	1.625

	0.375	2.375*	
Mean Differences			
	2.00*		

With a difference of 2.375, a small amount and a large amount of perfume were rated as smelling significantly different from each other. No perfume and a large amount were also different, with a difference value of 2.00. However, no perfume and a small amount were not significantly different from each other.

Plain English

We are finally ready to share the specifics of our results in plain English. Does the amount of perfume affect ratings of scent? Yes. The absence of perfume or a small amount smells better than a large amount of perfume. No perfume and a small amount smell equally pleasant.

Confidence Intervals

Confidence intervals should be calculated for each group that was significantly different from another group. In this example, no perfume and a small amount of perfume were different from a large amount of perfume; therefore, all three groups were represented in the discussion of significance, and all three groups will need confidence intervals calculated separately using the following formula:

$$\left(\sqrt{\frac{MS_{wg}}{n}}\right)(-t_{crit}) + \overline{X} \le \mu \le \left(\sqrt{\frac{MS_{wg}}{n}}\right)(+t_{crit}) + \overline{X}$$

The $\pm t_{crit}$ is found in the *t*-table using $N - k\ df$, which is 21 in this example. MS_{WG} for this example is 0.75. Small n and $\overline{X}$ are specific to each level of the IV under consideration.

First, in the population, what would be the likely range of smell ratings when someone wears no perfume? Concentrating on the no-perfume group, with an average odor rating of 3.625, the lower range for a 95% confidence interval is:

$$\left(\sqrt{\frac{0.75}{8}}\right)(-2.080) + 3.625 = 2.99$$

and the upper range for a 95% confidence interval is:

$$\left(\sqrt{\frac{0.75}{8}}\right)(2.080) + 3.625 = 4.26$$

Thus, wearing no perfume would be rated as smelling between 2.99 and 4.26 on our odor scale from 1 to 5, by 95% of the population:

$$2.99 \le \mu \le 4.26$$

Next, a small amount of perfume would be rated between 3.36 and 4.64 on the odor scale by most of the people in the population:

$$\left(\sqrt{\frac{0.75}{8}}\right)(-2.080) + 4.00 \le \mu \le \left(\sqrt{\frac{0.75}{8}}\right)(2.080) + 4.00$$

$$3.36 \le \mu \le 4.64$$

Finally, a large amount of perfume would be rated between 0.99 and 2.26 odor by the majority of the population of people who smelled it:

$$\left(\sqrt{\frac{0.75}{8}}\right)(-2.080) + 1.625 \le \mu \le \left(\sqrt{\frac{0.75}{8}}\right)(2.080) + 1.625$$

$$0.99 \le \mu \le 2.26$$

In summary, the amount of perfume worn affected ratings of odor by participants. The effect was quite large, with 62% of the variability in odor ratings explained by knowing how much perfume a person wore. Specific comparisons between group means revealed that a large amount of perfume smelled worse than a small amount or none at all. In the general population, a large amount of perfume is likely to be rated between 0.99 and 2.26 on an odor scale of 1 to 5, with lower numbers meaning a worse smell. A small amount of perfume is likely to be rated as better smelling, between 3.36 and 4.64. Finally, no perfume will be rated between 2.99 and 4.26 by most people in the population.

One-way, Between-groups ANOVA: Unequal n

The logic and calculations of ANOVA do not change when levels of the IV have an unequal number of participants (unequal n), but post-hoc testing will differ if the F_{obt} is found to be significant. For practice, we will examine a second ANOVA example, followed by a new type of post-hoc test for unequal n.

You have probably heard about DARE, a drug-use prevention program implemented in schools by law-enforcement officers and funded by federal dollars. Research suggests that students, teachers, parents, and administrators have a positive attitude toward the program (Berg, 1997; Blasik & Belsito, 1993; Curtis, 1999; Fife, 1994). Fictional data evaluating attitudes toward a drug-use prevention program are presented below using three levels of one IV. Students were randomly assigned to receive a drug-use prevention program provided by either their parents, teachers, or DARE police officers. The DV is students' attitudes toward the program on a scale from 1 to 10, with higher numbers representing more positive attitudes.

The null hypothesis indicates that the three groups will be equal.

$H_0: \mu_1 = \mu_2 = \mu_3$

In the alternative hypothesis:

H_1: At least two of the levels are significantly different from each other.

The analysis is the one-way, between-groups ANOVA.
Raw data from the study are as follow:

Parents' Program	Teachers' Program	DARE Officers
5	7	8
7	9	10
3	7	6
5	8	7
8	7	8
4	9	6
7		9
		8

First, calculate all of the variability in the data set with SS_{tot}. Then calculate SS_{BG} for the portion that contains treatment effect. Finally, subtract SS_{BG} from SS_{tot} to get SS_{WG}, the variability term that offers a pure measure of error.

X_1	$X_1{}^2$	X_2	$X_2{}^2$	X_3	$X_3{}^2$
Parents		Teachers		Officers	
5	25	7	49	8	64
7	49	9	81	10	100
3	9	7	49	6	36
5	25	8	64	7	49
8	64	7	49	8	64
4	16	9	81	6	36
7	49			9	81
				8	64
39	237	47	373	62	494

First, the SS_{tot}:

$$SS_{tot} = 1104 - \frac{(148)^2}{21} = 1104 - 1043.047619 = 60.952381$$

Second, SS_{BG}:

$$SS_{BG} = \left(\frac{(39)^2}{7} + \frac{(47)^2}{6} + \frac{(62)^2}{8}\right) - \left(\frac{(148)^2}{21}\right)$$

$$SS_{BG} = 217.285714 + 368.166667 + 480.50 - 1043.047619$$

$$SS_{BG} = 22.904762$$

Third, SS_{WG}:

$$SS_{WG} = 60.952381 - 22.904762 = 38.047619$$

At this point, you might find it useful to put the SS portions in a summary table.

Source	SS	df	MS	F	P
BG	22.904762				
WG	38.047619				
Total	60.952381				

The remaining calculations for MS and F_{obt} can be completed:

MS_{BG}:

$$MS_{BG} = \frac{SS_{BG}}{k-1} = \frac{22.904762}{2} = 11.452381$$

MS_{WG}:

$$MS_{WG} = \frac{SS_{WG}}{N-k} = \frac{38.047619}{18} = 2.113757$$

F_{obt}:

$$F_{\text{obt}} = \frac{MS_{\text{BG}}}{MS_{\text{WG}}} = \frac{11.452381}{2.113757} = 5.418022$$

Rounded, our final answer for F_{obt} is 5.42.

A comparison of F_{obt} and F_{crit} reveals that the F_{obt} falls in the region of rejection, allowing us to reject the null hypothesis:

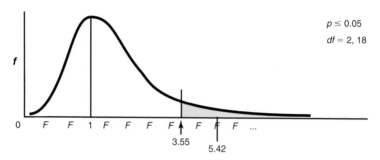

At least two of the groups were significantly different from each other.

Summary Table

Source	SS	df	MS	F_{obt}	F_{crit}	p	APA Style
Program	22.904762	2	11.452381	5.42	3.55	<0.05	$F(2, 18) = 5.42, p < 0.05$
Error	38.047619	18	2.113757				
Total	60.952381	20					

Notes

1. Instead of using *BG* and *WG* for sources of variability, the *BG* can be named for the IV being studied (Program), and *WG* can be labeled Error.
2. F_{crit} and APA style will not be found in the SPSS summary table. I have included them here for review.

Effect Size

Because the person offering the DARE program significantly affected attitudes toward the program, eta squared is calculated to indicate effect size:

$$\eta^2 = \frac{SS_{\text{BG}}}{SS_{\text{tot}}}$$

For this example

$$\eta^2 = \frac{22.904762}{60.952381} = 0.375781, \text{ rounded to } 0.38$$

Eta squared of 0.38 depicts a moderate amount of variability in attitudes explained by knowing who taught the program. In other words, 38% of the variability in the DV can be explained by knowing what level of the IV participants received.

Post-hoc Testing: Fisher's Protected t-tests

The ANOVA was significant, requiring post-hoc testing of the three means to identify which means are significantly different from each other. With unequal numbers (n) in the groups, Tukey's HSD is not appropriate because the formula only allows one n in the denominator. With unequal n, **Fisher's protected t-tests** are used. These tests are called protected because they are designed to remain conservative when looking for significant differences between several pairs of means. For our drug-use prevention example, the groups have unequal n; therefore, Fisher's t-tests offer the appropriate post-hoc analysis.

This post hoc employs t-tests, an analysis covered in Chapter 8. The formula for Fisher's protected t-test changes slightly for each comparison between two means. Below is the formula and outcome for a comparison of the first and second means using our DARE example:

$$t_{obt} = \frac{\overline{X}_1 - \overline{X}_2}{\sqrt{MS_{WG}\left(\dfrac{1}{n_1} + \dfrac{1}{n_2}\right)}} = \frac{5.571429 - 7.833333}{\sqrt{2.114\left(\dfrac{1}{7} + \dfrac{1}{6}\right)}} = -2.80$$

After we calculate the t_{obt} value, it is compared with t_{crit} based on $N - k\ df$ (18 in this example) for a two-tailed test: ± 2.101. As always, if the t_{obt} is further in the tail than t_{crit}, the two groups are significantly different from each other.

A t-test for groups 1 and 3, then groups 2 and 3, requires a change of means in the numerator and n in the denominator:

$$t_{obt} = \frac{\overline{X}_1 - \overline{X}_3}{\sqrt{MS_{WG}\left(\dfrac{1}{n_1} + \dfrac{1}{n_3}\right)}} = \frac{5.571429 - 7.75}{\sqrt{2.114\left(\dfrac{1}{7} + \dfrac{1}{8}\right)}} = -2.90$$

$$t_{obt} = \frac{\overline{X}_2 - \overline{X}_3}{\sqrt{MS_{WG}\left(\dfrac{1}{n_2} + \dfrac{1}{n_3}\right)}} = \frac{7.833333 - 7.75}{\sqrt{2.114\left(\dfrac{1}{6} + \dfrac{1}{8}\right)}} = 0.11$$

To keep these data organized, we might want to lay out our means again, and this time put in the t-values calculated for each pair. An asterisk in the upper right corner demonstrates a t_{obt} beyond t_{crit}:

	Parents	Teachers	Officers
Means	5.571429	7.833333	7.75

t_{obt} = 2.80* (Parents–Teachers)

t_{obt} = 0.11 (Teachers–Officers)

t_{obt} = -2.90* (Parents–Officers)

t_{obt} Values

Plain English

Based on Fisher's protected *t*-tests, we found that students who were taught drug-use prevention by teachers or DARE officers had better attitudes toward the program than students taught drug-use prevention by their parents. Students who received the program from teachers and those who learned from DARE officers reported similar attitudes.

Confidence Intervals

Each level of the IV (parents, teachers, and officers) was significantly different from at least one other group; therefore, confidence intervals for all three groups may be calculated:

$$\left(\sqrt{\frac{MS_{WG}}{n}}\right)(-t_{crit}) + \overline{X} \le \mu \le \left(\sqrt{\frac{MS_{WG}}{n}}\right)(t_{crit}) + \overline{X}$$

For parents:

$$\left(\sqrt{\frac{2.113757}{7}}\right)(-2.101) + 5.571429 \le \mu \le \left(\sqrt{\frac{2.113757}{7}}\right)(2.101) + 5.571429$$

$$4.42 \le \mu \le 6.73$$

In the general population, attitudes toward a parent-taught DARE course would have a 95% chance of falling between 4.42 and 6.73 on a scale of attitudes ranging from 1 to 10.

For teachers:

$$\left(\sqrt{\frac{2.113757}{6}}\right)(-2.101) + 7.833333 \le \mu \le \left(\sqrt{\frac{2.113757}{6}}\right)(2.101) + 7.833333$$

$$6.59 < \mu < 9.08$$

In the population, attitudes toward a DARE program taught by teachers would probably fall between 6.59 and 9.08.

Finally, for officers:

$$\left(\sqrt{\frac{2.113757}{8}}\right)(-2.101) + 7.75 \le \mu \le \left(\sqrt{\frac{2.113757}{8}}\right)(2.101) + 7.75$$

$$6.67 \le \mu \le 8.83$$

When the DARE program is taught by officers, approximately 95% of students in the population would rate their attitudes toward the program between 6.67 and 8.83.

In summary, attitudes toward the DARE program were significantly affected by who offered the program, with a moderate effect size of 0.38. Group comparisons illustrated that students had better attitudes toward the program when it was taught by teachers or officers than when it was taught by parents. In the general population of students, attitudes toward the program taught by parents are likely to range from 4.42 to 6.73; whereas, attitudes are likely to fall between 6.59 and 9.08 for teachers and 6.67 and 8.83 for officers who teach the program.

One-way, Between-groups ANOVA on SPSS

The one-way, between-groups ANOVA and post-hoc comparisons are analyzed on SPSS in the same data run, and both will be outlined here. In SPSS, Tukey's HSD can be used for post-hoc analysis regardless of unequal n; the program makes adjustments in the formula to accommodate unequal n. We will be analyzing our drug-use prevention program example in SPSS.

First, remember that participants in the independent-samples t-test and the between-groups ANOVA come into the experiment with nothing in common. When we analyzed an independent-samples t-test, we had to string out data into two columns for SPSS input. The same layout is needed for the between-groups ANOVA, but instead of only two levels of the IV, in this example we have three levels: programs from parents, teachers, and DARE officers. The first column, then, will be the IV (programs) with three levels, coded as 1, 2, and 3. The second column will be the DV (attitude), where we will enter the attitude ratings of each participant beside the appropriate level of the IV.

	programs	attitude
1	1.00	5.00
2	1.00	7.00
3	1.00	3.00
4	1.00	5.00
5	1.00	8.00
6	1.00	4.00
7	1.00	7.00
8	2.00	7.00
9	2.00	9.00
10	2.00	7.00
11	2.00	8.00
12	2.00	7.00
13	2.00	9.00
14	3.00	8.00
15	3.00	10.00
16	3.00	6.00
17	3.00	7.00
18	3.00	8.00
19	3.00	6.00
20	3.00	9.00
21	3.00	8.00

As in Chapter 8, click View+Variables to label the levels of the IV.

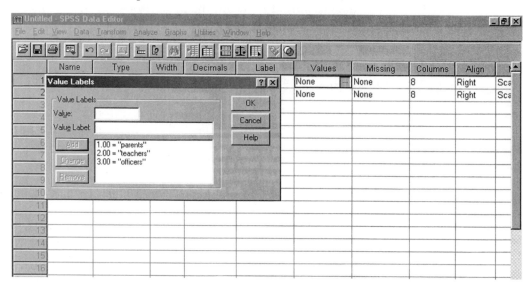

Click OK to remove the gray box, click View+Data to return to the data, then click View+Value Labels to reveal the names of IV levels.

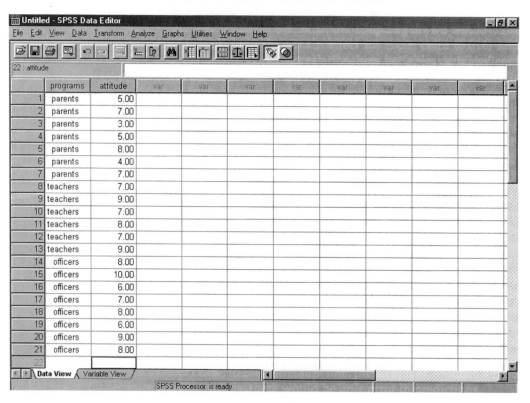

Click Analyze+General Linear Model+Univariate.

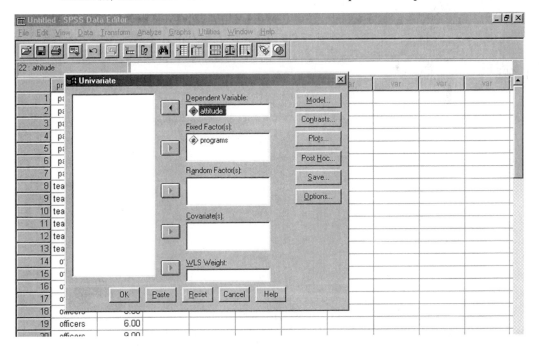

In the gray box that opens, select programs and click it into the space for Fixed Factor(s), then select **attitude** and click it into the space for Dependent Variable.

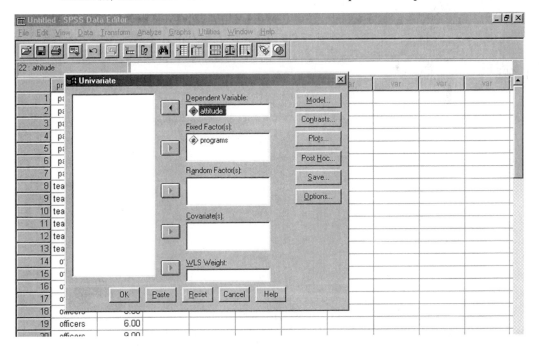

Next, click Options. In the gray box, select programs and click it over to the right. Then check Descriptive statistics and click Continue.

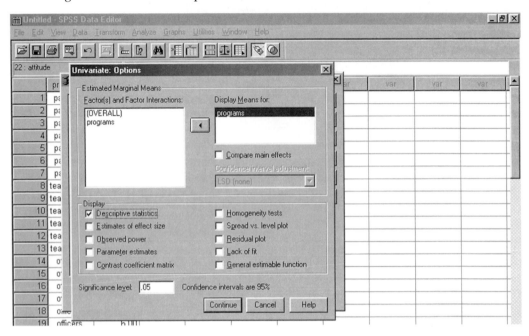

Again select programs and click it to the right. Check Tukey, then click Continue.

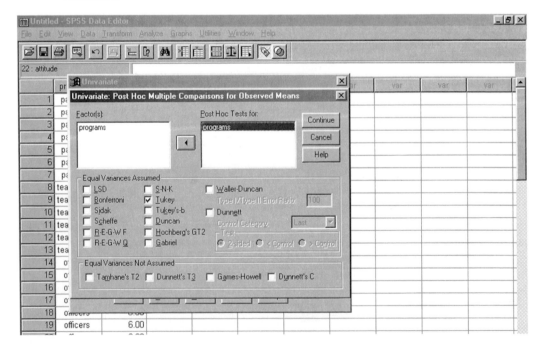

Click OK for output.

Univariate Analysis of Variance

Between-Subjects Factors

		Value Label	N
PROGRAMS	1.00	parents	7
	2.00	teachers	6
	3.00	officers	8

Descriptive Statistics

Dependent Variable: ATTITUDE

PROGRAMS	Mean	Std. Deviation	N
parents	5.5714	1.81265	7
teachers	7.8333	.98319	6
officers	7.7500	1.38873	8
Total	7.0476	1.74574	21

Tests of Between-Subjects Effects

Dependent Variable: ATTITUDE

Source	Type III Sum of Squares	df	Mean Square	F	Sig.
Corrected Model	22.905[a]	2	11.452	5.418	.014
Intercept	1029.918	1	1029.918	487.245	.000
PROGRAMS	22.905	2	11.452	5.418	.014
Error	38.048	18	2.114		
Total	1104.000	21			
Corrected Total	60.952	20			

a. R Squared = .376 (Adjusted R Squared = .306)

Estimated Marginal Means

PROGRAMS

Dependent Variable: ATTITUDE

PROGRAMS	Mean	Std. Error	95% Confidence Interval	
			Lower Bound	Upper Bound
parents	5.571	.550	4.417	6.726
teachers	7.833	.594	6.586	6.080
officers	7.750	.514	6.670	8.830

Post Hoc Tests

PROGRAMS

Multiple Comparisons

Dependent Variable: ATTITUDE
Tukey HSD

(I) PROGRAMS	(J) PROGRAMS	Mean Difference (I-J)	Std. Error	Sig.	95% Confidence Interval	
					Lower Bound	Upper Bound
parents	teachers	−2.2619*	.80886	.031	−4.3263	−.1975
	officers	−2.1786*	.75245	.025	−4.0990	−.2582
teachers	parents	−2.2619*	.80886	.031	.1975	4.3263
	officers	.0833	.78518	.994	−1.9206	2.0873
officers	parents	−2.1788*	.75245	.025	.2582	4.0990
	teachers	−.0833	.78518	.994	−2.0873	1.9206

Based on observed means.
* The mean difference is significant at the .05 level.

Homogeneous Subsets

ATTITUDE

Tukey HSD[a, b, c]

PROGRAMS	N	Subset	
		1	2
parents	7	5.5714	
officers	8		7.7500
teachers	6		7.8333
Sig.		1.000	.994

Means for groups in homogeneous subsets are displayed.
Based on Type III Sum of Squares
The error term is Mean Square(Error) = 2.114.
  a. Uses Harmonic Mean Sample Size = 6.904.
  b. The group sizes are unequal. The harmonic mean of the group sizes is used. Type I error levels are not guaranteed.
  c. Alpha = .05.

The Descriptive Statistics table provides the means and standard deviations, but the Estimated Marginal Means table is preferred, because it provides standard error of the mean (*SEM*). Means and *SEM*s are often reported in an APA-style result section and are used when graphing data. (We graphed with standard deviation in Chapter 4 because we needed a measure of variability, and *SEM* had not yet been introduced.)

The ANOVA summary table is labeled Tests of Between-Subjects Effects and contains more rows of data than were calculated by hand earlier in this chapter. Take this opportunity to notice which rows are relevant. The third row begins with a capitalized PROGRAMS, and the numbers should match what was calculated for between-groups variability. Immediately below that line is Error, which is also relevant and familiar. Finally, the Corrected Total row is needed, as indicated by the correct *MS* and *df* to the right.

The last important part of the output is the post-hoc table. Focus on the significance value for each mean comparison. Groups 1 and 2 (parents and teachers, respectively) were significantly different, since the significance value is 0.031, which is below the necessary 0.05 cut-off value needed. The next comparison on the chart is between groups 1 and 3 (parents and officers), and these groups were significantly different, with a p-value of 0.025. The third comparison is between groups 2 and 1, but it would of course be the same outcome as 1 vs. 2, so it is not necessary to restate the comparison. The fourth comparison in the chart is between groups 2 and 3, with a significance value of 0.994; therefore, programs offered by teachers and officers did not differ. The remaining two comparisons in the table are repeated comparisons and should be ignored. The post-hoc table gives specific p-values for each of the three comparisons needed, showing us once again that a drug-use prevention program offered by teachers or officers was liked better by students than a program offered by parents.

APA-style Results Section

A results section for these data follows:

Results

A one-way, between-groups ANOVA was used to analyze these data. A significant effect was further analyzed using Tukey's HSD comparisons ($p < 0.05$). Providers of drug-use prevention programs affected student attitudes, $F(2, 18) = 5.42, p < 0.05$, with an effect size of 0.38. When teachers ($M = 7.83$, $SEM = 0.59, n = 6$) or officers ($M = 7.75, SEM = 0.51, n = 8$) presented the program, student attitudes toward the program were more positive than when parents ($M = 5.57, SEM = 0.55, n = 7$) presented the drug-use prevention program. Student attitudes toward programs presented by teachers and officers were similar ($p > 0.05$).

In the results section above, the ANOVA value was reported as $F(2, 18) = 5.42$, $p < 0.05$ to be consistent with our hand calculations earlier in the chapter; however, SPSS provided a more specific result of $p = 0.01$, and this alternative can be used to report results:

$$F(2, 18) = 5.42, p = 0.01$$

Preview of Chapter 10

Now that you understand the one-way, between-groups ANOVA, you can analyze data sets that are larger than one IV with two levels, as long as different participants are in each condition. When the ANOVA is significant, move forward with Tukey's post-hoc comparisons if the data set contains equal n across conditions, or use Fisher's protected t-tests if conditions have unequal n. (SPSS is able to use Tukey's for both equal and unequal n.)

The repeated-measures ANOVA, in which each participant is tested under all IV conditions, will also require post-hoc analysis of means when significant. Appendix A covers analysis of the repeated-measures (within-groups) ANOVA using SPSS. Of course, post-hoc testing for a repeated-measure ANOVA will always be Tukey's HSD, because equal n is guaranteed when the same participants are tested under every level of the IV.

In Chapter 10, you will learn how to analyze a data set with two between-group IVs rather than just one, and you will need to follow up significant F-values with post-hoc tests again. One post-hoc for the two-way ANOVA must be analyzed by hand even when using SPSS, so it is helpful that you learned how to calculate both Tukey's HSD and Fisher's protected t-tests in this chapter.

Conceptual Items

1. Define the following:
   a. three-way ANOVA
   b. between-groups factor
   c. within-groups factor
   d. treatment variability
   e. error variability
   f. F_{crit}

2. What the null hypothesis is true, F_{obt} will equal _____.

3. Write the null hypothesis for a one-way ANOVA with five levels.

4. Write the alternative hypothesis for a one-way ANOVA with any number of levels.

5. How do the following pairs of terms differ from each other?
   a. Between-groups factor vs. between-groups variability
   b. Within-groups factor vs. within-groups variability
   c. One-tailed vs. one-way

6. What type of analysis is generally used to analyze an IV with two levels? Discuss the possibility that the ANOVA can be used to analyze a factor with only two levels.

7. Logically, if a MS_{tot} was created from the SS_{tot}, what formula would be used for degrees of freedom in the denominator?

8. A significant effect after random assignment to conditions indicates that the IV caused changes in the DV. If a study between year in college and maturity level yielded a significant F_{obt} value, would the result indicate that year in college *caused* changes in maturity levels? Why or why not?

Application Items

9. You want to figure out what kind of boy attracts high-school girls. High-school girls were randomly assigned to hear about either a guy with trendy clothes, a nice car, or a confident attitude, then they rated him on a scale from 1 to 10, with 1 being, "not interested" and 10 being "very interested." Here are the ratings given by your participants:

Trendy Clothes	Nice Car	Confident Attitude
8	6	10
6	7	9
9	8	10
6	6	10
8	4	8
6	5	9
7	5	10
6	6	9
6	8	8

   a. Lay out the H_0 and H_1 hypotheses.
   b. Choose a statistic to analyze this study (be specific).
   c. Sketch the distribution of normal people, and include the p-value, degrees of freedom, and F_{crit}.
   d. Analyze these data, and prepare a summary table of your results.
   e. Put your answer in APA style, and reject or fail to reject the null hypothesis.
   f. Were at least two groups significantly different from each other?
   g. If appropriate, calculate the size of the effect.
   h. If needed, conduct post-hoc testing in an organized way.
   i. Calculate confidence intervals for relevant groups means.
   j. Completely analyze this data set using SPSS.
   k. Based on your results, what did you learn from this study?

For the following items, address a-k from Application Item 9 above.

10. Vacation spot might affect length of vacation, with better locations causing people to stay longer. To test this possibility, we might randomly assign American participants to visit Paris, Madrid, Las Vegas, or New Orleans, then wait to see how many days they stay.

Paris	Madrid	Las Vegas	New Orleans
8	9	3	4
12	10	3	8
7	12	2	3
13	14	5	2
11	8	6	2
9		4	6

11. Examine the data below, representing several types of punishment used to discipline children and the effect of these punishers on behavior, on a scale from 1 to 10, with higher numbers indicating better behavior. Children were randomly assigned to receive one of the following types of punishers:

A Lecture	Yelling	Time-Out	Spanking
9	4	7	2
8	6	8	1
5	4	5	3
7	8	9	4
6	7	4	3
3	6	2	5

12. If someone told you that ethnicity and leadership were related, you might want to find out for yourself if the statement was true. To do this, you could collect data on the number of leadership activities people of different ethnicities engaged in over the past year. Your data might be similar to the following:

Native American	Asian	Hispanic
5	7	8
10	9	4
3	5	7
12	6	10
7	10	8
3	7	9
8		

13. Some people suggest that students become more comfortable with ambiguity as they experience higher education. Imagine that comfort with ambiguous knowledge is measured using a standardized test yielding scores from 0 to 100, with higher numbers indicating more comfort with ambiguous answers. Examine the following data and decide if this idea is supported. In addition to addressing items a-k (Application Item 9), decide if cause and effect have been established.

Freshperson	Sophomore	Junior	Senior
25	30	65	70
33	48	72	83
44	53	51	77
52	49	67	90
13	50	58	78

Computational formulas in this chapter

Total sum of squares

$$SS_{tot} = \sum X_{tot}{}^2 - \frac{\left(\sum X_{tot}\right)^2}{N}$$

Between-groups sum of squares

$$SS_{BG} = \sum \left(\frac{(\text{ColumnTotal})^2}{n} \right) - \left(\frac{\left(\sum X_{tot}\right)^2}{N} \right)$$

Within-groups sum of squares

$$SS_{WG} = SS_{tot} - SS_{BG}$$

Between-groups mean square

$$MS_{BG} = \frac{SS_{BG}}{k - 1}$$

Within-groups mean square

$$MS_{WG} = \frac{SS_{WG}}{N - k}$$

F-obtained value

$$F_{obt} = \frac{MS_{BG}}{MS_{WG}}$$

Effect size

$$\eta^2 = \frac{SS_{BG}}{SS_{tot}}$$

Confidence interval

$$\left(\sqrt{\frac{MS_{wg}}{n}} \right)(-t_{crit}) + \overline{X} \le \mu \le \left(\sqrt{\frac{MS_{wg}}{n}} \right)(+t_{crit}) + \overline{X}$$

Tukey's HSD for post hoc comparisons of means with equal n

$$HSD = q\left(\sqrt{\frac{MS_{WG}}{n}} \right)$$

Fisher's protected t-test for post hoc comparison of means with unequal n

$$t_{obt} = \frac{\overline{X}_1 - \overline{X}_2}{\sqrt{MS_{WG}\left(\frac{1}{n_1} + \frac{1}{n_2} \right)}}$$

References

In Text:

Berg, K. F. (1997). Drug abuse resistance (DARE) program for SY 94–95 and 95–96. Evaluation report. *Counseling and Personnel Services*, CG028501. (ERIC Document Reproduction Service No. ED420012)

Blasik, K. A., & Belsito, R. (1993). Drug abuse resistance education program (DARE). Evaluation report. *Teacher Education*, SP034939. (ERIC Document Reproduction Service No. ED440324)

Curtis, C. K. (1999). The efficacy of the drug abuse resistance education program (DARE) in West Vancouver schools. Part 1, Attitudes toward DARE: An examination of opinions, preferences, and perceptions of student, teachers, and parents. *Counseling and Personnel Services*, CG029859. (ERIC Document Reproduction Service No. ED383953)

Fife, B. L. (1994). An assessment of the drug abuse resistance education (DARE) program in Fort Wayne, Indiana. *Counseling and Personnel Services*, CG026071. (ERIC Document Reproduction Service No. ED383953)

Related Articles:

Becker, H. K., Agopian, M. W., & Yeh, S. (1992). Impact evaluation of Drug Abuse Resistance Program (DARE). *Journal of Drug Education, 22*, 283–291.

Harmon, M. A. (1993). Reducing the risk of drug involvement among early adolescents: An evaluation of Drug Abuse Resistance Education (DARE). *Evaluation Review, 17*, 221–239.

Lyman, D. R., Milich, R., Zimmerman, R., Novak, S. P., Logan, T. K., Martin, C., Leukefeld, C., & Clayton, R. (1999). Project DARE: No effects at 10-year follow-up. *Journal of Consulting & Clinical Psychology, 67*, 590–593.

Wysong, E., Aniskiewicz, R., & Wright, D. (1994). Truth and DARE: Tracking drug education to graduation as symbolic politics. *Social Problems, 41*, 448–472.

10

ANOVA: Two-Way, Between-Groups

One-way vs. Two-way ANOVA

The logic of the one-way, between-groups ANOVA can be applied to the two-way, between-groups ANOVA. Remember that a one-way ANOVA has 1 factor (IV or quasi-IV), with as many levels as you want. The **two-way ANOVA** has two factors, again with as many levels of each as chosen. But keep in mind that for something to be a variable, it must vary (take on more than one value). So, each factor (as a variable) must have at least two levels.

Logic of the Two-way, Between-groups ANOVA

As explained in Chapter 9, data layout for a one-way ANOVA appears in columns of numbers. But a two-way ANOVA relies on boxes rather than columns. Below is an example of a two-way ANOVA, with one IV having two levels and the second IV having three levels. Instead of simply calling this study a two-way design, we can be more specific by labeling it a 2 × 3 design, indicating the number of levels of each IV. The IV across the top is room color, and the IV down the side is level of lighting. Although numbers are not yet in the boxes, the DV will be mood on a scale from 1 to 10, with higher numbers representing better moods.

		IV: Room Color	
		Blue	Red
IV: Lighting	Dim		
	Moderate		
	Bright		

Each box in the two-way ANOVA is called a cell, and a 2 × 3 design has six cells. Because we are still using a between-groups design, each cell contains different people, with participants randomly assigned to conditions, or cells. People in the first cell (upper left corner) are exposed to dim lighting in a blue room; people in the cell to the right (top) are exposed to dim lighting in a red room, and so on.

Two-way ANOVA Effects

One way to learn about the effect of room color on mood and the effect of lighting on mood is to conduct two separate experiments. In this example of room color and lighting, separate experiments would allow us to analyze the first IV using a *t*-test, since room color has only two levels. The second IV, lighting, has three levels; therefore, this variable could be analyzed using a one-way ANOVA if we conducted a separate experiment. However, examining both IVs in the same experiment offers a bonus piece of information. Not only do we learn if room color affects mood and if lighting affects mood, but we also discover if the two IVs somehow work together to affect mood. A two-way ANOVA produces the same information that would be obtained by conducting two experiments at the same time, and a third piece of interesting information is produced as well. How might room color and lighting work together to affect mood? One possibility is that room color affects mood under only one type of lighting. Another possibility is that lighting affects mood in one room color but not the other.

When analyzing a one-way ANOVA, first look for main effects, then see if the two IVs work together somehow. A **main effect** is the effect of one IV on the DV while ignoring the other IV in the experiment. One way to talk about getting a main effect is *collapsing across* the levels of the other IV, which means we pretend for a moment that the other IV does not exist. For example, when looking for a main effect of color, we must collapse across lighting levels and ignore the lighting IV. If color affects mood, we have a main effect of color.

		IV: Room Color	
		Blue	Red
~~IV: Lighting~~	~~Dim~~		
	~~Moderate~~		
	~~Bright~~		

Next, levels of room color are ignored to find out if lighting affects mood. By collapsing across color, we might find a main effect of lighting.

	IV: Room Color	
	~~Blue~~	~~Red~~
IV: Lighting — Dim		
IV: Lighting — Moderate		
IV: Lighting — Bright		

Finally, if room color and lighting work together to affect mood, the outcome is called an **interaction effect.** When an interaction is found, the main effects become much less important, because they do not tell the entire story. The interaction moves beyond simple main effects and explains the intricacies of how both IVs work together to affect the DV.

Just as with the one-way ANOVA, all of the variability in the data set is first calculated with SS_{tot}. Then SS_{BG} and SS_{WG} are calculated exactly as in the one-way ANOVA. So far, we have made no changes in the procedure presented in Chapter 9.

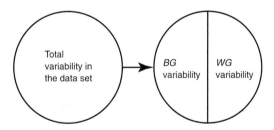

Recall from the one-way ANOVA that SS_{BG} was the portion of variability containing any treatment effect. The two-way ANOVA gives us not one, but three possibilities for treatment effect: room color, lighting, and the interaction between room color and lighting. Because this design has three pieces for potential effects, SS_{BG} will be divided into those three portions.

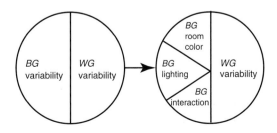

Next, we will move forward—getting a MS_{BG} for each of the three pieces and putting each MS_{BG} over the MS_{WG} (calculated the same as the one-way ANOVA, making the denominator the same across all three F-tests.)

In the following section, we will apply the logic of the two-way ANOVA to an example, then you might want to return to this section and read over the logic again.

Calculating the Two-way, Between-groups ANOVA

Below is the data layout with numbers in the cells for mood ratings. Begin by calculating the same three pieces of information used with the one-way ANOVA: first SS_{tot}, then SS_{BG}, then SS_{WG}. The SS_{BG} will be divided into three pieces (room color, lighting, and interaction) later.

		IV: Room Color	
		Blue Room	Red Room
	Dim Lighting	5 6 7 5	5 4 6 4
IV: Lighting	Moderate Lighting	4 5 6 5	7 6 4 4
	Bright Lighting	7 5 4 3	2 1 2 2

SS_{tot}

In the one-way ANOVA of Chapter 9, columns of numbers were used to calculate the values we needed to complete the SS_{tot} formula. The same will be done with the two-way ANOVA, but the data must first be placed in columns. Lay out each cell as its own column, like this:

Blue/Dim	Blue/Mod	Blue/Bright	Red/Dim	Red/Mod	Red/Bright
5	4	7	5	7	2
6	5	5	4	6	1
7	6	4	6	4	2
5	5	3	4	4	2

Recall that the SS_{tot} formula requires squared columns along with the original data (I have shortened the column headings to fit squared columns on the page):

B/D	B/D²	B/M	B/M²	B/B	B/B²	R/D	R/D²	R/M	R/M²	R/B	R/B²
5	25	4	16	7	49	5	25	7	49	2	4
6	36	5	25	5	25	4	16	6	36	1	1
7	49	6	36	4	16	6	36	4	16	2	4
5	25	5	25	3	9	4	16	4	16	2	4
23	135	20	102	19	99	19	93	21	117	7	13

Using the formula introduced in Chapter 9:

$$SS_{tot} = \sum X_{tot}^2 - \frac{\left(\sum X_{tot}\right)^2}{N}$$

$$SS_{tot} = 559 - \frac{(109)^2}{24} = 559 - \frac{11881}{24} = 559 - 495.041667 = 63.958333$$

This number represents all of the variability in the data set. Of course, no other numbers (SS_{BG} or SS_{WG}) can be higher than 63.958333.

SS_{BG} *and* SS_{WG}

With the data already presented in columns, it is a simple task to calculate SS_{BG} exactly as in the prior chapter:

$$SS_{BG} = \left(\frac{\left(\sum X_1\right)^2}{n_1} + \frac{\left(\sum X_2\right)^2}{n_2} + \frac{\left(\sum X_3\right)^2}{n_3} + \frac{\left(\sum X_4\right)^2}{n_4} + \frac{\left(\sum X_5\right)^2}{n_5} + \frac{\left(\sum X_6\right)^2}{n_6}\right) - \left(\frac{\left(\sum X_{tot}\right)^2}{N}\right)$$

Notice that more $\left(\sum X\right)^2 / n$ were added, because we have six columns of numbers now instead of the three columns from the previous chapter:

$$SS_{BG} = \left(\frac{(23)^2}{4} + \frac{(20)^2}{4} + \frac{(19)^2}{4} + \frac{(19)^2}{4} + \frac{(21)^2}{4} + \frac{(7)^2}{4}\right) - (495.041667)$$

$$SS_{BG} = 132.25 + 100.00 + 90.25 + 90.25 + 110.25 + 12.25 - 495.041667 = 40.208333$$

This number represents all of the treatment/effect information in the data set—all possible effects from our experiment.

Next, calculate the SS_{WG} by subtracting, SS_{BG} from the SS_{tot}. Recall that SS_{WG} is the measure of individual differences, or pure error:

$$SS_{WG} = SS_{tot} - SS_{BG} \qquad SS_{WG} = 63.958333 - 40.208333 = 23.75$$

SS_{WG} is not broken into three portions with the two-way ANOVA; therefore, a MS_{WG} can be created by dividing SS_{WG} by df_{WG}, just as in the one-way ANOVA. N is still the total number of values in the data set, and k is the number of cells, making $df_{WG} = 24 - 6 = 18$.

$$MS_{WG} = \frac{SS_{WG}}{N - k} = \frac{23.75}{18} = 1.319444$$

The MS_{WG}, the denominator of every F-test for this example, is 1.319444.

Separating SS_{BG} into Three Portions

In this section, we will finally calculate information differently from the one-way ANOVA, where we only had one effect and one SS_{BG}. With the two-way ANOVA, SS_{BG} will be divided into three pieces: SS_{RC} (for room color), SS_L (for lighting), and SS_{RCXL} for the interaction between the two IVs. Since we are looking for an effect of room color first, we must ignore the lighting variable. The best way to do this is to lay out the columns for the two levels of room color:

Blue Room	Red Room
5	5
6	4
7	6
5	4
4	7
5	6
6	4
5	4
7	2
5	1
4	2
3	2

Again, notice that the information about lighting is not listed. For now, we are only looking at room color and mood. We have collapsed across the lighting variable.

Now that we have a new data layout, we need to calculate the SS_{BG} formula again. Because the columns are different, the answer will be different. Calculate just the SS_{BG} piece for room color—the variability in mood associated with room color: (Hint: Don't bother doing squared columns; they're not needed in the SS_{BG} formula.)

$$SS_{RC} = \left(\frac{(62)^2}{12} + \frac{(47)^2}{12} \right) - (495.041667)$$

$$SS_{RC} = 320.333333 + 184.083333 - 495.041667 = 9.374999$$

The number 9.374999 is the variability associated with room color. To create a MS, divide by df_{RC}, which is $k - 1$. Because the variable of room color has two levels, k is 2, and $k - 1 = 1$:

$$MS_{RC} = \frac{9.374999}{1} = 9.374999$$

Next, calculate SS_{BG} for lighting by setting up columns of lighting levels, this time collapsing across room color. Because the columns are different again, the outcome of SS_{BG} will also be different:

Dim	Moderate	Bright
5	4	7
6	5	5
7	6	4
5	5	3
5	7	2
4	6	1
6	4	2
4	4	2

$$SS_L = \left(\frac{(42)^2}{8} + \frac{(41)^2}{8} + \frac{(26)^2}{8} \right) - (495.041667)$$

$$SS_L = 220.50 + 210.125 + 84.50 - 495.041667 = 20.083333$$

The number 20.083333 represents the between-groups variability associated with lighting. Calculate MS for lighting by dividing SS by df_L of $k-1$, which equals 2, since lighting has three levels:

$$MS_L = \frac{20.083333}{2} = 10.041667$$

Last, figure out how much of the SS_{BG} can be given to the interaction. Because all of the between-groups variability is 40.208333, room color takes 9.374999 of the variability, and lighting takes 20.083333 of the variability, subtraction will reveal how much between-groups variability remains for the interaction portion:

$$SS_{RCXL} = 40.208333 - 9.374999 - 20.083333 = 10.750001$$

Degrees of freedom for the interaction (df_{RCXL}) is calculated using df_{RC} and df_L. Multiply the two df values:

$$df_{RCXL} = (df_{RC})(df_L) = (1)(2) = 2$$

Prepare a MS for the interaction by dividing df_{RCXL} into SS_{RCXL}:

$$MS_{RCXL} = \frac{10.750001}{2} = 5.375001$$

F-tests for Each Effect

Because this example provides three pieces of between-groups information, or three possible effects to test, three F-tests must be calculated. Using the same approach as the one-way ANOVA, arrange each MS_{BG} portion over the MS_{WG} to create each F_{obt}. Then compare the F_{obt} value to the F_{crit} value from the F-table, using df_{BG} and df_{WG}.

The first main effect to test is room color:

$$F_{obt} = \frac{MS_{RC}}{MS_{WG}} = \frac{9.374999}{1.319444} = 7.105265$$

The F_{crit} is based on 1 and 18 df, since room color had 1 df and the error term had 18 df. (Keep in mind that df_{WG} is the same for all three F-tests in this example.) In the table, the F_{crit} is 4.41, and the F_{obt} of 7.105265 is beyond that value. A significant main effect exists.

Now test for a main effect of lighting:

$$F_{obt} = \frac{MS_L}{MS_{WG}} = \frac{10.041667}{1.319444} = 7.610529$$

The F_{crit} for this test is slightly different, because it is based on 2 degrees of freedom for lighting and 18 for the error term. The F_{crit} with 2 and 18 df is 3.55. F_{obt} for lighting is 7.610529, a value beyond an F_{crit} of 3.55. A second significant main effect was found.

Now for the final piece: the F-test for the interaction between room color and lighting:

$$F_{obt} = \frac{MS_{RCXL}}{MS_{WG}} = \frac{5.375001}{1.319444} = 4.073686$$

The F_{crit} for this final test is based on 2 and 18 df; therefore, the F_{crit} is again 3.55. F_{obt} for the interaction is 4.073686, which falls beyond 3.55. A significant interaction effect was revealed.

ANOVA information will be more organized in a summary table. Remember that we are dividing the SS_{BG} into three portions for the two-way ANOVA, a procedure followed in the summary table. The rest of the summary table relies on the same logic as the one-way ANOVA.

Source	SS	df	MS	F_{obt}	p	F_{crit}	APA Style
Between							
RC	9.374999	1	9.374999	7.105265	<0.05	4.41	$F(1, 18) = 7.11, p < 0.05$
L	20.083333	2	10.041667	7.610529	<0.05	3.55	$F(2, 18) = 7.61, p < 0.05$
RCXL	10.750001	2	5.375001	4.073686	<0.05	3.55	$F(2, 18) = 4.07, p < 0.05$
Within	23.75	18	1.319444				
Total	63.958333	23					

Notes

1. You should notice that the SS_{BG} across the top line is missing. We don't want to divide SS_{BG} into three pieces and still keep the sum on the top line; if we did, adding all the SS in the table would give us a number greater than SS_{tot}, and that is not logical.
2. F_{crit} is based on df for each test, so I've added a column for F_{crit}. F_{crit} is the same for the main effect of lighting and the interaction, because both have 2 and 18 df.
3. A final column of APA style shows that each result must be reported individually.

Hypothesis Testing and ANOVA Results

The components of hypothesis testing can be applied to the two-way ANOVA, but each potential effect (room color, lighting, and interaction) requires new null and alternative hypotheses. The type of statistic used in this chapter is the two-way, between-groups ANOVA, and the *F*-distribution is positively skewed (Chapter 9). In the sections that follow, hypothesis testing is presented for one effect at a time.

First Main Effect

For the main effect of room color, the null hypothesis would reflect that the IV has two levels:

$$H_0: \mu_1 = \mu_2$$

The alternative hypothesis would be:

H_1: The two groups are significantly different from each other.

Although the overall analysis is the two-way, between-groups ANOVA, the specific test for hypothesis testing will depend on which effect is being examined. Main effects allow comparisons of columns, whereas testing for an interaction requires comparisons between cells in the design. When testing for a main effect of room color, the type of analysis is a test of a *between-groups main effect*.

The specific test will also determine *df* and F_{crit} for the *F*-distribution. For the main effect of room color, the F_{crit} is based on 1 and 18 degrees of freedom, yielding a value of 4.41. The F_{crit} can be placed on the distribution as we did in Chapter 9.

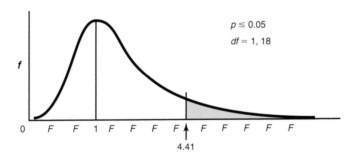

After calculating the F_{obt} for a main effect of room color, place the F_{obt} of 7.11 on the distribution to see that it falls in the region of rejection, allowing us to reject the null hypothesis.

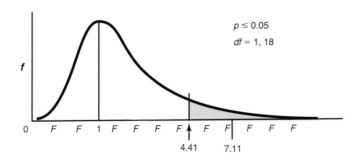

As reported earlier in the chapter, APA style is $F(1, 18) = 7.11, p < 0.05$. Room color affected mood.

Second Main Effect

For the main effect of lighting, the null hypothesis would reflect that the IV has three levels:

$H_0: \mu_1 = \mu_2 = \mu_3$

The alternative hypothesis would be:

H_1: At least two groups are significantly different from each other.

When testing for a main effect of lighting, the type of analysis is also a test of a *between-groups main effect*.

For the main effect of lighting, the F_{crit} is based on 2 and 18 degrees of freedom, yielding a value of 3.55. The F_{crit} can be placed on the distribution and compared with the F_{obt} (calculated earlier) of 7.61.

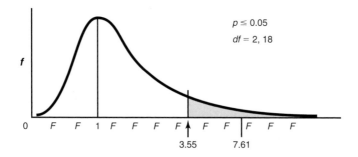

We reject the null hypothesis, and APA style communicates an effect: $F(2, 18) = 7.61, p < 0.05$. Lighting affected mood.

Interaction Effect

The only new effect portion in this chapter is the interaction. The null and alternative hypotheses will look a bit different, since the interaction is based on differences between cells rather than columns. The null hypothesis for the six cells would be:

$H_0: \mu_1 = \mu_2 = \mu_3 = \mu_4 = \mu_5 = \mu_6$

(In words, if nothing happens, all cell means will be the same.)

The alternative hypothesis would be:

H_1: At least two of the cells are significantly different from each other.

The specific type of test is a test of a *between-groups interaction*.

On the F-distribution, F_{crit} is again 3.55 based on 2 and 18 degrees of freedom for a test of the interaction. The F_{obt} of 4.07 falls in the critical region, allowing us to reject the null hypothesis.

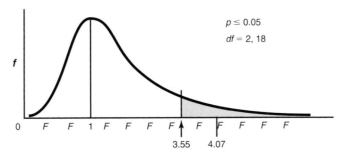

APA style is $F(2, 18) = 4.07, p < 0.05$. Room color and lighting work together (interact) to affect mood.

Notice when degrees of freedom for each effect change, the F_{crit} will change; therefore, F_{crit} for each effect must be found separately. Although the df_{WG} (denominator) will be the same for every F-test in an example, the df_{BG} for each test will be based on the number of levels of the IV $(k - 1)$ for main effects and df for each main effect multiplied to get df for the interaction.

Post-hoc Testing

As discussed in Chapter 9, a significant ANOVA only indicates that something is happening; it does not communicate specific results. We often need post-hoc tests to know exactly which groups are different from each other.

Post Hoc for a Significant Main Effect

First, the ANOVA revealed that room color affected mood. In other words, there was a main effect of room color on mood. Does that mean we must now conduct post-hoc testing? No. A significant ANOVA tells us that at least two groups were significantly different from each other, but since room color only had two levels, we know which two were different. Simply look at the group means for blue and red rooms, and state the result in plain English.

Second, did the ANOVA tells us that lighting affected mood? In other words, was there a main effect of lighting on mood? Yes. Do we need post-hoc testing? Yes, because we have a significant effect and more than two levels of the IV. We cannot know which levels were significantly different from each other without post-hoc testing.

Post-hoc testing for a significant main effect with more than two levels is accomplished in exactly the same way we analyzed the one-way ANOVA in Chapter 9. Find the mean for each group, then conduct Tukey's HSD comparisons (for equal n) or Fisher's protected t-tests (for unequal n) to learn which groups were significantly different from each other. With equal n across levels of lighting, Tukey's HSD comparisons are appropriate. Notice that n for each level of lighting is 8, because we are ignoring the room color variable for this analysis.

Use the layout from Chapter 9 to have a familiar procedure:

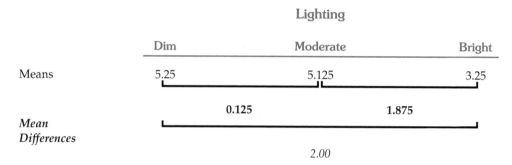

Next, calculate the HSD value:

$$HSD = q\left(\sqrt{\frac{MS_{WG}}{n}}\right)$$

$$HSD = 3.61\left(\sqrt{\frac{1.319444}{8}}\right) = 1.466080$$

With an HSD value of 1.466080, any mean differences at or above this number are considered large enough to indicate a significant difference between means. Place an asterisk in the upper right corner of each significant mean difference.

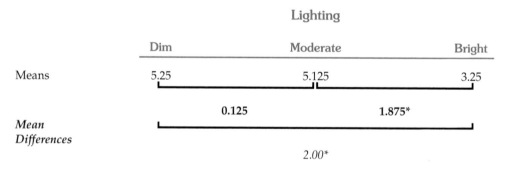

At this point, we have completely analyzed the significant main effect of lighting, and we know exactly which lighting levels differ from each other. Review the means for dim, moderate, and bright lighting to discuss this effect in plain English.

Post Hoc for a Significant Interaction Effect

For the third and final analysis, did room color and lighting somehow work together to affect mood? Yes. The ANOVA for the interaction was significant, suggesting that at least two of the cells were significantly different from each other. However, we do not yet know which two cells (or more) were different. To find out, conduct post-hoc testing.

Before we begin calculations, we must know which cells to compare. Only compare means from cells horizontally and vertically; no diagonal comparisons are possible. If we compare the top two cells and find a difference between the means, the difference was caused by room color, because lighting was the same across both cells. If the bottom two cells are different, room color again caused the difference, and so on. What about comparing cells diagonal to each other? If we do that, levels on both IVs differ, so the comparison does not specify which variable is responsible for the cell mean differences. In other words, diagonal comparisons do not provide firm answers, because either variable could be responsible for the effect.

For post-hoc comparisons of cells in this example, the same number of participants are found in each cell, so Tukey's HSD will be chosen to analyze the interaction.

The following cells contain means for the raw data from the original data layout. In addition, only horizontal and vertical cell mean differences have been calculated. Our next goal is to find out which cells means are different enough to report that they are significantly different from each other.

	Blue Room		**Red Room**	
Dim Lighting	5.75	1.00	4.75	
	0.75			0.50
Moderate Lighting	5.00	0.25	5.25	3.00
1.00				
	0.25			3.50
Bright Lighting	4.75	3.00	1.75	

To achieve our goal, we must calculate Tukey's HSD to see which cell mean differences are large enough to call them honestly significantly different:

$$\text{HSD} = q\left(\sqrt{\frac{MS_{\text{WG}}}{n}}\right)$$

Locate MS_{WG} in the summary table (1.319444), and recall the n for each cell is 4. Next, get the q from the q-table, but notice that the q-table requires adjusted k for an interaction. In the adjusted k-table, a 2×3 design (two levels of one IV and three levels of the second IV) does not use a k of 6 (for 6 cells being compared); an adjusted k of 5 is used. Always get adjusted k when analyzing an interaction before looking up the q value in the q-table. For this example, look up 5 across the top of the q-table and 18 down the left side, noticing that 18 df for the within-groups variability is what we used earlier when finding F_{crit}. Although k changes for the interaction, $N - k$ is still the df we pulled straight from the within-groups df on the summary table. The q value for this example is 4.28:

$$\text{HSD} = 4.28\left(\sqrt{\frac{1.319444}{4}}\right) = 4.28(.574335) = 2.458155$$

Any cell means different by at least 2.458155 are honestly significantly different from each other. Place an asterisk on the upper right corner of any differences at or above the HSD value.

	Blue Room		Red Room	
Dim Lighting	5.75	1.00	4.75	
	0.75		0.50	
Moderate Lighting 1.00	5.00	0.25	5.25	3.00*
	0.25		3.50*	
Bright Lighting	4.75	3.00*	1.75	

Plain English

Now that post-hoc testing is complete, state results in plain English. To keep results organized, state 1 outcome at a time, including the specific results of mean comparisons when the ANOVA was significant.

First, did room color affect mood? Yes. Participants in a blue room reported better moods than those in a red room.

Second, did lighting affect mood? Yes. Participants in a dimly lighted room and in a moderately-illuminated room reported better moods than those in a brightly lighted room.

Third, did room color and lighting work together to affect mood? Yes. When lighting was bright, people in a blue room reported better moods than those in a red room. Moods in a red room were better when lighting was dim or moderate, rather than bright.

Applying Results

Plain English results should make sense and answer logical questions. After all, research is about learning something useful, not just learning which group means are different. Based on the plain English from this example, test your ability to apply results to a real-life situation. But first, which of the three effects should be used?

When the interaction is significant, main effects become less important. For example, what type of lighting creates the best moods? Based on the main effect of lighting, dim and moderate light are better than bright. However, the interaction revealed more detailed effects: Dim and moderate lighting are better than bright only in a red room. Given our knowledge of the interaction, it is not accurate to simply rely on main effects. The following discussion is based on the interaction.

Imagine that you own a business where people have to sit in a waiting room. You assume blue is a common, likable color, so you paint the walls blue. You also must choose lighting for the waiting room, and you must decide between dim, moderate, and bright light. Which one do you choose? According to the results of our study, all three types of lighting evoke the same mood in a blue room; therefore, it doesn't matter which type of lighting you choose.

What if you painted the room red? Which type of lighting would put people in a better mood? In our study, participants rated their moods as equal across dim and moderate lighting in the red room. Only bright lighting in the red room impaired mood, so bright light should not be chosen.

What if your business partner wanted to decide on the paint later, but you needed to pick the lighting right away? It would be better for you to choose dim or moderate light, because these two types of lighting worked equally well in both room colors. If you choose bright illumination, and your partner later paints the room red, clients will experience low moods.

Two-way, Between-groups ANOVA on SPSS

To enter the data from this example into SPSS, string out the data as with the independent-samples *t*-test and the one-way, between-groups ANOVA. The only added feature is that we have two IVs instead of one. The first column will be the first IV, room color, with two levels represented by the numbers 1 and 2. The second column will be the second IV, lighting, with three levels represented by 1, 2, and 3. The third column will be the DV, with each number beside the appropriate IV_1 and IV_2 levels. For example, the first person in the study was in level 1 of room color (IV_1) and level 1 of lighting (IV_2); that person had a mood rating of 5. Take a few moments to look at the data layout for the two-way, between-groups ANOVA.

	color	lighting	mood
1	1.00	1.00	5.00
2	1.00	1.00	6.00
3	1.00	1.00	7.00
4	1.00	1.00	5.00
5	1.00	2.00	4.00
6	1.00	2.00	5.00
7	1.00	2.00	6.00
8	1.00	2.00	5.00
9	1.00	3.00	7.00
10	1.00	3.00	5.00
11	1.00	3.00	4.00
12	1.00	3.00	3.00
13	2.00	1.00	5.00

Recall that we can change the levels of the IV in a between-groups design to words rather than numbers. By labeling the levels so clearly, we're less likely to lose track of what level each number represented. In this example, we have two IVs, and each will need to be labeled. Begin with room color, the first IV. Label the levels "blue" and "red."

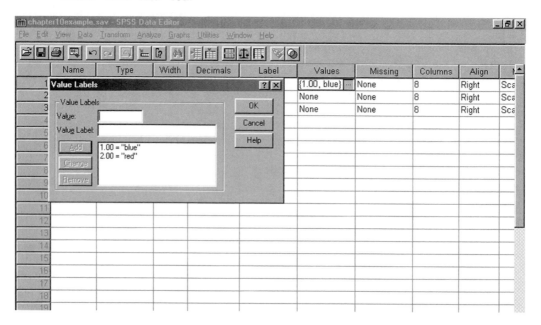

Using the same procedure, label the three levels of lighting.

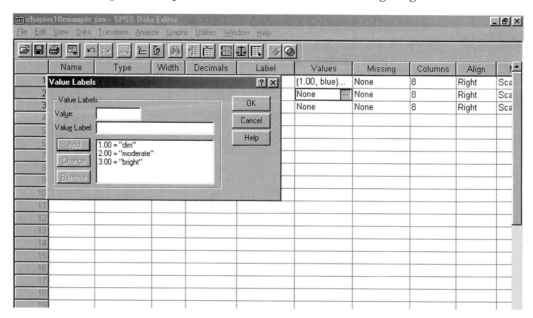

When you point to View and select Data, remember to also check Value Labels in order to see the labels on the data layout.

	color	lighting	mood	var	var	var	var	var	var	var
1	blue	dim	5.00							
2	blue	dim	6.00							
3	blue	dim	7.00							
4	blue	dim	5.00							
5	blue	moderat	4.00							
6	blue	moderat	5.00							
7	blue	moderat	6.00							
8	blue	moderat	5.00							
9	blue	bright	7.00							
10	blue	bright	5.00							
11	blue	bright	4.00							
12	blue	bright	3.00							
13	red	dim	5.00							
14	red	dim	4.00							
15	red	dim	6.00							
16	red	dim	4.00							
17	red	moderat	7.00							
18	red	moderat	6.00							
19	red	moderat	4.00							
20	red	moderat	4.00							
21	red	bright	2.00							

Point to Analyze, then select General Linear Model+Univariate.

chapter10example.sav - SPSS Data Editor

File Edit View Data Transform Analyze Graphs Utilities Window Help

Reports
Descriptive Statistics
Compare Means
General Linear Model ▶   Univariate...
Correlate
Regression
Classify
Data Reduction
Scale
Nonparametric Tests
Time Series

	color	lighting	mood
1	blue	dim	
2	blue	dim	
3	blue	dim	
4	blue	dim	
5	blue	moderat	
6	blue	moderat	
7	blue	moderat	6.00
8	blue	moderat	5.00
9	blue	bright	7.00
10	blue	bright	5.00
11	blue	bright	4.00
12	blue	bright	3.00
13	red	dim	5.00
14	red	dim	4.00
15	red	dim	6.00
16	red	dim	4.00
17	red	moderat	7.00
18	red	moderat	6.00
19	red	moderat	4.00

In the gray box, select color and lighting, and click them to the right under Fixed Factor(s). Select mood and click it to the right under Dependent Variable.

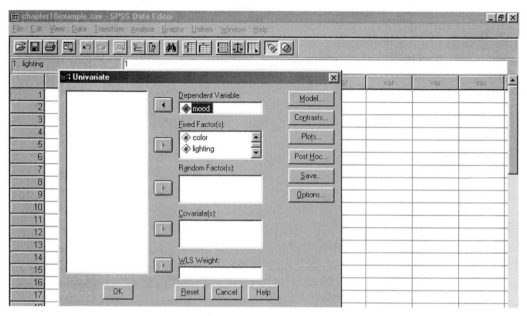

Click Options, select color, lighting, and color*lighting, and click them to the right under Display Means for. Then check the boxes next to Descriptive statistics and Estimates of effect size, and click Continue.

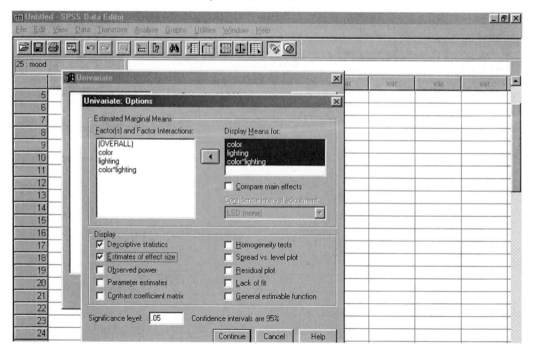

When at least one of the IVs has more than two levels, you can conduct post-hoc testing by clicking Post Hoc. SPSS runs the ANOVA and post hoc at the same time, so go ahead and ask for post hoc, even though the ANOVA has not yet been run by the computer.

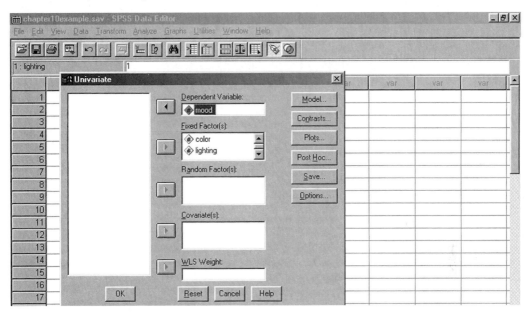

In the gray box, move the variable with more than two levels to the right and check Tukey. Then click Continue to return to the main gray box, where clicking OK will run the analysis.

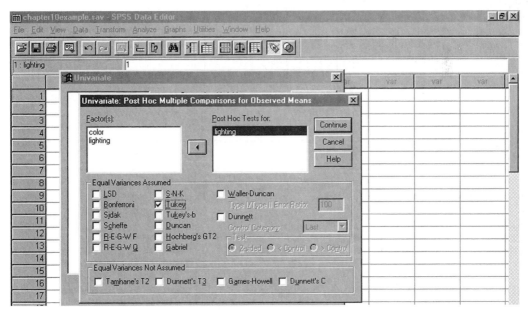

Don't ask for post hoc of color, because this variable only has two levels. If you ask for post-hoc testing, SPSS will refuse to conduct the tests, letting you know that it wouldn't be logical to see which two levels of an IV are different if you only have two levels. As for the interaction, you will need a post-hoc test to compare the cells, but since SPSS doesn't run cell comparisons without programming changes, it is much simpler to conduct post-hoc testing of the interaction by hand.

Output for the example from this chapter is below:

Univariate Analysis of Variance

Between-Subjects Factors

		Value Label	N
COLOR	1.00	blue	12
	2.00	red	12
LIGHTING	1.00	dim	8
	2.00	moderate	8
	3.00	bright	8

Descriptive Statistics

Dependent Variable: MOOD

COLOR	LIGHTING	Mean	Std. Deviation	N
blue	dim	5.7500	.95743	4
	moderate	5.0000	.81650	4
	bright	4.7500	1.70783	4
	Total	5.1667	1.19342	12
red	dim	4.7500	.95743	4
	moderate	5.2500	1.50000	4
	bright	1.7500	.50000	4
	Total	3.9167	1.88092	12
Total	dim	5.2500	1.03510	8
	moderate	5.1250	1.12599	8
	bright	3.2500	1.98206	8
	Total	4.5417	1.66757	24

Tests of Between-Subjects Effects

Dependent Variable: MOOD

Source	Type III Sum of Squares	df	Mean Square	F	Sig.	Partial Eta Squared
Corrected Model	40.208[a]	5	8.042	6.095	.002	.629
Intercept	495.042	1	495.042	375.189	.000	.954
COLOR	9.375	1	9.375	7.105	.016	.283
LIGHTING	20.083	2	10.042	7.611	.004	.458
COLOR*LIGHTING	10.750	2	5.375	4.074	.035	.312
Error	23.750	18	1.319			
Total	559.000	24				
Corrected Total	63.958	23				

a. R Squared = .629 (Adjusted R Squared = .526)

Estimated Marginal Means

1. COLOR

Dependent Variable: MOOD

COLOR	Mean	Std. Error	95% Confidence Interval	
			Lower Bound	Upper Bound
blue	5.167	.332	4.470	5.863
red	3.917	.332	3.220	4.613

2. LIGHTING

Dependent Variable: MOOD

LIGHTING	Mean	Std. Error	95% Confidence Interval	
			Lower Bound	Upper Bound
dim	5.250	.406	4.397	6.103
moderate	5.125	.406	4.272	5.978
bright	3.250	.406	2.397	4.103

3. COLOR * LIGHTING

Dependent Variable: MOOD

COLOR	LIGHTING	Mean	Std. Error	95% Confidence Interval	
				Lower Bound	Upper Bound
blue	dim	5.750	.574	4.543	6.957
	moderate	5.000	.574	3.793	6.207
	bright	4.750	.574	3.543	5.957
red	dim	4.750	.574	3.543	5.957
	moderate	5.250	.574	4.043	6.457
	bright	1.750	.574	.543	2.957

Post Hoc Tests
LIGHTING

Multiple Comparisons

Dependent Variable: MOOD
Tukey HSD

(I) LIGHTING	(J) LIGHTING	Mean Difference (I-J)	Std. Error	Sig.	95% Confidence Interval	
					Lower Bound	Upper Bound
dim	moderate	.1250	.57434	.974	−1.3408	1.5908
	bright	2.0000*	.57434	.007	.5342	3.4658
moderate	dim	−.1250	.57434	.974	−1.5908	1.3408
	bright	1.8750*	.57434	.011	.4092	3.3408
bright	dim	−2.0000*	.57434	.007	−3.4658	−.5342
	moderate	−1.8750*	.57434	.011	−3.3408	−.4092

Based on observed means.
*. The mean difference is significant at the .05 level.

Homogeneous Subsets

MOOD

Tukey HSD[a, b]

LIGHTING	N	Subset	
		1	2
bright	8	3.2500	
moderate	8		5.1250
dim	8		5.2500
Sig.		1.000	.974

Means for groups in homogeneous subsets are displayed.
Based on Type III Sum of Squares
The error term is Mean Square(Error) = 1.319.
   a. Uses Harmonic Mean Sample size = 8.000.
   b. Alpha = .05.

The first two tables of the output are not needed, because we asked for descriptive statistics to be calculated separately; means and standard errors are located at the end of the output under Estimated Marginal Means (three tables), where you will also find confidence intervals.

The summary table is labeled Tests of Between-Subjects Effects. Each potential effect is listed under Source in capital letters, so focus on those three rows of the table. In addition, we will need the Error row and the Corrected Total row. These five rows from the output summary table will recreate the same results we calculated and summarized by hand earlier in the chapter. As you can see, the significance values (p-values) indicate a main effect for room color (0.016) and lighting (0.004), and the interaction between the two variables is significant (0.035). In addition, effect sizes are available to report in an APA-style results section.

Post-hoc tests were conducted for lighting, and a table of comparisons is found near the end of the output. Compare the first and second levels of lighting to see that a significance value of 0.974 is not less than 0.05. Thus, dim and moderate lighting are not significantly different from each other. Dim and bright are significantly different from each other with a significance value of 0.007. Similarly, moderate and bright lighting are different at the 0.011 level.

APA-style Results Section

The results of this analysis are presented in the box on the next page.

In the first paragraph of the results section, the 2 × 3 has been defined by naming the first and second IV in parentheses. In the third paragraph, the p-value for lighting was less than 0.01, as indicated in the APA style of the first sentence. The interaction paragraph (fourth) begins with the word "however" to indicate that the main effects alone do not describe the data set as well as the more detailed interaction. Finally, do not expect the estimated standard errors to always be the same across columns or cells.

Results

A 2 × 3 (room color x lighting), between-groups ANOVA was used to analyze these data. Significant effects were further analyzed using Tukey's HSD ($p < 0.05$).

Room color affected mood, $F(1, 18) = 7.11, p < 0.05$, with an effect size of 0.28. Participants in a blue room ($M = 5.17, SEM = 0.33, n = 12$) reported better moods than those in a red room ($M = 3.92, SEM = 0.33, n = 12$).

In addition, lighting affected mood, $F(2, 18) = 7.61, p < 0.01$, with an effect size of 0.46. Participants in a dimly lighted room ($M = 5.25, SEM = 0.41, n = 8$) and in a moderately illuminated room ($M = 5.13, SEM = 0.41, n = 8$) reported better moods than those in a brightly lighted room ($M = 3.25, SEM = 0.41, n = 8$).

However, room color and lighting interacted to affect mood, $F(2, 18) = 4.07$, $p < 0.05$, with an effect size of 0.31. When lighting was bright, people in a blue room ($M = 4.75, SEM = 0.57, n = 4$) reported better moods than those in a red room ($M = 1.75, SEM = 0.57, n = 4$). Moods in a red room were better when lighting was dim ($M = 4.75, SEM = 0.57, n = 4$) or moderate ($M = 5.25, SEM = 0.57, n = 4$) rather than bright. No other cell comparisons were significant ($p > 0.05$).

Graphing the Two-way ANOVA

A results section is often enhanced with figures, which often take the form of graphs. Each main effect is graphed individually, and the format for graphing one IV on the *x*-axis and the DV (mean) on the *y*-axis was described in Chapter 4. Recall that an IV characterized by nominal or ordinal data is illustrated using a bar graph; an interval or ratio IV is depicted using a line graph. In the present example, neither room color not level of lighting reach interval or ratio data; therefore, each main effect would be represented by a bar graph.

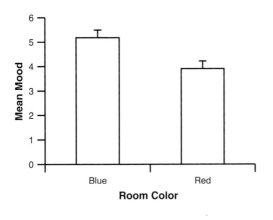
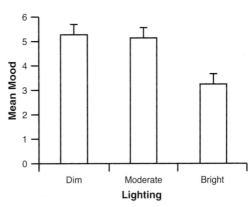

A graph of the interaction can also be either a line or a bar, depending on the level of measurement of the IV placed on the *x*-axis. The remaining IV will be identified by a legend on the graph. Either room color or lighting can be placed on the *x*-axis, and I have chosen lighting for the interaction graph. Because lighting condition represents nominal data, a bar graph is needed. An open bar will represent the blue room; a shaded bar will represent moods in the red room. Across levels of lighting, the blue room caused mood ratings of 5.75, 5.00, and 4.75 (refer to cell means earlier in the chapter). In fact, of all six cell means, 5.75 is the highest; therefore, the *y*-axis should be labeled to about 7.00 (to allow room for an error bar on top of the data bar). Put a bar above dim lighting to the 5.75 mark, draw a bar to 5.00 above moderate lighting, then draw a bar up to 4.75 to represent bright lighting in the blue room.

	Blue Room	Red Room
Dim Lighting	5.75	4.75
Moderate Lighting	5.00	5.25
Bright Lighting	4.75	1.75

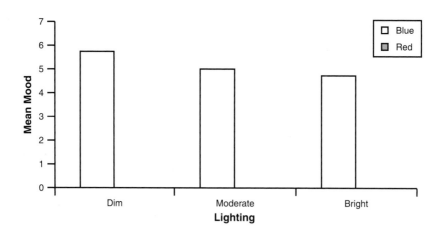

Next, create bars for the red room across dim, moderate, and bright lighting, with means of 4.75, 5.25, and 1.75, respectively.

	Blue Room	Red Room
Dim Lighting	5.75	**4.75**
Moderate Lighting	5.00	**5.25**
Bright Lighting	4.75	**1.75**

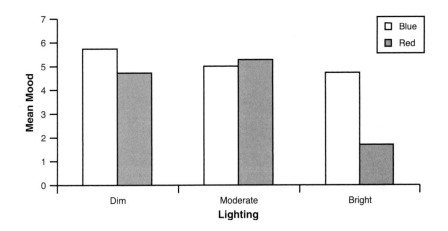

The only detail missing from this graph is standard error bars, and these *SEM*s can be taken from the SPSS printout we created earlier. Conveniently, the standard error was 0.57 for each of the six cells based on Estimated Marginal Means for COLOR * LIGHTING in the output. (Again, the estimated *SEM*s won't always be equal.) Complete the graph with error bars.

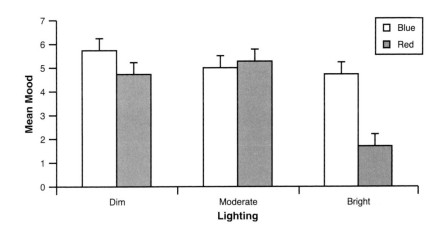

Instead of lighting level, room color could be placed on the *x*-axis, then levels of lighting would appear in the legend. The figure would again be a bar graph, because room color represents nominal data. Either graph would represent the data accurately.

If this study had operationally defined lighting as 60 watts, 120 watts, and 180 watts, lighting would have been a ratio variable, and a figure with lighting on the *x*-axis would have been a line graph. The graph below illustrates how the data would look if the *x*-axis variable represented interval or ratio data.

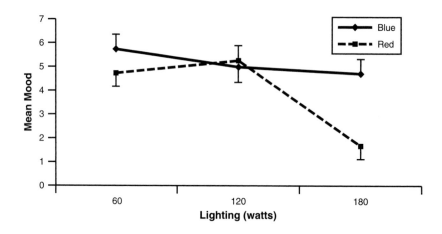

Preview of Chapter 11

In this chapter, you learned how to extend the between-groups ANOVA to encompass two IVs by separating SS_{BG} into the necessary portions. Effect size and confidence intervals can also be calculated just as they were in Chapter 9, and SPSS provides this information as well. Although the example from this chapter had two significant main effects and a significant interaction, any combination of effects (or no effect) is possible. A significant main effect with more than two levels requires post-hoc testing, and SPSS will conduct Tukey's for both equal and unequal *n*. However, a significant interaction should be analyzed by hand, using Tukey's HSD when the cells have equal *n*, and using Fisher's protected *t*-tests when the cells have unequal *n*.

Graphing can be accomplished for main effects the same way figures were created at the end of Chapters 3 and 4. Creating a figure for the interaction requires placing one factor on the *x*-axis (the one that defines whether the figure is a bar or line graph) and identifying the other factor in a legend.

In Chapter 11, we will step away from traditional experimental designs (and quasi-IVs) to discuss a specific correlational analysis. You probably recall that correlations measure the extent to which two variables are related. When a quasi-IV is used, we would define a significant outcome as a relationship between the quasi-IV and DV. Indeed, the relationship could be called a correlation. However, correlation also refers to a specific type of statistic used to measure how related two variables are. In most research, scientists try to choose correlational variables that are interval or ratio data in order to use a powerful statistic known as Pearson's correlation coefficient, a statistic you will learn in the next chapter.

Conceptual Items

1. How many cells would be found in a 3 × 4 design?
2. How is k obtained in a two-way ANOVA when calculating $N - k$?
3. What is the formula for degrees of freedom for the interaction MS?
4. How many effects are sought in a two-way ANOVA?
5. Why is it illogical to compare diagonal cell means after discovering a significant interaction?
6. When the factor on the x-axis is nominal or ordinal data, a _____ graph is used; when the factor on the x-axis is interval or ratio data, a _____ graph is created.
7. Why would an interaction be more important than main effects?

Application Items

8. Suppose you wanted to test the effectiveness of two different types of therapy on clients' levels of depression as measured by a depression inventory, where higher scores indicate more depression. In addition, you decide to examine the possible role of an emotionally uninvolved (cold) clinician vs. an emotionally involved (warm) clinician. Your data might be as follows:

	Psychoanalysis		Humanistic Therapy	
Emotionally Uninvolved (cold) Clinician	12	10	9	11
	9	11	9	5
	11	13	7	6
Emotionally Involved (warm) Clinician	8	6	6	7
	7	7	5	9
	8	9	5	8
	7		8	

a. Analyze these data, and put your results in a summary table.
b. Put each result in APA style.
c. Conduct post-hoc testing as needed.
d. Verify your results on SPSS.

e. Write your results in plain English. Address cause and effect or relationships between variables.

f. Graph each significant effect.

For the following items, address a-f from Application Item 8 above.

9. Giancola and colleagues (2002) recently reported that alcohol increased aggression in men but not women, and both genders showed increased aggression when they were highly provoked. Let's say we wanted to run a similar experiment to see if dosage of alcohol might also play a role in aggressive behavior. We could examine alcohol dose and level of provocation as our two IVs. (We won't include gender as a third factor, because we don't want this example to be a three-way ANOVA.) Our DV will be aggression as rated by independent observers using a scale from 1 to 20, with higher numbers representing greater levels of aggression. We might expect that higher doses of alcohol will increase aggression, and more provocation should increase aggression. In addition, the two variables might somehow interact in their effect on aggressive behavior.

Imagine that we randomly assigned participants to drink either 0, 5, or 10 ounces of alcohol. Within each dose of alcohol, some participants were mildly provoked and some were strongly provoked. Observers (researchers) watched participants' behavior and rated their aggression during the experiment. Remember that higher numbers indicate more aggression.

Here are the fictitious data:

	low provocation		high provocation	
0 ounces of alcohol	8	5	15	17
	9	5	16	18
	4	6	17	17
5 ounces of alcohol	8	9	16	18
	11	8	12	18
	9	11	16	14
10 ounces of alcohol	19	14	18	18
	17	15	20	16
	14	20	19	16

10. If college students were randomly assigned to receive either $25, $50, or $75 to spend at the grocery store, it would be interesting to see the percent of cash spent on junk food items. We might also take into consideration the number of hours per week students exercise. Those who are devoted to healthful living might not purchase as much junk food, regardless of the amount they have to spend. As students enter the store, we might ask them to report approximately how many hours a week they exercise. Below are possible data of percent of cash spent on junk food.

	$25	$50	$75
0 hours	20	25	45
	19	21	50
	15	18	29
	13	34	31
	22	32	34
	16		55
3 hours	5	25	35
	10	15	20
	13	21	30
	9	27	42
	17	35	
6 hours	0	11	22
	9	7	9
	10	13	18
	3	16	39

(Of course, it would be unlikely that all participants would report exactly 0, 3, or 6 hours of exercise per week. This is a fictional example.)

11. If a new carwash opened in your town, the owners might want to know how customers rate their three types of carwashes: regular, extra, or super. In addition, they might suspect that the color of car would make a difference, with dark colors showing dirt more clearly than light colors. At their grand opening, they could randomly hand out tokens for each of the three types of washes and have customers rate the cleanliness of their cars on a scale from 1 to 10, with 10 representing very clean. Of course, the owners would also need to keep track of whether or not each customer owned a light or dark car. The following data might be found.

	Regular wash	**Extra wash**	**Super wash**
Light cars	6	8	6
	7	5	5
	5	6	5
	4	7	7
	5		4
Dark cars	5	6	5
	3	5	2
	3	5	4
	4	2	5
	5	4	

Computational formulas in this chapter

Total sum of squares

$$SS_{tot} = \sum X_{tot}^2 - \frac{\left(\sum X_{tot}\right)^2}{N}$$

Between-groups sum of squares

$$SS_{BG} = \sum \left(\frac{(ColumnTotal)^2}{n}\right) - \left(\frac{\left(\sum X_{tot}\right)^2}{N}\right)$$

Within-groups sum of squares

$$SS_{WG} = SS_{tot} - SS_{BG}$$

Between-groups mean square

$$MS_{BG} = \frac{SS_{BG}}{k-1}$$

Within-groups mean square

$$MS_{WG} = \frac{SS_{WG}}{N-k}$$

F-obtained value

$$F_{obt} = \frac{MS_{BG}}{MS_{WG}}$$

Tukey's HSD for post hoc comparisons of means with equal n

$$HSD = q\left(\sqrt{\frac{MS_{WG}}{n}}\right)$$

References

In Text:

Giancola, P. R., Helton, E. L., Osborne, A. B., Terry, M. K., Fuss, A. M., & Westerfield, J. A. (2002). The effects of alcohol and provocation on aggressive behavior in men and women. *Journal of Studies on Alcohol, 63*, 64–73.

Related Articles:

Cheong, J., Patock-Peckham, J. A., & Nagoshi, C. T. (2001). Effects of alcoholic beverage, instigation, and inhibition on expectancies of aggressive behavior. *Violence & Victims, 16*, 173–184.

Gustafson, R. (1994). Alcohol and aggression. *Journal of Offender Rehabilitation, 21*, 41–80.

Ito, T. A., Miller, N., & Pollock, V. E. (1996). Alcohol and aggression: A meta-analysis on the moderating effects of inhibitory cues, triggering events, and self-focused attention. *Psychological Bulletin, 120*, 60–82.

CHAPTER 11

Correlational Data

Relationships Between Variables

The past several chapters have covered experimental designs in which an IV is manipulated (by definition), and we looked for changes in the DV. The same statistics procedures can be used to analyze non-experimental studies—those with quasi-IVs. A quasi-IV looks like a true IV, with separate levels to compare, but a significant effect indicates a relationship between the quasi-IV and DV. In other words, cause and effect cannot be established. The same holds true for more traditional correlational research in which a variable is not divided into levels. Data are simply collected on two interval or ratio variables, and statistics are used to see if the variables are related (co-related).

Logic of Pearson's *r*

This chapter will present the most common correlational statistic: **Pearson's *r*.** The entire name is Pearson's Product Moment Correlation Coefficient, therefore it is sometimes referred to as the **correlation coefficient.** Pearson's *r* evaluates the possibility that two interval- or ratio-level variables are related in a linear (straight line) way. For example, most instructors believe that the time a student spends studying (ratio data) and grades (ratio data) are linearly related. As time spent studying increases, so do grades. With numbers, Pearson's *r* could be calculated to see if the two variables are indeed related. But before we turn to calculations, we will cover the theory of correlations.

Perfect Linear Relationships

Values of Pearson's *r* can range from −1.00 to +1.00, a narrow range that will yield very small numbers. Because of this, it is important to continue using six decimal places until a final answer has been calculated. The ends of the range for Pearson's *r*, −1.00 and +1.00, indicate a strong relationship between two variables. In fact, these numbers indicate a perfect relationship. An example of a perfect relationship is the saying "a penny saved is a penny earned." The first variable (column) in the data is usually labeled X, and the second variable is Y.

X	Y
Pennies Saved	*Pennies Earned*
1	1
2	2
3	3
4	4
5	5

This is a one-to-one relationship, because for every penny saved (not spent), we might think of a penny being earned.

A perfect linear relationship between two variables does not have to reflect a one-to-one ratio. For example, a perfect relationship between time spent studying and grades might mean that for every hour of studying, grades increase by 12%. The data for a consistent 12% increase might look like this:

X	Y
Hours Spent Studying	*Grades*
1	51%
2	63%
3	75%
4	87%
5	99%

If we graphed these data points, the points would form a perfectly straight line. To create the graph, we generally put the first variable on the x-axis and the second variable on the y-axis. Then we put a dot at each intersection of X and Y values. Because we usually end up with a picture of many scattered dots, the graph is called a **scatterplot**.

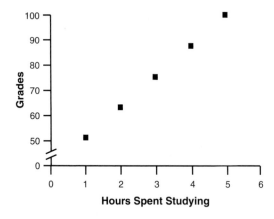

Hours spent studying and grades both increase, illustrating a positive relationship. The points form a line from the lower left corner of the graph to the upper right corner. If this relationship was given a number for Pearson's r, it would be $+1.00$. The sign can be omitted, since a number is positive if it does not have a negative sign in front of it. Data from this example represent a perfect, positive relationship with a Pearson's r of 1.00.

A perfect negative relationship would be found if one variable increased while the other decreased. For example, the number of hours per week spent at parties and grades might be negatively related. If we pretend that these variables form a perfect relationship, we might find the following data:

X	Y
Hours Spent at Parties	*Grades*
1	98%
2	93%
3	88%
4	83%
5	78%
6	73%
7	68%

A graph of these data would look like this:

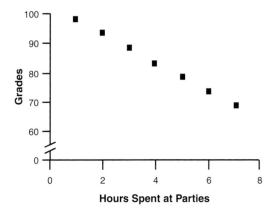

Notice that the points form a straight line from the upper left to the bottom right of the graph. When points form this type of pattern, the graph illustrates a negative relationship. In this case, the relationship is perfect; the Pearson's r value would be a -1.00.

Both positive and negative perfect linear relationships are indicated by all points falling in a straight line, but the imaginary line must have a slope. In other words, the pattern of points must be slanted either in the positive or negative direction. A line pattern with no slope illustrates no relationship, even if all of the data points fall in a straight line. Look at the examples on the next page.

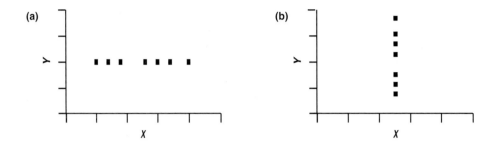

In graph (a), Y does not change across many levels of X. For example, X could be intelligence and Y could represent the number of ears people have. Intelligence scores (X) can vary widely, but number of ears (Y) will remain the same across all participants' intelligence scores. Even though the data fall in a perfect straight line, the line has no slope, therefore no relationship is depicted. In graph (b), X values do not change across many levels of Y. This could simply be a graph of intelligence as the Y variable and number of ears as the X variable. Again we see data in a perfect line pattern, but no slope means no relationship. A relationship is not possible when one variable remains constant.

Less-than-perfect Linear Relationships

Perfect relationships exist only in statistical theory and contrived examples. In the real world, Pearson's r will not be −1.00 or 1.00, but it will fall somewhere between these two numbers. The closer the relationship is to 0, the smaller the relationship. In fact, a Pearson's r of 0 means the two variables are not related to each other at all:

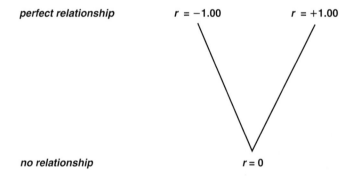

Pearson's r will rarely be 0. Even when there is no relationship between two variables, the value will not fall exactly at 0, because of sampling error. If a Pearson's r value is close to 0, the two variables are unlikely to be related. As a general rule, any value around ±0.10 is considered a weak relationship; values around ±0.30 are considered moderate relationships; and r values around ±0.50 (and beyond) represent strong relationships between two variables.

A popular way to discuss how much variability two variables have in common is called the **coefficient of determination,** which is calculated by squaring the r value. The coefficient of determination represents the proportion of variability the two variables have in common. For many people, it is more intuitive to calculate percent in common by multiplying the coefficient of determination (r^2) by 100. A Pearson's r of ±0.10 means the two variables have only 0.01 proportion, or 1%, in common. A moderate relationship of ±0.30 means the two variables have 0.09, or 9%, variability in common. A strong relationship of ±0.50 represents 0.25, or 25%, in common between the two variables.

It might seem odd to say that an r value of ±0.50 is a strong relationship, as the two variables only have 25% in common (leaving 75% of the variability in numbers not in common). Returning to the relationship between hours of studying and grades, a Pearson's r of 0.50 would mean that these two variables have 25% of the variability in their numbers in common, and 75% of the variability in their numbers has nothing to do with each other. But think of all the other reasons for getting different numbers across these variables. For example, what else other than studying might be related to grades? Grades might also be related to intelligence, mood, amount of sleep, and the difficulty of the test itself, to name a few. If hours of studying and grades have 25% in common, studying accounts for 25% of the variability in grades. Considering all the other possible influences on grades, that 25% was explained simply by looking at how many hours people study is excellent.

Pearson's *r* Calculations

To address calculations, we can turn to another example. Pearson's r can be calculated for the ratio variables of the number of hours students sleep each night and their grades. Before data are collected, we should decide what kind of relationship we might expect. Research has suggested that the less students sleep, the lower their grades (Kelly, Kelly, & Clanton, 2001). Based on this wording, as numbers on sleep decrease, so do grades. Because both sets of numbers go in the same direction, sleep and grades would represent a positive relationship. This is not likely to be a weak relationship, since it is a well-known effect, but it might not be a strong relationship given all the other variables that might influence grades. Perhaps we can imagine that a moderate relationship exists between these two variables. We should always have an idea of how the data from a study will turn out so we can logically assess our results. In this example, if a negative relationship was found, it would not be logical; a mistake might have been made during calculations.

Here are some data we might expect if we asked people to report the number of hours they sleep per night and their semester average across classes. Notice that the number of hours people sleep is not manipulated. If hours of sleep were manipulated, this project would become an experiment with only a few IV levels, and we would probably analyze it using statistics from earlier chapters. Participants were simply asked to report how much sleep they normally get, providing correlational data:

X	Y
Hours of Sleep	*Grades*
8	92
7	82
5	64
6	74
6	77
8	91
9	88
5	53

Some researchers can view numbers in column format (above) and see possible relationships. Others begin with a scatterplot to illustrate their data. For now, we will examine the scatterplot of these data, then we will calculate the *r* value. Notice on the graph below that the two points above 8 hours of sleep are almost on top of one another:

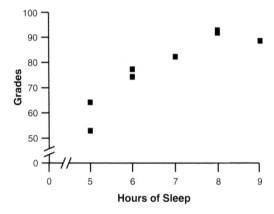

The points fall in a line pattern that begins in the lower left corner and ends in the upper right corner. This indicates a positive relationship, which is what we expected. Now look at the scatter of points around the imaginary line. If the points are widely scattered, the *r* value will be low. On the other hand, if they fall in an exact straight line, a perfect relationship is depicted. Because the points are not in a precise line, the relationship is not a 1.00. Nor is the relationship a 0, since the points are not scattered widely across the graph.

Now that the relationship between sleep and grades has been overviewed, Pearson's *r* will provide an exact number for the relationship. At first glance, the formula looks complicated, but the pieces should be familiar; several parts were used when variability was calculated in previous chapters:

$$r = \frac{N\left(\sum XY\right) - \left(\sum X\right)\left(\sum Y\right)}{\sqrt{\left[N\left(\sum X^2\right) - \left(\sum X\right)^2\right]\left[N\left(\sum Y^2\right) - \left(\sum Y\right)^2\right]}}$$

Recall that *N* generally stands for the number of values in a data set. However, in correlational research, each row is paired. That is, each participant provides two pieces of information about herself or himself, and these two pieces must stay beside each other. In correlational research, N stands for the number of pairs in the data set (8 in this example).

The only other new piece of information in the formula is the ΣXY. To get this number, multiply each X by the Y found beside it, then sum the XY column. The set-up calculations should look like this:

X	X^2	Y	Y^2	XY
Hours of Sleep	*Hours^2*	*Grades*	*Grades^2*	*Hours x Grades*
8	64	92	8464	736
7	49	82	6724	574
5	25	64	4096	320
6	36	74	5476	444
6	36	77	5929	462
8	64	91	8281	728
9	81	88	7744	792
5	25	53	2809	265
$\Sigma X = 54$	$\Sigma X^2 = 380$	$\Sigma Y = 621$	$\Sigma Y^2 = 49523$	$\Sigma XY = 4321$

Use the necessary pieces to complete the formula and calculate:

$$r = \frac{8(4321) - (54)(621)}{\sqrt{[8(380) - (2916)][8(49523) - (385641)]}} = 0.904331$$

A Pearson's r of 0.904331 indicates a strong relationship between sleep and grades. To quantify how much variability the two variables have in common, simply calculate r^2 to be 0.82, or 82% variability in common. In other words, 82% of the variability in grades was explained by knowing how many hours of sleep students get per night. (Keep in mind that these data are fictional, and a correlation as strong as 0.90 between the two variables is unlikely.)

Inferential Correlations: Hypothesis Testing

Correlations can be used to indicate whether or not two variables from a sample are related, which describes a sample. But if the goal is to estimate the relationship in a population, inferential statistics are needed. You already know that inferential statistics allow us to make statements about a population based on a sample. With correlations, we will often want to make a guess about whether or not the relationship we found in the sample is likely to be true in the larger population.

A sampling distribution for Pearson's r is based on looking for a relationship in the population between two variables. The null hypothesis, the idea that no relationship exists, is characterized by an r value of 0, so 0 is the highest simple frequency on the distribution. Positive r values are found on the right side of the distribution, and negative values fall on the left side of the distribution. The further in the tails a value is found, the lower the likelihood of finding such a strong relationship in the population in which the null hypothesis is true. Therefore, if a value falls far in the tail of the distribution, a true relationship probably exists:

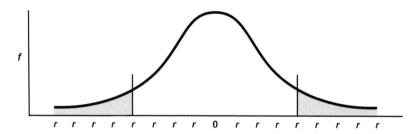

If an r value in a sample is large enough, the relationship between two variables is significant, meaning the relationship is not just chance or sampling error. As mentioned earlier, psychologists generally rely on a significance value of 0.05 or less to decide if an r-value is unlikely enough to be considered unusual. In correlational research, an interesting discovery would be a relationship between two variables.

In the example of sleep and grades, we expected a positive correlation. Rho (ρ) represents correlation in the population, so our hypotheses would be:

$H_0: \rho \leq 0$

$H_1: \rho > 0$

Notice that the alternative hypothesis represents a one-tailed Pearson's r in the positive direction. The null hypothesis represents all other possibilities, including a zero relationship and the unlikely possibility of a negative relationship between sleep and grades.

On the normal distribution, r_{crit} is based on a one-tailed test and df for this study. In correlational research, df is calculated using $N - 2$ (number of pairs minus 2 pairs). Since we have 8 pairs in this example, $df = 6$. In the correlation table, a one-tailed test with 6 degrees of freedom has an r_{crit} of 0.622 for a p-value of 0.05. Place the r_{obt} of 0.90 (calculated earlier) on the distribution to see if it falls in the critical region:

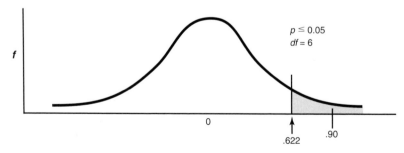

Because r_{obt} fell in the rejection region, we can reject the null hypothesis of no relationship and report that sleep and grades were significantly related.

When reporting results for inferential statistics, we will need all the pieces used in prior inferential tests. These include the *df*, calculated statistic (r_{obt}), and *p*-value. For this example, APA style is:

$$r(6) = 0.90, p < 0.05.$$

Because we are conducting inferential statistics, and we were able to reject the null hypothesis, we can say that a positive relationship between sleep and grades is likely to be found in the population of all college students.

The size of the effect can be quantified with the coefficient of determination by squaring Pearson's *r*. In this example:

$$r^2 = 0.90^2 = 0.81$$

In plain English, hours of sleep and grades are related. As hours of sleep increase, grades increase.

Correlations on SPSS

This example can be placed in SPSS by entering the two original columns of data (X: sleep and Y: grades) in the spreadsheet. There is no need to string out the data as we did with the independent-samples *t*-test and the between-groups ANOVA. In fact, this data layout is identical to the related-samples *t*-test, because we are again focusing on pairs of scores.

	sleep	grades
1	8.00	92.00
2	7.00	82.00
3	5.00	64.00
4	6.00	74.00
5	6.00	77.00
6	8.00	91.00
7	9.00	88.00
8	5.00	53.00

Scatterplot on SPSS

First, create a scatterplot of these data. Point to Graphs on the tool bar at the top of your screen. Then select Scatter.

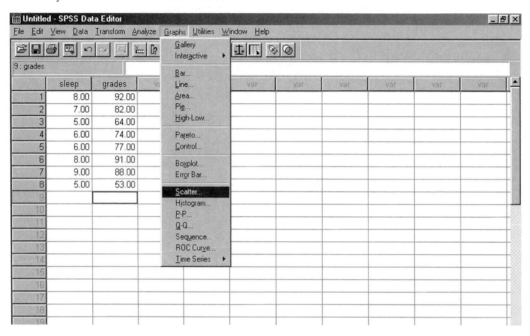

A Simple graph will be selected as the default setting.

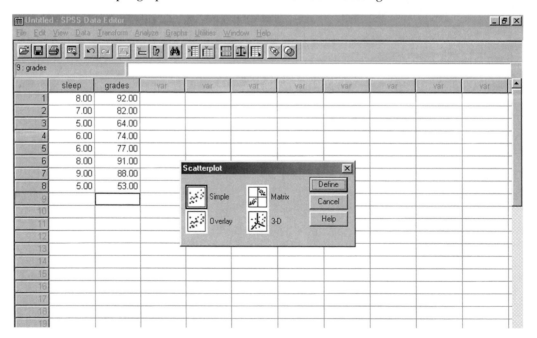

Click Define. Put the X variable (sleep) on the X-axis by clicking it into the appropriate box, then move the Y variable (grades) to the Y-axis box.

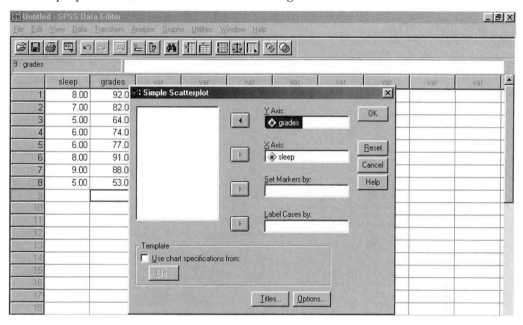

Click OK to get the following scatterplot.

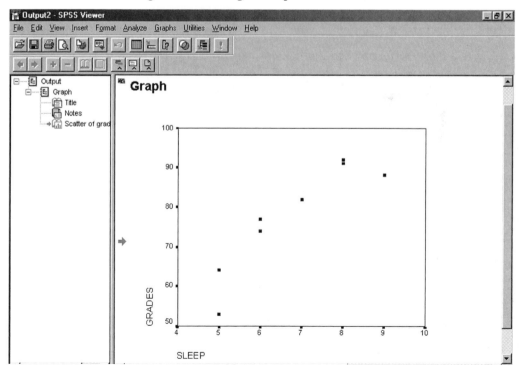

Pearson's r on SPSS

To analyze these data, point to Analyze at the top of the screen, then select Correlate+Bivariate. Bivariate is chosen to provide the relationship between two (bi) variables.

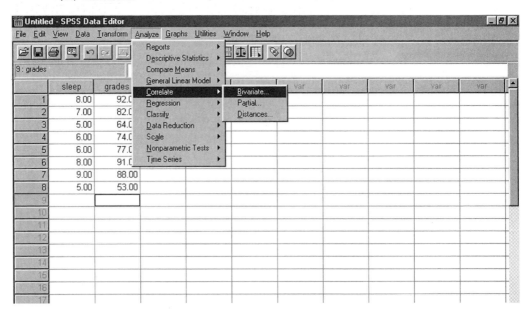

When the gray box opens, select sleep+grades and move them to the right side. Notice that Pearson is already checked as the statistic of choice. Check One-tailed test based on your expectations for this study.

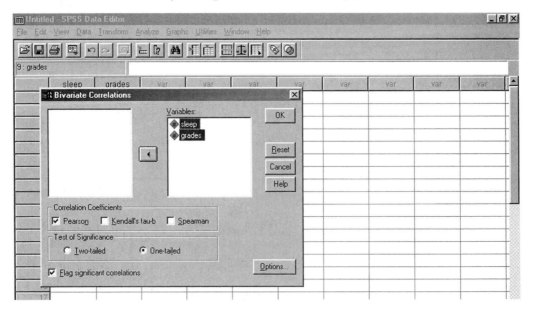

Click OK to get the output.

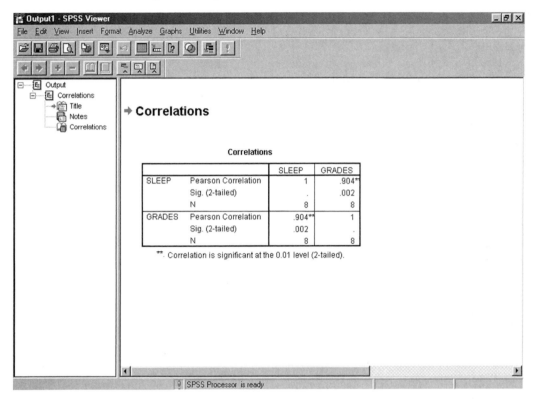

The output table is called a correlation matrix, meaning that every possible combination of the two variables is shown. As you can see, sleep and grades are correlated on one corner, and grades and sleep are also correlated on the diagonal corner. It should make sense that they are the same number. On the remaining corners, sleep has been correlated with itself, and grades has been correlated with itself. A variable always correlates with itself for a perfect 1.00, an obvious fact that is not reported by researchers. The only relevant box contains the correlation between sleep and grades; we can look at either the upper right box or the lower left box, since they both hold the same results.

Notice that the Pearson's r is 0.90, which is exactly what was calculated by hand. Also notice that the N is 8, indicating the number of pairs in this data set. We will need to subtract 2 from N to get *df*. A third number of importance is the significance value, or the p-value. This is not new and was seen on output from previous chapters on *t*-tests and ANOVA. Because we already found the critical value in the table, we knew the p-value would be less than 0.05, indicating a significant relationship between sleep and grades. In fact, the SPSS printout showed us a significance value of 0.002. With this information, we could choose to report our results using the following APA style altered to show a more accurate p-value:

$$r(6) = 0.90, p < 0.01$$

APA-style Results Section

Results from the correlation analysis are below:

Results

These data were analyzed using Pearson's correlation coefficient. Number of hours students sleep and grades were positively related, $r(6) = 0.90, p < 0.01$. The coefficient of determination was 0.81.

In addition to the results section above, it is useful to report the mean and standard deviation of each variable. Although we did not request descriptive statistics from SPSS, descriptives are found under Options in the gray box where a one-tailed test was checked.

Inaccurate Correlations

Data problems can result in a Pearson's r that is artificially low or high. In either case, the result is inaccurate and should not be reported as valid. Since Pearson's r is based on data representing a line pattern, all six possible problems are caused by errors in defining a linear relationship between two variables. Fortunately, four of the errors can be seen by graphing data on a scatterplot. The final two problems cannot be identified as easily and rely on careful review of data-collection methodology to be detected.

Artificially Low Correlations

First, Pearson's r may inaccurately show no relationship between two variables if the relationship is not linear. A common example is when data represent a U-shaped function:

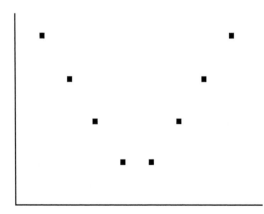

or an inverted U-shaped function:

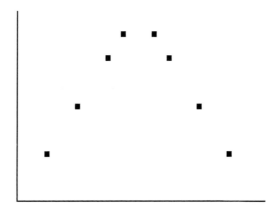

Both relationships are called curvilinear, since they are illustrated by lines that curve. Using the example of an inverted U-shaped function, the Pearson's r will be close to 0, because the positive slope found at the beginning of the relationship will cancel out the negative slope found at the end of the relationship. Thus, the Pearson's r will communicate that no relationship exists, but in reality the two variables are related, though not in a linear fashion.

Curvilinear relationships are not restricted to U- and inverted U-shaped functions. Below are two additional graphs of curvilinear data. Keep in mind that any non-linear relationship will not be characterized well by Pearson's r.

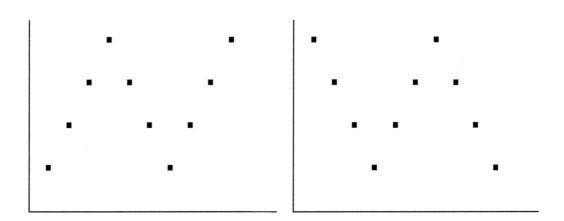

The best way to find a curvilinear function is to create a scatterplot of your data. If Pearson's r is low, a graph will reveal whether or not you have a non-linear relationship.

As a second reason for an artificially low correlation, Pearson's *r* will reflect a weak linear relationship when a few data points fall outside of the line pattern formed by the majority of points in a data set:

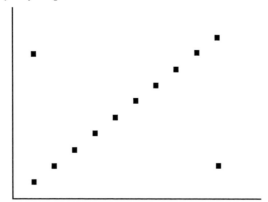

The two points off to the sides of the line pattern are called *outliers*. They are clearly out of the normal range of points and would be dropped from the data set by most researchers. In a manuscript, the method of dropping data points should be explained, and the data should be reanalyzed without the outliers. Most psychologists are interested in forming theories of behavior, and as a result, focus on patterns of behavior across the majority of people. Outliers are highly unusual and will reduce Pearson's *r*, communicating that no relationship exists between the two variables, even though a clear relationship exists for the majority of people.

The best way to find outliers in a data set is to create a scatterplot. If a true relationship exists, it will be visible on a graph, and any outliers should be obvious, too.

As a third reason for an artificially low correlation, Pearson's *r* may indicate no relationship if the range of at least one variable is restricted, resulting in a problem called restriction of range. In this situation, only a small portion of the relationship between two variables is seen. For example, suppose we looked again at the relationship between sleep and grades, but this time we only selected participants who sleep 7, 8, or 9 hours a night, on average. A scatterplot of our data might illustrate a weak relationship between sleep and grades:

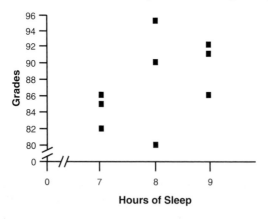

However, if we had chosen a wider range of sleep hours, we might have seen that a relationship exists after all:

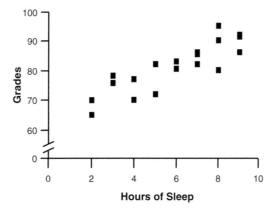

The relationship was not revealed because the range of sleep was restricted. A scatterplot of sample data will not illustrate a restriction-of-range problem; we would need to notice that one of our variables has a restricted range of values. When designing a study, try to get a wide range of values on each variable to reduce the possibility of restriction of range. Avoiding this problem certainly does not guarantee that two variables will be related, but you will have a better chance of finding a relationship if one indeed exists.

Artificially High Correlations

Just as Pearson's *r* can be erroneously low, it can also depict a linear relationship when, in fact, there is no linear relationship. First, Pearson's *r* may inaccurately indicate that a relationship exists between two variables if few people participate in a study. By chance, a few data points might fall into a line pattern and result in a high Pearson's *r* value:

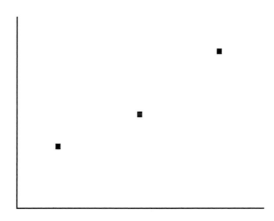

Fortunately, inferential testing requires extremely high *r* values when *N* is low, so this problem is often solved by examining the significance value in addition to

Pearson's r. At any rate, competent researchers would not conduct a study with few participants.

A second reason for an artificially high correlation occurs when outliers are in the same general direction as the rest of the data points. In the graph below, the majority of points do not indicate a strong relationship between the two variables, but outliers will increase the r value to communicate a stronger relationship than actually exists:

Just as with outliers that create artificially low correlations, these outliers must be dropped from the data set. Then reanalyze the data to see that Pearson's r is substantially lower. A scatterplot will illustrate outliers when the problem occurs.

As a third problem, Pearson's r will be artificially high if there is a curvilinear relationship with a restriction-of-range problem. An example is the training of athletes to perform a sport.

Intense training increases performance, but when training becomes too intense (or the duration too long), performance suffers (Kreider, Fry, & O'Toole, 1998). The full relationship is an inverted U-shaped function:

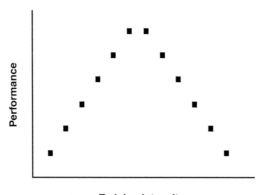

Training Intensity

If this function is combined with a restriction of range such that only low to moderate levels of training intensity are tested, Pearson's r will indicate a strong, positive relationship between the two variables:

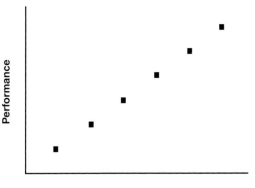

Training Intensity

As a result, we might be led to believe that training at ever-increasing intensities can only enhance performance. You might imagine that this faulty conclusion could lead coaches to push athletes beyond their peak training needs.

Thus, when restriction of range and a curvilinear relationship are combined, r may falsely indicate a linear relationship. Unfortunately, this type of r inflation is the most difficult to detect. A scatterplot will not show the problem, and a strong relationship between two variables is tempting to believe. Try to have a wide range of values on each variable, and subsequent research will fine-tune the theory over time.

Preview of Chapter 12

Recall that t-tests and ANOVA were used to analyze data that fell into specific levels, with some variables being true IVs and some being quasi-IVs. The analysis did not change when a quasi-IV was used; we merely learned to alter our discussion of cause and effect to a discussion of relationships. Likewise, although Pearson's r is generally used to imply a relationship between two variables, cause and effect can indeed be established if one of the variables is manipulated. For example, we could randomly assign participants to eat: 1,000 calories; 1,050 calories; 2,000 calories; 2,500 calories; 3,000 calories; 3,500 calories; or 4,000 calories per day for a year and measure their weight at the end of the year. Participants would be manipulated, allowing a significant result to be discussed as cause and effect: Calories cause changes in weight. From this discussion, please be reminded that the statistical analysis used does not imply causation (or relationship); the design of your study—whether or not participants were manipulated—guides discussion of your results.

Before we leave Chapter 11, I should point out that although this chapter was restricted to Pearson's r for two interval or ratio variables, other correlations are available for variables that do not reach interval level. Because the focus of this text is essential statistics, and Pearson's r is used far more often than other correlations, additional types of calculations were not addressed.

Pearson's r is used to quantify linear relationships between two interval or ratio variables, but careful evaluation of a scatterplot is necessary to help identify artificially low or high correlations. When you are confident that the r value is accurate, the coefficient of determination can communicate the proportion the two variables have in common.

If two variables are related, we should be able to predict one variable from the other. In Chapter 12, you will learn how to predict based on a linear relationship between two variables. In addition, you will learn how far from the truth you might be each time you make a prediction.

Conceptual Items

1. What is the full name of Pearson's r?
2. Pearson's r is used when both variables are _____ or _____ data.
3. Pearson's r can range from _____ to _____.
4. The coefficient of determination can range from _____ to _____.
5. Sketch 2 scatterplots with straight lines and a 0 relationship.
6. Pearson's r captures only _____ relationships between variables.
7. Write the null hypothesis for a two-tailed correlational test.
8. Which problem(s) associated with an artificially low r-value can be identified with a scatterplot of the data? Which problem(s) are not apparent in a graph?
9. Which problem(s) associated with an artificially high r-value can be identified with a scatterplot of the data? Which problem(s) are not apparent in a graph?

Application Items

10. For each of the following, choose whether the relationship is weak, moderate, or strong.
    a. 0.09   c. 0.48
    b. −0.32   d. −0.75
11. For each of the following scatterplots, make an educated guess about the direction of the relationship (positive or negative) and the strength of the relationship (weak, moderate, or strong):

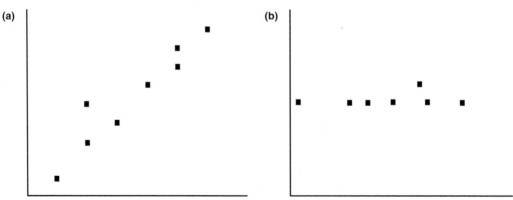

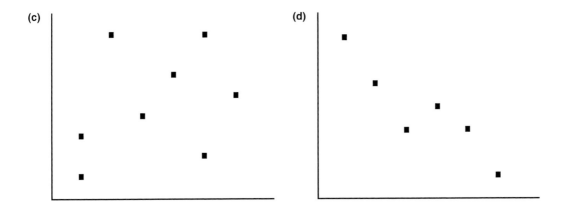

12. Based on your knowledge of linear relationships, analyze the following data set and draw conclusions from your results. Your job is to clearly communicate exactly what this data set reveals about the relationship between age (in years) and the amount of respect given to people in our society, with the expectation that age brings increasing respect. For the respect variable, assume each person was asked to rate the amount of respect received on a daily basis using a scale from 0 to 100, with higher numbers indicating more respect. Using the following data, address items a–i:

Age	Respect
39	90
75	63
15	48
62	85
19	59
21	60
26	78
37	84
40	96
82	40
45	87
12	35
50	95
35	81
67	78
20	62
72	66
29	76
80	45

a. Lay out the H_0 and H_1 hypotheses.
b. Choose a specific statistic to analyze these data.

    c. Sketch the distribution of normal people, and include the p-value, degrees of freedom, and r_{crit}.

    d. Analyze these data, and write the result in APA style.

    e. Reject or fail to reject the null hypothesis.

    f. Calculate the coefficient of determination. What is the percent of variability in common between the two variables?

    g. Sketch a scatterplot of these data to see if your calculations accurately depict the relationship.

    h. Based on your results, what did you learn from this study? (That is, put your results in plain English.)

    i. Analyze this example in SPSS and provide data layout, output, and a scatterplot.

Use a–i from Application Item 12 to analyze the following examples.

13. Most people report that they get nervous as the day for a speech approaches; therefore, we would expect a specific type of relationship between days until the deadline to give a speech and ratings of nervousness on a scale from 1 to 20, with higher numbers representing more nervousness:

Days Before Speech	Nervousness
8	9
3	13
10	7
1	18
10	2
14	4
2	13
11	9
5	12

14. For some odd reason, the more money people earn, the more bills they seem to acquire. Rely on the following fabricated data set to assess this possibility:

Monthly pay	Monthly bills
2500	2000
1000	500
3200	2500
5000	4000
1800	500
2900	2100
3700	2600
4000	2200
6000	5400
2000	800
1100	750
650	325

15. If we looked at the potential relationship between the length of a comedy show and the length of clapping, we might expect people to appreciate a long perform- ance and reward the comedian with more clapping, or become bored and clap less when the performance ends. Examine the following data to see if either of these suppositions is supported:

Length of comedy (minutes)	Length of clapping (seconds)
30	10
20	11
30	10
50	35
10	10
40	9
10	13
20	16
20	12
10	5
30	15

Computational formula in this chapter

Pearson's correlation coefficient

$$r = \frac{N\left(\sum XY\right) - \left(\sum X\right)\left(\sum Y\right)}{\sqrt{\left[N\left(\sum X^2\right) - \left(\sum X\right)^2\right]\left[N\left(\sum Y^2\right) - \left(\sum Y\right)^2\right]}}$$

References

In Text:

Kelly, W. E., Kelly, K. E., & Clanton, R. C. (2001). The relationship between sleep length and grade-point average among college students. *College Student Journal, 35*, 84–86.

Related Articles:

Brown, F. C., Soper, B., Buboltz, W. C. (2001). Prevalence of delayed sleep syndrome in uni- versity students. *College Student Journal, 35*, 472–476.

Buboltz, W. C., Brown, F., & Soper, B. (2001). Sleep habits and patterns of college students: A preliminary study. *Journal of American College Health, 50*, 131–135.

Gray, E. K., & Watson, D. (2002). General and specific traits of personality and their relation to sleep and academic performance, *Journal of Personality, 70*, 177–206.

Overtraining of Athletes Book:

Kreider, R. B., Fry, A. C., & O'Toole, M. L. (Eds.). (1998). *Overtraining in sport*. Champaign, IL: Human Kinetics.

12

Linear Regression

Correlation Before Prediction

When two variables are correlated (have variability in common), we can predict one from the other. In fact, prediction is a logical application or extension of the correlations presented in the previous chapter. Imagine a perfect correlation of 1.00 between two variables. The coefficient of determination multiplied by 100 indicates that the two variables have 100% of their variability in common. With 100% overlap, we would have perfect prediction. A correlation of −1.00 between two variables also means they have 100% in common, and again we would have perfect prediction of Y from X.

Recall that life rarely produces perfect relationships between variables, and less-than-perfect relationships will not allow perfect prediction. In other words, prediction of Y values from X values will not be entirely accurate. Not surprisingly, this is called prediction error, which will be calculated later in the chapter.

Linear Regression Theory

Predicting Y values from X values when a linear relationship exists (Pearson's r) can be accomplished using **linear regression.** The most logical way to think of linear regression at this point is to estimate a line through a scatterplot that best represents the linear relationship seen on the graph. For example, points on the scatterplot on the next page fall roughly in the pattern of a straight line, so a line through the points can easily be visualized.

The line is called the **regression line,** or the line of prediction. We will be able to choose any point on the x-axis, look up to the prediction line, then move to the left to find a predicted value of Y. Notice on the following graphs that any prediction might not be entirely correct, since not all data points would fall directly on the regression line, but the line would provide a guide for a good guess. If most of the data points cluster close to the regression line, prediction of Y values would be fairly accurate. In other words, there would be little error in predictions.

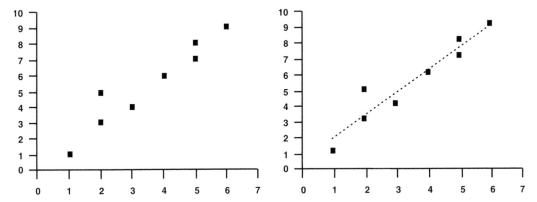

You might remember from math courses that the formula for a line is $y = mx + b$. The m refers to the slope of the line, and b stands for the point where the line crosses the y-axis (also called the Y-intercept). In psychology, the same formula is represented by different letters: $Y' = bX + a$. In this formula, b is the slope, and a is the Y-intercept. Y' is pronounced Y prime, and represents the predicted value. Finally, X represents any value of X you choose to insert in the formula when predicting a specific outcome (value of Y').

Prediction

Prediction of one variable from another is common, and decisions about your life have already been made based on regression analysis. For example, colleges and universities often try to predict college GPA from SAT scores, because the two variables are correlated. Administrators predicted your college GPA (Y' value) from your SAT score (X value). A low SAT predicts a low college GPA, so students with low SAT scores have a poorer chance of succeeding in college.

To be able to predict college GPA from SAT scores, a regression equation was created. First, a sample of students completed the SAT, and those students were allowed to attend college. After they graduated, college GPA and SAT were correlated to see if there was any relationship at all. If no relationship had been found, it would have been a waste of time to try to predict one from the other. However, the two variables were found to be related, and sample data might have looked like this:

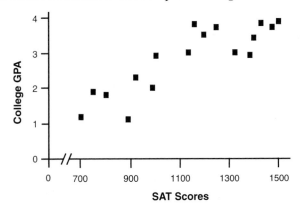

The scatterplot (like the Pearson's r) depicts a clear positive relationship between SAT scores and college GPA. Since a relationship existed, regression analysis was conducted, which placed a prediction line on the graph and also provided a formula to predict college GPA (Y') from SAT scores (X). After numbers were filled in for b (the slope) and a (the Y-intercept), predictions began. Incoming students took the SAT, and college GPA was predicted from SAT by inserting each student's SAT score (X) and predicting college GPA (Y'). Every time another group completed college, students' GPAs were collected and used to recalculate the regression equation again to be ready for the next group of students who took the SAT. In this way, the regression equation is always evolving.

As you know, the SAT and college GPAs have existed for a long time, and the prediction equation used by schools has been fine-tuned over and over again. With a limited number of spaces in each incoming class, schools must find a way to guess about each applicant's academic performance.

Error in Predictions

Recall that predictions are not perfect, so predicting college GPA from an SAT score is not always accurate; there is error. For example, highly motivated students might make better grades than were predicted by their SAT scores. Likewise, some bright students (with high SAT scores) might earn worse grades than predicted because they partied more than they should have (or didn't bother to study or attend every class). Although prediction of college GPA from SAT scores is not perfect, it is reasonably good; therefore, the prediction equation is used.

I should mention here that colleges and universities use more than SAT scores to predict how well students will perform. They also use variables such as high-school grades. The regression formula can be extended to include many predictors without much difficulty, as long as a computer is used to analyze data. Then we could insert values for SAT score (X_1), high-school GPA (X_2), and any other variables that might be useful when predicting how well a student will perform in college. Additional predictors not only reduce error in predictions, they also seem fairer than relying only on one predictor to capture all of a student's potential for success. When more than one predictor is used, the statistical analysis is called **multiple regression,** and SPSS handles this analysis efficiently. At the end of this chapter, you will be directed to Appendix B for multiple regression on SPSS.

Calculating the Regression Equation

Creating a regression equation requires a group of people to provide data on both the X and Y variables in order for the regression equation to be calculated and used to predict future samples. We collect data on the first sample, analyze whether or not the two variables are correlated, then move on to regression analysis only if the variables are related. For calculations, we will consider a new example based on exposure to the sun. Research suggests that tanning is prevalent among young adults (Cokkinides et al., 2001; Vail-Smith & Felts, 1993), and at least one study indicates that warning people of the damaging effects to appearance may reduce unprotected sun exposure (Jones & Leary, 1994). Below is a fabricated data set of the amount of exposure to the sun (average hours per week) and skin health at age 50 on a scale from 1 to 100, with higher numbers representing more healthful.

Sun Exposure	Skin Health
9	34
3	75
5	78
6	56
3	82
1	93
4	69

First, whether or not these two variables are correlated must be assessed with Pearson's r.

$$r = \frac{N\left(\sum XY\right) - \left(\sum X\right)\left(\sum Y\right)}{\sqrt{\left[N\left(\sum X^2\right) - \left(\sum X\right)^2\right]\left[N\left(\sum Y^2\right) - \left(\sum Y\right)^2\right]}}$$

The necessary pieces of information are below:

X		**Y**		
Sun Exposure	X^2	*Skin Health*	Y^2	XY
9	81	34	1156	306
3	9	75	5625	225
5	25	78	6084	390
6	36	56	3136	336
3	9	82	6724	246
1	1	93	8649	93
4	16	69	4761	276
$\sum X = 31$	$X^2 = 177$	$\sum Y = 487$	$\sum Y^2 = 36135$	$\sum XY = 1872$

Pearson's r can now be completed:

$$r = \frac{7(1872) - (31)(487)}{\sqrt{[7(177) - (31)^2][7(36135) - (487)^2]}} = -0.951670$$

With an r-value of -0.95, the relationship between these two variables is strong. We might also want to create a scatterplot (see next page) to make sure this is not an artificially high r-value due to outliers (refer to Chapter 11).

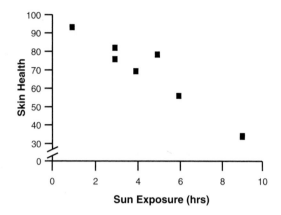

Based on the scatterplot, the data set has no obvious problems (other than a rather small number of participants); therefore, it would be reasonable to continue with the prediction analysis.

Calculate the slope (b) of the line.

$$b = \frac{N(\sum XY) - (\sum X)(\sum Y)}{N(\sum X^2) - (\sum X)^2}$$

Notice that this formula is similar to the formula for Pearson's r, a reasonable comparison since prediction is based on a relationship between the two variables. In addition, the slope and the r-value should have the same sign; for this example, both the r-value and the slope should be negative.

The completed formula for the slope is:

$$b = \frac{7(1872) - (31)(487)}{7(177) - (31)^2} = \frac{13104 - 15097}{1239 - 961} = -7.169065$$

Next, complete the formula for the Y-intercept (a). The Y-intercept requires the slope (above) and $\overline{X}$ and $\overline{Y}$ values.

$$a = \overline{Y} - (b)(\overline{X}) = 69.571429 - (-7.169065)(4.428571) = 101.320142$$

Now fill in the slope and Y-intercept to produce the regression equation for this data set. Six decimal places are maintained in the regression equation because further calculations are required for Y'.

$$\hat{Y} = (-7.169065)(X) + 101.320142$$

If prediction is good, we should be able to ask a person approximately how many hours are spent in the sun per week, then predict skin health at age 50. Insert the number of hours per week in the X location in the formula, and calculate skin health in older age if hours of sun exposure continue. For example, if a friend said he spends an average of 8.5 hours in the sun each week, his predicted skin health at 50 years old would be 40.383090.

$$Y' = (-7.169065)(8.5) + 101.320142 = 40.383090$$

Because the skin health scale ranges from 1 to 100, a score of 40.38 is poor. Based on our research, you can explain to your friend the relationship between sun exposure and skin health. Perhaps he decides he can reduce his sun exposure to 3 hours a week, but he wants to know if this change will improve his skin health substantially. By calculating Y' for 3 hours, you can tell him that 3 hours of sun exposure will nearly double his skin-health score.

$$Y' = (-7.169065)(3) + 101.320142 = 79.812947$$

As a final example, if you spend an average of 1 hour in the sun each week, you could use the equation to predict your own skin health at age 50.

$$Y' = (-7.169065)(1) + 101.320142 = 94.151077$$

A skin-health score of 94.15 is excellent, and you can feel confident in your decision to stay out of the sun (at least without sunscreen).

Graphing the Regression Line

Now that the regression equation for this data set has been calculated, a regression line can be sketched on the scatterplot of the original sample. Recall that the scatterplot for this data set was created earlier in the chapter.

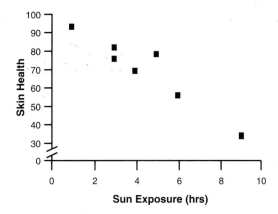

To place the regression line on the graph, a minimum of two points are required for a straight line. Insert two values of X (one at a time) to get two predicted values. Since the line of regression is the prediction line, all predicted values will fall on it. Be careful to choose X values that are found on the x-axis so the predicted values will fall within the range of the graph. I recommend an X value at the far left of the x-axis and one at the far right, to create an accurate line that stretches across the entire figure.

An X value of 1 is found at the far left.

$$Y' = (-7.169065)(1) + 101.320142 = 94.151077$$

A point intersecting at 1 and 94.15 can be placed on the graph. You could use an asterisk rather than a dot to identify the predicted value.

An X value of 9 is found at the far right of the x-axis.

$$Y' = (-7.169065)(9) + 101.320142 = 36.798557$$

Place an asterisk on the graph at the intersection of 9 and 36.80. Next, connect the two asterisks to create a straight line—the regression line or the line of prediction.

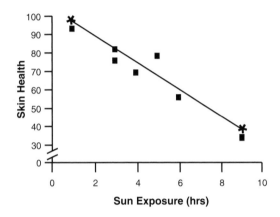

The new graph (with the prediction line) will facilitate estimates about skin health at age 50 from the number of hours of sun exposure. Choose a value of sun exposure on the x-axis, move up to the regression line, and look left to the y-axis to predict skin health. The graph illustrates the relationship between the two variables and allows estimates of skin health using the prediction line.

Of course, for more mathematically exact predictions, use the regression equation itself to predict skin health from sun exposure, by inserting a specific value of X (as discussed earlier). Regardless of the method chosen, will predictions be perfect? No. Countless other factors influence skin health at 50 (for example, smoking damages skin). So, our guesses will not be perfect; predictions will have some error.

Standard Error of the Estimate

The average amount of error during prediction is called the **standard error of the estimate.** If two variables were perfectly related (± 1.00), prediction would be perfect every time, and there would be no error in predictions. In real life, however, error exists. In the example of sun exposure and skin health, prediction of someone's skin health from amount of sun exposure will not be exactly correct.

Standard Error Calculations

We can find out how far from truth we are when predicting skin health. To do this, use the same sample of people who first provided information about sun exposure and skin health. Using the regression equation for this example, we can predict their skin health and check to see how far off we were, because members of the sample have already reached 50 years of age. Below is a table of their actual scores and what we would have predicted with our regression equation. Simple subtraction provides us with error (how far off we would have been) for each participant.

X	Y		
Sun Exposure	*Skin Health*	Y'	$(Y - Y')$
9	34	36.80	−2.80
3	75	79.81	−4.81
5	78	65.47	12.53
6	56	58.31	−2.31
3	82	79.81	2.19
1	93	94.15	−1.15
4	69	72.64	−3.64

An average amount of error will quantify about how far off we are most of the time when predicting skin health from sun exposure. If we follow the logic of calculating an average (the mean), we might add all the errors and divide by the number in the sample. We have tried this before when we discussed standard deviation in Chapter 4. Unfortunately, adding all the error scores equals 0, making it impossible to get an average error score that way.

X	Y		
Sun Exposure	*Skin Health*	Y'	$(Y - Y')$
9	34	36.80	−2.80
3	75	79.81	−4.81
5	78	65.47	12.53
6	56	58.31	−2.31
3	82	79.81	2.19
1	93	94.15	−1.15
4	69	72.64	−3.64
			0.01

(Note that rounding each Y' to two decimal places to fit the numbers neatly in the table caused a bit of rounding error, and as a result, the $\Sigma(Y - Y') = 0.01$. We consider this the same as a 0.)

In Chapter 4, the solution to a sum of 0 was to square all the error values, then add them up and divide by N. We know this works (since we've done it before), but we also know it gives us a large value for error because we squared every error value. To reduce the error term back to where it should be, we simply take the square root of the final number. The logic is illustrated in the following definitional formula:

$$S_{Y'} = \sqrt{\frac{\Sigma(Y - Y')^2}{N}}$$

If this discussion sounds like the one we had for standard deviation, it is. If you recall that discussion, you probably also know that we do not actually use the

definitional formula to calculate average error. Instead, we use a formula that results in the same answer: the computational formula for the standard error of the
estimate.

$$S_{Y'} = S_Y \sqrt{1 - (r)^2}$$

To complete this formula, Pearson's r (calculated earlier to be -0.951670) and
the sample standard deviation of Y are required. As a reminder, below is the sample standard deviation calculation, with X replaced by Y to indicate that the Y column is used:

$$S_Y = \sqrt{\dfrac{\sum Y^2 - \dfrac{(\sum Y)^2}{N}}{N}}$$

$$S_Y = \sqrt{\dfrac{36135 - \dfrac{(487)^2}{7}}{7}} = 17.943221$$

Now fill in the components of the standard error of the estimate formula to find
out how far off we will be when predicting someone's skin health from amount of
sun exposure.

$$S_{Y'} = 17.943221 \sqrt{1 - (-0.951670)^2}$$

Six decimal places of the r-value were used in this calculation, because the final
answer is $S_{Y'}$, and only the final answer can be rounded to two decimal places.

$$S_{Y'} = 17.943221 \left(\sqrt{1 - 0.905676} \right) = 5.510760$$

On average, we will be off about 5.51 when predicting someone's skin health
in older age from the amount of sun exposure during college years. For example,
we would predict a skin health rating of 40.38 for someone who spends approximately 8.5 hours a week in the sun. Based on the standard error of the estimate, we
would be off approximately 5.51 points. We can subtract and add the standard
error of the estimate from the estimated value of 40.38 to see the likely range in
which the real score for skin health would fall. The actual rating of skin health in
old age for someone who spent about 8.5 hours per week in the sun is likely to fall
between 34.87 and 45.89 on a scale from 1 to 100.

Thus, prediction is not perfect, but the standard error of the estimate can
be used to tell people a range of skin health in which they are likely to fall at the
age of 50. The more error, the wider the range will be, and the less meaningful
predictions will be. (For example, if we predicted a skin health rating of 55, but
the likely range for that person was between 15 and 95, our prediction wouldn't
be useful.)

Prediction on SPSS

Data layout in SPSS is the same as correlation and the related-samples *t*-test. All three of these analyses are based on pairs of scores, so it is important to lay out each pair side-by-side on the spreadsheet.

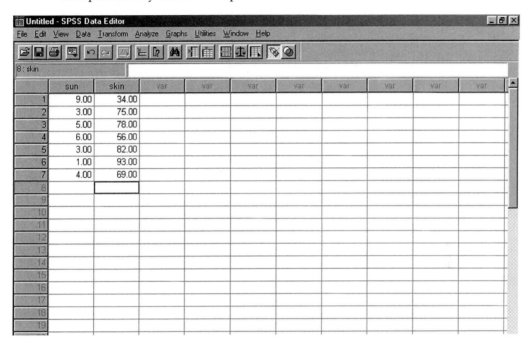

Correlation on SPSS

First, analyze the data using bivariate correlation as we did in Chapter 11.

Correlations

Correlations

		SUN	SKIN
SUN	Pearson Correlation	1	−.952**
	Sig. (2-tailed)	.	.001
	N	7	7
SKIN	Pearson Correlation	−.952**	1
	Sig. (2-tailed)	.001	.
	N	7	7

** Correlation is significant at the 0.01 level

The output shows that the two variables are related, with a strong negative correlation of −0.95 (and a significance value of 0.001). With such a strong correlation, it is perfectly reasonable to continue with prediction analysis.

Linear Regression on SPSS

Point to Analyze and select Regression+Linear.

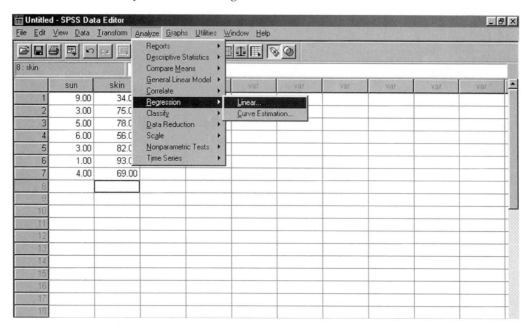

In the gray box that opens, select sun and click it under Independent(s). Select skin and move it to Dependent. (Of course, this is not an experiment, so the words don't mean that we have independent and dependent variables.)

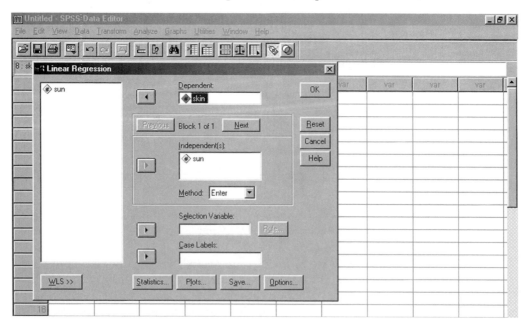

Click OK for output.

Regression

Variables Entered/Removed[b]

Model	Variables Entered	Variables Removed	Method
1	CIGS, SUN[a]	.	Enter

a. All requested variables entered.

b. Dependent Variable: SKIN

Model Summary

Model	R	R Square	Adjusted R Square	Std. Error of the Estimate
1	.987[a]	.973	.960	3.87044

a. Predictors: (Constant), CIGS, SUN

ANOVA[b]

Model		Sum of Squares	df	Mean Square	F	Sig.
1	Regression	2193.793	2	1096.896	73.222	.001[a]
	Residual	59.921	4	14.980		
	Total	2253.714	6			

a. Predictors: (Constant), CIGS, SUN

b. Dependent Variable: SKIN

Coefficients[a]

Model		Unstandardized Coefficients		Standardized Coefficients	t	Sig.
		B	Std. Error	Beta		
1	(Constant)	97.512	3.311		29.454	.000
	SUN	-4.367	1.071	-.580	-4.077	.015
	CIGS	-.926	.290	-.454	-3.192	.033

a. Dependent Variable: SKIN

The ANOVA summary table reveals that the model of prediction of skin health from sun exposure is a good one, as indicated by the significance level of 0.001 (less than the required 0.05 for significance). The regression output table is found under Coefficients, and relevant information for the equation is found under the column marked B. Based on earlier hand calculations, we know that a Constant of 101.320 represents the Y-intercept of the equation, or the a. The -7.169 beside SUN is the slope value, or b for the regression equation. Under the significance column, the predictor SUN has a significance value of 0.001, so we know that sun significantly predicts skin health (although we already knew sun was a useful predictor based on the significance value in the ANOVA summary table). The significance value for Constant on the first line of the regression table is not relevant. You might find it useful to rewrite the regression equation from the table, then you can plug in any X value for prediction when you're ready.

In the table labeled Model Summary, the output shows R^2, which we know to be the same as the coefficient of determination. Because correlation and prediction both rely on overlap between variables, R^2 captures the strength of the relationship in both analyses. In regression analysis, rely on the adjusted R^2, which takes into account the sample size and number of predictors.

The Model Summary table also contains the standard error of the estimate. Notice that the number is slightly different from the one we calculated. This is because SPSS calculates standard error using the estimated population standard deviation of $Y (\hat{S}_Y)$, rather than the sample standard deviation of $Y (S_Y)$. (Remember that SPSS also calculated estimated population variability instead of sample variability when we covered the material in Chapter 4.) Your instructor will decide which number to use—standard error calculated by hand using the sample standard deviation, or the standard error calculated by SPSS using the estimated population standard deviation. Either way, the numbers will be similar.

APA-style Results Section

Results of our analyses in APA style follow:

Results

These data were analyzed using correlation and linear regression. The number of hours of skin exposure to the sun was significantly related to ratings of skin health at age 50, $r(5) = -0.95, p < 0.01$.

Hours of skin exposure significantly predicted skin health, $F(1, 5) = 48.01$, $p < 0.01$. The Y-intercept was 101.32, and the slope for sun exposure was -7.17 $(p = 0.001)$. Eighty-nine percent of the variability in skin health was explained by knowing hours of sun exposure, and the standard error of the estimate was 6.52.

Preview of Chapter 13

This chapter presented how to predict one variable (usually Y) from another variable (usually X) when the two variables are correlated. The variable used to predict is sometimes referred to as a predictor variable, and the variable predicted can be termed the criterion variable. Prediction is not perfect, and you can quantify error and provide a range in which the actual score is likely to fall. Keep in mind that correlation and regression designs generally do not deal with cause and effect. We are able to find out if two variables are related, and if they are, we can predict one from the other. In Appendix B, multiple regression is used to predict skin health from more than one variable.

The next chapter also provides what is primarily considered to be non-experimental information. Chapter 13 covers how to analyze the number of people (or rats or whatever is relevant) who fall in each group of a variable. For example, if we went to the park and found out how many people have children and how many don't, we would have information on how many people fell in each category. If you tried to run a *t*-test or correlation on these data, you would quickly see that one number in each of the two categories is not sufficient.

No Children	Have Children
17	55

In both the *t*-test and correlation, several values (of interval or ratio data) were found under each column; now only one number is in each category. To analyze a single value in each category, we turn to chi-square.

Conceptual Items

1. Before we predict values on one variable from another variable, we must first know that they are _____.
2. In the linear regression equation, *a* refers to _____.
3. In the linear regression equation, *b* stands for _____.
4. Finally, in the linear regression equation, *X* represents _____.
5. When graphing the regression line, the *X* variable is generally labeled on the _____-axis, and the *Y* variable is on the _____-axis.
6. The standard error of the estimate is calculated using the standard deviation of _____ values.
7. If the standard error of the estimate is 0, the correlation must be _____ or _____.
8. In the creation of the regression equation, which formula is most similar to Pearson's *r*?
9. When graphing the regression line, two values of *X* are generally used to yield two values of *Y'*; however, an alternate method would be to predict *Y'* for one *X* and use the *Y*-intercept as the second point. Under what qualifications would the latter approach be possible?
10. Returning to the sun exposure and skin health example in this chapter, could you estimate the number of hours spent in the sun during college years from a 50-year-old person's skin? Why or why not?
11. Although correlation and regression analyses generally do not draw conclusions about cause and effect, imagine that you randomly assigned people to levels of sleep (3, 6, or 9 hours) and examined their grades. Sleep is the IV, and the DV is measured in grades on a test. Assume you analyzed these data using correlation and regression and found a significant relationship. Would you be able to determine cause and effect from the outcome? Why or why not?

Application Items

12. Imagine that your instructor has noticed a relationship between grades on Test 1 and final grades in the course. If the relationship between these two variables is strong and significant, (s)he will adopt a class policy of giving students their final grade in the course based on their grades on Test 1. From last term, (s)he pulls the following grades:

Test 1	Final Grade
90	65
65	74
94	90
77	81
40	56
96	84
59	73
81	84

a. Are grades on Test 1 and final grades in the course related? Support your answer with a hand calculation and SPSS printout.

b. What proportion of variability do these two variables have in common? In other words, how much variability in final grades can be explained by knowing scores on Test 1?

c. If grades on Test 1 and final grades are significantly related, calculate the regression equation by hand and verify your work on SPSS.

d. Sketch a scatterplot of the data, and place the regression line on the graph.

e. Since predictions are not perfect, how far off (on average) will predictions fall?

f. If you made an 85 on Test 1, what final grade would be predicted? About how far off would the prediction be (on average) in either direction? Calculate the range in which your final grade would probably fall.

13. Based on Application Item 13 in Chapter 11, would it be reasonable to predict nervousness from the number of days remaining prior to giving a speech? For example, can an instructor predict how nervous her students will be based on how many more days they have to prepare a speech?

As a reminder, here are the data:

Days Before Speech	Nervousness
8	9
3	13
10	7
1	18
10	2
14	4
2	13
11	9
5	12

a. Calculate the regression equation by hand and verify your work on SPSS.

b. Place a regression line on a scatterplot of these data.

c. Since predictions are not perfect, how far off (on average) will predictions of nervousness fall?

d. If a student had 7 days remaining until his speech, how nervous do you think he would be? About how far off would the prediction be (on average) in either direction? Calculate the range in which his nervousness would probably fall.

14. Suppose you randomly assigned people to drink different amounts of caffeinated coffee: 0 ounces, 4 ounces, 8 ounces, 12 ounces, 16 ounces, and 20 ounces. One hour after they consumed the beverage, you measured their heartrate in beats per minute (BPM). Imagine you found the following data:

Coffee	BPM
0	65
0	50
0	78
4	73
4	80
4	69
4	75
8	71
8	88
12	72
12	89
12	87
16	70
16	88
16	83
20	90
20	78

a. Are amount of coffee and BPM related? If so, does this example allow us to discuss more than just a relationship between the two variables? In other words, can cause and effect be established? Explain your answer.

b. What proportion of variability do these two variables have in common? In other words, how much variability in BPM can be explained by knowing the amount of coffee consumed?

c. To be able to predict BPM from amount of coffee, calculate the regression equation by hand.

d. Sketch a scatterplot of the data, and place the regression line on the graph.

e. Since predictions are not perfect, how far off (on average) will predictions fall?

f. Verify all work on SPSS.

g. If you drank 6 ounces of coffee, what heartrate would you expect to have an hour later? About how far off would the prediction be (on average) in either direction? Calculate the range in which your BPM would probably fall.

15. If you wanted to examine note-taking and final grades in the course, you might ask participants to report the number of pages written from lecture each week as well as their final grades. Perhaps the following would be typical:

Number of pages	Grade
7.5	72
2	43
20	94
18	75
5	68
15	82
15.5	60
22	82
3.5	55
12	69
2	50
29	48
18.5	83
10	77
17	85
20.5	87
3	71

a. Is amount of note-taking related to grades? Quantify the relationship with a calculation.

b. Sketch a scatterplot of these data to see if any problems exist. If a problem is found, adjust the data set before continuing.

c. What proportion of variability do these two variables have in common? In other words, how much variability in grades can be explained by knowing the amount of notes taken?

d. To be able to predict grades from number of pages of notes, calculate the regression equation by hand.

e. Since predictions are not perfect, how far off (on average) will predictions fall?

f. Verify all work on SPSS.

g. If you wrote 23 pages of notes per week, what grade might you expect in this course? About how far off would the prediction be (on average) in either direction? Calculate the range in which your grade would probably fall.

Note: For additional practice, refer to Chapter 11. Use any example in which the two variables were significantly related.

Computational formulas in this chapter

Pearson's correlation coefficient

$$r = \frac{N\left(\sum XY\right) - \left(\sum X\right)\left(\sum Y\right)}{\sqrt{\left[N\left(\sum X^2\right) - \left(\sum X\right)^2\right]\left[N\left(\sum Y^2\right) - \left(\sum Y\right)^2\right]}}$$

Linear regression (prediction) equation

$$Y' = bX + a$$

Slope of the regression line

$$b = \frac{N\left(\sum XY\right) - \left(\sum X\right)\left(\sum Y\right)}{N\left(\sum X^2\right) - \left(\sum X\right)^2}$$

Y Intercept of the regression line

$$a = \overline{Y} - (b)(\overline{X})$$

Standard error of the estimate

$$S_{Y'} = S_Y\sqrt{1 - (r)^2}$$

References

In Text:

Cokkinides, V. E., Johnston-Davis, K., Weinstock, M., O'Connell, M. C., Kalsbeek, W., Thun, M. J., Wingo, P. A. (2001). Sun exposure and sun-protection behaviors and attitudes among U.S. youth, 11 to 18 years of age. *Preventive Medicine: An International Journal Devoted to Practice & Theory, 33*, 141–152.

Jones, J. L., & Leary, M. R. (1994). Effects of appearance-based admonitions against sun exposure on tanning intentions in young adults. *Health Psychology, 13*, 86–90.

Vail-Smith, K., & Felts, W. M. (1993). Sunbathing: College students' knowledge, attitudes, and perceptions of risk. *Journal of American College Health, 42*, 21–26.

Related Articles:

Jackson, K. M., Aiken, L. S. (2000). A psychosocial model of sun protection and sunbathing in young women: The impact of health beliefs, attitudes, norms, and self-efficacy for sun protection. *Health Psychology, 19*, 469–478.

Prentice-Dunn, S., Jones, A. L., Jones, J. L., & Floyd, D. L. (1997). Persuasive appeals and the reduction of skin cancer risk: The roles of appearance concern, perceived benefits of a tan, and efficacy information. *Journal of Applied Social Psychology, 27*, 1041–1047.

Robinson, J. K., Rademaker, A. W. (1995). Skin cancer risk and sun protection learning by helpers of patients with nonmelanoma skin cancer. *Preventive Medicine: An International Journal Devoted to Practice & Theory, 24*, 333–341.

13

Chi-Square Analyses

Simple Frequency Counts

The early chapters of this book presented descriptive statistics, which are simply used to describe a sample. Then several chapters were devoted to inferential statistics, which are used to learn about a population based on a sample. The specific type of inferential statistics we have been covering is **parametric statistics,** and this type is based on data (DVs or correlational variables) that are at interval or ratio level. This chapter explains two final inferential statistics, both of which are based on simpler data: frequency counts (how frequently a category is represented). These analyses are called **nonparametric statistics.** Without interval or ratio data, *t*-tests, ANOVA, and Pearson's *r* would not be appropriate. Instead **chi square** will be used, symbolized by χ^2.

One-way χ^2: Goodness-of-fit Test

The first type of χ^2 is called the **goodness-of-fit test**. It is also called the **one-way** χ^2, because only one variable is examined. The variable cannot be called an IV, because participants are not manipulated to experience an IV level, but the variable will look like an IV split into levels. For example, a variable might be whether or not people on a college campus like dogs, with yes as one level and no as another level of the variable. To keep this simple, no one will be allowed to answer maybe. Of course, people are not randomly assigned to like or dislike dogs, they just report their preference. Then we can record frequency counts, or in other words, we can see how many people fall into each category. This is called the **observed frequency** and is symbolized by f_o, where f is the simple frequency introduced in Chapter 2, and o represents observed.

Null and Alternative Hypotheses

Before data collection, the null and alternative hypotheses must be outlined. For the one-way χ^2, that means setting up our expectations of how many people will like dogs and how many will not like dogs. Lay out **expected frequency** for each category, with expected frequency symbolized by f_e. The null hypothesis indicates that we will find exactly what is expected: Observed frequencies will be the same as expected frequencies.

H_0: Expected frequencies and observed frequencies are the same.

It would also be acceptable to use symbols with the plural form of expected and observed frequencies indicated by an *s* at the end of each symbol.

H_0: $f_e s = f_o s$

The alternative hypothesis would say that what we observed was significantly different from what we expected to find.

H_1: Expected frequencies and observed frequencies are not equal.

Or in symbols,

H_1: $f_e s \neq f_o s$

If we find (observe) different numbers of people in each group than expected, the outcome is considered unusual, and the results may be of interest to the scientific community. Notice that with the one-way χ^2, observed frequencies are not compared to each other, they are compared with expected frequencies.

Chosen Statistic

When expected frequencies are hypothesized prior to data collection, the statistic of choice will be the one-way χ^2 (goodness-of-fit test). Another hint for using the one-way χ^2 is having only one variable and simple frequency counts for data.

Sampling Distribution for χ^2

Using the same example of liking dogs, half of the people in our sample might be expected to like dogs and half to not like them. If the sample consists of 50 people, that means 50%, or 25 people, would be expected to like dogs and 50%, or 25 people, would be expected to not like dogs, making expected frequencies 25 and 25 across the two categories.

The format for these data is as follows:

Do you like dogs?

Yes	**No**
$f_e = 25$	$f_e = 25$

After indicating expectations, data are collected from a sample of 50 people. Each person is asked the question and put in a category of either liking or not liking dogs. As mentioned earlier, the actual data (rather than expectations) are symbolized by observed frequency (f_o).

Do you like dogs?

Yes	No
$f_e = 25$	$f_e = 25$
$f_o = 25$	$f_o = 25$

Since this is the goodness-of-fit test, does it look like the 25/25 observed lay-out fits our expectations? Yes, observed frequencies of 25 and 25 exactly fit our expected frequencies of 25 and 25. Thus, nothing unusual has been found, and the null hypothesis has been supported. If we take this opportunity to calculate the x^2 for these data, we will discover the value of x^2 when the null hypothesis is true.

The formula for x^2_{obt} is below:

$$x^2_{obt} = \Sigma \left(\frac{(f_o - f_e)^2}{f_e} \right)$$

Each cell (level) is calculated individually before adding the components of the x^2 together.

$$x^2 = \left(\frac{(25 - 25)^2}{25} + \frac{(25 - 25)^2}{25} \right) = 0$$

As illustrated above, when the null hypothesis is true, x^2 is 0. Therefore, to sketch this distribution, the highest part of the graph is above the 0 point to reflect the idea that x^2 is most likely to be 0 in the normal population.

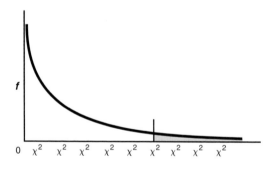

To reject this picture of the null hypothesis, a x^2 value would have to fall far enough to the right of the graph to be significantly different from normal. Since the x^2 for this example was 0, the lowest possible value, we failed to reject the null hypothesis. Inferring to the population, about 50% of people on a college campus like dogs and 50% do not like them.

x^2_{obt} Above Zero

The same study using a sample of people visiting an animal shelter would address the possibility that these customers answer the question in the same expected pattern of an equal split. In this study, 100 people will be sampled rather than 50, so the expected frequencies would be 50/50 rather than the 25/25 split from the previous study.

Do you like dogs?

Yes	No
$f_e = 50$	$f_e = 50$

Now that expectations have been specified, 100 people at an animal shelter can be asked whether or not they like dogs. Observed frequencies are below.

Do you like dogs?

Yes	No
$f_e = 50$	$f_e = 50$
$f_o = 65$	$f_o = 35$

The observed frequencies are not 50/50, but are they different enough from expectations to decide that they are significantly different? Or is the 65/35 split only different from a 50/50 split because of sampling error? We will rely on the x^2 statistic to answer this question.

$$x^2 = \left(\frac{(65 - 50)^2}{50} + \frac{(35 - 50)^2}{50} \right) = 4.50 + 4.50 = 9.00$$

The obtained value of x^2 is 9.00, a value to be compared with a critical value of x^2 based on $k - 1$ df, where k is the number of groups (in this case, 2). On the x^2 table, 1 df at $p = 0.05$ is 3.84. Because the obtained value of 9.00 is beyond 3.84, what was found (observed frequencies) was significantly different from what was expected (expected frequencies).

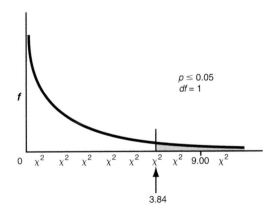

The one-way x^2 tested the goodness of fit for our 50/50 split and found that it was not a good fit for this sample of people. In other words, we found an interesting outcome.

APA Style

The result of this study is reported to the scientific community in APA style:

$$\chi^2(1, N = 100) = 9.00, p < 0.05$$

The null hypothesis was rejected; our observations were significantly different from our expectations. A 65/35 split on the question of liking dogs was significantly different from the expected 50/50 split.

Plain English

Results are discussed in plain English using descriptive statistics. For this example, we would say that although 50% of the sample was expected to like dogs, 65% did. Since only two categories were used, it is not necessary to mention the percent who did not like dogs. The fact that only 35% is leftover is logical. However, if three categories were used (perhaps not liking dogs, liking them slightly, and strongly liking them), it would be necessary to describe at least two of the three categories.

A second way to discuss the outcome in plain English would be to simply report that 65% of the people at an animal shelter liked dogs, and 35% did not like dogs. (Again, the 35% is logical, since 65% was already mentioned, but both percentages can be reported if you prefer.)

Inferring Back to the Population

Keep in mind that we are conducting inferential statistics. A sample of participants is used as a tool to learn something about the population from which they were drawn. Based on the results from our sample, we know it is likely that 65% of all people who visit animal shelters like dogs, and only 35% of these people do not like dogs.

Goodness-of-Fit for Three Levels

The one-way χ^2 is not limited to a variable with only two levels. For example, suppose a fast-food restaurant introduced a seaweed burger and wanted to know how many people would purchase it. The owners decided to have 200 people taste the burger and say they would either (a) definitely buy it, (b) definitely not buy it, or (c) maybe buy it. Since the owners had no information on how many people might fall in each category, they distributed their expected percentages equally across the three levels:

$$fe = \frac{N}{3} = \frac{200}{3} = 66.67$$

Would you buy this burger?

Yes	No	Maybe
$f_e = 66.67$	$f_e = 66.67$	$f_e = 66.67$

When data were collected from the 200 participants, the owner found the following observed frequencies.

Would you buy this burger?

Yes	No	Maybe
$f_e = 66.67$	$f_e = 66.67$	$f_e = 66.67$
$f_o = 50$	$f_o = 80$	$f_o = 70$

Insert the appropriate numbers in the x^2 formula and compare the x^2_{obt} value to the x^2_{crit}.

$$x^2 = \left(\frac{(50 - 66.67)^2}{66.67} + \frac{(80 - 66.67)^2}{66.67} + \frac{(70 - 66.67)^2}{66.67} \right) =$$

$$4.168125 + 2.6652 + .166325 = 6.99965$$

The critical value of x^2 is based on $k - 1$ degrees of freedom ($k = 3$, so $k - 1$ is 2 for this example).

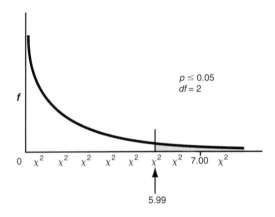

APA style is:

$$x^2(2, N = 200) = 7.00, p < 0.05$$

Reject the null hypothesis. What was observed was significantly different from what was expected. Rejecting the null simply means that one-third of potential customers did not fall in each category. This could be good news, if substantially more than one-third said they would buy the seaweed burger, or bad news, if a great deal more than one-third said they absolutely would not purchase the burger. Descriptive statistics clarify the significant result.

Divide each observed frequency by the size of the sample (200) and multiply by 100 to report the percent in each category. In this example, 25% would purchase the burger, 40% would not, and 35% might buy it.

Because we are conducting inferential statistics, the owners assume the same percentages would be found in the larger population. Based on the results from this sample, it might not be wise to market the seaweed burger after all.

Goodness-of-Fit with Unequal Expectations

In the previous two data sets, expected frequencies were equal across levels; however, equal frequencies will not always be expected. For example, we certainly would not expect to find an equal number of left-handed and right-handed people in any population. Neither would we expect to find an equal number of men and women in political office. Further, we would not expect to find every ethnic group equally represented in the field of medicine. Thus, expected frequencies will often be unequal, and we will need to locate numbers in previous research to let us know what would be expected for a given variable. Existing data in the literature help guide expectations, and it might be of interest to find if participants in our study deviate from those expectations.

For example, based on the finding by Goetestam (2001) that homosexuals are highly creative, we might want to see if we have a large number of homosexuals in a sample of 150 creative people. But first we would need to know the percentage of homosexuals in the normal population. Estimates have indicated that 10% of the adult population is homosexual; therefore, the same percentage could be expected in our sample.

10% of 150 expected to be homosexual:

$$150 \times 0.10 = 15$$

90% of 150 expected to be heterosexual:

$$150 \times 0.90 = 135$$

Even with unequal expected frequencies, the null hypothesis would be:

H_0: $f_e s = f_o s$

and the alternative hypothesis would be:

H_1: $f_e s \neq f_o s$

Lay out expected frequencies in the correct format:

Homosexuals	Heterosexuals
$f_e = 15$	$f_e = 135$

With these expectations, we could conduct our study on people who rate themselves as highly creative to see if the incidence of homosexuality is higher than 10%. Imagine we found the following data.

Homosexuals	Heterosexuals
$f_e = 15$	$f_e = 135$
$f_o = 23$	$f_o = 127$

Calculation of the χ^2_{obt} will reveal if a 23/127 split is significantly different from the 15/135 split we expected.

$$\chi^2 = \left(\frac{(23 - 15)^2}{15} + \frac{(127 - 135)^2}{135} \right) = 4.266667 + .474074 = 4.740741$$

Compare the obtained value of χ^2 to the critical value of χ^2 based on $k - 1$, or 1 degree of freedom.

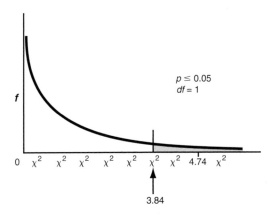

In APA style,

$$\chi^2(1, N = 150) = 4.74, p < 0.05$$

Reject the null hypothesis. Observed frequencies were significantly different from expected frequencies.

Based on these data, while we expected 10% of our sample of creative people to be homosexual, 15% were. Further, we expected 90% of our sample to be heterosexual, but only 85% were. Thus, a higher percentage of creative people were homosexual than would be expected in the normal population.

We might also infer back to the larger population of all creative people. Our sample data indicate that among all creative people, approximately 15% are homosexual, and 85% are heterosexual.

One-way χ^2 on SPSS

Although SPSS will conduct the one-way χ^2, the analysis is straightforward enough to be completed by hand most efficiently.

APA-style Results Section

Below is an APA-style results section for the most recent one-way χ^2 example:

Results

A one-way χ^2 test was used to analyze these data. We expected 10% of our sample of creative people to be homosexual and 90% to be heterosexual; however, observed frequencies were significantly different from expectations, $\chi^2(1, N = 150) = 4.74$, $p < 0.05$. Fifteen percent of our sample of creative people was homosexual, and 85% of our sample was heterosexual.

Two-way χ^2: Test of Independence

The second type of χ^2 is the **two-way** χ^2, or the **test of independence,** which is used when we have two variables with at least two categories each. Do not try to link the two-way χ^2 with the logic of the goodness-of-fit test, because they have completely different purposes. In the test of independence (two-way χ^2), the goal is to learn if two variables are independent of each other. For example, the previous example of homosexuality and creativity could be extended to a different question: Are the two variables independent of each other or related? We could pull a sample of college students and ask each participant to report sexual orientation and label themselves as either low or high in creativity:

	Homosexual	Heterosexual
Low Creativity		
High Creativity		

Null and Alternative Hypotheses

The null hypothesis specifies that the two variables are independent of each other. The alternative hypothesis indicates they are related to each other. No symbols are used to state the hypotheses:

H_0: The two variables are independent.

H_1: The two variables are not independent. (Or: The two variables are related to each other.)

Although this terminology sounds like Pearson's r, we will only have simple frequency in each condition, so a different statistic is needed for calculations of the relationship between the two variables.

Chosen Statistic

The statistic of choice when two variables contain only simple frequency data is the two-way χ^2. To symbolize two levels of each variable in this example, this design is labeled a $2 \times 2 \, \chi^2$.

Sampling Distribution

The sampling distribution for the two-way χ^2 is the same as the one-way χ^2, because both are based on the χ^2 calculation (even though the questions they answer are quite different). However, the two-way χ^2 requires a new calculation for degrees of freedom:

$$df = (\text{number of rows} - 1)(\text{number of columns} - 1)$$

Significantly Related

In the test of independence, expectations are not indicated first (that's only for the goodness-of-fit test). Instead, data are collected (observed frequencies) by asking participants to answer the two questions of the study. The observed frequencies might look like this:

	Homosexual	Heterosexual
Low Creativity	$f_o = 5$	$f_o = 25$
High Creativity	$f_o = 30$	$f_o = 15$

Adding all the observed frequencies equals N, which is 75 in this example.

To complete χ^2_{obt}, expected frequencies are needed and are calculated with the following formula:

$$f_e = \frac{(\text{cell's row total } f_o)(\text{cell's column total } f_o)}{N}$$

Recall that in the goodness-of-fit test, f_e was based on expectations, and expected frequencies were stated before data collection. However, in the test of independence, expected frequencies are completed after data collection, and they are calculated. For this example, we must calculate f_e for each of the four cells in the design:

	Homosexual	Heterosexual
Low Creativity	$f_o = 5$	$f_o = 25$
	$f_e = \dfrac{(30)(35)}{75} = 14.00$	$f_e = \dfrac{(30)(40)}{75} = 16.00$
High Creativity	$f_o = 30$	$f_o = 15$
	$f_e = \dfrac{(45)(35)}{75} = 21.00$	$f_e = \dfrac{(45)(40)}{75} = 24.00$

All information to complete the χ^2 is now available:

$$\chi^2 = \left(\frac{(5-14)^2}{14} + \frac{(25-16)^2}{16} + \frac{(30-21)^2}{21} + \frac{(15-24)^2}{24} \right)$$

$$\chi^2 = 5.785714 + 5.0625 + 3.857143 + 3.375 = 18.080357$$

The χ^2 obtained is 18.08. This value is compared with a critical value based on the *df* calculation:

$$(2-1)(2-1) = (1)(1) = 1$$

As in a prior example, the critical value for 1 *df* at the 0.05 level is 3.84.

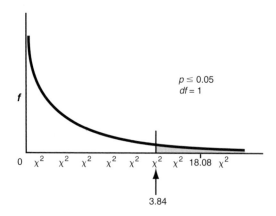

The x^2_{obt} value falls beyond the x^2_{crit} of 3.84, and in the critical region.

APA Style

In APA style:

$$x^2(1, N = 75) = 18.08, p < 0.05$$

Reject the null hypothesis that the two variables are independent. The two variables are significantly related to each other. That is, sexual orientation and creativity are related.

Strength of Effect

After a significant effect has been found in the two-way x^2, report the strength of that effect. Strength ranges from 0 to 1, with higher numbers indicating a stronger effect. For a 2×2 x^2, as illustrated by this example, the strength of the relationship is calculated using the **phi coefficient:**

$$\Phi = \sqrt{\frac{x^2_{obt}}{N}}$$

For this example, the phi coefficient is:

$$\Phi = \sqrt{\frac{18.08}{75}} = \sqrt{0.241067} = 0.490985$$

Therefore, the strength of the relationship is 0.49. Just as the Pearson's *r* was squared in Chapter 11 to get the proportion of variability in common, the phi coefficient is squared to get 0.24 variability in common between sexual orientation and creativity. Likewise, 0.24 can be multiplied by 100 to get percent in common: 24% in common between sexual orientation and creativity.

For a two-way χ^2 larger than 2×2, a different coefficient, the **contingency co-efficient**, provides the same information. The calculation for the contingency coefficient is only slightly different from the phi coefficient.

$$C = \sqrt{\frac{\chi^2_{obt}}{N + \chi^2_{obt}}}$$

Plain English

Just as with the one-way χ^2, descriptive statistics clarify the results. Since we collected data from 75 people, we could put the observed frequency for each cell over 75 and multiply by 100 to report the percent of the sample found in each cell. If we did, it would look like this:

	Homosexual	Heterosexual
Low Creativity	$f_o = 5$ $\frac{5}{75} \times 100 = 7\%$	$f_o = 25$ $\frac{25}{75} \times 100 = 33\%$
High Creativity	$f_o = 30$ $\frac{30}{75} \times 100 = 40\%$	$f_o = 15$ $\frac{15}{75} \times 100 = 20\%$

We could write the results to say 7% of our sample are homosexuals with low creativity, and 40% are homosexual and have high creativity. Thirty-three percent of the participants are heterosexual and rate themselves as low on creativity, and 20% are highly creative heterosexuals.

Another approach to describing our sample would be to discuss 1 column at a time. Since the first column contains 35 total observed frequency, 5 over 35×100 is 14%.

	Homosexual
Low Creativity	$f_o = 5$ $\frac{5}{35} \times 100 = 14\%$
High Creativity	$f_o = 30$ $\frac{30}{35} \times 100 = 86\%$

In other words, 14% of homosexuals are low on creativity, and 86% of homosexuals are highly creative. Now do the second column, with a total observed frequency of 40.

Heterosexual

Low Creativity	$f_o = 25$
	$\dfrac{25}{40} \times 100 = 63\%$
High Creativity	$f_o = 15$
	$\dfrac{15}{40} \times 100 = 38\%$

Twenty-five over 40 $\times$ 100 is 63%, so 63% of heterosexuals are low on creativity, and only 38% of heterosexuals are highly creative. (Percentages of heterosexuals who are low and high on creativity sum to 101% due to simple rounding error.) As you can see, breaking the data set into columns (or rows, if you prefer) and describing them separately sometimes makes more sense than putting each cell's observed frequency over the total N. Either way is accurate, but the goal is to make the results as clear as possible.

Inference to the Real Population

Before we complete this example in SPSS, I should make three points. First, it would be highly unlikely that 47% of a sample would be homosexual, since we already know that only about 10% of the general population is homosexual. Second, as a reminder, χ^2 generally does not tell us that 1 variable causes the other; the two-way χ^2 merely indicates that the two variables are related (like Pearson's r). Thus, the results of this example do not support the idea that homosexuality causes creativity or that creativity causes people to become homosexual. Indeed, research suggests that both homosexuality and creativity may result from brain asymmetry associated with the prenatal environment (McCormick, Witelson, & Kingstone, 1990). Third, alternate research suggests that homosexuals are not more creative than heterosexuals (e.g., Domino, 1977).

Two-way χ^2 in SPSS

The two-way χ^2 can be analyzed by SPSS, but of course data entry is different from previous chapters.

The variable that labels columns can be placed in the first column of SPSS. Based on our example, label the column sexual. Label levels 1 and 2 homosexual and heterosexual, respectively. The row variable in the example is creative and should be placed in the second column of the SPSS spreadsheet. Levels 1 and 2 are low creativity and high creativity. Because five people are found in the first cell (level 1 of sexual and level 1 of creative), this combination will be entered five times. Examine the first five rows below for clarification. Next, 30 participants reported that they were homosexual and highly creative; therefore, this combination is entered in the next 30 rows. The remaining combinations are heterosexuals who are low and high in creativity, with 25 and 15 combinations (rows), respectively.

	sexual	creative
1	homosex	low creat
2	homosex	low creat
3	homosex	low creat
4	homosex	low creat
5	homosex	low creat
6	homosex	high cre
7	homosex	high cre
8	homosex	high cre
9	homosex	high cre
10	homosex	high cre
11	homosex	high cre
12	homosex	high cre
13	homosex	high cre
14	homosex	high cre
15	homosex	high cre
16	homosex	high cre
17	homosex	high cre
18	homosex	high cre
19	homosex	high cre
20	homosex	high cre
21	homosex	high cre
22	homosex	high cre
23	homosex	high cre
24	homosex	high cre
25	homosex	high cre
26	homosex	high cre
27	homosex	high cre
28	homosex	high cre
29	homosex	high cre
30	homosex	high cre
31	homosex	high cre
32	homosex	high cre
33	homosex	high cre
34	homosex	high cre
35	homosex	high cre
36	heterose	low creat
37	heterose	low creat
38	heterose	low creat

	sexual	creative
39	heterose	low creat
40	heterose	low creat
41	heterose	low creat
42	heterose	low creat
43	heterose	low creat
44	heterose	low creat
45	heterose	low creat
46	heterose	low creat
47	heterose	low creat
48	heterose	low creat
49	heterose	low creat
50	heterose	low creat
51	heterose	low creat
52	heterose	low creat
53	heterose	low creat
54	heterose	low creat
55	heterose	low creat
56	heterose	low creat
57	heterose	low creat
58	heterose	low creat
59	heterose	low creat
60	heterose	low creat
61	heterose	high cre
62	heterose	high cre
63	heterose	high cre
64	heterose	high cre
65	heterose	high cre
66	heterose	high cre
67	heterose	high cre
68	heterose	high cre
69	heterose	high cre
70	heterose	high cre
71	heterose	high cre
72	heterose	high cre
73	heterose	high cre
74	heterose	high cre
75	heterose	high cre

After the data are entered, point to Analyze and select Descriptive Statistics+Crosstabs.

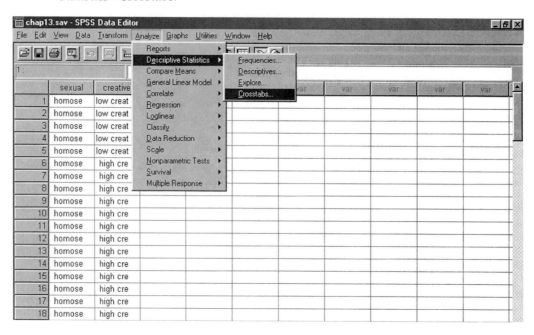

In the box that opens, move sexual to the Column(s) box and creative to the Row(s) box. Next, click Statistics.

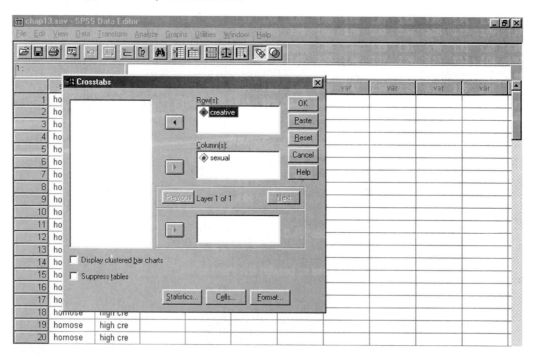

Check Chi-square and Phi and Cramer's to request effect size. Then click Continue.

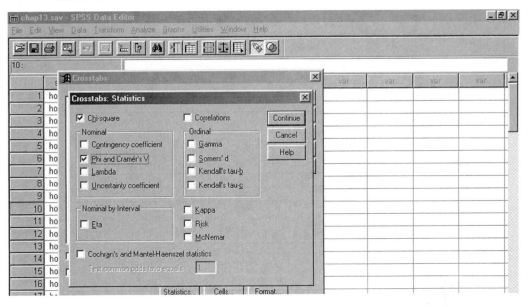

Notice that the Contingency coefficient is available for a design larger than 2×2.

Next, click Cells. Observed frequencies will be checked by default, and that is needed. In addition, check Column under Percentages, because we decided to discuss plain English results using percentage of homosexuals who are low and high on creativity separately from heterosexual creativity levels. Allowing SPSS to report percentages will save us the trouble of calculating these descriptive statistics by hand.

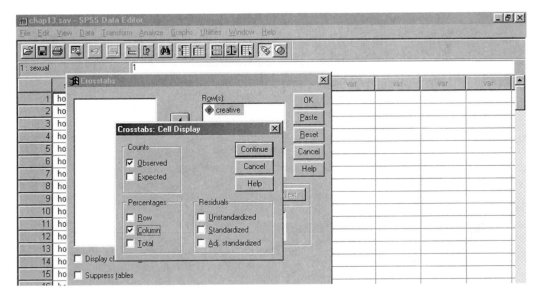

Click Continue+OK for the following output.

Crosstabs

Case Processing Summary

	Cases					
	Valid		Missing		Total	
	N	Percent	N	Percent	N	Percent
CREATIVE* SEXUAL	75	100.0%	0	.0%	75	100.0%

CREATIVE* SEXUAL Crosstabulation

			SEXUAL		
			homosexual	heterosexual	Total
CREATIVE	low creative	Count	5	25	30
		% within SEXUAL	14.3%	62.5%	40.0%
	high creative	Count	30	15	45
		% within SEXUAL	85.7%	37.5%	60.0%
Total		Count	35	40	75
		% within SEXUAL	100.0%	100.0%	100.0%

Chi-Square Tests

	Value	df	Asymp. Sig. (2-sided)	Exact Sig. (2-sided)	Exact Sig. (1-sided)
Pearson Chi-Square	18.080[b]	1	.000		
Continuity Correction[a]	16.127	1	.000		
Likelihood Ration	19.319	1	.000		
Fisher's Exact Test				.000	.000
Linear-by-Linear Association	17.839	1	.000		
N of Valid Cases	75				

a. Computed only for a 2x2 table

b. 0 cells (.0%) have expected count less than 5. The minimum expected count is 14.00.

Symmetric Measures

		Value	Approx. Sig.
Nominal by Nominal	Phi	-.491	.000
	Cramer's V	.491	.000
N of Valid Cases		75	

a. Not assuming the null hypothesis.

b. Using the asymptotic standard error assuming the null hypothesis.

From the output, examine the Chi-square Tests table first. In it you will see that the Pearson's Chi-square Value (on the first row) is 18.08, which is exactly what was calculated earlier in this chapter. Of course, $df = 1$, and the significance value is less than 0.05. In fact, it is less than 0.001.

In the Symmetric Measures table, the phi coefficient is -0.491, but the negative sign is irrelevant. Report the phi coefficient as the absolute value, which is 0.491. Remember also to square the value to report proportion of variability in common. Further, multiplying Φ by 100 provides percent in common.

With a significant χ^2 value, descriptive statistics become important to explain the result in plain English. The table labeled CREATIVE * SEXUAL Cross-tabulation shows that 14.3% of homosexuals in our sample were low on creativity, and 85.7% were highly creative. Percentages for heterosexuals in the sample are also reported, and all four of the percentages match what we calculated by hand earlier.

APA-style Results Section

APA-style results for the two-way χ^2 are as follows:

Results

A 2 × 2 (sexual orientation × creativity) χ^2 was used to analyze these data. Sexual orientation and high vs. low creativity were significantly related, $\chi^2(1, N = 75) = 18.08$, $p < 0.05$, with 24% of variability in common. Fourteen percent of homosexuals were low on creativity, and 86% of homosexuals were highly creative. Among heterosexuals, 62.5% were low on creativity, and only 37.5% were highly creative.

Conceptual Items

1. Define the following:
   a. one-way
   b. two-way
   c. observed frequencies
   d. expected frequencies
2. When the null hypothesis is true for the one-way χ^2, the χ^2_{obt} will be _____.
3. When the null hypothesis is true for the two-way χ^2, the χ^2_{obt} will be _____.
4. The formula for degrees of freedom in the one-way χ^2 is _____.
5. The formula for degrees of freedom in the two-way χ^2 is _____.
6. A significant 2 × 2 χ^2 is further analyzed for effect size using _____.
7. A significant 3 × 3 χ^2 is further analyzed for effect size using _____.
8. APA style for χ^2 includes a value not reported in the *t*-test or ANOVA. What is this value, and why must it be included in the χ^2 result?
9. What makes the one-way and two-way χ^2 different conceptually? What makes these two analyses different mathematically?
10. Instead of post-hoc analyses, a significant χ^2 result is often discussed in what way?

Application Items

11. Suppose you want to know what percentage of men and women are lawyers. Since approximately 50% of people in the general population are women, you expect the same percentage to be found among lawyers. After you collect data from a sample of 200 lawyers, you find that 75% were men, and only 25% were women. Your job is to find out if these percentages are significantly different from percentages of men and women in the general population.

    a. Lay out the null and alternative hypotheses.

    b. Choose an appropriate statistic to analyze these data.

    c. Sketch the sampling distribution with p-value, degrees of freedom, and χ^2_{crit}.

    d. Calculate χ^2_{obt} and compare it with χ^2_{crit}.

    e. Write your result in APA style.

    f. Discuss the outcome in plain English (be specific, and use descriptive statistics where necessary).

For the remaining items, follow instructions a–f from Application Item 11, and calculate effect size when relevant. Verify your work on SPSS for two-way χ^2 examples.

12. Executives of a cola company have decided to market a new type of cherry soda, but they need to know that significantly more than 30% of people who drink cherry soda would purchase their product. They will set their expectations at 30% and 60% for their competition made by another cola company. Then, at grocery stores, they'll have people who like cherry soda conduct taste tests of their cola and their competitor's cola. One thousand participants will simply choose which one tastes better.

    Analyze the data, assuming that 33% of the sample chose the new cherry soda over the established cola company's cherry soda.

13. Analyze the following data set of hair color and intelligence:

	Blonde	Brunette
Below Average Intelligence	$f_o = 18$	$f_o = 13$
Average Intelligence	$f_o = 15$	$f_o = 14$
Above Average Intelligence	$f_o = 10$	$f_o = 17$

14. An airline is trying to decide if it should charge more for certain types of seats in coach class based on their demand. Researchers set up a study of the number of customers who request aisle, window, or middle seats. They set their expectations at an equal distribution of people across the three types of seats and plan to collect information from 150 customers. If the χ^2 is significant, the airline will charge more for the popular type(s) of seats.

    Imagine the researchers discovered that 70 people chose window seats, 58 people chose aisle seats, and 22 people chose seats between the window and aisle seats.

15. A sample of psychology majors at your institution was asked if they believed statistics was a useful course. Because a researcher at another university found that 65% of her students thought statistics was useful, we might expect 65% of our sample to say that a statistics course is useful, and 35% to say that a statistics course isn't useful.

    Using our randomly selected sample, we found that 44 students think the course is useful and 56 think it's not.

16. After much thought, we decided that the question investigated by the experiment above (Application Item 15) was not sufficiently answered by knowing how many people thought statistics was a useful course and how many did not. We thought it might be important to know if participants had actually taken statistics yet. We now want to know if people's opinions about the usefulness of statistics is related to whether or not they've taken the course.

    Using a new random sample from the same population, we found the following:

Is Statistics a useful course?

	Yes	**No**
Have Taken Statistics	$f_o = 26$	$f_o = 8$
Have Not Taken Statistics	$f_o = 9$	$f_o = 17$

Computational formulas in this chapter

Chi square obtained value	$$\chi^2_{obt} = \sum \left(\frac{(f_o - f_e)^2}{f_e} \right)$$
Expected frequency (calculated only for a two-way χ^2)	$$f_e = \frac{(\text{cell's row total } f_o)(\text{cell's column total } f_o)}{N}$$
Phi coefficient (effect size for a significant 2×2 χ^2)	$$\Phi = \sqrt{\frac{\chi^2_{obt}}{N}}$$
Contingency coefficient (effect size for a significant χ^2 larger than a 2×2 design)	$$C = \sqrt{\frac{\chi^2_{obt}}{N + \chi^2_{obt}}}$$

References

In Text:

Domino, G. (1977). Homosexuality and creativity. *Journal of Homosexuality, 2,* 261–267.

Goetestam, K. O. (2001). Handedness and creativity in a sample of homosexual men. *Perceptual & Motor Skills, 92,* 1069–1074.

McCormick, C. M., Witelson, S. F., Kingstone, E. (1990). Left-handedness in homosexual men and women: Neuroendocrine implications. *Psychoneuroendocrinology, 15,* 69–76.

ANOVA: One-Way,
Repeated-Measures Using SPSS

Testing the Same Participants

Recall from Chapter 9 that the repeated-measures ANOVA is also called the within-groups ANOVA, and this design tests the same participants across every level of the IV. Because this is a one-way design, only one IV is used, but the IV can have any number of levels beyond one.

A repeated-measures design controls for individual differences across the data set, and is therefore more powerful than a between-groups design. Although it might seem that a repeated-measures design would always be a better choice than different people in the levels of the IV, the within-groups design has a unique set of problems. For example, participants tested under every level of the IV might get tired, and their fatigue could affect DV values across time. Also, exposure to the first level(s) of the IV might create a long-term or permanent change in participants, affecting performance on all subsequent levels of the IV. It is beyond the scope of this book to elaborate further on problems with the repeated-measure design, but these pitfalls and potential solutions may be addressed by your professor or in other courses.

In Chapter 9, we analyzed an example in which participants (students) were randomly assigned to one of three types of a drug-use prevention program. Some students received a program from parents; others were taught a program by teachers; and still others learned from police officers. Since participants were randomly assigned to conditions, the design was a between-groups ANOVA. Each participant received only one level of the drug program IV.

As an alternative, this study could be conducted as a repeated-measures design by having each participant receive the program from all three types of instructors: parents, teachers, and police officers. That is, each participant would participate in all programs, or levels, of the IV. After each program ended, participants would rate their attitude toward the program on a scale from 1 to 10, with higher numbers indicating a more positive attitude toward the program.

On paper, data layout would look the same for both types of studies; however, the repeated-measures design will always yield equal numbers of participants (n) across groups as a result of the same people experiencing all of the levels. Participants would not learn from one type of instructor and then quit the study; if they did, their data would be dropped from the analysis.

Below are data from this repeated-measures example:

Parents	Teachers	Officers
5	7	8
5	7	5
3	8	9
4	6	5
4	9	7
8	10	8
2	4	5
6	6	8

One-way, Repeated-measures ANOVA on SPSS

The Base Version (student version) of SPSS will not analyze a repeated-measures ANOVA. The following analysis was conducted using the complete version of SPSS.

Each student was asked to rate all three programs, with each row of the data representing responses from one participant. It is important to keep all three responses from a participant together, so we'll need to enter the data in SPSS as we did the related- samples t-test.

Point to Analyze and select General Linear Model+Repeated-Measures.

A small gray box will open, and you'll notice that the Within-Subject Factor Name is factor1.

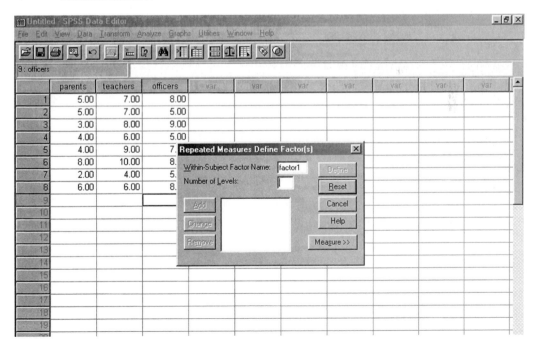

A more appropriate name than factor1 for our IV would be Program, so select factor1 and type **program** in its place. Then type **3** in the Number of Levels box.

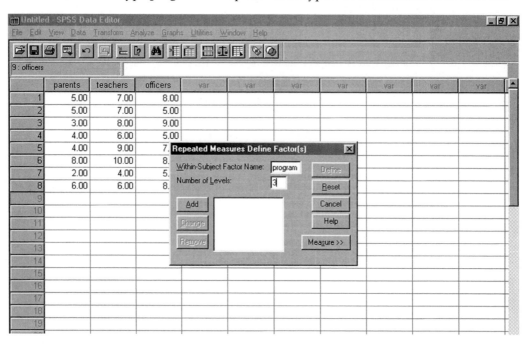

Click Add to move the IV name and number of levels to the lowest white box, then click Define.

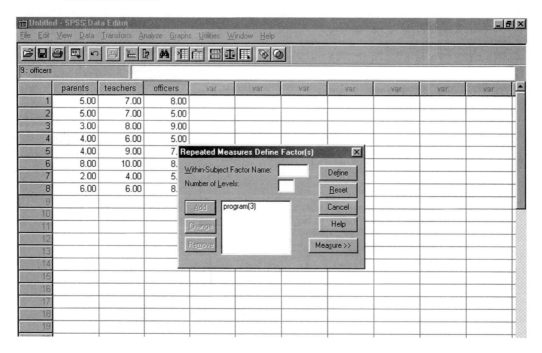

Select parents+teachers+officers, and move them to the right. By doing this, we are labeling the three levels of the IV. Level 1 is Parents, Level 2 is Teachers, and Level 3 is Officers.

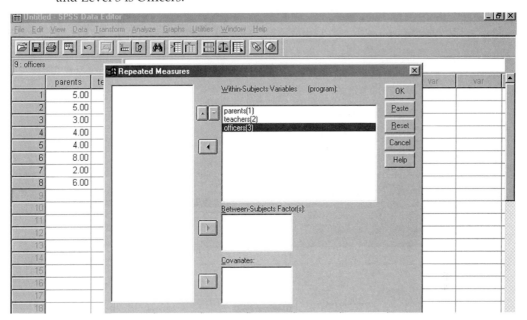

Click Options, select Program under Display Means for, and check Compare main effects just under that box. Then check Descriptive statistics+Estimates of effect size. Then click Continue. On the original gray box, click OK.

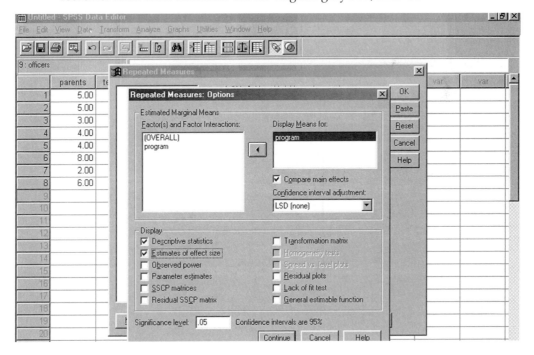

The detailed output is as follows:

General Linear Model

Within-Subjects Factors

Measure: MEASURE_1

PROGRAM	Dependent Variable
1	PARENTS
2	TEACHERS
3	OFFICERS

Descriptive Statistics

	Mean	Std. Deviation	N
PARENTS	4.6250	1.84881	8
TEACHERS	7.1250	1.88509	8
OFFICERS	6.8750	1.64208	8

Multivariate Tests[b]

Effect		Value	F	Hypothesis df	Error df	Sig.
PROGRAM	Pillai's Trace	.723	7.839[a]	2.000	6.000	.021
	Wilks' Lambda	.277	7.839[a]	2.000	6.000	.021
	Hotelling's Trace	2.613	7.839[a]	2.000	6.000	.021
	Roy's Largest Root	2.613	7.839[a]	2.000	6.000	.021

a. Exact statistic

b.
   Design: Intercept
   Within Subjects Design: PROGRAM

Mauchly's Test of Sphericity[b]

Measure: MEASURE_1

Within Subjects Effect	Mauchly's W	Approx. Chi-Square	df	Sig.
PROGRAM	.946	.331	2	.847

Tests the null hypothesis that the error covariance matrix of the orthonormalized transformed dependent variables is proportional to an identity matrix.

Mauchly's Test of Sphericity[b]

Measure: MEASURE_1

| Within Subjects Effect | Epsilon[a] | | |
	Greenhouse-Geisser	Huynh-Feldt	Lower-bound
PROGRAM	.949	1.000	.500

Tests the null hypothesis that the error covariance matrix of the orthonormalized transformed dependent variables is proportional to an identity matrix.

a. May be used to adjust the degrees of freedom for the averaged tests of significance. Corrected tests are displayed in the Tests of Within-subjects Effects table.

b.
Design: Intercept
Within Subjects Design: PROGRAM

Tests of Within-Subjects Effects

Measure: MEASURE_1

Source		Type III Sum of Squares	df	Mean Square	F	Sig.	Partial Eta Squared
PROGRAM	Sphericity Assumed	30.333	2	15.167	9.507	.002	.576
	Greenhouse-Geisser	30.333	1.898	15.981	9.507	.003	.576
	Huynh-Feldt	30.333	2.000	15.167	9.507	.002	.576
	Lower-bound	30.333	1.000	30.333	9.507	.018	.576
Error(PROGRAM)	Sphericity Assumed	22.333	14	1.595			
	Greenhouse-Geisser	22.333	13.287	1.681			
	Huynh-Feldt	22.333	14.000	1.595			
	Lower-bound	22.333	7.000	3.190			

Tests of Within-Subjects Contrasts

Measure: MEASURE_1

Source	PROGRAM	Type III Sum of Squares	df	Mean Square	F	Sig.	Partial Eta Squared
PROGRAM	Linear	20.250	1	20.250	10.309	.015	.596
	Quadratic	10.083	1	10.083	8.223	.024	.540
Error(PROGRAM)	Linear	13.750	7	1.964			
	Quadratic	8.583	7	1.226			

Tests of Between-Subjects Effects

Measure: MEASURE_1
Transformed Variable: Average

Source	Type III Sum of Squares	df	Mean Square	F	Sig.	Partial Eta Squared
Intercept	925.042	1	925.042	142.969	.000	.953
Error	45.292	7	6.470			

Estimated Marginal Means

PROGRAM

Estimates

Measure: MEASURE_1

PROGRAM	Mean	Std. Error	95% Confidence Interval	
			Lower Bound	Upper Bound
1	4.625	.653	3.081	6.169
2	7.125	.666	5.549	8.701
3	6.875	.581	5.502	8.248

Pairwise Comparisons

Measure: MEASURE_1

(I)PROGRAM	(J) PROGRAM	Mean Difference (I-J)	Std. Error	Sig.[a]	95% Confidence Interval for Difference[a]	
					Lower Bound	Upper Bound
1	2	−2.500*	.598	.004	−3.913	−1.087
	3	−2.250*	.701	.015	−3.907	−.593
2	1	2.500*	.598	.004	1.087	3.913
	3	.250	.590	.685	−1.145*	1.645
3	1	2.250*	.701	.015	.593	3.907
	2	−.250	.590	.685	−1.645	1.145

Based on estimated marginal means

  *. The mean difference is significant at the .05 level.

a. Adjustment for multiple comparisons: Least Significant Difference (equivalent to no adjustments).

Multivariate Tests

	Value	F	Hypothesis df	Error df	Sig.	Partial Eta Squared
Pillai's trace	.723	7.839[a]	2.000	6.000	.021	.723
Wilks' lambda	.277	7.839[a]	2.000	6.000	.021	.723
Hotelling's trace	2.613	7.839[a]	2.000	6.000	.021	.723
Roy's largest root	2.613	7.839[a]	2.000	6.000	.021	.723

Each F tests the multivariate effect of PROGRAM. These tests are based on the linearly independent pairwise comparisons among the estimated marginal means.

  a. Exact statistic

    The first table of interest is Tests of Within-Subjects Effects. We need an effect line for Program; look at the row labeled Sphericity Assumed to find the effect degrees of freedom (2), the *F*-value (9.51), the *p*-value (0.002), and effect size (0.58). To write this result in APA style, we also need error degrees of freedom, and the relevant row is also Sphericity Assumed, where we find 14 degrees of freedom. Although the effect *df* is still $k − 1$, the error *df* is based on a formula different from the between-groups ANOVA, so don't be concerned that the 14 seems odd.

At the end of the output, look under Estimated Marginal Means, Estimates for group means and standard error terms. There you will also find confidence intervals, if you choose to use them.

Finally, you will see comparisons between pairs of means under the table labeled Pairwise Comparisons. As you can see from the significance values, parents and teachers differ (groups 1 and 2), and parents and officers differ (groups 1 and 3), but mean attitudes toward the program taught by teachers and officers did not differ.

APA-style Results Section

The direction of effects is contained in the following APA-style results section:

Results

A one-way, repeated-measures ANOVA was used to analyze these data. A significant effect was further analyzed using pairwise comparisons ($p < 0.05$).

Students' attitudes toward drug-use prevention programs were affected by who presented the program, $F(2, 14) = 9.51$, $p < 0.01$, with an effect size of 0.58. Students rated programs offered by teachers ($M = 7.13$, $SEM = 0.67$) and officers ($M = 6.88$, $SEM = 0.58$) higher than the program offered by parents ($M = 4.63$, $SEM = 0.65$). Ratings of programs offered by teachers and officers did not differ.

Summary of the One-way, Repeated-measures ANOVA

The one-way, repeated-measures (within-groups) ANOVA is used when each participant is tested under every level of the IV. Because individual differences are equally distributed across IV levels, the potential effect of the manipulation is easier to find. The full version of SPSS analyzes the repeated-measures ANOVA efficiently, offering F- and p-values, effect size, descriptive statistics, and mean comparisons.

Conceptual Items

1. Another name for the repeated-measures ANOVA is _____.
2. Which is more powerful, a repeated-measures or between-groups ANOVA? Explain your answer.
3. In SPSS output, the relevant rows are labeled (choose one)
   a. Sphericity Assumed
   b. Greenhouse-Geisser
   c. Huynh-Feldt
   d. Lower-bound

4. If post-hoc comparisons between means were conducted by hand for the repeated-measures ANOVA, which type of post-hoc test would be used and why?

5. List two potential problems resulting from repeatedly testing the same participants.

Application Items

6. Imagine that you wanted to know if water temperature significantly affects how long people stay in the shower. You ask a group of participants to shower across 4 days with water at 60°F, then at 70°F, next at 80°F, and finally in water at 90°F. After each shower, you ask them to write down how many minutes the shower lasted. Notice that you did not randomly assign participants to conditions, but participants were definitely manipulated–treated differently in each of the conditions. Therefore, water temperature is a true independent variable, and cause and effect can be established if the following data reveal a significant result:

60°F	70°F	80°F	90°F
3	5	7	10
5	4	9	13
6	5	12	20
2	3	5	11
8	8	10	18
2	3	6	9

a. Analyze these data using SPSS.
b. Write the result in APA style.
c. Discuss the results in plain English.

For Application Items 7 and 8, address a–c from Application Item 6 above.

7. Suppose you want to find out if type of anniversary gift affects a woman's love, as measured on a rating scale from 0 to 30, with higher numbers indicating more love. Participants will receive anniversary gifts over 3 years. The first year, the gift will be a card; the second year, the gift will be a few roses; and the third year, the gift will be diamond earrings. The following data might be found:

Card	Roses	Diamonds
13	18	27
20	27	28
25	30	30
17	17	21
10	8	15

(Just for fun, think about what else might explain changes in love over 3 years besides gifts! You should begin to see why a repeated-measures design has its own problems.)

8. If you suffer from allergies, you might take medication to reduce discomfort. Examine the following fictional data of allergy treatments (and a control group) and number of sneezes per hour. Because people differ in how serious their allergies are, it is useful to use a repeated-measures design to partial out individual differences. Each participant in the study receives no medication for the first week, an over-the-counter antihistamine the second week, and a prescription drug for allergies the third week.

No Medication	Antihistamine	Prescription Medication
20	15	12
7	6	6
14	10	8
9	6	7
11	10	11
8	8	6
15	9	9
10	5	4

9. For the following, continue with the example of allergies and medication (above). You may want to refer to Chapter 9 (one-way, between-groups ANOVA) to refresh your memory of the hypothesis-testing procedure, effect size, and confidence intervals.

    a. Lay out the H_0 and H_1 hypotheses.

    b. Choose a statistic to analyze this study (be specific).

    c. Sketch the distribution of normal people, and include the p-value, degrees of freedom, and F_{crit}.

    d. Reject or fail to reject the null hypothesis.

    e. If appropriate, calculate the size of the effect.

    f. Based on post-hoc testing, calculate confidence intervals for group means.

B

Multiple Regression Using SPSS

More Than One Predictor Variable

For multiple regression, we rely on linear relationships between variables, just as we did in Chapter 12. We are also still using variables to predict other variables, as long as they are related to each other. Recall our example of predicting skin health (scores 1 to 100) at age 50 from the number of hours of sun exposure during younger years. We were able to show that sun exposure significantly predicted skin health at age 50 by looking first at the ANOVA summary table to see if the significance value for the prediction model was less than 0.05, then examining the Coefficients table to see if Sun specifically predicted skin health. It came as no surprise that Sun significantly predicted skin health, since the ANOVA model was already significant at 0.001, and Sun was the only predictor used.

However, when more than one predictor is used, significance of each predictor must be assessed in addition to the overall predictive ability of all predictors together. For the sun exposure and skin health example, another predictor might be average number of cigarettes smoked per day. SPSS will tell us if cigarettes smoked can help predict skin health in old age based on the following data:

Sun Exposure	Cigarettes	Skin Health
9	25	34
3	3	75
5	0	78
6	17	56
3	5	82
1	1	93
4	14	69

Multiple Regression in SPSS

Data entry in SPSS is based on sets of scores; each participant's sun exposure, number of cigarettes smoked, and skin health must be on the same row. In linear regression with only one predictor, we used pairs of scores; with two predictors, we have a set of three scores on a row.

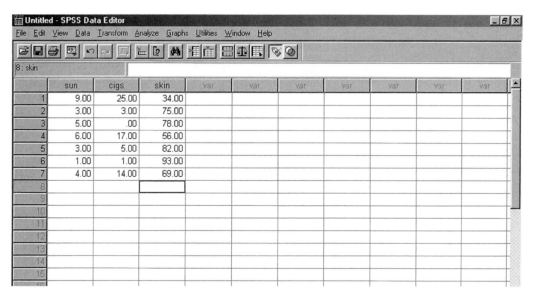

Point to Analyze and click Regression+Linear. Even though we are using more than one predictor, we still expect linear relationships between predictors and the predicted variable of skin health.

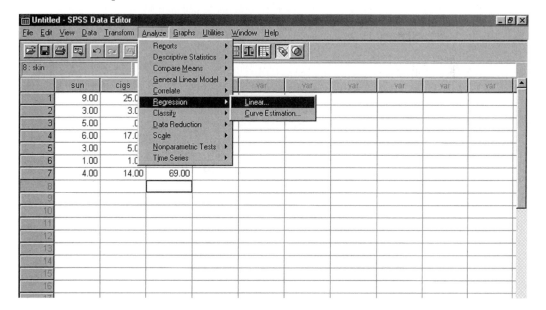

In the gray box, select each predictor and move it to the right under Independent(s). Then select the predicted variable (skin) and move it into the open box under Dependent. Notice in the middle of the gray box that the method of entering predictors is called Enter. This is the default setting on SPSS, and it should not be changed until you have taken an advanced course in regression analysis that explains alternate methods of entering predictors into the equation.

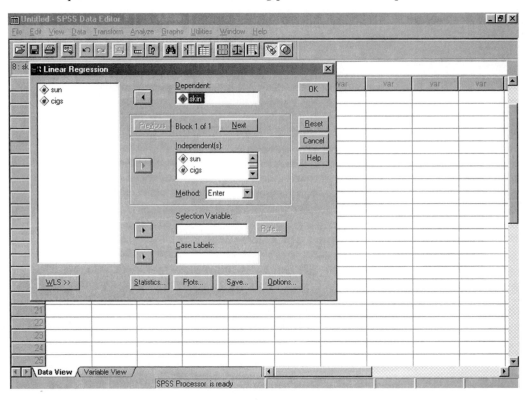

Click OK for output.

Regression

Variables Entered/Removed[b]

Model	Variables Entered	Variables Removed	Method
1	CIGS. SUN[a]		Enter

a. All requested variables entered.

b. Dependent Variable: SKIN

Model Summary

Model	R	R Square	Adjusted R Square	Std. Error of the Estimate
1	.987*	.973	.960	3.87044

a. Predictors: (Constant), CIGS, SUN

ANOVA[b]

Model		Sum of Squares	df	Mean Square	F	Sig.
1	Regression	2193.793	2	1096.896	73.222	.001[a]
	Residual	59.921	4	14.980		
	Total	2253.714	6			

a. Predictors: (Constant), CIGS, SUN
b. Dependent Variable: SKIN

Coefficients[a]

Model		Unstandardized Coefficients		Standardized Coefficients	t	Sig.
		B	Std. Error	Beta		
1	(Constant)	97.512	3.311		29.454	.000
	SUN	−4.367	1.071	−.580	−4.077	.015
	CIGS	−.926	.290	−.454	−3.192	.033

a. Dependent Variable: SKIN

The model of prediction with these two predictors is significant at 0.001 based on the ANOVA table. Also, the Coefficients table shows that Sun significantly predicts skin health with a *p*-value of 0.015, and Cigs (Cigarettes) also predict skin health at a *p*-value of 0.033. From this analysis, we can see that both Sun and Cigarettes are significant predictors of skin health.

In the Model Summary table, adjusted R^2 is 0.960, indicating excellent prediction using sun exposure and number of cigarettes smoked. In fact, if we compare this R^2 value with the analysis in Chapter 12 where one predictor was used, we can see that using only Sun as a predictor of skin health provided an adjusted R^2 value of 0.906. Adding the predictor of Cigarettes to the equation significantly increased prediction to an R^2 value of 0.960.

Further, our standard error of the estimate using one predictor was 6.52042. Using two predictors, the standard error of the estimate has been reduced to 3.87044, providing less error in predictions of skin health when both sun exposure and number of cigarettes are used as predictors.

As a reminder, the prediction equation with only Sun was:

$$Y' = -7.169X + 101.320$$

The new equation looks like this:

$$Y' = -4.367X_1 + -0.926X_2 + 97.512,$$

where X_1 is number of hours of sun exposure, and X_2 is the number of cigarettes smoked.

If this equation was based on an actual study, hours of sun exposure could be entered for X_1, and number of cigarettes could be entered for X_2. The resultant predicted value (Y') would indicate likely future skin health, with error in predictions of approximately 3.87 below or above the predicted value.

APA-style Results Section

Multiple regression analysis is written in much the same way as linear regression with only one predictor.

> **Results**
>
> These data were analyzed using regression analysis. Hours of sun exposure and the number of cigarettes smoked significantly predicted skin health, $F(1, 4) = 73.22$, $p < 0.01$. The Y-intercept was 97.51, and slopes for sun exposure and number of cigarettes were -4.37 ($p < 0.05$) and -0.93 ($p < 0.05$), respectively. Ninety-six percent of skin health was explained by knowing hours of sun exposure and number of cigarettes smoked, and the standard error of the estimate was 3.87 on a scale from 1 to 100 for skin health.

Summary of Multiple Regression

In multiple regression, we can use as many predictors as we would like. When the data are analyzed, we can look at the SPSS printout to see if our chosen set of predictors significantly predicts the variable of interest. If the model is significant based on the ANOVA summary table, we must see if each of the predictors improves prediction by looking at individual significance values in the Coefficients table of the output. Each predictor with a p-value of less than or equal to 0.05 is a significant predictor and can remain in the final equation. However, predictors with p-values above 0.05 must be dropped from the equation, because they are not useful predictors.

Conceptual Items

1. The overall predictive ability of all predictors is evaluated using _____.
2. The predictive relevance of individual predictors is signified by _____.
3. What does R^2 represent in multiple regression?

Application Items

4. Use the regression equation in this chapter to predict skin health for someone who spends an average of 5 hours in the sun per week and smokes an average of 10 cigarettes per day. Calculate the likely range in which this person's skin-health score will actually fall.
5. Now predict skin health for someone who spends an average of 8 hours in the sun per week and smokes an average of 14 cigarettes per day. Calculate the likely range in which this person's skin-health score will actually fall.

6. Finally, predict skin health for someone who spends an average of 3 hours in the sun per week and smokes an average of 6 cigarettes per day. Calculate the likely range in which this person's skin-health score will actually fall.

7. People in charge of fundraising would find it useful to know what variables affect the amount of money people give to charities such as those associated with cancer research. It might be possible to collect data on people who donate to charity and learn what variables affect giving. It is likely that more than 1 variable influences donating to charity, with the following variables of potential importance: the number of family and friends who have suffered with cancer, a person's available cash, and the amount of money given to other charities. Assume the data are as follows, and use SPSS to provide a complete analysis of these variables as predictors, including the regression equation with relevant predictors, R^2, and the average amount of error that can be expected when predicting amount of money donated to cancer research based on the equation you produce.

# of Sufferers	Cash	Other Charities	Donation
6	20	5	15
3	35	7	12
5	140	20	40
2	50	0	10
0	10	0	0
2	85	15	10
7	100	0	50
3	48	5	20
4	67	10	25
1	5	30	2

8. Using SPSS, produce the regression equation for the following data set in which duration of massage and how much the masseuse talks during the massage are predictors, and relaxation is the predicted variable. Relaxation is rated on a scale from 1 to 50, with higher numbers meaning more relaxed.

Massage (in minutes)	Talking (in minutes)	Relaxation
50	45	30
30	0	47
60	30	24
15	15	10
30	20	28
45	25	35
60	59	20
75	20	40
20	0	42
60	10	48
45	5	50

Examine the regression equation. Is it reasonable that one predictor has a positive slope and the other has a negative slope? Do they both significantly contribute to prediction? What does this mean for prediction from each variable? (For example, would the predictor with the negative slope have less predictive ability than the predictor with the positive slope?)

Table 1   z-table: Proportions of Area Under the Standard Normal Curve

Column (A) lists z-score values. Column (B) lists the proportion of the area between the mean and the z-score value. Column (C) lists the proportion of the area beyond the z-score in the tail of the distribution. *Note:* Because the normal distribution is symmetrical, areas for negative z-scores are the same as those for positive z-scores.

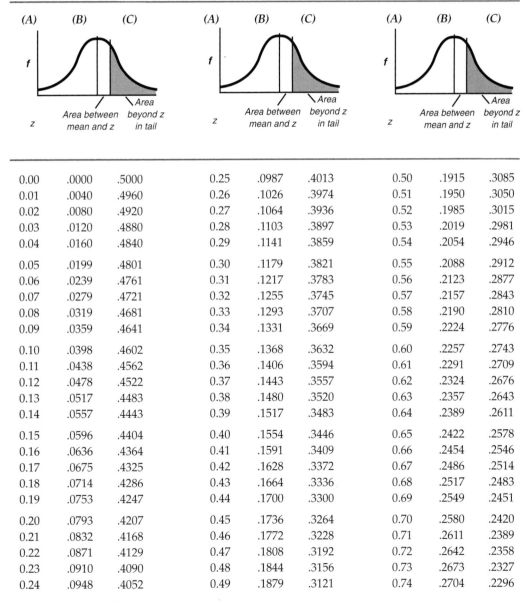

(A)	(B)	(C)	(A)	(B)	(C)	(A)	(B)	(C)
0.00	.0000	.5000	0.25	.0987	.4013	0.50	.1915	.3085
0.01	.0040	.4960	0.26	.1026	.3974	0.51	.1950	.3050
0.02	.0080	.4920	0.27	.1064	.3936	0.52	.1985	.3015
0.03	.0120	.4880	0.28	.1103	.3897	0.53	.2019	.2981
0.04	.0160	.4840	0.29	.1141	.3859	0.54	.2054	.2946
0.05	.0199	.4801	0.30	.1179	.3821	0.55	.2088	.2912
0.06	.0239	.4761	0.31	.1217	.3783	0.56	.2123	.2877
0.07	.0279	.4721	0.32	.1255	.3745	0.57	.2157	.2843
0.08	.0319	.4681	0.33	.1293	.3707	0.58	.2190	.2810
0.09	.0359	.4641	0.34	.1331	.3669	0.59	.2224	.2776
0.10	.0398	.4602	0.35	.1368	.3632	0.60	.2257	.2743
0.11	.0438	.4562	0.36	.1406	.3594	0.61	.2291	.2709
0.12	.0478	.4522	0.37	.1443	.3557	0.62	.2324	.2676
0.13	.0517	.4483	0.38	.1480	.3520	0.63	.2357	.2643
0.14	.0557	.4443	0.39	.1517	.3483	0.64	.2389	.2611
0.15	.0596	.4404	0.40	.1554	.3446	0.65	.2422	.2578
0.16	.0636	.4364	0.41	.1591	.3409	0.66	.2454	.2546
0.17	.0675	.4325	0.42	.1628	.3372	0.67	.2486	.2514
0.18	.0714	.4286	0.43	.1664	.3336	0.68	.2517	.2483
0.19	.0753	.4247	0.44	.1700	.3300	0.69	.2549	.2451
0.20	.0793	.4207	0.45	.1736	.3264	0.70	.2580	.2420
0.21	.0832	.4168	0.46	.1772	.3228	0.71	.2611	.2389
0.22	.0871	.4129	0.47	.1808	.3192	0.72	.2642	.2358
0.23	.0910	.4090	0.48	.1844	.3156	0.73	.2673	.2327
0.24	.0948	.4052	0.49	.1879	.3121	0.74	.2704	.2296

Table 1 (cont.)   z-table: Proportions of Area Under the Standard Normal Curve

(A) z	(B) Area between mean and z	(C) Area beyond z in tail	(A) z	(B) Area between mean and z	(C) Area beyond z in tail	(A) z	(B) Area between mean and z	(C) Area beyond z in tail
0.75	.2734	.2266	1.05	.3531	.1469	1.35	.4115	.0885
0.76	.2764	.2236	1.06	.3554	.1446	1.36	.4131	.0869
0.77	.2794	.2206	1.07	.3577	.1423	1.37	.4147	.0853
0.78	.2823	.2177	1.08	.3599	.1401	1.38	.4162	.0838
0.79	.2852	.2148	1.09	.3621	.1379	1.39	.4177	.0823
0.80	.2881	.2119	1.10	.3643	.1357	1.40	.4192	.0808
0.81	.2910	.2090	1.11	.3665	.1335	1.41	.4207	.0793
0.82	.2939	.2061	1.12	.3686	.1314	1.42	.4222	.0778
0.83	.2967	.2033	1.13	.3708	.1292	1.43	.4236	.0764
0.84	.2995	.2005	1.14	.3729	.1271	1.44	.4251	.0749
0.85	.3023	.1977	1.15	.3749	.1251	1.45	.4265	.0735
0.86	.3051	.1949	1.16	.3770	.1230	1.46	.4279	.0721
0.87	.3078	.1922	1.17	.3790	.1210	1.47	.4292	.0708
0.88	.3106	.1894	1.18	.3810	.1190	1.48	.4306	.0694
0.89	.3133	.1867	1.19	.3830	.1170	1.49	.4319	.0681
0.90	.3159	.1841	1.20	.3849	.1151	1.50	.4332	.0668
0.91	.3186	.1814	1.21	.3869	.1131	1.51	.4345	.0655
0.92	.3212	.1788	1.22	.3888	.1112	1.52	.4357	.0643
0.93	.3238	.1762	1.23	.3907	.1093	1.53	.4370	.0630
0.94	.3264	.1736	1.24	.3925	.1075	1.54	.4382	.0618
0.95	.3289	.1711	1.25	.3944	.1056	1.55	.4394	.0606
0.96	.3315	.1685	1.26	.3962	.1038	1.56	.4406	.0594
0.97	.3340	.1660	1.27	.3980	.1020	1.57	.4418	.0582
0.98	.3365	.1635	1.28	.3997	.1003	1.58	.4429	.0571
0.99	.3389	.1611	1.29	.4015	.0985	1.59	.4441	.0559
1.00	.3413	.1587	1.30	.4032	.0968	1.60	.4452	.0548
1.01	.3438	.1562	1.31	.4049	.0951	1.61	.4463	.0537
1.02	.3461	.1539	1.32	.4066	.0934	1.62	.4474	.0526
1.03	.3485	.1515	1.33	.4082	.0918	1.63	.4484	.0516
1.04	.3508	.1492	1.34	.4099	.0901	1.64	.4495	.0505

Table 1 (cont.)   *z*-table: Proportions of Area Under the Standard Normal Curve

(A) z	(B) Area between mean and z	(C) Area beyond z in tail	(A) z	(B) Area between mean and z	(C) Area beyond z in tail	(A) z	(B) Area between mean and z	(C) Area beyond z in tail
1.65	.4505	.0495	1.95	.4744	.0256	2.25	.4878	.0122
1.66	.4515	.0485	1.96	.4750	.0250	2.26	.4881	.0119
1.67	.4525	.0475	1.97	.4756	.0244	2.27	.4884	.0116
1.68	.4535	.0465	1.98	.4761	.0239	2.28	.4887	.0113
1.69	.4545	.0455	1.99	.4767	.0233	2.29	.4890	.0110
1.70	.4554	.0446	2.00	.4772	.0228	2.30	.4893	.0107
1.71	.4564	.0436	2.01	.4778	.0222	2.31	.4896	.0104
1.72	.4573	.0427	2.02	.4783	.0217	2.32	.4898	.0102
1.73	.4582	.0418	2.03	.4788	.0212	2.33	.4901	.0099
1.74	.4591	.0409	2.04	.4793	.0207	2.34	.4904	.0096
1.75	.4599	.0401	2.05	.4798	.0202	2.35	.4906	.0094
1.76	.4608	.0392	2.06	.4803	.0197	2.36	.4909	.0091
1.77	.4616	.0384	2.07	.4808	.0192	2.37	.4911	.0089
1.78	.4625	.0375	2.08	.4812	.0188	2.38	.4913	.0087
1.79	.4633	.0367	2.09	.4817	.0183	2.39	.4916	.0084
1.80	.4641	.0359	2.10	.4821	.0179	2.40	.4918	.0082
1.81	.4649	.0351	2.11	.4826	.0174	2.41	.4920	.0080
1.82	.4656	.0344	2.12	.4830	.0170	2.42	.4922	.0078
1.83	.4664	.0336	2.13	.4834	.0166	2.43	.4925	.0075
1.84	.4671	.0329	2.14	.4838	.0162	2.44	.4927	.0073
1.85	.4678	.0322	2.15	.4842	.0158	2.45	.4929	.0071
1.86	.4686	.0314	2.16	.4846	.0154	2.46	.4931	.0069
1.87	vv.4693	.0307	2.17	.4850	.0150	2.47	.4932	.0068
1.88	.4699	.0301	2.18	.4854	.0146	2.48	.4934	.0066
1.89	.4706	.0294	2.19	.4857	.0143	2.49	.4936	.0064
1.90	.4713	.0287	2.20	.4861	.0139	2.50	.4938	.0062
1.91	.4719	.0281	2.21	.4864	.0136	2.51	.4940	.0060
1.92	.4726	.0274	2.22	.4868	.0132	2.52	.4941	.0059
1.93	.4732	.0268	2.23	.4871	.0129	2.53	.4943	.0057
1.94	.4738	.0262	2.24	.4875	.0125	2.54	.4945	.0055

Table 1 (cont.)   z-table: Proportions of Area Under the Standard Normal Curve

(A) z	(B) Area between mean and z	(C) Area beyond z in tail	(A) z	(B) Area between mean and z	(C) Area beyond z in tail	(A) z	(B) Area between mean and z	(C) Area beyond z in tail
2.55	.4946	.0054	2.82	.4976	.0024	3.09	.4990	.0010
2.56	.4948	.0052	2.83	.4977	.0023	3.10	.4990	.0010
2.57	.4949	.0051	2.84	.4977	.0023	3.11	.4991	.0009
2.58	.4951	.0049	2.85	.4978	.0022	3.12	.4991	.0009
2.59	.4952	.0048	2.86	.4979	.0021	3.13	.4991	.0009
2.60	.4953	.0047	2.87	.4979	.0021	3.14	.4992	.0008
2.61	.4955	.0045	2.88	.4980	.0020	3.15	.4992	.0008
2.62	.4956	.0044	2.89	.4981	.0019	3.16	.4992	.0008
2.63	.4957	.0043	2.90	.4981	.0019	3.17	.4992	.0008
2.64	.4959	.0041	2.91	.4982	.0018	3.18	.4993	.0007
2.65	.4960	.0040	2.92	.4982	.0018	3.19	.4993	.0007
2.66	.4961	.0039	2.93	.4983	.0017	3.20	.4993	.0007
2.67	.4962	.0038	2.94	.4984	.0016	3.21	.4993	.0007
2.68	.4963	.0037	2.95	.4984	.0016	3.22	.4994	.0006
2.69	.4964	.0036	2.96	.4985	.0015	3.23	.4994	.0006
2.70	.4965	.0035	2.97	.4985	.0015	3.24	.4994	.0006
2.71	.4966	.0034	2.98	.4986	.0014	3.25	.4994	.0006
2.72	.4967	.0033	2.99	.4986	.0014	3.30	.4995	.0005
2.73	.4968	.0032	3.00	.4987	.0013	3.35	.4996	.0004
2.74	.4969	.0031	3.01	.4987	.0013	3.40	.4997	.0003
2.75	.4970	.0030	3.02	.4987	.0013	3.45	.4997	.0003
2.76	.4971	.0029	3.03	.4988	.0012	3.50	.4998	.0002
2.77	.4972	.0028	3.04	.4988	.0012	3.60	.4998	.0002
2.78	.4973	.0027	3.05	.4989	.0011	3.70	.4999	.0001
2.79	.4974	.0026	3.06	.4989	.0011	3.80	.4999	.0001
2.80	.4974	.0026	3.07	.4989	.0011	3.90	.49995	.00005
2.81	.4975	.0025	3.08	.4990	.0010	4.00	.49997	.00003

Table 2   t-table: Critical values of t

Note: Values of $-t_{crit}$ = values of $+t_{crit}$.

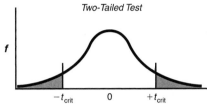

	Two-Tailed Test			One-Tailed Test	
	Alpha Level			*Alpha Level*	
df	$\alpha = .05$	$\alpha = .01$	df	$\alpha = .05$	$\alpha = .01$
1	12.706	63.657	1	6.314	31.821
2	4.303	9.925	2	2.920	6.965
3	3.182	5.841	3	2.353	4.541
4	2.776	4.604	4	2.132	3.747
5	2.571	4.032	5	2.015	3.365
6	2.447	3.707	6	1.943	3.143
7	2.365	3.499	7	1.895	2.998
8	2.306	3.355	8	1.860	2.896
9	2.262	3.250	9	1.833	2.821
10	2.228	3.169	10	1.812	2.764
11	2.201	3.106	11	1.796	2.718
12	2.179	3.055	12	1.782	2.681
13	2.160	3.012	13	1.771	2.650
14	2.145	2.977	14	1.761	2.624
15	2.131	2.947	15	1.753	2.602
16	2.120	2.921	16	1.746	2.583
17	2.110	2.898	17	1.740	2.567
18	2.101	2.878	18	1.734	2.552
19	2.093	2.861	19	1.729	2.539
20	2.086	2.845	20	1.725	2.528
21	2.080	2.831	21	1.721	2.518
22	2.074	2.819	22	1.717	2.508
23	2.069	2.807	23	1.714	2.500
24	2.064	2.797	24	1.711	2.492
25	2.060	2.787	25	1.708	2.485
26	2.056	2.779	26	1.706	2.479
27	2.052	2.771	27	1.703	2.473
28	2.048	2.763	28	1.701	2.467
29	2.045	2.756	29	1.699	2.462
30	2.042	2.750	30	1.697	2.457
40	2.021	2.704	40	1.684	2.423
60	2.000	2.660	60	1.671	2.390
120	1.980	2.617	120	1.658	2.358
∞	1.960	2.576	∞	1.645	2.326

Table 3 *F*-table (ANOVA): Critical Values of *F*

Critical values for $\alpha = .05$ are in **dark numbers**.
Critical values for $\alpha = .01$ are in light numbers.

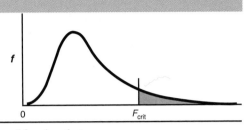

Degrees of freedom within groups (degrees of freedom in denominator of F ratio)	α	\multicolumn{15}{c}{*Degrees of freedom between groups (degrees of freedom in numerator of F ratio)*}

df within	α	1	2	3	4	5	6	7	8	9	10	11	12	14	16	20
1	.05	**161**	**200**	**216**	**225**	**230**	**234**	**237**	**239**	**241**	**242**	**243**	**244**	**245**	**246**	**248**
	.01	4,052	4,999	5,403	5,625	5,764	5,859	5,928	5,981	6,022	6,056	6,082	6,106	6,142	6,169	6,208
2	.05	**18.51**	**19.00**	**19.16**	**19.25**	**19.30**	**19.33**	**19.36**	**19.37**	**19.38**	**19.39**	**19.40**	**19.41**	**19.42**	**19.43**	**19.44**
	.01	98.49	99.00	99.17	99.25	99.30	99.33	99.34	99.36	99.38	99.40	99.41	99.42	99.43	99.44	99.45
3	.05	**10.13**	**9.55**	**9.28**	**9.12**	**9.01**	**8.94**	**8.88**	**8.84**	**8.81**	**8.78**	**8.76**	**8.74**	**8.71**	**8.69**	**8.66**
	.01	34.12	30.82	29.46	28.71	28.24	27.91	27.67	27.49	27.34	27.23	27.13	27.05	26.92	26.83	26.69
4	.05	**7.71**	**6.94**	**6.59**	**6.39**	**6.26**	**6.16**	**6.09**	**6.04**	**6.00**	**5.96**	**5.93**	**5.91**	**5.87**	**5.84**	**5.80**
	.01	21.20	18.00	16.69	15.98	15.52	15.21	14.98	14.80	14.66	14.54	14.45	14.37	14.24	14.15	14.02
5	.05	**6.61**	**5.79**	**5.41**	**5.19**	**5.05**	**4.95**	**4.88**	**4.82**	**4.78**	**4.74**	**4.70**	**4.68**	**4.64**	**4.60**	**4.56**
	.01	16.26	13.27	12.06	11.39	10.97	10.67	10.45	10.27	10.15	10.05	9.96	9.89	9.77	9.68	9.55
6	.05	**5.99**	**5.14**	**4.76**	**4.53**	**4.39**	**4.28**	**4.21**	**4.15**	**4.10**	**4.06**	**4.03**	**4.00**	**3.96**	**3.92**	**3.87**
	.01	13.74	10.92	9.78	9.15	8.75	8.47	8.26	8.10	7.98	7.87	7.79	7.72	7.60	7.52	7.39
7	.05	**5.59**	**4.47**	**4.35**	**4.12**	**3.97**	**3.87**	**3.79**	**3.73**	**3.68**	**3.63**	**3.60**	**3.57**	**3.52**	**3.49**	**3.44**
	.01	12.25	9.55	8.45	7.85	7.46	7.19	7.00	6.84	6.71	6.62	6.54	6.47	6.35	6.27	6.15
8	.05	**5.32**	**4.46**	**4.07**	**3.84**	**3.69**	**3.58**	**3.50**	**3.44**	**3.39**	**3.34**	**3.31**	**3.28**	**3.23**	**3.20**	**3.15**
	.01	11.26	8.65	7.59	7.01	6.63	6.37	6.19	6.03	5.91	5.82	5.74	5.67	5.56	5.48	5.36
9	.05	**5.12**	**4.26**	**3.86**	**3.63**	**3.48**	**3.37**	**3.29**	**3.23**	**3.18**	**3.13**	**3.10**	**3.07**	**3.02**	**2.98**	**2.93**
	.01	10.56	8.02	6.99	6.42	6.06	5.80	5.62	5.47	5.35	5.26	5.18	5.11	5.00	4.92	4.80
10	.05	**4.96**	**4.10**	**3.71**	**3.48**	**3.33**	**3.22**	**3.14**	**3.07**	**3.02**	**2.97**	**2.94**	**2.91**	**2.86**	**2.82**	**2.77**
	.01	10.04	7.56	6.55	5.99	5.64	5.39	5.21	5.06	4.95	4.85	4.78	4.71	4.60	4.52	4.41
11	.05	**4.84**	**3.98**	**3.59**	**3.36**	**3.20**	**3.09**	**3.01**	**2.95**	**2.90**	**2.86**	**2.82**	**2.79**	**2.74**	**2.70**	**2.65**
	.01	9.65	7.20	6.22	5.67	5.32	5.07	4.88	4.74	4.63	4.54	4.46	4.40	4.29	4.21	4.10
12	.05	**4.75**	**3.88**	**3.49**	**3.26**	**3.11**	**3.00**	**2.92**	**2.85**	**2.80**	**2.76**	**2.72**	**2.69**	**2.64**	**2.60**	**2.54**
	.01	9.33	6.93	5.95	5.41	5.06	4.82	4.65	4.50	4.39	4.30	4.22	4.16	4.05	3.98	3.86
13	.05	**4.67**	**3.80**	**3.41**	**3.18**	**3.02**	**2.92**	**2.84**	**2.77**	**2.72**	**2.67**	**2.63**	**2.60**	**2.55**	**2.51**	**2.46**
	.01	9.07	6.70	5.74	5.20	4.86	4.62	4.44	4.30	4.19	4.10	4.02	3.96	3.85	3.78	3.67
14	.05	**4.60**	**3.74**	**3.34**	**3.11**	**2.96**	**2.85**	**2.77**	**2.70**	**2.65**	**2.60**	**2.56**	**2.53**	**2.48**	**2.44**	**2.39**
	.01	8.86	6.51	5.56	5.03	4.69	4.46	4.28	4.14	4.03	3.94	3.86	3.80	3.70	3.62	3.51
15	.05	**4.54**	**3.68**	**3.29**	**3.06**	**2.90**	**2.79**	**2.70**	**2.64**	**2.59**	**2.55**	**2.51**	**2.48**	**2.43**	**2.39**	**2.33**
	.01	8.68	6.36	5.42	4.89	4.56	4.32	4.14	4.00	3.89	3.80	3.73	3.67	3.56	3.48	3.36
16	.05	**4.49**	**3.63**	**3.24**	**3.01**	**2.85**	**2.74**	**2.66**	**2.59**	**2.54**	**2.49**	**2.45**	**2.42**	**2.37**	**2.33**	**2.28**
	.01	8.53	6.23	5.29	4.77	4.44	4.20	4.03	3.89	3.78	3.69	3.61	3.55	3.45	3.37	3.25
17	.05	**4.45**	**3.59**	**3.20**	**2.96**	**2.81**	**2.70**	**2.62**	**2.55**	**2.50**	**2.45**	**2.41**	**2.38**	**2.33**	**2.29**	**2.23**
	.01	8.40	6.11	5.18	4.67	4.34	4.10	3.93	3.79	3.68	3.59	3.52	3.45	3.35	3.27	3.16
18	.05	**4.41**	**3.55**	**3.16**	**2.93**	**2.77**	**2.66**	**2.58**	**2.51**	**2.46**	**2.41**	**2.37**	**2.34**	**2.29**	**2.25**	**2.19**
	.01	8.28	6.01	5.09	4.58	4.25	4.01	3.85	3.71	3.60	3.51	3.44	3.37	3.27	3.19	3.07

Table 3 (cont.) *F*-table (ANOVA): Critical Values of *F*

Critical values for $\alpha = .05$ are in **dark numbers.**
Critical values for $\alpha = .01$ are in light numbers.

Degrees of freedom within groups (degrees of freedom in denominator of F ratio)	α	1	2	3	4	5	6	7	8	9	10	11	12	14	16	20
19	.05	4.38	3.52	3.13	2.90	2.74	2.63	2.55	2.48	2.43	2.38	2.34	2.31	2.26	2.21	2.15
	.01	8.18	5.93	5.01	4.50	4.17	3.94	3.77	3.63	3.52	3.43	3.36	3.30	3.19	3.12	3.00
20	.05	4.35	3.49	3.10	2.87	2.71	2.60	2.52	2.45	2.40	2.35	2.31	2.28	2.23	2.18	2.12
	.01	8.10	5.85	4.94	4.43	4.10	3.87	3.71	3.56	3.45	3.37	3.30	3.23	3.13	3.05	2.94
21	.05	4.32	3.47	3.07	2.84	2.68	2.57	2.49	2.42	2.37	2.32	2.28	2.25	2.20	2.15	2.09
	.01	8.02	5.78	4.87	4.37	4.04	3.81	3.65	3.51	3.40	3.31	3.24	3.17	3.07	2.99	2.88
22	.05	4.30	3.44	3.05	2.82	2.66	2.55	2.47	2.40	2.35	2.30	2.26	2.23	2.18	2.13	2.07
	.01	7.94	5.72	4.82	4.31	3.99	3.76	3.59	3.45	3.35	3.26	3.18	3.12	3.02	2.94	2.83
23	.05	4.28	3.42	3.03	2.80	2.64	2.53	2.45	2.38	2.32	2.28	2.24	2.20	2.14	2.10	2.04
	.01	7.88	5.66	4.76	4.26	3.94	3.71	3.54	3.41	3.30	3.21	3.14	3.07	2.97	2.89	2.78
24	.05	4.26	3.40	3.01	2.78	2.62	2.51	2.43	2.36	2.30	2.26	2.22	2.18	2.13	2.09	2.02
	.01	7.82	5.61	4.72	4.22	3.90	3.67	3.50	3.36	3.25	3.17	3.09	3.03	2.93	2.85	2.74
25	.05	4.24	3.38	2.99	2.76	2.60	2.49	2.41	2.34	2.28	2.24	2.20	2.16	2.11	2.06	2.00
	.01	7.77	5.57	4.68	4.18	3.86	3.63	3.46	3.32	3.21	3.13	3.05	2.99	2.89	2.81	2.70
26	.05	4.22	3.37	2.98	2.74	2.59	2.47	2.39	2.32	2.27	2.22	2.18	2.15	2.10	2.05	1.99
	.01	7.72	5.53	4.64	4.14	3.82	3.59	3.42	3.29	3.17	3.09	3.02	2.96	2.86	2.77	2.66
27	.05	4.21	3.35	2.96	2.73	2.57	2.46	2.37	2.30	2.25	2.20	2.16	2.13	2.08	2.03	1.97
	.01	7.68	5.49	4.60	4.11	3.79	3.56	3.39	3.26	3.14	3.06	2.98	2.93	2.83	2.74	2.63
28	.05	4.20	3.34	2.95	2.71	2.56	2.44	2.36	2.29	2.24	2.19	2.15	2.12	2.06	2.02	1.96
	.01	7.64	5.45	4.57	4.07	3.76	3.53	3.36	3.23	3.11	3.03	2.95	2.90	2.80	2.71	2.60
29	.05	4.18	3.33	2.93	2.70	2.54	2.43	2.35	2.28	2.22	2.18	2.14	2.10	2.05	2.00	1.94
	.01	7.60	5.42	4.54	4.04	3.73	3.50	3.33	3.20	3.08	3.00	2.92	2.87	2.77	2.68	2.57
30	.05	4.17	3.32	2.92	2.69	2.53	2.42	2.34	2.27	2.21	2.16	2.12	2.09	2.04	1.99	1.93
	.01	7.56	5.39	4.51	4.02	3.70	3.47	3.30	3.17	3.06	2.98	2.90	2.84	2.74	2.66	2.55
32	.05	4.15	3.30	2.90	2.67	2.51	2.40	2.32	2.25	2.19	2.14	2.10	2.07	2.02	1.97	1.91
	.01	7.50	5.34	4.46	3.97	3.66	3.42	3.25	3.12	3.01	2.94	2.86	2.80	2.70	2.62	2.51
34	.05	4.13	3.28	2.88	2.65	2.49	2.38	2.30	2.23	2.17	2.12	2.08	2.05	2.00	1.95	1.89
	.01	7.44	5.29	4.42	3.93	3.61	3.38	3.21	3.08	2.97	2.89	2.82	2.76	2.66	2.58	2.47
36	.05	4.11	3.26	2.86	2.63	2.48	2.36	2.28	2.21	2.15	2.10	2.06	2.03	1.98	1.93	1.87
	.01	7.39	5.25	4.38	3.89	3.58	3.35	3.18	3.04	2.94	2.86	2.78	2.72	2.62	2.54	2.43
38	.05	4.10	3.25	2.85	2.62	2.46	2.35	2.26	2.19	2.14	2.09	2.05	2.02	1.96	1.92	1.85
	.01	7.35	5.21	4.34	3.86	3.54	3.32	3.15	3.02	2.91	2.82	2.75	2.69	2.59	2.51	2.40
40	.05	4.08	3.23	2.84	2.61	2.45	2.34	2.25	2.18	2.12	2.07	2.04	2.00	1.95	1.90	1.84
	.01	7.31	5.18	4.31	3.83	3.51	3.29	3.12	2.99	2.88	2.80	2.73	2.66	2.56	2.49	2.37
42	.05	4.07	3.22	2.83	2.59	2.44	2.32	2.24	2.17	2.11	2.06	2.02	1.99	1.94	1.89	1.82
	.01	7.27	5.15	4.29	3.80	3.49	3.26	3.10	2.96	2.86	2.77	2.70	2.64	2.54	2.46	2.35
44	.05	4.06	3.21	2.82	2.58	2.43	2.31	2.23	2.16	2.10	2.05	2.01	1.98	1.92	1.88	1.81
	.01	7.24	5.12	4.26	3.78	3.46	3.24	3.07	2.94	2.84	2.75	2.68	2.62	2.52	2.44	2.32
46	.05	4.05	3.20	2.81	2.57	2.42	2.30	2.22	2.14	2.09	2.04	2.00	1.97	1.91	1.87	1.80
	.01	7.21	5.10	4.24	3.76	3.44	3.22	3.05	2.92	2.82	2.73	2.66	2.60	2.50	2.42	2.30
48	.05	4.04	3.19	2.80	2.56	2.41	2.30	2.21	2.14	2.08	2.03	1.99	1.96	1.90	1.86	1.79
	.01	7.19	5.08	4.22	3.74	3.42	3.20	3.04	2.90	2.80	2.71	2.64	2.58	2.48	2.40	2.28

Table 3 (cont.)   *F*-table (ANOVA): Critical Values of *F*

Critical values for $\alpha = .05$ are in **dark numbers**.
Critical values for $\alpha = .01$ are in light numbers.

Degrees of freedom within groups (degrees of freedom in denominator of F ratio)	α	1	2	3	4	5	6	7	8	9	10	11	12	14	16	20
50	.05	**4.03**	**3.18**	**2.79**	**2.56**	**2.40**	**2.29**	**2.20**	**2.13**	**2.07**	**2.02**	**1.98**	**1.95**	**1.90**	**1.85**	**1.78**
	.01	7.17	5.06	4.20	3.72	3.41	3.18	3.02	2.88	2.78	2.70	2.62	2.56	2.46	2.39	2.26
55	.05	**4.02**	**3.17**	**2.78**	**2.54**	**2.38**	**2.27**	**2.18**	**2.11**	**2.05**	**2.00**	**1.97**	**1.93**	**1.88**	**1.83**	**1.76**
	.01	7.12	5.01	4.16	3.68	3.37	3.15	2.98	2.85	2.75	2.66	2.59	2.53	2.43	2.35	2.23
60	.05	**4.00**	**3.15**	**2.76**	**2.52**	**2.37**	**2.25**	**2.17**	**2.10**	**2.04**	**1.99**	**1.95**	**1.92**	**1.86**	**1.81**	**1.75**
	.01	7.08	4.98	4.13	3.65	3.34	3.12	2.95	2.82	2.72	2.63	2.56	2.50	2.40	2.32	2.20
65	.05	**3.99**	**3.14**	**2.75**	**2.51**	**2.36**	**2.24**	**2.15**	**2.08**	**2.02**	**1.98**	**1.94**	**1.90**	**1.85**	**1.80**	**1.73**
	.01	7.04	4.95	4.10	3.62	3.31	3.09	2.93	2.79	2.70	2.61	2.54	2.47	2.37	2.30	2.18
70	.05	**3.98**	**3.13**	**2.74**	**2.50**	**2.35**	**2.23**	**2.14**	**2.07**	**2.01**	**1.97**	**1.93**	**1.89**	**1.84**	**1.79**	**1.72**
	.01	7.01	4.92	4.08	3.60	3.29	3.07	2.91	2.77	2.67	2.59	2.51	2.45	2.35	2.28	2.15
80	.05	**3.96**	**3.11**	**2.72**	**2.48**	**2.33**	**2.21**	**2.12**	**2.05**	**1.99**	**1.95**	**1.91**	**1.88**	**1.82**	**1.77**	**1.70**
	.01	6.96	4.88	4.04	3.56	3.25	3.04	2.87	2.74	2.64	2.55	2.48	2.41	2.32	2.24	2.11
100	.05	**3.94**	**3.09**	**2.70**	**2.46**	**2.30**	**2.19**	**2.10**	**2.03**	**1.97**	**1.92**	**1.88**	**1.85**	**1.79**	**1.75**	**1.68**
	.01	6.90	4.82	3.98	3.51	3.20	2.99	2.82	2.69	2.59	2.51	2.43	2.36	2.26	2.19	2.06
125	.05	**3.92**	**3.07**	**2.68**	**2.44**	**2.29**	**2.17**	**2.08**	**2.01**	**1.95**	**1.90**	**1.86**	**1.83**	**1.77**	**1.72**	**1.65**
	.01	6.84	4.78	3.94	3.47	3.17	2.95	2.79	2.65	2.56	2.47	2.40	2.33	2.23	2.15	2.03
150	.05	**3.91**	**3.06**	**2.67**	**2.43**	**2.27**	**2.16**	**2.07**	**2.00**	**1.94**	**1.89**	**1.85**	**1.82**	**1.76**	**1.71**	**1.64**
	.01	6.81	4.75	3.91	3.44	3.14	2.92	2.76	2.62	2.53	2.44	2.37	2.30	2.20	2.12	2.00
200	.05	**3.89**	**3.04**	**2.65**	**2.41**	**2.26**	**2.14**	**2.05**	**1.98**	**1.92**	**1.87**	**1.83**	**1.80**	**1.74**	**1.69**	**1.62**
	.01	6.76	4.71	3.88	3.41	3.11	2.90	2.73	2.60	2.50	2.41	2.34	2.28	2.17	2.09	1.97
400	.05	**3.86**	**3.02**	**2.62**	**2.39**	**2.23**	**2.12**	**2.03**	**1.96**	**1.90**	**1.85**	**1.81**	**1.78**	**1.72**	**1.67**	**1.60**
	.01	6.70	4.66	3.83	3.36	3.06	2.85	2.69	2.55	2.46	2.37	2.29	2.23	2.12	2.04	1.92
1000	.05	**3.85**	**3.00**	**2.61**	**2.38**	**2.22**	**2.10**	**2.02**	**1.95**	**1.89**	**1.84**	**1.80**	**1.76**	**1.70**	**1.65**	**1.58**
	.01	6.66	4.62	3.80	3.34	3.04	2.82	2.66	2.53	2.43	2.34	2.26	2.20	2.09	2.01	1.89
∞	.05	**3.84**	**2.99**	**2.60**	**2.37**	**2.21**	**2.09**	**2.01**	**1.94**	**1.88**	**1.83**	**1.79**	**1.75**	**1.69**	**1.64**	**1.57**
	.01	6.64	4.60	3.78	3.32	3.02	2.80	2.64	2.51	2.41	2.32	2.24	2.18	2.07	1.99	1.87

The header "Degrees of freedom between groups (degrees of freedom in numerator of F ratio)" spans the numerator columns 1 through 20.

Reprinted by permission from *Statistical Methods*, 8th edition by G. Snedecor and W. Cochran. © 1989 by The Iowa State University Press, Ames, Iowa.

Table 4   *q*-table

For a one-way ANOVA, or a comparison of the means from a main effect, the value of *k* is the number of means in the factor.

To compare the means from an interaction, find the appropriate design (or number of cell means) in the table below and obtain the adjusted value of *k*. Then use adjusted *k* as *k* to find the value of *q*.

Values of Adjusted *k*

Design of study	Number of cell means in study	Adjusted value of k
2 × 2	4	3
2 × 3	6	5
2 × 4	8	6
3 × 3	9	7
3 × 4	12	8
4 × 4	16	10
4 × 5	20	12

Values of *q* for $\alpha = .05$ are **dark numbers** and for $\alpha = .01$ are light numbers.

Degrees of freedom within groups (degrees of freedom in denominator of F ratio)	α	k = number of means being compared										
		2	3	4	5	6	7	8	9	10	11	12
1	.05	18.00	27.00	32.80	37.10	40.40	43.10	45.40	47.40	49.10	50.60	52.00
	.01	90.00	135.00	164.00	186.00	202.00	216.00	227.00	237.00	246.00	253.00	260.00
2	.05	6.09	8.30	9.80	10.90	11.70	12.40	13.00	13.50	14.00	14.40	14.70
	.01	14.00	19.00	22.30	24.70	26.60	28.20	29.50	30.70	31.70	32.60	33.40
3	.05	4.50	5.91	6.82	7.50	8.04	8.48	8.85	9.18	9.46	9.72	9.95
	.01	8.26	10.60	12.20	13.30	14.20	15.00	15.60	16.20	16.70	17.10	17.50
4	.05	3.93	5.04	5.76	6.29	6.71	7.05	7.35	7.60	7.83	8.03	8.21
	.01	6.51	8.12	9.17	9.96	10.60	11.10	11.50	11.90	12.30	12.60	12.80
5	.05	3.64	4.60	5.22	5.67	6.03	6.33	6.58	6.80	6.99	7.17	7.32
	.01	5.70	6.97	7.80	8.42	8.91	9.32	9.67	9.97	10.20	10.50	10.70
6	.05	3.46	4.34	4.90	5.31	5.63	5.89	6.12	6.32	6.49	6.65	6.79
	.01	5.24	6.33	7.03	7.56	7.97	8.32	8.61	8.87	9.10	9.30	9.49
7	.05	3.34	4.16	4.69	5.06	5.36	5.61	5.82	6.00	6.16	6.30	6.43
	.01	4.95	5.92	6.54	7.01	7.37	7.68	7.94	8.17	8.37	8.55	8.71
8	.05	3.26	4.04	4.53	4.89	5.17	5.40	5.60	5.77	5.92	6.05	6.18
	.01	4.74	5.63	6.20	6.63	6.96	7.24	7.47	7.68	7.87	8.03	8.18

Table 4 (cont.)   *q*-table

Degrees of freedom within groups (degrees of freedom in denominator of F ratio)	α	2	3	4	5	6	7	8	9	10	11	12
					k = *number of means being compared*							
9	.05	3.20	3.95	4.42	4.76	5.02	5.24	5.43	5.60	5.74	5.87	5.98
	.01	4.60	5.43	5.96	6.35	6.66	6.91	7.13	7.32	7.49	7.65	7.78
10	.05	3.15	3.88	4.33	4.65	4.91	5.12	5.30	5.46	5.60	5.72	5.83
	.01	4.48	5.27	5.77	6.14	6.43	6.67	6.87	7.05	7.21	7.36	7.48
11	.05	3.11	3.82	4.26	4.57	4.82	5.03	5.20	5.35	5.49	5.61	5.71
	.01	4.39	5.14	5.62	5.97	6.25	6.48	6.67	6.84	6.99	7.13	7.26
12	.05	3.08	3.77	4.20	4.51	4.75	4.95	5.12	5.27	5.40	5.51	5.62
	.01	4.32	5.04	5.50	5.84	6.10	6.32	6.51	6.67	6.81	6.94	7.06
13	.05	3.06	3.73	4.15	4.45	4.69	4.88	5.05	5.19	5.32	5.43	5.53
	.01	4.26	4.96	5.40	5.73	5.98	6.19	6.37	6.53	6.67	6.79	6.90
14	.05	3.03	3.70	4.11	4.41	4.64	4.83	4.99	5.13	5.25	5.36	5.46
	.01	4.21	4.89	5.32	5.63	5.88	6.08	6.26	6.41	6.54	6.66	6.77
16	.05	3.00	3.65	4.05	4.33	4.56	4.74	4.90	5.03	5.15	5.26	5.35
	.01	4.13	4.78	5.19	5.49	5.72	5.92	6.08	6.22	6.35	6.46	6.56
18	.05	2.97	3.61	4.00	4.28	4.49	4.67	4.82	4.96	5.07	5.17	5.27
	.01	4.07	4.70	5.09	5.38	5.60	5.79	5.94	6.08	6.20	6.31	6.41
20	.05	2.95	3.58	3.96	4.23	4.45	4.62	4.77	4.90	5.01	5.11	5.20
	.01	4.02	4.64	5.02	5.29	5.51	5.69	5.84	5.97	6.09	6.19	6.29
24	.05	2.92	3.53	3.90	4.17	4.37	4.54	4.68	4.81	4.92	5.01	5.10
	.01	3.96	4.54	4.91	5.17	5.37	5.54	5.69	5.81	5.92	6.02	6.11
30	.05	2.89	3.49	3.84	4.10	4.30	4.46	4.60	4.72	4.83	4.92	5.00
	.01	3.89	4.45	4.80	5.05	5.24	5.40	5.54	5.56	5.76	5.85	5.93
40	.05	2.86	3.44	3.79	4.04	4.23	4.39	4.52	4.63	4.74	4.82	4.91
	.01	3.82	4.37	4.70	4.93	5.11	5.27	5.39	5.50	5.60	5.69	5.77
60	.05	2.83	3.40	3.74	3.98	4.16	4.31	4.44	4.55	4.65	4.73	4.81
	.01	3.76	4.28	4.60	4.82	4.99	5.13	5.25	5.36	5.45	5.53	5.60
120	.05	2.80	3.36	3.69	3.92	4.10	4.24	4.36	4.48	4.56	4.64	4.72
	.01	3.70	4.20	4.50	4.71	4.87	5.01	5.12	5.21	5.30	5.38	5.44
∞	.05	2.77	3.31	3.63	3.86	4.03	4.17	4.29	4.39	4.47	4.55	4.62
	.01	3.64	4.12	4.40	4.60	4.76	4.88	4.99	5.08	5.16	5.23	5.29

Table 5   *r*-table (Pearson's correlation coefficient): Critical values of *r*

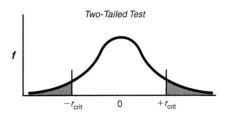

Two-Tailed Test

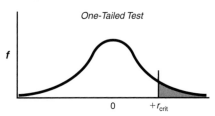

One-Tailed Test

df (no. of pairs − 2)	Alpha Level		df (no. of pairs − 2)	Alpha Level	
	$\alpha = .05$	$\alpha = .01$		$\alpha = .05$	$\alpha = .01$
1	.997	.9999	1	.988	.9995
2	.950	.990	2	.900	.980
3	.878	.959	3	.805	.934
4	.811	.917	4	.729	.882
5	.754	.874	5	.669	.833
6	.707	.834	6	.622	.789
7	.666	.798	7	.582	.750
8	.632	.765	8	.549	.716
9	.602	.735	9	.521	.685
10	.576	.708	10	.497	.658
11	.553	.684	11	.476	.634
12	.532	.661	12	.458	.612
13	.514	.641	13	.441	.592
14	.497	.623	14	.426	.574
15	.482	.606	15	.412	.558
16	.468	.590	16	.400	.542
17	.456	.575	17	.389	.528
18	.444	.561	18	.378	.516
19	.433	.549	19	.369	.503
20	.423	.537	20	.360	.492
21	.413	.526	21	.352	.482
22	.404	.515	22	.344	.472
23	.396	.505	23	.337	.462
24	.388	.496	24	.330	.453
25	.381	.487	25	.323	.445
26	.374	.479	26	.317	.437
27	.367	.471	27	.311	.430
28	.361	.463	28	.306	.423
29	.355	.456	29	.301	.416
30	.349	.449	30	.296	.409
35	.325	.418	35	.275	.381
40	.304	.393	40	.257	.358

Table 5 (cont.) r-table (Pearson's correlation coefficient): Critical values of r

df (no. of pairs $-$ 2)	Alpha Level		df (no. of pairs $-$ 2)	Alpha Level	
	$\alpha = .05$	$\alpha = .01$		$\alpha = .05$	$\alpha = .01$
45	.288	.372	45	.243	.338
50	.273	.354	50	.231	.322
60	.250	.325	60	.211	.295
70	.232	.302	70	.195	.274
80	.217	.283	80	.183	.256
90	.205	.267	90	.173	.242
100	.195	.254	100	.164	.230

From Table IV of R. A. Fisher and F. Yates, *Statistical Tables for Biological, Agricultural and Medical Research*, 6th ed. (London: Longman Group Ltd., 1974). Reprinted by permission of Pearson Education Limited.

Table 6 χ^2-table: Critical values of chi square

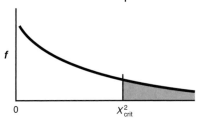

df	Alpha Level	
	$\alpha = .05$	$\alpha = .01$
1	3.84	6.64
2	5.99	9.21
3	7.81	11.34
4	9.49	13.28
5	11.07	15.09
6	12.59	16.81
7	14.07	18.48
8	15.51	20.09
9	16.92	21.67
10	18.31	23.21
11	19.68	24.72
12	21.03	26.22
13	22.36	27.69
14	23.68	29.14
15	25.00	30.58
16	26.30	32.00
17	27.59	33.41
18	28.87	34.80
19	30.14	36.19
20	31.41	37.57
21	32.67	38.93
22	33.92	40.29
23	35.17	41.64
24	36.42	42.98
25	37.65	44.31
26	38.88	45.64
27	40.11	46.96
28	41.34	48.28
29	42.56	49.59
30	43.77	50.89
40	55.76	63.69
50	67.50	76.15
60	79.08	88.38
70	90.53	100.42

From Table IV of R. A. Fisher and F. Yates, *Statistical Tables for Biological, Agricultural and Medical Research*, 6th ed. (London: Longman Group Ltd., 1974). Reprinted by permission of Pearson Education Limited.

ANSWERS TO ODD-NUMBERED EXERCISES

Chapter 1

1. Statistics are useful because they organize and summarize data. Statistics help us to communicate results of our studies efficiently and effectively.

3. Symbols are used in statistics for convenience, so the entire name of a formula does not have to be written each time.

5. Random selection from the population means that all people in the population have an equal chance of being selected to be in a sample; whereas, random assignment to conditions means that all people in the sample have an equal chance of being put into the various levels of the IV.

7. a. 45.93   d. 11.36
   b. 7.51   e. 3.00
   c. 36.80   f. 0.98

9. a. 0.50   d. 0.67
   b. 1.00   e. 0.31
   c. 0.25   f. 0.11

11. a. 6.00   e. 0.06
    b. 36.00   f. 5.00
    c. 5.33   g. 3.07
    d. 2.31   h. 14.56

13. a. passing or failing   d. having patience or not
    b. short or long   e. red or brown
    c. batting average below or above 0.300   f. good or poor

15. a. IV: Playing violent video games
    Levels: playing them or not
    DV: Violence in real life
    b. IV: Smiling
    Levels: none, once, or twice
    DV: How long it takes someone to join in a conversation
    c. IV: Exercising
    Levels: 3 or 6 times per week
    DV: Self-esteem
    d. IV: TV watching
    Levels: watching TV or not
    DV: Everyday motivation
    e. IV: Taking this course
    Levels: taking this course or not taking it
    DV: Happiness

17. 1.02

Chapter 2

1. a.   A nominal variable has levels that are categories.

   b.   An ordinal variable has levels that are rankings.

   c.   An interval variable has levels with equal intervals.

   d.   A ratio variable has levels with equal intervals and an absolute 0 point.

3. Interval and ratio variables reflect quantity (are quantitative).

5. Yes, it would be possible for an interval or ratio variable to be discrete, if decimals were not possible between levels. For example, a census of the number of people in the country represents ratio data, but fractions of people are not possible, demonstrating discrete, ratio data.

7. a.   A bar graph is used to illustrate nominal or ordinal data on the x-axis.

   b.   A histogram is used to illustrate discrete interval or ratio data on the x-axis.

   c.   A line graph is used to illustrate continuous interval or ratio data on the x-axis.

9. A simple frequency polygon is a graph of continuous interval or ratio data on the x-axis.

11.

Variable	Nominal, Ordinal, Interval, Ratio	Qualitative vs. Quantitative	Discrete vs. Continuous
Ink colors	Nominal	Qualitative	Discrete
Number of research paper rough drafts	Ratio	Quantitative	Discrete
Time spent writing research paper	Ratio	Quantitative	Continuous
Rank boyfriend/ girlfriend from best to worst	Ordinal	Qualitative	Discrete
Gallons of water in the bathtub	Ratio	Quantitative	Continuous
Test difficulty on a scale from 1 to 10	Interval	Quantitative	Discrete (with only whole numbers)
Number of notebooks in a book bag	Ratio	Quantitative	Discrete
Price the bookstore pays to buy back used textbooks	Ratio	Quantitative	Continuous

13.

Attend	f
0	6
1	3
2	4
3	3
4	9
5	2
6	1
7	0
8	2

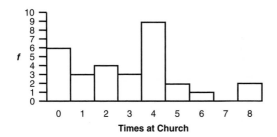

Times at Church

15.

Hours	f
0	2
1	1
2	2
3	5
4	6
5	8
6	9
7	7

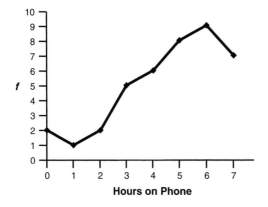

Hours on Phone

17.

Pain	f
41–50	3
51–60	2
61–70	4
71–80	3
81–90	3
91–100	5

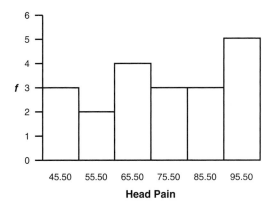

Head Pain

Chapter 3

1. Measures of central tendency summarize a data set using 1 number that best represents the data set.

3. The median is a measure of central tendency used to indicate the point at which 50% of the values in a data set falls at or below, and 50% of the distribution falls above the median. The median is used to summarize data on an ordinal variable and to represent skewed interval or ratio values.

5. An interval or ratio data set with clear outliers is summarized using the median. If the data set contains an even number of values, the average of the 2 values is used as the median.

7. A simple frequency distribution graph of interval or ratio values is a line graph (polygon), with simple frequency on the y-axis. Conversely, a graph of experimental data with an interval or ratio DV is labeled with the mean DV on the y-axis. The type of graph depends on the level of measurement of the IV.

9. a. 58.42
   b. 56.81
   c. 54.71

11. a. ratio
    b. The most appropriate measure of central tendency is the mean, because the data are ratio values with no obvious outliers.
    c. 54.71

13.

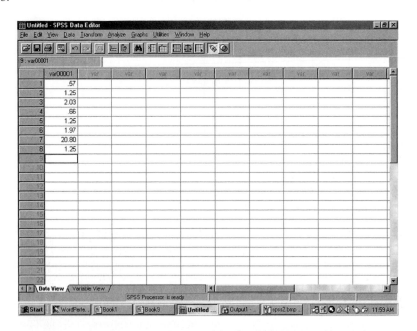

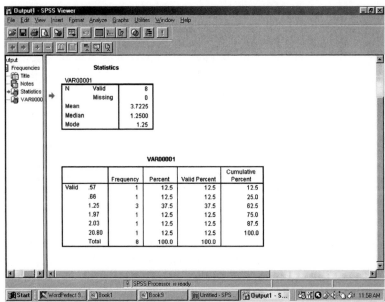

15. a.   These data represent ratio data.

   b.   The most appropriate measure of central tendency would be the median due to the out-
         lier of 298 students enrolled in one class.

   c.   36.00

17. a.   The IV represents nominal data (alone vs. with a friend).

b. With a nominal variable on the *x*-axis, a bar graph is needed.

c.

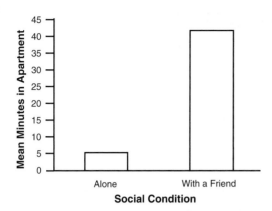

d.

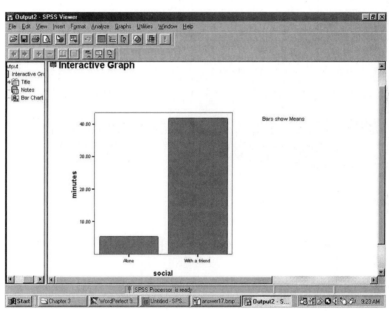

Chapter 4

1. These graphs have different levels of kurtosis. The first is mesokurtic, the second is leptokurtic, and the third is platykurtic. Also, these distributions differ in their variability, which can be measured using standard deviation or variance.

3. To describe a sample, the best measure of variability is the sample standard deviation.

5. Definitional formulas are used to explain the logic behind a calculation, whereas calculational formulas provide a shortcut to a final answer.

7. Skewed interval or ratio data require the range as a measure of variability.

9. a. 7.10
    b. 5.18
    c. 2.28

   d.   5.83

   e.   2.41

   f.   These data are best described by the standard deviation, because time is a ratio variable, and no outliers are found in the data set. The sample standard deviation is the best choice to simply describe these data.

11. a.   These data represent an ordinal variable.

   b.   The appropriate measure of variability, the range, is from 1st to 4th place.

13. a.   This quasi-IV is a ratio variable.

   b.   A ratio variable on the *x*-axis requires a line graph.

   c.

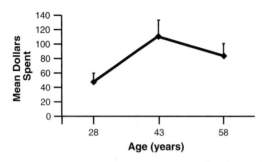

   d.

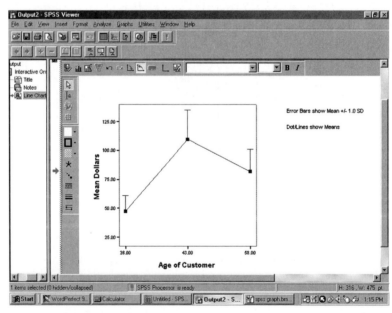

Chapter 5

1.   Standardized values are more meaningful than raw values because they allow you to compare scores across any distribution. In addition, the value of the score is easier to understand because it reflects number of standard deviations from the mean (by the absolute value), and whether the score is lower or higher than the mean (by the sign of the number).

3. A z-score is rarely found beyond ±3.00. That is, about 0.13 percent of the distribution is found below a z-score of −3.00 or above a z-score of +3.00.

5. Percent can never be a negative value, because it ranges from 0% to 100%. In terms of a distribution of values, 0% means no area under a distribution, and 100% means all of the area under a curve.

7. $X = S_x(z) + \overline{X}$

9. a. −1.28
   b. 1.67
   c. 2.82
   d. −0.64
   e. 0.00

11. a. 0.1003
    b. 0.9525
    c. 0.9976
    d. 0.2611
    e. 0.5000

13. Stats Test 1

15. a. 0.0329
    b. 0.9671
    c. 0.0329
    d. 0.9342
    e. 0.0658

17. 84th percentile

19. 41.65

21. 0.4812

23. 0.11

25. 5%

27. 8%

Chapter 6

1. a. Probability is the likelihood of an event.
   b. Sampling error occurs when a sample characteristic does not reflect the population from which it was drawn.
   c. The critical region is the area under the curve (in the tail) that is likely to occur in a normal population less than 5% of the time (or 1% in a more conservative test).
   d. A critical value is a number that sets the edge of the critical region.
   e. An obtained value is a number calculated from a sample to compare with the critical value.

3. A sample distribution of means is a simple frequency distribution of means on the dependent variable.

5. $\dfrac{1}{4} = 0.25$

7. 0.3944

9. 0.0495

11. 0.0500

13. a./b.

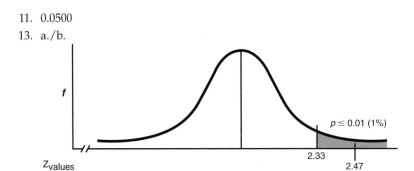

c.   Yes, completing homework increases grades.

15. 0.2881

17. First, the standard error is calculated to be 0.166667, then the z_{obt} is calculated to be -4.67. Because the upper region (tail) of the distribution was shaded for an expected increase in memory capacity, -4.67 falls in an unshaded region. Obviously, this drug does not improve memory.

19. The standard error is 6.50, and the z_{obt} is 3.08. The expectation was that the physician was overcharging, so the upper tail of the distribution was shaded, with a z_{crit} of 1.65. The z_{obt} of 3.08 falls above a z_{crit} of 1.65, in the critical region; therefore, this physician does overcharge.

Chapter 7

1. a.   The null hypothesis is an expectation laid out prior to data collection that indicates what will happen if the sample is not different from the normal population. In a one-tailed test, the null hypothesis will also represent the direction in which the sample is not expected to fall.

   b.   The alternate hypothesis is an expectation laid out prior to data collection that indicates what the research imagines will happen if the sample is different from the population.

   c.   The rejection region is the area under the curve (in the tail or tails) that is likely to occur in a normal population less than 5% of the time (or 1% in a more conservative test).

   d.   A confidence interval is an estimate of the range in which 95% of a population is likely to fall if members of the population experienced what members of the sample experienced.

   e.   Statistical power is the ability to reject the null hypothesis when the rules of hypothesis testing have been followed. If a researcher had access to reality, power would mean the ability to reject the null hypothesis when it is indeed false.

3. μ is used rather than $\overline{X}$ when stating hypotheses, because we are inferring what would happen in the entire population if they were treated the same way as the sample.

5. Failing to reject the null hypothesis could mean that no effect exists in the real world, or it could mean that the researcher conducted sloppy research. An editor cannot know which is true.

7. a.   moderate

   b.   weak

   c.   strong

   d.   strong

   e.   moderate

9. a. 250
   b. 50
   c. $H_0: \mu = 250$
       $H_1: \mu \neq 250$
   d. two-tailed z-test
   e.

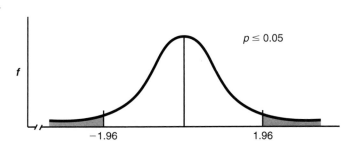

   f. 240
   g. The standard error of the mean is 5.00, and z_{obt} is 2.00.
   h.

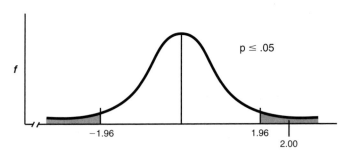

   i. Yes, there was an effect. The sample mean was significantly different from the population mean.
   j. $z_{obt} = 2.00, p < 0.05$
   k. Reject H_0
   l. If we went back to the population and made people exercise, their self-esteem would change.
   m. 0.20
   n. People who exercised had higher self-esteem than those who did not exercise.
   o. $250.20 \rightarrow 269.80$
11. a. 15
   b. 7
   c. $H_0: \mu \leq 15$
       $H_1: \mu > 15$
   d. one-tailed z-test (in the positive direction)

e.

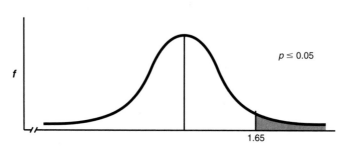

$p \leq 0.05$

f.   17
g.   The standard error of the mean is 1.00, and the z_{obt} is 2.00.
h.

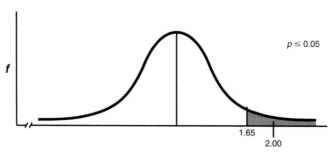

$p \leq 0.05$

i.   Yes, there was an effect. The sample mean was significantly different from the population mean.
j. $z_{obt} = 2.00, p < 0.05$
k.   Reject H_0
l.   If you went back to the population of rats and encouraged them all, their speed would increase.
m.   0.29
n.   Encouraging rats made them move faster than those who were not encouraged.
o. $15.04 \rightarrow 18.96$
13. a.   7.00
    b.   1.34
    c. $H_0: \mu \leq 15$
          $H_1: \mu > 15$
    d.   one-tailed z-test (in the positive direction)
    e.

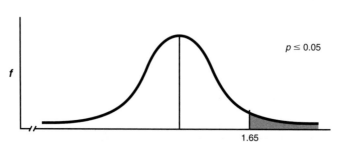

$p \leq 0.05$

    f.   6.111111

g. The standard error of the mean is 0.446667, and the z_{obt} is -1.99.

h.

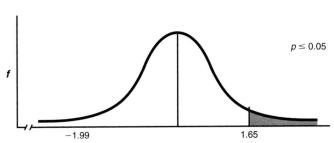

i. No, there was not a significant effect. The sample mean was not significantly different from the population mean.

j. $z_{obt} = -1.99, p > 0.05$

k. Fail to reject H_0

l. If we went back to the population of students and gave them all soft mattresses, they would not hit the snooze button more often.

m. Effect size can't be calculated for no effect.

n. Students with new, soft mattresses did not hit the snooze button more often than students without new, soft mattresses.

o. A confidence interval is restricted to a significant effect.

Chapter 8

1. single-sample t-test

3. independent-samples t-test

5. a. $\mathcal{S}_{\overline{X}}$

    b. $\mathcal{S}_{\overline{D}}$

    c. $\mathcal{S}_{\overline{X}_1-\overline{X}_2}$

7. In inferential statistics, we are always testing the preconception that the sample will not be different from the population or the 2 samples will not be different from each other; thus, we must accept the null hypothesis unless we can find strong evidence to reject it. When calculating t_{obt}, we have not yet rejected the null hypothesis, which indicates that $\mu_1 - \mu_2 = 0$ (and $\mu_D = 0$).

9. a. $H_0: \mu = 8$

      $H_1: \mu \neq 8$

    b. two-tailed, single-sample t-test

    c.

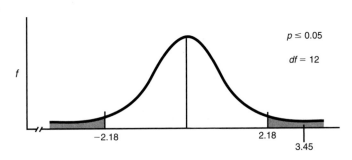

    d.   The estimated standard error of the mean is 0.779420, and the t_{obt} is 3.45. In APA style, $t(12) = 3.45, p < 0.05$. Reject the null hypothesis.

    e.   The sample mean was significantly different from the population mean.

    f.   The effect size is 0.96, and the confidence interval ranges from 8.99 to 12.39.

    g.   People who learn the rules of baseball enjoy the game more than the normal population.

11. a. $H_0: \mu_1 - \mu_2 \geq 0$

       $H_1: \mu_1 - \mu_2 < 0$

    b.   one-tailed, independent-samples t-test (in the negative direction)

    c.

$p \leq 0.05$

$df = 12$

f

-1.782

-4.44

    d.   The estimated standard error of the difference between means is 4.928744, and the t_{obt} is -4.44. In APA style, $t(12) = -4.44, p < 0.05$. Reject the null hypothesis.

    e.   The 2 groups were significantly different from each other.

    f.   The effect size is 0.62. The confidence interval for nonsmokers is -3.31 (0) to 11.88; the confidence interval for people who smoke 2 packs of cigarettes a day is 18.55 to 33.74 coughs and chokes.

    g.   Smoking 2 packs of cigarettes a day for a month causes more coughing and choking than not smoking.

       Work verified on SPSS:

T-Test

Group Statistics

SMOKE		N	Mean	Std. Deviation	Std. Error Mean
COUGH	nonsmokers	7	4.2857	5.55921	2.10118
	smokers	7	26.1429	11.79588	4.45842

Independent Samples Test

		Levene's Test for Equality of Variances		t-test for Equality of Means					95% Confidence Interval of the Difference	
		F	Sig.	t	df	Sig. (2-talled)	Mean Difference	Std. Error Difference	Lower	Upper
COUGH	Equal variances assumed	5.091	.043	−4.435	12	.001	−21.8571	4.92874	−32.59595	−11.11833
	Equal variances not assumed			−4.435	8.540	.002	−21.8571	4.92874	−33.09896	−10.61533

13. a. $H_0: \mu_D \leq 0$

       $H_1: \mu_D > 0$

    b.   one-tailed, related-samples t-test (in the positive direction based on the friend column being first in the data set)

c.

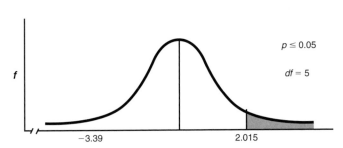

$p \leq 0.05$

$df = 5$

d.   The estimated standard error of the mean difference is 12.292730, and the t_{obt} is -3.39. APA style is $t(5) = -3.39, p > 0.05$, indicating that we fail to reject the null hypothesis.

e.   The 2 groups were not significantly different from each other.

f.   Effect size and confidence intervals should not be calculated, because a significant effect was not found based on a one-tailed test in the positive direction.

g.   Middle school students who were asked not to watch TV by their mothers watched just as much TV as their siblings who were asked not to watch TV by their friends.

Work verified on SPSS:

T-Test

Paired Samples Statistics

		Mean	N	Std. Deviation	Std. Error Mean
Pair 1	FRIEND	58.3333	6	27.68875	11.30388
	MOTHER	100.0000	6	53.38539	21.79449

Paired Samples Correlations

	N	Correlation	Sig.
Pair 1 FRIEND & MOTHER	6	.917	.010

Paired Samples Test

	Paired Difference							
				95% Confidence Interval of the Difference				
	Mean	Std. Deviation	Std. Error Mean	Lower	Upper	t	df	Sig. (2-tailed)
Pair 1 FRIEND & MOTHER	-41.6667	30.11091	12.29273	-73.2661	-10.0672	-3.390	5	.019

Chapter 9

1.   a.   A three-way ANOVA has 3 factors, with at least 2 levels for each factor.

b.   A between-groups factor is a variable (either an IV or quasi-IV) with levels containing different participants. With a true IV, participants are randomly assigned to conditions.

c.   A within-groups factor is an IV with levels containing the sample participants, with participants experiencing something different under each level.

d.   Treatment variability is associated with effect. It is found in differences between levels of a factor.

e. Error variability is associated with individual differences. It is found in differences within each level of a factor.

f. F_{crit} is the ANOVA value that delineates the beginning of the rejection region in ANOVA. It generally identifies the upper 5% of the F-distribution.

3. $H_0: \mu_1 = \mu_2 = \mu_3 = \mu_4 = \mu_5$

5. a. A between-groups factor is an IV or quasi-IV with different participants in the levels, and between-groups variability is the differences in DV numbers between the levels.

   b. A within-groups factor is an IV with the same people tested under every level, and within-groups variability is the differences in the DV numbers within each level of the IV.

   c. A one-tailed test is often used in t-tests to indicate a directional alternate hypothesis, and one-way is an ANOVA term to indicate one IV or quasi-IV in the analysis.

7. The SS_{tot} df would be $N - 1$ if a MS_{tot} was created.

9. a. $H_0: \mu_1 = \mu_2 = \mu_3$

   H_1: At least 2 of the groups are significantly different from each other.

   b. one-way, between-groups ANOVA

   c.

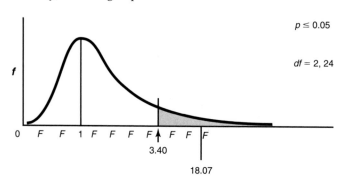

   d.

Source	SS	df	MS	F_{obt}
Attributes	47.19	2	23.59	18.07
Error	31.33	24	1.31	
Total	78.52	26		

   e. $F(2, 24) = 18.07, p < 0.05$; reject H_0

   f. At least 2 of the groups were significantly different from each other.

   g. 0.60

   h. $HSD = 3.53 \sqrt{\dfrac{1.306}{9}} = 1.34$

Clothes	Car	Confidence
6.89	6.11	9.22

0.78   3.11*

2.33*

i.   The confidence interval for trendy clothes is from 6.10 to 7.68; the confidence interval for a nice car is 5.33 to 6.90; the confidence interval for a confident attitude is 8.44 to 10.01.

j.   Work verified on SPSS:

Univariate Analysis of Variance

Between-Subjects Factors

		Value Label	N
ATTRIBUT	1.00	clothes	9
	2.00	car	9
	3.00	confidence	9

Descriptive Statistics

Dependent Variable: INTEREST

ATTRIBUT	Mean	Std. Deviation	N
clothes	6.8889	1.16667	9
car	6.1111	1.36423	9
confidence	9.2222	.83333	9
Total	7.4074	1.73780	27

Tests of Between-Subjects Effects

Dependent Variable: INTEREST

Source	Type III Sum of Squares	df	Mean Square	F	Sig.	Partial Eta Squared
Corrected Model	47.185[a]	2	23.593	18.071	.000	.601
Intercept	1481.481	1	1481.481	1134.752	.000	.979
ATTRIBUT	47.185	2	23.593	18.071	.000	.601
Error	31.333	24	1.306			
Total	1560.000	27				
Corrected Total	78.519	26				

a. R Squared = .601 (Adjusted R Squared = .588)

Estimated Marginal Means

ATTRIBUT

Dependent Variable: INTEREST

ATTRIBUT	Mean	Std. Error	95% Confidence Interval	
			Lower Bound	Upper Bound
clothes	6.889	.381	6.103	7.675
car	6.111	.381	5.325	6.897
confidence	9.222	.381	8.436	10.008

Post Hoc Tests

ATTRIBUT

Multiple Comparisons

Dependent Variable: INTEREST
Tukey HSD

(I) ATTRIBUT	(J) ATTRIBUT	Mean Difference (I-J)	Std. Error	Sig.	95% Confidence Interval	
					Lower Bound	Upper Bound
clothes	car	.7778	.53863	.335	−.5873	2.1229
	confidence	−2.3333*	.53863	.001	−3.6784	−.9882
car	clothes	−.7778	.53863	.335	−2.1229	.5673
	confidence	−3.1111*	.53863	.001	−4.4562	−1.7660
confidence	clothes	2.3333*	.53863	.001	.9882	3.6784
	car	3.1111*	.53863	.000	1.7660	4.4562

Based on observed means.
  *. The mean difference is significant at the .05 level.

Homogeneous Subsets

INTEREST

Tukey HSD[a,b]

ATTRIBUT	N	Subset	
		1	2
car	9	6.1111	
clothes	9	6.8889	
confidence	9		9.2222
Sig.		.335	1.000

Means for groups In homogeneous subsets are displayed.
Based on Type III Sum of Squares
The error term is Mean Square(Error) = 1.306.
  a. Uses Harmonic Mean Sample Size = 9.000.
  b. Alpha = .05.

  k. A guy with a confident attitude attracted more interest from high school girls than a guy with trendy clothes or a nice car. Boys with trendy clothes or a nice car were not rated differently from each other.

11. a. $H_0: \mu_1 = \mu_2 = \mu_3 = \mu_4$
      H_1: Not all μs are equal.

    b. one-way, between-groups ANOVA

c.

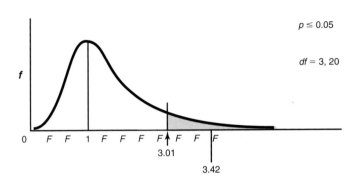

$p \le 0.05$

$df = 3, 20$

d.

Source	SS	df	MS	F_{obt}
Discipline	41.50	3	13.83	3.42
Error	81.00	20	4.05	
Total	122.50	23		

e. $F(3, 20) = 3.42, p < 0.05$; reject H_0
f. At least 2 of the groups were significantly different from each other.
g. 0.34
h. $\text{HSD} = 3.90\sqrt{\dfrac{4.05}{6}} = 3.20$

Lecture	Yelling	Time-out	Spanking
6.33	5.83	5.83	3.00

0.50   0   2.83

0.50

2.83

3.33*

i. The confidence interval for a lecture is 4.62 to 8.05; the confidence interval for yelling is 4.12 to 7.55; the confidence interval for time-out is also 4.12 to 7.55; the confidence interval for spanking is behavioral scores ranging from 1.29 to 4.71, with higher numbers indicating better behavior.

j. Work verified on SPSS:

Univariate Analysis of Variance

Between-Subjects Factors

		Value Label	N
DISCIPLN	1.00	lecture	6
	2.00	yelling	6
	3.00	time-out	6
	4.00	spanking	6

Descriptive Statistics

Dependent Variable: BEHAVIOR

DISCIPLN	Mean	Std. Deviation	N
lecture	6.3333	2.16025	6
yelling	5.8333	1.60208	6
time-out	5.8333	2.63944	6
spanking	3.0000	1.41421	6
Total	5.2500	2.30783	24

Tests of Between-Subjects Effects

Dependent Variable: BEHAVIOR

Source	Type III Sum of Squares	df	Mean Square	F	Sig.	Partial Eta Squared
Corrected Model	41.500[a]	3	13.833	3.416	.037	.339
Intercept	661.500	1	661.500	163.333	.000	.891
DISCIPLN	41.500	3	13.833	3.416	.037	.339
Error	81.000	20	4.050			
Total	784.000	24				
Corrected Total	122.500	23				

a. R Squared = .339 (Adjusted R Squared = .240)

Estimated Marginal Means

DISCIPLN

Dependent Variable: BEHAVIOR

DISCIPLN	Mean	Std. Error	95% Confidence Interval	
			Lower Bound	Upper Bound
lecture	6.333	.822	4.620	8.047
yelling	5.833	.822	4.120	7.547
time-out	5.833	.822	4.120	7.547
spanking	3.000	.822	1.288	4.714

Post Hoc Tests

DISCIPLN

Multiple Comparisons

Dependent Variable: BEHAVIOR
Tukey HSD

(1) DISCIPLN	(J) DISCIPLN	Mean Difference (I-J)	Std. Error	Sig.	95% Confidence Interval	
					Lower Bound	Upper Bound
lecture	yelling	.5000	1.16190	.973	−2.7521	3.7521
	time-out	.5000	1.16190	.973	−2.7521	3.7521
	spanking	3.3333*	1.16190	.043	.0813	6.5854
yelling	lecture	−.5000	1.16190	.973	−3.7521	2.7521
	time-out	.0000	1.16190	1.000	−3.2521	3.2521
	spanking	2.8333	1.16190	.102	−.4187	6.0854
time-out	lecture	−.5000	1.16190	.973	−3.7521	2.7521
	yelling	.0000	1.16190	1.000	−3.7521	3.2521
	spanking	2.8333	1.16190	.102	−.4187	6.0854
spanking	lecture	−3.3333*	1.16190	.043	−6.5854	−.0813
	yelling	−2.8333	1.16190	.102	−6.0854	.4187
	time-out	−2.8333	1.16190	.102	−6.5854	.4187

Based on observed means.
 *. The mean difference is significant at the .05 level.

Homogeneous Subsets

BEHAVIOR

Tukey HSD[a,b]

DISCIPLN	N	Subset	
		1	2
spanking	6	3.0000	
yelling	6	5.8333	5.8333
time-out	6	5.8333	5.8333
lecture	6		6.3333
Sig.		.102	.973

Means for groups in homogeneous subsets are displayed.
Based on Type III Sum of Squares
The error term is Mean Square(Error) = 4.050.
 a. Uses Harmonic Mean Sample Size = 6.000.
 b. Alpha = .05.

k.   Children behave better after a lecture than after a spanking. No other discipline groups were different from each other as measured by behavior.

13. a. $H_0: \mu_1 = \mu_2 = \mu_3 = \mu_4$
H_1: Not all μs are equal.

b.   one-way, between-groups ANOVA

c.

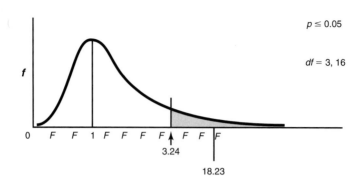

d.

Source	SS	df	MS	F_{obt}
Year	6049.20	3	2016.40	18.23
Error	1769.60	16	110.60	
Total	7818.80	19		

e. $F(3, 16) = 18.23, p < 0.05$; reject H_0

f.   At least 2 of the groups were significantly different from each other.

g.   0.77

h. $\text{HSD} = 4.05\sqrt{\dfrac{110.60}{5}} = 19.05$

Freshperson	Sophomore	Junior	Senior
33.40	46.00	62.60	79.60

12.60   16.60   17.00

29.20*

33.60*

46.20*

i.   The confidence interval for freshpersons is 23.43 to 43.37; the confidence interval for sophomores is 36.03 to 55.97; the confidence interval for juniors is 52.63 to 72.57; the confidence interval for seniors is 69.63 to 89.57.

j.   Work verified on SPSS:

Univariate Analysis of Variance

Bewteen-Subjects Factors

		Value Label	N
YEAR	1.00	freshperson	5
	2.00	sophomore	5
	3.00	junior	5
	4.00	senior	5

Descriptive Statistics

Dependent Variable: COMFORT

YEAR	Mean	Std. Deviation	N
freshperson	33.4000	15.37205	5
sophomore	46.0000	9.13783	5
junior	62.6000	8.20366	5
senior	79.6000	7.43640	5
Total	55.4000	20.28585	20

Tests of Between-Subjects Effects

Dependent Variable: COMFORT

Source	Type III Sum of Squares	df	Mean Square	F	Sig.	Partial Eta Squared
Corrected Model	6049.200[a]	3	2016.400	18.231	.000	.774
Intercept	61383.200	1	61383.200	555.002	.000	.972
YEAR	6049.200	3	2016.400	18.231	.000	.774
Error	1769.600	16	110.600			
Total	69202.000	20				
Corrected Total	7818.800	19				

a. R Squared = .774 (Adjusted R Squared = .731)

Estimated Marginal Means

YEAR

Dependent Variable: COMFORT

YEAR	Mean	Std. Error	95%Confidence Interval Lower Bound	Upper Bound
freshperson	33.400	4.703	23.430	43.370
sophomore	46.000	4.703	36.030	55.970
junior	62.600	4.703	52.630	72.570
senior	79.600	4.703	69.630	89.570

Post Hoc Tests

YEAR

Multiple Comparisons

Dependent Variable: COMFORT
Tukey HSD

(I) YEAR	(J) YEAR	Mean Difference (I-J)	Std. Error	Sig.	95% Confidence Interval	
					Lower Bound	Upper Bound
freshperson	sophomore	−12.6000	6.65132	.269	−31.6295	6.4295
	junior	−29.2000*	6.65132	.002	−48.2295	−10.1705
	senior	−46.2000*	6.65132	.000	−85.2295	−27.1705
sophomore	freshperson	12.6000	6.65132	.269	−5.4295	31.6295
	junior	−16.6000	6.65132	.099	−35.6295	2.4295
	senior	−33.6000	6.65132	.001	−52.6295	−14.5705
junior	freshperson	29.2000*	6.65132	.002	10.1705	48.2295
	sophomore	16.6000	6.65132	.099	−2.4295	35.6295
	senior	−17.0000	6.65132	.089	−36.0295	2.0295
senior	freshperson	48.2000*	6.65132	.000	27.1705	65.2295
	sophomore	33.6000*	6.65132	.001	14.5705	52.6295
	junior	17.0000	6.65132	.089	−2.0295	36.0295

Based on observed means.
*, The mean difference is significant at the .05 level.

Homogeneous Subsets

COMFORT

Tukey HSD[a,b]

YEAR	N	Subset		
		1	2	3
freshperson	5	33.4000		
sophomore	5	46.0000	46.0000	
junior	5		62.6000	62.6000
senior	5			79.6000
Sig.		.269	.099	.089

Means for groups in homogeneous subsets are displayed.
Based on Type III Sum of Squares
The error term is Mean Square(Error) =110.600.
  a. Uses Harmonic Mean Sample Size = 5.000.
  b. Alpha = .05.

k. Juniors and seniors were more comfortable with ambiguity than freshpersons. In addition, seniors were more comfortable with ambiguity than sophomores. No other groups were different from each other as measured by comfort with ambiguous answers.

Evaluation of cause and effect:

Although this design may look like an experiment with 4 levels of an IV, participants were not manipulated. They entered the study already existing in one of the conditions: year in college. Thus, cause and effect cannot be established. Instead, we have learned from these data that year in school and comfort with ambiguous answers are related. Of course, we also still know which groups are significantly different from each other based on post-hoc comparisons.

Chapter 10

1. Twelve cells would be found in a 3×4 design.

3. The formula for degrees of freedom (*df*) for the interaction *MS* is $(k_A - 1)(k_B - 1)$, where *A* is the first factor, and *B* is the second factor.

5. Diagonal cell means would differ across levels of both factors; therefore, a diagonal comparison could not be explained as due to changes on one factor. If either factor could be responsible for diagonal means differing, no clear information is gained.

7. An interaction is more important than main effects because an interaction provides the details of results. That is, an interaction reveals how the effect of one factor depends on the level of the other factor (in a two-way design). Main effects merely offer a simple overview of each factor individually.

9. a.

Source	SS	df	MS	F_{obt}
Provoke	330.03	1	330.03	92.39
Alcohol	224.06	2	112.03	31.36
Prov × Alc	126.39	2	63.19	17.69
Error	107.17	30	3.57	
Total	787.64	35		

   b. Provoke: $F(1, 30) = 92.39, p < 0.05$
       Alcohol: $F(2, 30) = 31.36, p < 0.05$
       Provoke × Alcohol $F(2, 30) = 17.69, p < 0.05$

   c. Post hoc for the main effect of provocation is not needed, because a significant *F*-value means at least 2 groups are significantly different from each other, and provocation only has 2 groups. Post hoc for the main effect of alcohol is needed because a significant effect was found, and the factor has 3 levels.

$$HSD = 3.49\sqrt{\frac{3.572}{12}} = 1.90$$

0 ounces	5 ounces	10 ounces
11.42	12.50	17.17

1.08

4.67*

5.75*

Post hoc for the interaction is needed because a significant effect was found, and 6 cells are in this design. Because an interaction will always have more than 2 means (cells) to compare, post hoc will always be needed to further analyze a significant effect.

$$HSD = 4.10\sqrt{\frac{3.572}{6}} = 3.16$$

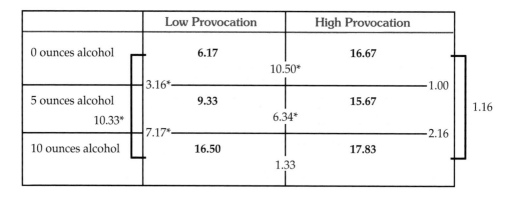

d. Work verified on SPSS:

Univariate Analysis of Variance

Between-Subjects Factors

		Value Label	N
PROVOKE	1.00	low	18
	2.00	high	18
ALCOHOL	1.00	0 ounces	12
	2.00	5 ounces	12
	3.00	10 ounces	12

Descriptive Statistics

Dependent Variable: AGGESS

PROVOKE	ALCOHOL	Mean	Std. Deviation	N
low	0 ounces	6.1667	1.94079	6
	5 ounces	9.3333	1.36626	6
	10 ounces	16.5000	2.58844	6
	Total	10.6667	4.83857	18
high	0 ounces	18.6667	1.03280	6
	5 ounces	15.6667	2.33809	6
	10 ounces	17.8333	1.60208	6
	Total	16.7222	1.87257	18
Total	0 ounces	11.4167	5.68024	12
	5 ounces	12.5000	3.77793	12
	10 ounces	17.1667	2.16725	12
	Total	13.6944	4.74383	36

Tests of Between-Subjects Effects

Dependent Variable: AGGESS

Source	Type III Sum of Squares	df	Mean Square	F	Sig.	Partial Eta Squared
Corrected Model	680.472*	5	136.094	38.098	.000	.864
Intercept	6751.361	1	6751.361	1889.961	.000	.984
PROVOKE	330.028	1	330.028	92.387	.000	.755
ALCOHOL	224.056	2	112.028	31.361	.000	.676
PROVOKE* ALCOHOL	126.389	2	63.194	17.691	.000	.541
Error	107.167	30	3.572			
Total	7539.000	36				
Corrected Total	787.639	35				

a. R Squared = .884 (Adjusted R Squared = .841)

Estimated Marginal Means

1. PROVOKE

Dependent Variable: AGGESS

PROVOKE	Mean	Std. Error	95% Confidence Interval	
			Lower Bound	Upper Bound
low	10.667	.445	9.757	11.576
high	16.722	.445	15.812	17.632

2. ALCOHOL

Dependent Variable: AGGESS

ALCOHOL	Mean	Std. Error	95% Confidence Interval	
			Lower Bound	Upper Bound
0 ounces	11.417	.546	10.302	12.531
5 ounces	12.500	.546	11.386	13.614
10 ounces	17.167	.546	16.052	18.281

3. PROVOKE* ALCOHOL

Dependent Variable: AGGESS

PROVOKE	ALCOHOL	Mean	Std. Error	95% Confidence Interval	
				Lower Bound	Upper Bound
low	0 ounces	6.167	.772	4.591	7.742
	5 ounces	9.333	.772	7.758	10.909
	10 ounces	16.500	.772	14.924	18.076
high	0 ounces	16.667	.772	15.091	18.242
	5 ounces	15.667	.772	14.091	17.242
	10 ounces	17.833	.772	16.258	19.409

Post Hoc Tests

ALCOHOL

Multiple Comparisons

Dependent Variable: AGGESS
Tukey HSD

(I) ALCOHOL	(J) ALCOHOL	Mean Difference (I-J)	Std. Error	Sig.	95% Confidence Interval	
					Lower Bound	Upper Bound
0 ounces	5 ounces	−1.0833	.77160	.352	−2.9855	.8189
	10 ounces	−5.7500*	.77160	.000	−7.6522	−3.8478
5 ounces	0 ounces	1.0833	.77160	.352	−.8189	2.9855
	10 ounces	−4.6667*	.77160	.000	−6.5689	−2.7645
10 ounces	0 ounces	5.7500*	.77160	.000	3.8478	7.6522
	5 ounces	4.6667*	.77160	.000	2.7645	6.5689

Based on observed means.

*. The mean difference is significant at the .05 level.

Homogeneous Subsets

AGGESS

Tukey HSD[a,b]

ALCOHOL	N	Subset	
		1	2
0 ounces	12	11.4167	
5 ounces	12	12.5000	
10 ounces	12		17.1667
Sig.		.352	1.000

Means for groups in homogeneous subsets are displayed.
Based on Type III Sum of Squares.
The error term is Mean Square(Error) = 3.572.
   a. Uses Harmonic Mean Sample Size = 12.000.
   b. Alpha = .05

e. Level of provocation affected aggression, with those highly provoked showing more aggression than those provoked at a low level. In addition, alcohol affected aggression. People who consumed 10 ounces of alcohol were more aggressive than those who drank 5 ounces or none. Aggression levels between 0 and 5 ounces of alcohol did not differ.

However, level of provocation and amount of alcohol interacted to affect aggression. High provocation caused more aggression than low provocation when participants drank 0 or 5 ounces of alcohol. Aggression was high across both levels of provocation when participants drank 10 ounces of alcohol. Under low provocation, participants who consumed 10 ounces of alcohol were more aggressive than those who drank 0 or 5 ounces, and those who drank 5 ounces were more aggressive than those who did not drink alcohol. Under high provocation, aggression was high across 0, 5, and 10 ounces of alcohol, with no differences between groups.

f.

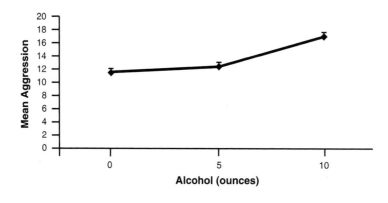

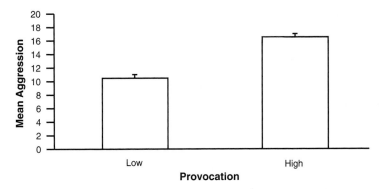

The interaction can be graphed with either alcohol or provocation on the *x*-axis. Both graphs appear below.

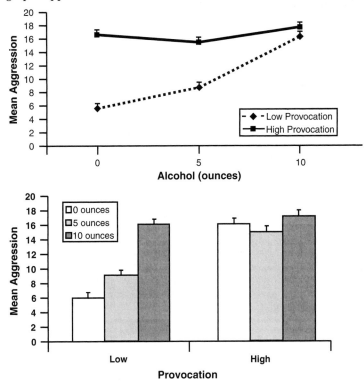

11. a.

Source	SS	df	MS	F_{obt}
Wash	3.40	2	1.70	1.08
Color	18.47	1	18.47	11.74
Wash × Color	0.74	2	0.37	0.235
Error	34.60	22	1.57	
Total	55.86	27		

b.   Wash: $F(2, 22) = 1.08, p > 0.05$
     Color: $F(1, 22) = 11.74, p < 0.05$
     Wash $\times$ Color: $F(2, 22) = 0.24, p > 0.05$

c.   Post hoc for type of carwash is not needed because no main effect was found. Although a main effect of car color was revealed, post hoc is not needed because only 2 levels, light and dark, were used. Simply compare the means for light and dark cars to see which customers rated their cars as cleaner. Finally, type of carwash and color of car did not interact to affect ratings of cleanliness; therefore, no post hoc is needed for an interaction. (Notice that with unequal n in this design, post-hoc analyses by hand would have required Fisher's protected t-tests, not Tukey's HSD.)

d.   Work verified on SPSS:

Univariate Analysis of Variance

Between-Subjects Factors

		Value Label	N
WASH	1.00	regular	10
	2.00	extra	9
	3.00	super	9
COLOR	1.00	light	14
	2.00	dark	14

Descriptive Statistics

Dependent Variable: CLEAN

WASH	COLOR	Mean	Std. Deviation	N
regular	light	5.4000	1.14018	5
	dark	4.0000	1.00000	5
	Total	4.7000	1.25167	10
extra	light	6.5000	1.29099	4
	dark	4.4000	1.51658	5
	Total	5.3333	1.73205	9
super	light	5.4000	1.14018	5
	dark	4.0000	1.41421	4
	Total	4.7778	1.39443	9
Total	light	5.7143	1.20439	14
	dark	4.1429	1.23146	14
	Total	4.9286	1.43833	28

Tests of Between-Subjects Effects

Dependent Variable: CLEAN

Source	Type III Sum of Squares	df	Mean Square	F	Sig.	Partial Eta Squared
Corrected Model	21.257*	5	4.251	2.703	.047	.381
Intercept	678.531	1	678.531	431.436	.000	.951
WASH	3.400	2	1.700	1.081	.357	.089
COLOR	18.469	1	18.469	11.743	.002	.348
WASH* COLOR	.740	2	.370	.235	.792	.021
Error	34.600	22	1.573			
Total	736.000	28				
Corrected Total	55.857	27				

a. R Squared = .381 (Adjusted R Squared =.240)

Estimated Marginal Means

1. WASH

Dependent Variable: CLEAN

WASH	Mean	Std. Error	95% Confidence Interval	
			Lower Bound	Upper Bound
regular	4.700	.397	3.878	5.522
extra	5.450	.421	4.578	6.322
super	4.700	.421	3.828	5.572

2. COLOR

Dependent Variable: CLEAN

COLOR	Mean	Std. Error	95% Confidence Interval	
			Lower Bound	Upper Bound
light	5.767	.337	5.068	6.466
dark	4.133	.337	3.434	4.832

3. WASH * COLOR

Dependent Variable: CLEAN

WASH	COLOR	Mean	Std. Error	95% Confidence Interval	
				Lower Bound	Upper Bound
regular	light	5.400	.561	4.237	6.563
	dark	4.000	.561	2.837	5.163
extra	light	6.500	.627	5.200	7.800
	dark	4.400	.561	3.237	5.563
super	light	5.400	.561	4.237	6.563
	dark	4.000	.627	2.700	5.300

Post Hoc Tests

WASH

Multiple Comparisons

Dependent Variable: CLEAN
Tukey HSD

(i) WASH	(J) WASH	Mean Difference (I-J)	Std.Error	Sig.	95% Confidence Interval	
					Lower Bound	Upper Bound
regular	extra	−.6333	.57621	.525	−2.0808	.8141
	super	−.0778	.57621	.990	−1.5253	1.3697
extra	regular	−.6333	.57621	.525	−.8141	2.0808
	super	.5556	.59118	.622	−.9295	2.0406
super	regular	.0778	.57621	.990	−1.3697	1.5253
	extra	−.5556	.59118	.622	−2.0406	.9295

Based on observed means.

Homogeneous Subsets

CLEAN

Tukey HSD[a,b,c]

WASH	N	Subset
		1
regular	10	4.7000
super	9	4.7778
extra	9	5.3333
Sig.		.530

Means for groups in homogeneous subsets are displayed.
Based on Type III Sum of Squares
The error term is Mean Square(Error) = 1.573.
 a. Uses Harmonic Mean Sample Size = 9.310.
 b. The group sizes are unequal. The harmonic mean of the group sizes is used. Type I error levels are not guaranteed.
 c. Alpha = .05.

e.   Type of carwash did not affect customers' ratings of cleanliness. Conversely, the color of customers' cars was related to their ratings of cleanliness, with light cars rated as cleaner than dark cars after the wash. No interaction was found between type of carwash and color of car.

(Notice that participants were randomly assigned to receive different types of car-washes, thus, type of carwash was manipulated, and cause and effect—or lack of effect in this case—could be discussed. However, color of car was not manipulated; customers already owned their cars. Because this factor was not manipulated, color of car did not affect cleanliness. Instead, a relationship was discussed in the plain English section above.)

f.

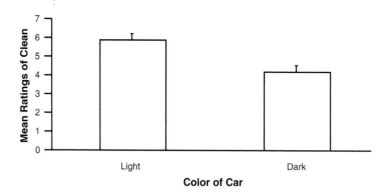

Chapter 11

1. Pearson's product moment correlation coefficient
3. Pearson's r can range from -1.00 to $+1.00$.
5.

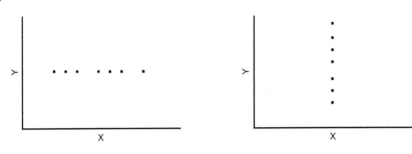

7. $H_0: \rho = 0$
9. When an r-value is artificially high, a scatterplot of the data will reveal a problem due to outliers and few participants with points that just happen to fall in a line pattern (although researchers would not conduct a study with few participants). A graph will not reveal a problem due to restriction of range on a curvilinear relationship.
11. a. positive and strong   b. very close to 0
    c. positive and weak   d. negative and strong
13. a. $H_0: \rho \geq 0$
       $H_1: \rho < 0$
    b. one-tailed Pearson's r (in the negative direction)
    c.

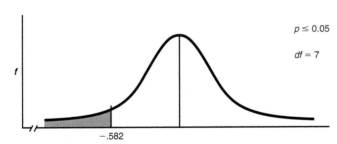

    d. $r(7) = -0.88, p < 0.05$
    e. Reject the null hypothesis.
    f. The coefficient of determination is 0.78, which indicates that the 2 variables have 78% of their variability in common with each other.

g.

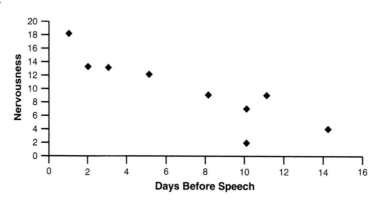

h.   The number of days before a speech and nervousness are related, with nervousness increasing as the number of days before a speech decrease.

i.   Work verified on SPSS:

	days	nervous
1	8.00	9.00
2	3.00	13.00
3	10.00	7.00
4	1.00	18.00
5	10.00	2.00
6	14.00	4.00
7	2.00	13.00
8	11.00	9.00
9	5.00	12.00

Graph

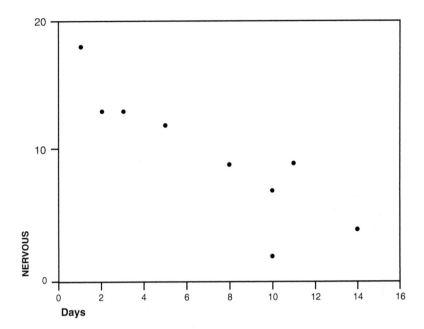

Correlations

Correlations

		DAYS	NERVOUS
DAYS	Pearson Correlation	1	−.883**
	Sig. (1-tailed)	.	.001
	N	9	9
NERVOUS	Pearson Correlation	−.883**	1
	Sig. (1-tailed)	.001	.
	N	9	9

**. Correlation is significant at the 0.01 level (1-tailed).

15. a. $H_0: \rho = 0$
     $H_1: \rho \neq 0$
   b.   two-tailed Pearson's r

c.

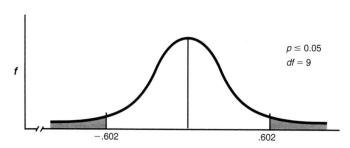

$p \leq 0.05$
$df = 9$

d. $r(9) = 0.24, p > 0.05$
e.   Fail to reject the null hypothesis.
f.   Although a significant effect does not exist, the coefficient of determination is 0.06. These 2 variables have approximately 6% in common.

g.

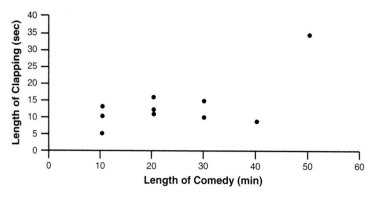

h.   Length of comedy show and length of clapping appeared to be related, but this relationship may be explained by a single outlier.
i.   Work verified on SPSS:

	comedy	clapping
1	30.00	10.00
2	20.00	11.00
3	30.00	10.00
4	50.00	35.00
5	10.00	10.00
6	40.00	9.00
7	10.00	13.00
8	20.00	16.00
9	20.00	12.00
10	10.00	5.00
11	30.00	15.00

Correlations

Correlations

		COMEDY	CLAPPING
COMEDY	Pearson Correlation	1	.631*
	Sig. (2-tailed)	.	.037
	N	11	11
CLAPPING	Pearson Correlation	.631*	1
	Sig. (2-tailed)	.037	.
	N	11	11

*.Correlation is significant at the 0.05 level (2-tailed).

Graph

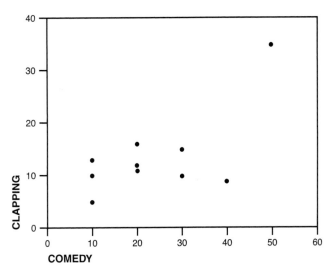

The scatterplot indicates that an outlier is present in the data. Removal of the outlier results in no relationship between length of comedy and length of applause. Analysis of the data with 1 outlier removed revealed a Pearson's r-value of 0.10. SPSS output and scatterplot are below.

Correlations

Correlations

		COMEDY	CLAPPING
COMEDY	Pearson Correlation	1	.096
	Sig. (2-tailed)	.	.792
	N	10	10
CLAPPING	Pearson Correlation	.096	1
	Sig. (2-tailed)	.792	.
	N	10	10

Graph

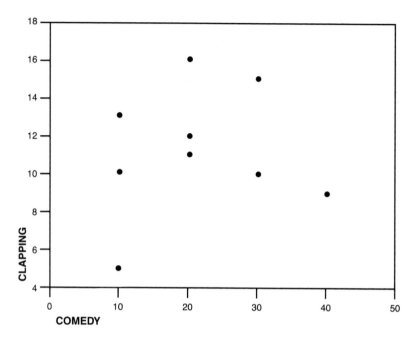

Chapter 12

1. Before we predict values on one variable from another variable, we must first know they are related (correlated).

3. In the linear regression equation, b stands for the slope.

5. When graphing the regression line, the X variable is generally labeled on the x-axis, and the Y variable is on the y-axis.

7. If the standard error of the estimate is 0, the correlation must be -1.00 or $+1.00$.

9. The Y-intercept can be used as the second point when it is located on the pictured graph and when no values have been skipped at the beginning of the x- or y-axis.

11. Yes, in this case causation could be determined because participants were manipulated. The statistical analysis used does not dictate cause and effect vs. relationships; the design itself is responsible for that distinction.

13. a. $Y' = -0.962X + 16.509$

Work verified on SPSS:

Correlations

Correlations

		DAYS	NERVOUS
DAYS	Pearson Correlation	1	−.883**
	Sig. (1-tailed)	.	.001
	N	9	9
NERVOUS	Pearson Correlation	-.883**	1
	Sig. (1-tailed)	.001	.
	N	9	9

**. Correlation is significant at the 0.01 level (1-tailed).

Regression

Variables Entered/Removed[b]

Model	Variables Entered	Variables Removed	Method
1	DAYS[a]		Enter

a. All requested variables entered.
b. Dependent Variable: NERVOUS

Model Summary

Model	R	R Square	Adjusted R Square	Std. Error of the Estimate
1	.883[a]	.779	.747	2.48771

a. Predictors: (Constant), DAYS

ANOVA[b]

Model		Sum of Squares	df	Mean Square	F	Sig.
1	Regression	152.679	1	152.679	24.671	.002[a]
	Residual	43.321	7	6.189		
	Total	196.000	8			

a. Predictors: (Constant), DAYS
b. Dependent Variable: NERVOUS

Coefficients[a]

Model		Unstandardized Coefficients		Standardized Coefficients	t	Sig.
		B	Std. Error	Beta		
1	(Constant)	16.509	1.608		10.267	.000
	DAYS	−.962	.194	−.883	−4.967	.002

a. Dependent Variable: NERVOUS

b.

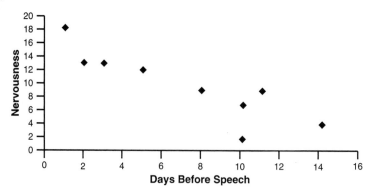

c. The standard error of the estimate is 2.49.

d. He would have a nervousness rating of 9.78 on a scale from 1 to 20. The average error is 2.49; therefore, his actual nervousness rating is likely to fall between 7.29 and 12.27.

15. a. Based on a Pearson's r-value of 0.43 and p-value of 0.08, note-taking is not related to grades.

Work verified on SPSS:

Correlations

Correlations

		NOTES	GRADE
NOTES	Pearson Correlation	1	.431
	Sig. (2-tailed)	.	.084
	N	17	17
GRADE	Pearson Correlation	.431	1
	Sig. (2-tailed)	.084	.
	N	17	17

b.

Graph

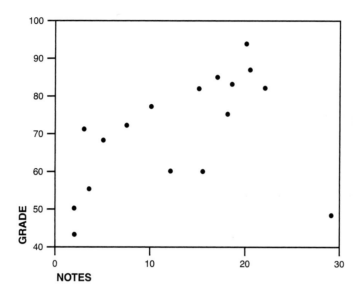

Based on one outlier, these data should be adjusted and reanalyzed without the unusual data point. SPSS output with the outlier removed follows:

Correlations

Correlations

		NOTES	GRADE
NOTES	Pearson Correlation	1	.780**
	Sig. (2-tailed)	.	.000
	N	16	16
GRADE	Pearson Correlation	.780**	1
	Sig. (2-tailed)	.000	.
	N	16	16

**. Correlation is significant at the 0.01 level (2-tailed).

Graph

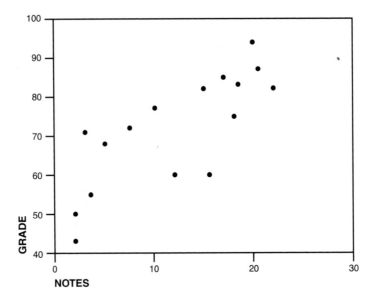

c. These variables have 0.61 proportion in common with each other.

d. $Y' = 1.559X + 52.841$

e. The standard error of the estimate is 9.39.

f.

Regression

Variables Entered/Removed[b]

Model	Variables Entered	Variables Removed	Method
1	NOTES[a]		Enter

a. All requested variables entered.
b. Dependent Variable: GRADE

Model Summary

Model	R	R Square	Adjusted R Square	Std. Error of the Estimate
1	.780[a]	.608	.580	9.39146

a. Predictors: (Constant), NOTES

ANOVA[b]

Model		Sum of Squares	df	Mean Square	F	Sig.
1	Regression	1913.207	1	1913.207	21.692	.000[a]
	Residual	1234.793	14	88.199		
	Total	3148.000	15			

a. Predictors: (Constant), NOTES
b. Dependent Variable: GRADE

Coefficients[a]

Model		Unstandardized Coefficients		Standardized Coefficients	t	Sig.
		B	Std. Error	Beta		
1	(Constant)	52.841	4.643		11.380	.000
	NOTES	1.559	.335	.780	4.657	.000

a. Dependent Variable: GRADE

g. If you wrote 23 pages of notes per week, you might expect a grade of 88.70. The standard error of the estimate is 9.39; therefore, your actual grade would probably fall between 79.31 and 98.09.

Chapter 13

1. a. One-way indicates the use of 1 variable in a chi-square design.
   b. Two-way indicates the use of 2 variables in a chi-square design.
   c. Observed frequencies are collected sample data on simple frequency for each category.
   d. Expected frequencies are expected simple frequencies for each category in a one-way x^2, and expected frequencies are calculated in the two-way x^2.
3. When the null hypothesis is true for the two-way x^2, the x^2_{obt} will be 1.00.
5. The formula for degrees of freedom in the two-way x^2 is (number of rows $-$ 1)(number of columns $-$ 1).
7. A significant 3×3 x^2 is further analyzed for effect size using the contingency coefficient.
9. The one-way and two-way x^2 differ in the questions they answer. The one-way x^2 examines whether data fit expectations, and the two-way x^2 examines whether 2 variables are related to each other. Mathematically, the one-way x^2 does not require f_e to be calculated; f_e values are based on expectations. On the other hand, the two-way x^2 requires f_e values to be calculated from observed frequencies.
11. a. $H_0: f_e s = f_o s$
       $H_1: f_e s \neq f_o s$
    b. one-way x^2 (goodness-of-fit test)

c.

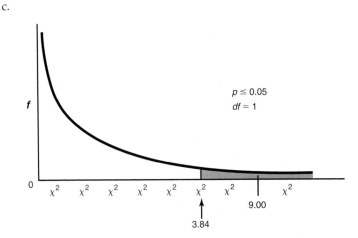

d. $\chi^2 = 25.00 + 25.00 = 50.00$

e. $\chi^2(1, N = 200) = 50.00, p < 0.05$

f.   Although we expected 50% of lawyers to be women, only 25% were.

13. a. H_0: The 2 variables are independent

      H_1: The 2 variables are related to each other.

  b. $2 \times 3 \; \chi^2$ (test of independence)

  c.

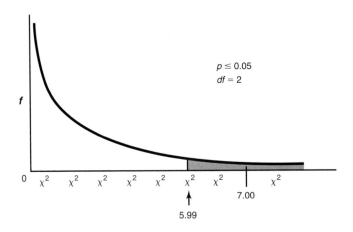

d. $\chi^2 = 0.468125 + 0.031008 + 0.838367 + 0.457486 + 0.030303 + 0.819314 = 2.64$

e. $\chi^2(2, N = 87) = 2.64, p > 0.05$

f.   Hair color and intelligence were not related to each other.

Work verified on SPSS:

Crosstabs

Case Processing Summary

	Cases					
	Valid		Missing		Total	
	N	Percent	N	Percent	N	Percent
HAIR *IQ	87	100.0%	0	0%	87	100.0%

HAIR *IQ Crosstabulation

Count

		IQ			
		1.00	2.00	3.00	Total
HAIR	1.00	18	15	10	43
	2.00	13	14	17	44
Total		31	29	27	87

Chi-Square Tests

	Value	df	Asymp. Sig. (2-sided)
Pearson Chi-Square	2.645[a]	2	.267
Likelihood Ratio	2.669	2	.263
Linear-by-Linear Association	2.481	1	.115
N of Valid Cases	87		

a. 0 cells (.0%) have expected count less than 5. The minimum expected count is 13.34.

15. a. $H_0: f_e s = f_o s$
        $H_1: f_e s \neq f_o s$
    b. one-way χ^2 (goodness-of-fit test)
    c.

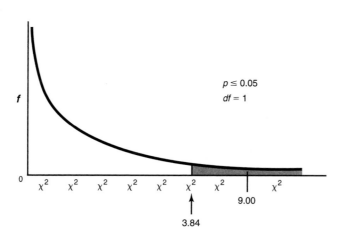

d. $\chi^2 = 1.246154 + 2.314286 = 3.56$

e. $\chi^2(1, N = 100) = 3.56, p < 0.05$

f.   The expectation that 65% of psychology majors would agree that statistics is a useful course and 35% would say that statistics is not useful, was supported.

Appendix A

1. Another name for the repeated-measures ANOVA is within-groups.

3. In SPSS output, the relevant rows are labeled sphericity assumed.

5. Two potential problems with the repeated measures ANOVA are tiring out participants, and having exposure to 1 level change responses under subsequent levels.

7. a.   SPSS output:

General Linear Model

Within-Subjects Factors

Measure: MEASURE_1

GIFTS	Dependent Variable
1	CARD
2	ROSES
3	DIAMONDS

Descriptive Statistics

	Mean	Std. Deviation	N
CARD	17.0000	5.87367	5
ROSES	20.0000	8.74643	5
DIAMONDS	24.2000	6.14003	5

Multivariate Tests[b]

Effect		Value	F	Hypothesis df	Error df	Sig.	Partial Eta Squared
GIFTS	Pillai's Trace	.797	5.876[a]	2.000	3.000	.092	.797
	Wilks' Lambda	.203	5.876[a]	2.000	3.000	.092	.797
	Hotelling's Trace	3.917	5.876[a]	2.000	3.000	.092	.797
	Roy's Largest Root	3.917	5.876[a]	2.000	3.000	.092	.797

a. Exact statistic

b.
    Design: Intercept
    Within Subjects Design: CARD

Mauchiy's Test of Sphericity[b]

Measure: MEASURE_1

Within Subjects Effect	Mauchly's W	Approx. Chi-Square	df	Sig.	Epsilon[a]		
					Greenhouse -Geisser	Huynh-Feldt	Lower-bound
GIFTS	.992	.025	2	.967	.992	1.000	.500

Tests the null hypothesis that the error covariance matrix of the orthonormalized transformed dependent variables is proportional to an identity matrix.

　　a. May be used to adjust the degrees of freedom for the averaged tests of significance. Corrected tests
　　are displayed in the Tests of Within-subjects Effects table.

　　b.
　　Design: Intercept
　　Within Subjects Design: GIFTS

Tests of Within-Subjects Effects

Measure: MEASURE_1

Source		Type III Sum of Squares	df	Mean Square	F	Sig.	Partial Eta Squared
GIFTS	Sphericity Assumed	130.800	2	66.400	8.548	.010	.681
	Greenhouse-Geisser	130.800	1.983	65.951	8.548	.011	.681
	Huynh-Feldt	130.800	2.000	65.400	8.548	.010	.681
	Lower-bound	130.800	1.000	130.800	8.548	.043	.681
Error(GIFTS)	Sphericity Assumed	61.200	8	7.650			
	Greenhouse-Geisser	61.200	7.933	7.714			
	Huynh-Feldt	61.200	8.000	7.650			
	Lower-bound	61.200	4.000	15.300			

Tests of Within-Subjects Contrasts

Measure: MEASURE_1

Source	GIFTS	Type III Sum of Squares	df	Mean Square	F	Sig.	Partial Eta Squared
GIFTS	Linear	129.600	1	129.600	15.521	.017	.795
	Quadratic	1.200	1	1.200	.173	.699	.041
Error(GIFTS)	Linear	33.400	4	6.350			
	Quadratic	27.800	4	6.950			

Tests of Between-Subjects Effects

Measure: MEASURE_1
Transformed Variable: Average

Source	Type III Sum of Squares	df	Mean Square	F	Sig.	Partial Eta Squared
Intercept	6242.400	1	6242.400	46.795	.002	.921
Error	533.600	4	133.400			

Estimated Marginal Means

GIFTS

Estimates

Measure: MEASURE_1

			95% Confidence Interval	
GIFTS	Mean	Std. Error	Lower Bound	Upper Bound
1	17.000	2.627	9.707	24.293
2	20.000	3.612	9.140	30.660
3	24.200	2.746	16.576	31.624

Pairwise Comparisons

Measure: MEASURE_1

		Mean Difference (I-J)	Std. Error	Sig.[a]	95% Confidence Interval for Difference[a]	
(I) GIFTS	(J) GIFTS				Lower Bound	Upper Bound
1	2	−3.000	1.703	.153	−7.728	1.728
	3	−7.200*	1.828	.017	−12.274	−2.126
2	1	3.000	1.703	.153	−1.728	7.728
	3	−4.200	1.715	.070	−8.961	.561
3	1	7.200*	1.828	.017	2.126	12.274
	2	4.200	1.715	.070	−.561	8.961

Based on estimated marginal means

*. The mean difference is significant at the .05 level.

a. Adjustment for multiple comparisons: Least Significant Difference (equivalent to no adjustments).

Multivariate Tests

	Value	F	Hypothesis df	Error df	Sig.	Partial Eta Squared
Pillai's trace	.797	5.878[a]	2.000	3.000	.092	.797
Wilks'lambda	.203	5.878[a]	2.000	3.000	.092	.797
Hotelling's trace	3.917	5.878[a]	2.000	3.000	.092	.797
Roy's largest root	3.917	5.878[a]	2.000	3.000	.092	.797

Each F tests the multivariate effect of PROGRAM. These tests are based on the linearly independent pairwise comparisons among the estimated marginal means.

a. Exact statistic

 b. $F(2, 8) = 8.55, p < 0.05$

 c. Women love their husbands more when they are given diamonds than when they are given a card for their anniversary.

9. a. $H_0: \mu_1 = \mu_2 = \mu_3$

    H_1: At least 2 of the groups are significantly different from each other.

 b. one-way, repeated-measures ANOVA

c.

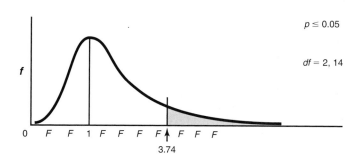

$p \leq 0.05$

$df = 2, 14$

0   F   F   1   F   F   F   F↑ F   F   F
                              3.74

d.   Reject the null hypothesis.

e.   0.65

f.   The confidence interval for no medication is 8.13 to 15.37; the confidence interval for over-the-counter antihistamine is from 5.95 to 11.30 sneezes per hour; the confidence interval for prescription allergy medication is from 5.62 to 10.13.

Appendix B

1.   The overall predictive ability of all predictors is evaluated using the F-value and p-value for the overall model.

3. R^2 represents the proportion of variability in an outcome variable explained by knowing values on the predictor variables.

5. $Y' = -4.367(8) + -0.926(14) + 97.512 = 49.61$; the likely range in which this person's skin-health score will fall is between 45.74 and 53.48.

7.   Work verified on SPSS:

Regression

Variables Entered/Removed[b]

Model	Variables Entered	Variables Removed	Method
1	OTHER CASH, SUFFERE R[a]		Enter

a. All requested variables entered.
b. Dependent Variable: SKIN

Model Summary

Model	R	R Square	Adjusted R Square	Std. Error of the Estimate
1	.947[a]	.896	.844	6.32546

a. Predictors: (Constant), OTHER, CASH, SUFFERER

ANOVA[b]

Model		Sum of Squares	df	Mean Square	F	Sig.
1	Regression	2072.332	3	690.777	17.265	.002[a]
	Residual	240.068	6	40.011		
	Total	2312.400	9			

a. Predictors: (Constant), OTHER, CASH, SUFFERER
b. Dependent Variable: DONATION

Coefficients[a]

Model		Unstandardized Coefficients		Standardized Coefficients	t	Sig.
		B	Std. Error	Beta		
1	(Constant)	−4.786	4.599		−1.041	.338
	SUFFERER	4.038	1.164	.558	3.411	.014
	CASH	.192	.060	.513	3.184	.019
	OTHER	−.097	.224	.060	−.433	.680

a. Dependent Variable: DONATION

Overall, this set of predictors significantly predicts amount of money donated to cancer research; however, closer inspection of each variable reveals that only the number of sufferers and a person's available cash significantly aid in prediction. The amount of money given to other charities is not necessary in the equation and must be dropped.

$$Y' = 4.038(X_{\text{sufferers}}) + .192(X_{\text{cash}}) + -4.786$$

Adjusted R^2 is 0.84, indicating that 84% of the variability in amount donated to cancer research can be explained by knowing number of friends and family members who suffered from cancer, and amount of cash on hand.

The average amount of error in predictions is $6.33 donated to cancer research.

INDEX

absolute zero, 12, 27
adjusted k-table, 183
alternative hypothesis, 99, 105, 145
American Psychological Association style (APA), 3, 4
    results section in SPSS, 125–126, 135–136, 165,
        192–193, 214, 236, 259
    symbols, 3–4, 29, 102
analysis of variance (ANOVA)
    APA style, 150
    dependent variables, 143
    hypothesis testing, 143–159, 178–181
    independent variables, 143
    obtained value, *see F*-ratio
    one-way, between-groups design, 143
        equal n, 146–153
        logic of, 144–146
        unequal n, 154–159
        variability, 144
            calculating, 148
    organizing results, 150, 156
    post-hoc testing, 151, 181
        Fisher's protected t-tests, 157
        Fisher's protected t-tests, formula, 157
        for significant interaction effect, 182–183
        for significant main effect, 181–182
        Tukey's HSD, 151–152, 183
            formula, 152
    repeated-measures design, 144
    summary table, 150, 156, 178, 235
    total variability, 147
    two-way, between-groups design, 171–196
        graphing, 193–196
        interaction effect, 173, 180–181
        logic of, 171–173
        main effect, 172, 179–180
        variability, 173, 174–178
            between-groups, 177
    variability, *see* sum of squares
    within-groups design, 143–144
    within-groups variability, 148
area, 75. *See also* proportion
average, *see* mean

bar graphs, 16, 17–18, 19, 193–196
bell-shaped curve, *see* normal curve
between-groups design, 143
    defined, 143
    variability, 144, 148, 174–176

categorical variables, *see* variables, nominal
Central Limit Theorem, 85, 86, 116

central tendency, 26–50, 51. *See also* mean, median,
    mode
chi-square analyses, 242–259
    goodness-of-fit, 242–249
        for three levels, 246
        with unequal expectations, 248
        one-way, *see* chi-square analyses,
            goodness-of-fit
    test of independence, 250–259
        two-way, *see* chi-square analyses, test of
            independence
coefficient of determination, 205, 236
confidence intervals, 104–105, 106, 108, 117,
    152–153, 158
contingency coefficient, 253
continuous data, 20–21, 27
    graphing, 19, 20–21, 27
continuous variables, *see* variables, continuous
correlation coefficient, *see* Pearson's r
correlations, 4, 5, 207
    data, 201–219
    inaccurate, 214–219
        artificially high, 217–219
        artificially low, 215–217
    SPSS, 209–214
        matrix, 213
    use of, 6, 207
    vs. experiments, 6
critical region, 88, 101
    decreasing, 92–94
critical value
    F-test, 149, 156, 178
    Pearson's r, 208
    t-score, 116
    z-score, 88
curve, *see* distribution

data collection, 101
data summarization, 26, 28, 40–41
    using means, 40
data, graphing, 14–23
decimal places, 3
degrees of freedom, 116
denominator, 2
dependent variables, *see* variables, dependent
dependent-samples t-test, *see* related-samples t-test
descriptive statistics, 7, 246, 253, 259
deviation score, 52–53
    formula for, 52
dichotomous variables, *see* variables, dichotomous
discrete variables, *see* variables, discrete

distributions
    bimodal, 23
    tails of, 21–22
    trimodal, 23
    normal, 21–22
    shapes of, 21–23
    skewed, 22, 145

effect size, 103–104, 106, 108, 117, 150, 156
error bar, 61, 63. *See also* T-bar
error in prediction, *see* prediction error
estimated population standard deviation, 56–57,
        114, 115
    formula for, 57
estimated population variance, 57–58
    formula for, 58
estimated standard error of the difference between
        means, 121
    calculating, 122
estimated standard error of the mean difference, 120
    calculating, 121
eta squared, 150–151
expected frequency
    for one-way chi-square, 242–243, 244, 245,
        247–249
    for two-way chi-square, 251
        formula, 251
experiments, 4
exponents, 2

factor, 143
fractions, 14
F-ratio, 149, 156, 178
frequency
    counts, 242
    expected, 242
    observed, 242
F-table, 149, 177
F-test, 149–150, 177–178

goodness-of-fit, *see* chi-square analyses,
        goodness-of-fit
graphs, 14–16, 17–18, 19–20, 21–23
    creating, 15
    scatterplot, 202
    shapes of, *see* distributions, shapes of
grouped frequency distributions, 20–21

histogram, 19
hypothesis testing
    ANOVA
        one-way, between-groups, 146–159
        two-way, between-groups, 178–181
    correlations (Pearson's *r*), 201–209, 224
    defined, 98
    independent-samples *t*-test, one-tailed, 127–130
    truth, 108–109
    t-test
        independent-samples, 127–130
        related-samples, 120–123
        single-sample, 116–118

Type I error, 109
Type II error, 109
z-test
    one-tailed
        in the negative direction, 107–108
        in the positive direction, 105–107
    two-tailed, 99, 101, 105
hypothesis
    alternative, 99
    defined, 98
    null, 98

independent variables, *see* variables, independent
independent-samples *t*-test, 126–135
    hypothesis testing, 127–130
individual differences, 144, 149
inferential statistics, 7
interval data, 20–21, 51
intervals, equal, 12

kurtosis, 22–23

leptokurtic, 22–23
levels of measurement, *see* scales of measurement
levels, 4–5. *See also* conditions, groups, *and* treatment
        groups
line graph, 19, 27
line of prediction, 224, 229, 230. *See also* linear
        regression
    calculating, 226–229
    graphing, 229–230
linear regression, 224–236
    defined, 224
linear relationships, *see* relationships, linear

manipulating samples, *see* samples, manipulating
matched-samples *t*-test, *see* related-samples *t*-test
mean square, 148
mean, 29–31, 51
    central tendency, 30, 41, 51
    formula, 29
    graphing, 41–42
    interval and ratio data, 30
    symbol, 3
    vs. median, 30–31
means, sampling distribution of, 85
    creating, 86
    standardizing, 86–87
measurement scales, *see* scales of measurement
measures of central tendency, *see* central tendency
median, 28–29, 31
    defined, 28
    interval data when skewed, 28
    skewed, 30, 52
    ordinal data, 52
    range, *see* range, with median
    ratio data, 28, 30, 52
    vs. mode, 28
mesokurtic, 22–23
mode, 26–28, 31, 51
    defined, 26

nominal data, 28
  use of, 26
multiple regression, 226

negative skew, 22, 23
nominal data, 13
  graphing, 15–16
nonparametric statistics, 242
normal curve, 21–22
normal distribution, 85
normal population mean, vs. sample mean,
    and hypothesis testing, 100
null hypothesis, 98
  Type I error, 109
  Type II error, 109
numerator, 2

observed frequency,
  for one-way chi-square, 242–243, 244, 245,
    247–249
  for two-way chi-square, 251
one-tailed z-test, 86–88
  in the negative direction, 107–108
  in the positive direction, 105–107
one-way chi-square test, *see* chi-square analyses,
    goodness-of-fit
one-way, between-groups design, 143–165
operationally defined variables, *see* variables,
    operationally defined
operations, order of, 2
order of operations, *see* operations, order of
ordinal data, 13, 51
  graphing, 16
ordinal variables, *see* variables, ordinal
organizing data, *see* data, organizing
outliers, 216, 218

p value, *see* significance value
paired-samples *t*-test, *see* related-samples *t*-test
parametric statistics, 242
Pearson's *r* (Pearson's Product Moment Correlation
    Coefficient), 201–209, 224
  alternative hypothesis, 208
  null hypothesis, 207
  formula, 206
  inaccurate correlations, 214–219
  logic of, 201–205
  SPSS, 212–213
percent, 3
percent, changing to proportion, 88
percentile, 77–78
phi coefficient, 252
platykurtic, 22–23
population, 6–7
  average, *see* population mean
  mean, 57, 84, 86
  standard deviation, 86
  variability
    compensating for, 57
positive skew, 22, 145
post-hoc testing

ANOVA, 151
  Fisher's protected *t*-tests, 157
    formula, 157
  significant interaction effect, 182–183
  significant main effect, 181–182
  Tukey's HSD, 151–152, 183
    formula, 152
power, 109
prediction
  equation, 226
  error, 224, 226
  line, *see* line of prediction
  mathematical, 230
probability(ies), 82
  calculating, 82
  defined, 82
proportion, 2–3, 73, 75. *See also* area

q-table, 152, 183
qualitative variables, *see* variables, qualitative
quantitative variables, *see* variables, quantitative
quasi-independent variables, *see* variables,
    quasi-independent

random assignment, 5
random sampling, 7
range, 51–52
  ordinal data, 51–52
  ratio data, 52
  skewed interval data, 52
  use of, 52
  with median, 52
ratio data, graphing, 27
ratio variables, *see* variables, ratio
raw scores, 29
  converting to z-scores, 70–71
regression
  analysis, 225, 226
  equation, 225, 226, 230
    calculating, 226
  line, 224, 230. *See also*, line of prediction
    graphing, 229–230
  output table, 235
rejection (critical) region, 102
related samples, 118, 119
related-samples *t*-test, 118–125
  within-groups design and, 143–144
  hypothesis testing, 120–123
relationships, 201–207
  curvilinear, 214–215, 218
    Pearson's *r* and, 215, 218
  less-than-perfect, 204–205
    Pearson's *r* and, 204–205
  linear, 201–207, 224
  moderate, 204, 205
  negative, 203
  one-to-one, *see* relationships, linear
  perfect, 201–204
    Pearson's *r* and, 203
  positive, 203, 205, 206, 226
  slope, 203–204

strong, 204, 205
    weak, 204, 205
    y-intercept, 225
repeated-measures design, 144
restriction of range, 216, 218
rounding, 3

sample mean, 84–86
    probabilities of, 84–85
    Central Limit Theorem and, 85
sample standard deviation, 55–56, 61–62
    formula, 55
    graphing, 61–63
sample variance, 52–54
    formula for, 54
samples, 7
    independent, *see* independent samples
    manipulating, 88–94
        higher than normal, 89–91
        lower than normal, 91–92
        not different from normal, 89
    picking, 6–7, 84, 126
    related, *see* related samples
    representative, 7
sampling distribution
    of differences between means, 126
    of mean differences, 119, 120
    of means, 84–88
    for Pearson's *r*, 207
sampling error, 84–85
    simple frequency distribution and, 85
scale(s) of measurement, 11. *See also* variables
    choosing, 12–13
    interval, 12, 51
    nominal, 11, 51
    ordinal, 11, 51
    ratio, 12, 51
scatterplot, 202, 206, 224, 225, 226, 227
significance value (*p* value), 213
simple frequency, 14
    distribution, 14, 85
    graphing, 15–19
    polygon, 19
single-sample *t*-test, 114–118
    estimated population standard deviation,
        114, 115
    estimated standard error of the mean, 115
    z-test vs. 114–115
skewed data, 22
    median, 30–31, 52
slope, 203–204, 225
spread of scores, *see* variability
SPSS, 7–8, 31–33
    APA-style results, 125–126, 135–136, 165,
        192–193, 214, 249
    bivariate correlation, 212–213, 233
    central tendency, 33–47
    changing numbers to names, 43
    Chi-square Tests Table, 258
    correlation, 209–214, 233
        matrix, 213

    Descriptive Statistics Table, 164
    error bars, 64–65
    Estimated Marginal Means Table, 164, 192
    graphing standard deviation, 63–66
    independent-samples *t*-test, 130–135
    labels
        for columns, 33
        viewing, 45
        for *x*- and *y*-axes, 46, 65
    linear regression on, 234–236
    means, 42–47
    Model Summary Table, 236
    one-way, between-groups ANOVA, 159–165
    Pearson's *r*, 212–214
    post-hoc table, 164–165
    prediction on, 233–236
    printing output, 40
    related-samples *t*-test, 123–125
    scatterplot, 210–211
    significance value (*p* value), 213
    Symmetric Measures table, 258
    Test of Between-Subjects Effects, 164, 192
    two-way chi-square analysis, 254–259
    two-way, between-groups ANOVA, 185–196
        graphing, 193–196
    variability, 58–60
standard deviation, 73
    estimated population, *see* estimated population
        standard deviation
    sample, *see* sample standard deviation
standard error
    calculations, 230–232
    of the difference between means, estimated *see*
        estimated standard error of the difference
        between means
    of the estimate, 230, 236
        formula, 230
    of the mean, 86–87, 89, 115
        formula, 87
    of the mean difference, estimated *see* estimated
        standard error of the mean difference
standardized distribution, *see* *z*-distribution
standardized scores, *see* *z*-scores
statistics, use of, 1–2
sum of squares, 147, 174–175
    formula, 147
    separating, 176–177
summary table, ANOVA, 150, 156, 178, 235

tables, 14–15, 17, 19, 20
    creating, 15
tails of distribution, *see* distribution, tails of
T-bar, 61, 63. *See also* error bar
t-distribution, 12, 116, 122
total variability, in ANOVA, *see* sum of squares
truth, 108–109
t-test, 114
    independent-samples, *see* independent samples
        t-test
    Fisher's protected, *see* Fisher's protected *t*-tests
    related-samples, *see* related-samples *t*-test

single-sample, *see* single-sample *t*-test
  z-tests vs., 114
Tukey's honestly significant difference (HSD),
      151–152, 183
  formula, 152
  SPSS, 159
two-tailed *z*-test, 99, 100, 101
  distribution for, 101
Type I error, 109
Type II error, 109

variability, 51–58. *See also* estimated population stan-
      dard deviation, estimated population vari-
      ance range, sample variance, sample
      standard deviation
  defined, 51
  for interval or ratio data, not skewed, 31
  for ordinal data, 51–52
  for a sample of numbers, 54
  for skewed interval or ratio data, 51–52
  sum of squares
variables, 4
  categorical, *see* variables, nominal
  continuous, 14, 19
  dependent (DV), 4–5, 41, 143
  dichotomous, 14
  discrete, 14, 19
  independent (IV), 4–5, 41, 143
      ANOVA, 143
      independent-samples *t*-test, 126
      related-samples *t*-test, 118
  linear relationship between, 201–207. *See also*
      linear relationships
  nominal, 11
  operationally defined, 4
  ordinal, 11

predicting, 224, 225
  qualitative, 13
  quantitative, 13
  quasi-independent, 118, 201, 201
  ratio, 12, 14
  relationships between, 5–6, 201
      Pearson's *r*, 208
variance pooled, 128

within-groups design, 143–144
  defined, 143
  variability, 148, 174–176

x-axis
  defined, 15

y-axis
  defined, 15
Y-intercept, 225

z-distribution, 72–73, 86
  mean of, 72–73
  standard deviation of, 73
z-obtained value, 87, 89
z-scores, 71–72, 73–75, 87
  for area under curve, 73–78
  from different samples, 70–72
  formula
      descriptive, 71
      inferential, 87
z-table, 74, 87, 88
z-test
      one-tailed, *see* one-tailed *z*-test
      two-tailed, *see* two-tailed *z*-test